Business and environmental leaders
extol the promise — and the proven e

Natural Capitalism

"*Natural Capitalism* introduces a visionary concept that regards business, environmental, and social interests as an integrated, harmonious system. . . . Business types traditionally cry 'unrealistic!' when confronted with such ideas, but the dozens of documented success stories presented in this book are hard to dismiss. . . . Not a manual but the elucidation of a new spirit, this book reveals the many opportunities available to those who apply its concepts. Leaders need to know this stuff."
— J. Baldwin, *I.D.*

"You had better have a copy of this book on your shelf or you will not be able to identify tomorrow's companies and industries as they appear before your eyes."
— Professor Stuart Hart, Kenan-Flagler Business School,
University of North Carolina

"*Natural Capitalism* is the most important book of the century, a handbook of solutions and restoration that will have CEOs and ecologists cheering together. . . . Paul, Amory, and Hunter are your expert guides to how companies and individuals are redesigning commerce to put back more than they take from the earth. . . . Required reading for all crewmembers of Spaceship Earth. That means you, so get to reading."
— David R. Brower, Chairman and Founder, Earth Island Institute

"Both a call to arms and a revelation. The authors not only show how today's industrialists and economists can change to work in harmony with the environment, they reveal how many of them already are doing so — and improving profitability in the process. . . . This is radical stuff."
— Brad Knickerbocker, *Christian Science Monitor*

"Three world-class minds. One giant leap for sustainability."
— John Elkington, Chairman, SustainAbility Ltd.
and author of *Cannibals with Forks*

"This is an important book, not for environmentalists, but for business owners and executives who have the power to reorganize their operations based on the four principles of natural capitalism. The more this book influences *Wall Street Journal* readers, the better chance we have to leave our children a livable planet."

— Dana Jackson, *Land Stewardship Letter*

"Proof that America's environmental movement has come of age. Built upon the groundbreaking work of such authors as Rachel Carson, Aldo Leopold, and Wendell Berry, *Natural Capitalism* erects a new framework for discussing how we're affecting the planet.... The message in *Natural Capitalism* is both huge and simple: The industrial revolution is over. We don't have to drive gas-guzzling cars fueled by dead dinosaurs anymore. We don't have to live with toilets flushed by gallons of drinking water. We don't have to accept toxic waste as a byproduct of industry.... Time and again, the book demonstrates how the United States is lagging behind Japan, Germany, and Sweden in environmental entrepreneurship.... But for every tale of horror, *Natural Capitalism* offers an inspiring story.... What's particularly likable about *Natural Capitalism* is that now, between two covers, there exists a way for ordinary consumers — people who buy food at supermarkets, live in houses, and drive cars — to get an insider's glimpse of the vast industries that essentially control their lives, and how those industries may soon change dramatically."

— Christine Colasurdo, *San Francisco Chronicle*

"Paul Hawken and Amory and Hunter Lovins are the advocates and technicians most responsible for shaping this emerging, pro-investment, win-win (profitable and preservationist) brand of environmentalism. . . . *Natural Capitalism* brilliantly details their most recent thinking about hyper-efficiency.... If it has to do with commerce and environmentalism, it's here."

— Allen Hershkowitz, *Amicus Journal*

"There is not an idea in this powerful book that doesn't make intuitive, obvious, immediate, calculable sense. We are at one of the historical moments of crisis when those forces must be routed, and change unleashed; *Natural Capitalism* comes not a moment too soon."

— Bill McKibben, author of *The End of Nature* and *The Age of Missing Information*

"Stunning. . . . If Adam Smith's *The Wealth of Nations* was the bible for the first industrial revolution, then *Natural Capitalism* may well prove to be it for the next."

— Peter Senge, author of *The Fifth Discipline*

"Ambitious, visionary. . . . In looking at options for transportation, energy use, building design, and waste reduction and disposal, the book's reach is phenomenal. It belongs to the galvanizing tradition of Frances Moore Lappé's *Diet for a Small Planet* and Stewart Brand's *The Whole Earth Catalog.*"

— *Publishers Weekly*

"*Natural Capitalism* reads like a manifesto, a touching and powerful credo, for the second industrial revolution. . . . A work that future historians may look back upon as a milestone on our way to a new, sustainable economy."

— Tachi Kiuchi, Managing Director of Mitsubishi Electric Corporation and Chairman of The Future 500

"For those seeking long-term investment strategies, *Natural Capitalism* makes a convincing case that sustainable solutions to the problems caused by industrialization are increasingly business-oriented and financially, as well as environmentally, beneficial to all."

— Kira L. Gould, *Architecture*

"Empowering. . . . The whole concept of natural capital manages to be both pragmatic and idealistic, which, in my book, adds up to inspirational."

— Anita Roddick, Founder, The Body Shop International

"Nothing less than an up-to-date business manual for the next century. . . . *Natural Capitalism* redefines how businesses and ultimately the entire planet should grow to sustain a prosperous and equitable quality of life for the indefinite future."

— Jim Durrett, Vice President, Environmental Affairs, Metro Atlanta Chamber of Commerce

"By illuminating the common ground between economics, environment, and society with crystal clarity and eloquence, *Natural Capitalism* is the design manual for the 21st century. Read it! Read it again!"

— David W. Orr, Oberlin College, author of *Earth in Mind*

ALSO BY PAUL HAWKEN

The Ecology of Commerce

Growing a Business

The Next Economy

ALSO BY AMORY AND L. HUNTER LOVINS

Energy/War: Breaking the Nuclear Link

Least-Cost Energy: Solving the CO_2 Problem *(with Florentin Krause & Wilfrid Bach)*

Brittle Power: Energy Strategy for National Security

Factor Four: Doubling Wealth, Halving Resource Use *(with Ernst von Weizsäcker)*

ALSO BY AMORY LOVINS

World Energy Strategies: Facts, Issues, and Options

Non-Nuclear Futures: The Case for an Ethical Energy Strategy *(with John Price)*

Soft Energy Paths: Toward a Durable Peace

ALSO BY L. HUNTER LOVINS

Green Development: Integrating Ecology and Real Estate *(with RMI colleagues)*

Paul Hawken, Amory Lovins,
and L. Hunter Lovins

Natural
Capitalism

CREATING THE

NEXT INDUSTRIAL

REVOLUTION

LITTLE, BROWN AND COMPANY

BOSTON NEW YORK LONDON

To Dana, David, Herman, and Ray

Originally published in hardcover by Little, Brown and Company, September 1999
First Back Bay paperback edition, October 2000

"Hypercar" is a trademark of Hypercar, Inc. "The Hypercar Center" is a service mark of Rocky Mountain Institute. Other marks used in this book are the property of their respective holders.

The authors are grateful to David Whyte for permission to use his poem "Loaves and Fishes" from *The House of Belonging: Poems* by David Whyte (Many Rivers Press). Copyright © 1996 by David James Whyte.

This book is printed with soy-based inks on New Leaf Eco Offset paper. The paper has 100% recycled fiber content, including 80% post-consumer waste, and is Processed Chlorine Free.

The authors wish to thank both the supplier, New Leaf Paper, and Little, Brown and Company's paper buyer, Barry Lenick, for their help, as well as Rocky Mountain Institute's Chris Lotspeich. Other vendors and RMI researchers also assisted in the selection process. For more information about the production decision, visit www.natcap.org.

Library of Congress Cataloging-in-Publication Data

Hawken, Paul.
    Natural capitalism : creating the next industrial revolution /
    Paul Hawken, Amory Lovins, and L. Hunter Lovins.
        p.   cm.
    Includes bibliographical references and index.
    ISBN 0-316-35316-7 (hc) / 0-316-35300-0 (pb)
       1. Economic forecasting — United States.   2. United States —
Economic policy — 1993–   3. Capitalism — United States — Forecasting.
4. Twenty-first century — Forecasts.   I. Lovins, Amory B.
II. Lovins, L. Hunter.   III. Title.
HC106.82.H39   1999
338.973 — dc21   99-24067

10 9 8 7 6 5 4 3 2

Q-FF

Book design by Elizabeth Elsas

Printed in the United States of America

CONTENTS

LOAVES AND FISHES

This is not the age of information.
This is *not*
the age of information.

Forget the news,
and the radio,
and the blurred screen.

This is the time
of loaves
and fishes.

People are hungry,
and one good word is bread
for a thousand.

— *David Whyte*

PREFACE

Natural Capitalism as an idea and thesis for a book emerged in 1994, the year after the publication of *The Ecology of Commerce*. After meeting with and speaking to different business, government, and academic institutions in the aftermath of the book's publication, it became clear to Hawken that industry and government needed an overall biological and social framework within which the transformation of commerce could be accomplished and practiced. To that end, articles and papers were written that became the basis of a book about natural capitalism. A key element of this theory was the idea that the economy was shifting from an emphasis on human productivity to a radical increase in resource productivity. This shift would provide more meaningful family-wage jobs, a better worldwide standard of living to those in need, and a dramatic reduction of humankind's impact upon the environment. So while the context for *Natural Capitalism* existed in a theoretical framework, the exposition did not.

Contemporaneously, Amory and Hunter Lovins were coming to the same conclusion: that a shared framework was needed that could harness the talent of business to solve the world's deepest environmental and social problems. Both were writing *Factor Four: Doubling Wealth, Halving Resource Use* for publication in Germany in 1995. The senior author of *Factor Four*, Ernst von Weizsäcker, among Europe's top innovators in environmental policy, had teamed up with the Lovinses to pool the experience of their respective nonprofit research centers — Wuppertal Institute in Germany and Rocky Mountain Institute (RMI) in Colorado. The three authors had assembled fifty case studies of at least quadrupled resource productivity to detail how, across whole economies, people could live twice as well but use half as much material and energy. *Factor Four* showed that such striking gains in resource efficiency could be profitable, and that obstacles to their implementation could be hurdled by combining innovations in business practice and in public policy.

Both *Factor Four* and *The Ecology of Commerce* urged the private sector to move to the vanguard of environmental solutions. *Factor Four* described a creative policy framework that could foster fair and open competition in achieving that success. *The Ecology of Commerce* suggested techniques that when combined with business's unique strengths could enable it to meet this challenge successfully.

Hunter Lovins sent a draft of *Factor Four* to Paul Hawken in early 1995. He saw that it was the exposition that natural capitalism needed if it were to make its theoretical claims credible and demonstrable. The ideas not only meshed, they were absolutely complementary. We agreed to work together toward one book, under the title of *Natural Capitalism,* that would contain both theory and practice. After the work began, we discovered it wasn't that simple. *Factor Four* was anecdotal, Europe-oriented (by 1997 it had also been published in England after being a German bestseller for nearly two years), and written more for policy and environmental activists than for business practitioners. It needed not adaptation but complete rewriting. Further, the examples offered concentrated mainly on efficiency and did not take fully into account the need for the restoration of natural capital nor for several other important elements of natural capitalism that go far beyond mere resource efficiency. Fortunately, Rocky Mountain Institute's researchers in buildings, industry, water, agriculture, forestry, and vehicles had been compiling information on ways to turn the expanding returns of advanced resource productivity into a common business practice. Cultural shifts within the business community had started to accelerate the pace of change, providing practical examples even more compelling than those available in 1995. A wider and more ambitious agenda was becoming possible and profitable.

As we sought to make the American public aware of an emerging resource productivity revolution, we realized that there was a larger message. Eco-efficiency, an increasingly popular concept used by business to describe incremental improvements in materials use and environmental impact, is only one small part of a richer and more complex web of ideas and solutions. Without a fundamental rethinking of the structure and the reward system of commerce, narrowly focused eco-efficiency could be a disaster for the environment by overwhelming resource savings with even larger growth in the production of the wrong products, produced by the wrong processes, from the wrong materials, in the wrong place, at the wrong scale, and delivered using the wrong business models. With so many wrongs outweighing one right, more efficient production by itself could become not the servant but the enemy of a durable economy. Reconciling ecological with economic goals requires not just eco-efficiency alone, but also three additional principles, all interdependent and mutually reinforcing. Only that combination of all four principles can yield the full benefits and the logical consistency of natural capitalism.

Hundreds of exciting examples emerged from rapidly evolving business experience in many sectors: transportation and land use, buildings and real estate, industry and materials, forests, food, water. But as we sifted and distilled those new business cases, we realized that the conventional wisdom is mistaken in seeing priorities in economic, environmental, and social policy as competing. The best solutions are based not on tradeoffs or "balance" between these objectives but on design integration achieving all of them together — at every level, from technical devices to production systems to companies to economic sectors to entire cities and societies. This book tells that story of design integration, unfolding through the interaction of successive topical chapters and interleaved with explanations of the design concepts they reveal.

The story is neither simple nor complete. Each of these ideas deserves far greater explanation than space allows. Its conclusion is tantalizing if not yet wholly clear. Although it is a book abounding in solutions, it is not about "fixes." Nor is it a how-to manual. It is a portrayal of opportunities that if captured will lead to no less than a transformation of commerce and of all societal institutions. Natural capitalism maps the general direction of a journey that requires overturning long-held assumptions, even questioning what we value and how we are to live. Yet the early stages in the decades-long odyssey are turning out to release extraordinary benefits. Among these are what business innovator Peter Senge calls "hidden reserves within the enterprise" — "lost energy," trapped in stale employee and customer relationships, that can be channeled into success for both today's shareholders and future generations. All three of us have witnessed this excitement and enhanced total factor productivity in many of the businesses we have counseled. It is real; it is replicable; its principles and practice are documented in this book and its roughly eight hundred references.

The order of the chapters bears some explanation. Chapter 1, The Next Industrial Revolution, sets out the principles and underlying theory of natural capitalism. Here, the four main strategies are spelled out and elaborated. Chapter 2, about Hypercars and neighborhoods, demonstrates immediately how the four principles of natural capitalism are

transforming one of the world's largest and most destructive industries —
automobiles — and how sensible land use and fair competition between
modes of access can reduce car dependence to an optimal level. Chapter 3, Waste Not, further establishes the foundation for radical changes
in resource use. It tells how we are needlessly losing materials, energy,
money, and even people, a critical point because the potential and opportunities inherent in natural capitalism cannot be fathomed or accepted
without understanding the extraordinary wastefulness of the current
industrial system. Chapter 4, Making the World, outlines the ingenious
and fundamental principles of resource productivity in industry and
materials. Chapter 5, Building Blocks, like the chapter on cars, shows how
the natural capitalism principles are becoming manifest in revolutionizing the building and real estate industries. Chapter 6, Tunneling
Through the Cost Barrier, returns again to a set of counterintuitive
design principles to show that very large gains in resource productivity
are often much more profitable than smaller ones. Chapter 7, *Muda,*
Service, and Flow, describes how the relentless elimination of waste
combined with business redefinition can vault companies into new
commercial terrain and help to stabilize the entire economy. Chapter 8,
Capital Gains, defines and addresses the loss of natural capital and
what can be done to reverse the loss of "our only home." The next three
chapters discuss natural processes, showing how biologically inspired
design can radically reduce human impact on farmland, forests, and
water, while retaining the ability to increase the quality of life for all.
Chapter 12, Climate, combines principles and examples to show how to
literally end the threat of global warming at a profit to all nations,
rich and poor. Chapter 13, Making Markets Work, explores the virtues
and misconceptions surrounding market-based principles and how to
harness them for both short- and long-term gains for all sectors. Chapter 14, about a near-legendary city in Brazil called Curitiba, describes
how a small group of designers, with scant money but brilliant conceptual integration and entrepreneurship, changed the concept of what a
city can be, vastly improving the quality of life of both citizens and the
environment. Finally, chapter 15 explores how the move toward a
durable and sustaining economy is becoming the most powerful movement in the world today, and what that augurs for the decades to come.

    If the book seems more like a tapestry than a straight-line exposi-
tion of theory and fact, it is because the subject itself is far from linear.
In all respects, *Natural Capitalism* is about integration and restoration,

a systems view of our society and its relationship to the environment, that defies categorization into subdisciplines. Readers may wonder that the book largely ignores the market darlings of biotechnology, nano-technology, e-commerce, and the burgeoning Internet. There are armfuls of books describing how technology is revolutionizing our lives. While that is undeniably so, at least for a minority of the world's population, our purpose is almost the opposite. We are trying to describe how our lives and life itself will revolutionize all technologies. Regardless of whether a business is an Internet retailer in California or a tool-and-die shop in Cleveland or a software company in India, the reconciliation of the relationship between human, in this case business, and living systems will dominate the twenty-first century.

Critics on the left may argue that businesspeople pursue only short-term self-interest unless guided by legislation in the public interest. However, we believe that the world stands on the threshold of basic changes in the conditions of business. Companies that ignore the mes-sage of natural capitalism do so at their peril. Thus our strategy here is not to approach business as a supplicant, asking corporations to change and make a better world by respecting the limits of the environment. Actually, there are growing numbers of business owners and managers who are changing their enterprises to become more environmentally responsible because of deeply rooted beliefs and values. This is a won-derful change to witness. But what we are saying is more pressing than a request. The book teems with examples and references, included to show that the move toward radical resource productivity and natural capitalism is beginning to feel inevitable rather than merely possible. It is similar to a train that is at the station about to go. The train doesn't know if your company, country, or city is safely on board, nor whether your ticket is punched or not. There is now sufficient evidence of change to suggest that if your corporation or institution is not paying attention to this revolution, it will lose competitive advantage. In this changed business climate, those who incur that loss will be seen as remiss if not irresponsible. The opportunity for constructive, meaning-ful change is growing and exciting. If at times we seem to lean more to enthusiasm than reportage, it is because we can see the tremendous array of possibilities for healing the most intransigent problems of our time. This is what we have tried to share with you.

There are far too many good examples to include here. Many of the ideas beg for greater explication. Many more examples, and hundreds of notes amplifying the text, are therefore posted on the World Wide Web at http://www.natcap.org. Those postings will be frequently improved by incorporating new cases and discussions of ideas. Readers are warmly invited to add new cases through the website's interactive features, thereby making this book not a static document but a living body of practice.

In offering this book and site, we hope to serve a rapidly growing network of people in the world who see the world as it can be, not merely as it is. Wendell Berry writes in his *Recollected Essays:*

> We have lived by the assumption that what was good for us would be good for the world. We have been wrong. We must change our lives, so that it will be possible to live by the contrary assumption that what is good for the world will be good for us. And that requires that we make the effort to know the world and to learn what is good for it. We must learn to cooperate in its processes, and to yield to its limits. But even more important, we must learn to acknowledge that the creation is full of mystery; we will never clearly understand it. We must abandon arrogance and stand in awe. We must recover the sense of the majesty of the creation, and the ability to be worshipful in its presence. For it is only on the condition of humility and reverence before the world that our species will be able to remain in it.

— *PGH, ABL, LHL*
Sausalito, California, and Old Snowmass, Colorado

ACKNOWLEDGMENTS

It is not possible to mention all the individuals who have helped this book come to be. We have benefited from the work of many who have preceded us, as well as those we consider our colleagues in this work. We also acknowledge some of the many institutions that have served as laboratories, teachers, and supporters of our work. These include both for- and non-profits.

It was difficult to select, from a far larger set, the particular firms and examples presented in *Natural Capitalism*. Selection was based solely on substantive and pedagogic merit; no firm asked or paid to be mentioned. Nonetheless, since we are writing from our experience, much of it gained by working with and for companies mentioned in this book, it seems proper to declare that interest by listing our personal and institutional private-sector clienteles (omitting our larger public-sector and non-profit clienteles) during the past decade, ranging from one-day engagements to long-term consulting or research relationships. In listing the companies, no endorsement is implied or given, either from us or by the companies. In alphabetical order, these include: Aerovironment, American Development Group, Arthur D. Little, Ashland Chemical, Aspen Ski Co., Atlantic Electric, AT&T, Baxter, Bayernwerk, Bechtel, Ben & Jerry's, Bosal, Boston Consulting Group, Boston Edison, BP, Calvert, Carrier div. of UTC, Cesar Pelli, CH2M Hill, Ciba-Geigy, Citicorp, Collins & Aikman, ComEd, Continental Office, Daimler-Chrysler, Datafusion, Delphi, Diamonex, Dow Chemical, Emmett Realty, Esprit de Corps, First Chicago Building, Florida P&L, General Mills, GM, Gensler, Global Business Network, Grand Wailea Resort, Herman Miller, Hexcel, Hines, Honda, Hong Kong Electric, HP, IBM, Imagine Foods, Interface, Landis & Gyr, Levi Strauss & Co., Lockheed Martin, Michelin, Minnesota Power, Mitsubishi Electric, Mitsubishi Motor Sales America, Monsanto, Motorola, Nike, Nissan, Nokia, Norsk Hydro, Northface, NYSE&G, Odwalla, Ontario Hydro, OG&E, Osaka Gas, Patagonia, PG&E, PGE, Phillips Petroleum, Prince div. of Johnson Controls, Rieter, Royal Dutch/Shell, SAGE J.B. Goodman Properties,

Schott Glas, Schweizer, SDG&E, Searle, Shearson Lehmann Amex, STMicroelectronics, Stonyfield Farms, Sun Microsystems, Sun [Oil], Swiss Bank Corp./UBS, UniDev, Unipart, US West, Volvo, VW, Xerox, and Zoltek. Some of these companies have generously aided this research with data and insights, but no proprietary data have been used here. For this assistance, and for the help of their pioneering managers and practitioners, the authors are grateful.

Our research and work were partly supported by grants from the Surdna, Columbia, Geraldine R. Dodge, MacArthur, Energy, Joyce, Aria, William and Flora Hewlett, Sun Hill, Charles Stewart Mott, Turner, and Goldman foundations, as well as the Educational Foundation of America, Environmental Protection Agency, G.A.G. Charitable Corporation, Merck Family Fund, J. M. Kaplan Fund, and Wallace Global Fund. Our appreciation for this support extends far beyond the publication of this book. These and other funders are investing in the preservation and restoration of the life on this planet, and are leaders all.

A similar debt is owed to hundreds of other colleagues, researchers, and reviewers. Much of the underlying research was done by the staff of Rocky Mountain Institute. Chapter 2 reports the work of RMI's Hyper-car Center: Mike Brylawski, Dave Cramer, Jonathan Fox-Rubin, Timothy Moore, Dave Taggart, and Brett Williams. Chapter 5 summarizes the experience of RMI's Green Development Services, chiefly Bill Browning, Huston Eubank, Alexis Karolides, and Jen Seal-Uncapher, and of the ACT² experiment cosponsored by Pacific Gas and Electric Co., Natural Resources Defense Council, and Lawrence Berkeley National Laboratory. Chapter 9 (fiber) draws heavily on a Yale master's thesis by Chris Lotspeich and on outside collaborators in RMI's Systems Group on Forests, notably Dana Meadows, Jim Bowyer, Eric Brownstein, Jason Clay, Sue Hall, and Peter Warshall. Chapter 10 (agriculture) owes much to RMI director Dana Jackson and adviser Allan Savory. Chapter 11 relies on numerous studies by RMI water researchers Scott Chaplin, Richard Pinkham, and Bob Wilkinson. Much of the reported energy-efficiency work builds on the definitive research by RMI's COMPETITEK group, spun out in 1992 from RMI to its subsidiary E SOURCE, led then by Michael Shepard and now by Jim Newcomb. Chapter 14 could not have been written without the work and help of Jonas Rabinovitch, and was informed by the writings of Bill McKibben and the insights of RMI's Economic Renewal efforts led by Michael Kinsley. Many of the lean-clean-and-green concepts reported here were identified early by Joe Romm, who wrote *Lean and Clean Management* (1994) as an RMI researcher. We have relied frequently on the essential publications of our friends at Worldwatch Institute. And of course the godfather of our resource-productivity work is the lead author of *Factor Four,* now a member of the German Bundestag, the extraordinary Ernst von Weizsäcker.

We want especially to acknowledge Herman Daly, whose pioneering work in ecological economics provided the basis for the thesis of this work. His seminal contributions to a truly integrated economics discipline are made all the more remarkable by his modesty and humility. Equal acknowledgment for her extraordinary contributions to understanding our society and environment as a system we extend to Dana Meadows. Her wisdom and balance are a touchstone to us and many others.

Much of what we've learned comes from other outstanding practitioners and teachers, many of whom were also reviewers of the manuscript. They include Rebecca Adamson, Jan Agri, Abigail Alling, Mohamed El-Ashry, Bob Ayres, J. Baldwin, Spencer Beebe, Janine Benyus, Wendell Berry, Paul Bierman-Lytle, Dick Bourne, Peter Bradford, Michael Braungart, Chip Bupp, Jody Butterfield, Ralph Cavanagh, Nancy Clanton, John Clarke, Jim Clarkson, Gordon Conway, Mike and Judy Corbett, Robert Costanza, Peter Coyote, Robert Cumberford, Mike Curzan, Gretchen Daily, Joan Davis, Steve DeCanio, Murray Duffin, Paul and Anne Ehrlich, John Elkington, Don Falk, Chris Flavin, Peter Forbes, Greg Franta, Ashok Gadgil, Thomas Gladwin, Peter Gleick, Jose Goldemberg, David Goldstein, Robert Goodland, Tom Graedel, Sue Hall, Ted Halstead, Stuart Hart, Randy Hayes, Allen Hershkowitz, Buzz Holling, John Holmberg, Wes Jackson, Dan Jones, Thomas B. Johansson, Joel Jamison, Greg Kats, Phillipp Kauffman, Yoichi Kaya, Byron Kennard, Tachi Kiuchi, Florentin Krause, Jonathan Lash, Eng Lock Lee, Nick Lenssen, Jaime Lerner, Paul MacCready, Bob Massie, Gil Masters, William McDonough, Dennis Meadows, Niels Meyer, Norman Myers, Steve Nadel, Jon Olaf Nelson, Jørgen Nørgård, Joan Ogden, Ron Perkins, John Picard, Amulya Reddy, Bob Repetto, Karl-Henrik Robèrt, Tina Robinson, Jim Rogers, Dan Roos, Art Rosenfeld, Marc Ross, Peter Rumsey, Wolfgang Sachs, Yasushi Santo, Robert Sardinsky, Anjali Sastry, Jan Schilham, Bio Schmidt-Bleek, Steve Schneider, Peter Schwartz, Floyd Segel, Sarah Severn, Ed Skloot, Rob Socolow, Jim Souby, Walter Stahel, Maurice Strong, David Suzuki, Nickolas Themelis, Sandy

Thomas, Andy Tobias, John and Nancy Jack Todd, Michael Totten, Haruki Tsuchiya, Christine von Weizsäcker, Stuart White, Bob Williams, Daniel Yergin, Susumu Yoda, and Vlatko Zagar.

Included in this group are a smaller group of reviewers — Alan AtKisson, Dave Brower, Fritjof Capra, Diana Cohn, Robert Day, Christopher Juniper, Fran and David Korten, Scott McVay, David Orr, Peter Raven, Bill Rees, Peter Senge, Frank Tugwell, Joanna Underwood, Sarah Van Gelder, Mathis Wackernagel, Peter Warshall, Jim Womack, and others — who provided exceptionally thoughtful critiques which greatly improved the book and for which we are both grateful and beholden. We are also hugely indebted to Bio Schmidt-Bleek and his pioneering work in resource productivity. His leadership has propelled the subject to the very top of the environmental agenda in Europe and richly informs this work. A very special mention goes to architect Tom Bender who was proposing the possibility of Factor Ten productivity in the early 1970s in the magazine *RAIN*, heard then by only a few, now echoed back in this and other works to many. Special thanks to Ray Anderson, Chairman of Interface, for his support and leadership, as well as his innovative colleagues including Charlie Eitel, Mike Bertolucci, Jim Hartzfeld, and John McIntosh, who are creating perhaps the best archetypal firm so far of the next industrial revolution.

Vital research support came from, among others, RMI's Dan Bakal, Jennifer Constable, Rick Heede, Ross Jacobs, Dan LeBlanc, André Lehmann, Louis Saletan, Auden Schendler, and Kipchoge Spencer, and from Paul Hawken's assistants — Kelly Costa, Andre Heinz, and Jeanne Trombly; special thanks also to Paul's associates at The Natural Step who were extraordinarily helpful and generous: Catherine Gray, Jill Rosenblum, John Hagen, Dane Nichols, Kate Fish, Karl-Henrik Robèrt, and Ed Skloot. Kerry Tremaine provided key insights and help in an early draft of a magazine article that preceded the book. We are also grateful for graphics help to Ema Tibbetts, for editorial counsel to Norm Clasen, Dave Reed, and Farley Sheldon, and for logistical support to JoAnn Glassier, Marty Hagen, Ruth Klock, Chad Laurent, Lisa Linden, Robert Noiles, Jennifer Schwager, and Marilyn Wien.

A special thank-you also to the following individuals whose contributions to this book cannot be easily summarized or acknowledged, but surpass expectations and generosity: Michael Baldwin, Jennifer Beckman, Maniko Dadigan, Cindy Roberts, Reed Slatkin, and Roz Zander.

Ultimately, it is the editor who brings a work to life and the public. For his endurance, patience, and skill, we thank Rick Kot of Little, Brown. His belief in this work and its implications was invaluable.

Many of the facts, ideas, and lessons in this book have come from these hundreds of collaborators. Our interpretations, and any mistakes that eluded detection, remain our sole responsibility. Readers who point out errors and omissions, and who add even better stories and ways to tell them, will earn our special thanks and the gratitude of all who labor to build further on these foundations.

The authors can be reached at:

Paul Hawken
Natural Capital Institute
P.O. Box 2938
Sausalito, CA 94966
phone: 415/332-6990
fax: 415/332-7933
e-mail: info@naturalcapital.org

Amory B. Lovins
L. Hunter Lovins
Rocky Mountain Institute
1739 Snowmass Creek Road
Snowmass, CO 81654
phone: 970/927-3851
fax: 970/927-4178
e-mail: natcap@rmi.org

CHAPTER 1

The Next Industrial Revolution

Emerging possibilities — A new type of industrialism — The loss of living systems — Valuing natural capital — The industrial mind-set — The emerging pattern of scarcity — Four strategies of natural capitalism — Radical resource productivity — Putting the couch potato of industrialism on a diet — An economy of steady service and flow — Restoring the basis of life and commerce

IMAGINE FOR A MOMENT A WORLD WHERE CITIES HAVE BECOME PEACEFUL and serene because cars and buses are whisper quiet, vehicles exhaust only water vapor, and parks and greenways have replaced unneeded urban freeways. OPEC has ceased to function because the price of oil has fallen to five dollars a barrel, but there are few buyers for it because cheaper and better ways now exist to get the services people once turned to oil to provide. Living standards for all people have dramatically improved, particularly for the poor and those in developing countries. Involuntary unemployment no longer exists, and income taxes have largely been eliminated. Houses, even low-income housing units, can pay part of their mortgage costs by the energy they *produce;* there are few if any active landfills; worldwide forest cover is increasing; dams are being dismantled; atmospheric CO_2 levels are decreasing for the first time in two hundred years; and effluent water leaving factories is cleaner than the water coming into them. Industrialized countries have reduced resource use by 80 percent while improving the quality of life. Among these technological changes, there are important social changes. The frayed social nets of Western countries have been repaired. With the explosion of family-wage jobs, welfare demand has fallen. A progressive and active union movement has taken the lead to work with business, environmentalists, and government to create "just transitions" for workers as society phases out coal, nuclear energy, and oil. In communities and towns, churches, corporations, and labor groups promote a new living-wage social contract as the least expensive way to ensure the growth and preservation of valuable social capital. Is this the vision of a utopia? In fact, the changes described here could come about in the decades to come as the result of economic and technological trends already in place.

This book is about these and many other possibilities.

It is about the possibilities that will arise from the birth of a new type of industrialism, one that differs in its philosophy, goals, and fundamental processes from the industrial system that is the standard today. In the next century, as human population doubles and the resources available per person drop by one-half to three-fourths, a remarkable transformation of industry and commerce can occur. Through this transformation, society will be able to create a vital economy that uses radically less material and energy. This economy can free up resources, reduce taxes on personal income, increase per-capita spending on social ills (while simultaneously reducing those ills), and begin to restore the damaged environment of the earth. These necessary changes done properly can promote economic efficiency, ecological conservation, and social equity.

The industrial revolution that gave rise to modern capitalism greatly expanded the possibilities for the material development of humankind. It continues to do so today, but at a severe price. Since the mid-eighteenth century, more of nature has been destroyed than in all prior history. While industrial systems have reached pinnacles of success, able to muster and accumulate human-made capital on vast levels, *natural capital*, on which civilization depends to create economic prosperity, is rapidly declining,[1] and the rate of loss is increasing proportionate to gains in material well-being. *Natural capital* includes all the familiar resources used by humankind: water, minerals, oil, trees, fish, soil, air, et cetera. But it also encompasses living systems, which include grasslands, savannas, wetlands, estuaries, oceans, coral reefs, riparian corridors, tundras, and rainforests. These are deteriorating worldwide at an unprecedented rate. Within these ecological communities are the fungi, ponds, mammals, humus, amphibians, bacteria, trees, flagellates, insects, songbirds, ferns, starfish, and flowers that make life possible and worth living on this planet.

As more people and businesses place greater strain on living systems, limits to prosperity are coming to be determined by natural capital rather than industrial prowess. This is not to say that the world is running out of commodities in the near future. The prices for most raw materials are at a twenty-eight-year low and are still falling. Supplies are cheap and appear to be abundant, due to a number of reasons: the collapse of the Asian economies, globalization of trade, cheaper transport costs, imbalances in market power that enable commodity traders and middlemen to squeeze producers, and in large measure the success of powerful new extractive technologies, whose correspondingly extensive damage to ecosystems is seldom given a monetary value. After richer ores are exhausted, skilled mining companies can now level and grind up whole mountains of poorer-quality ores to extract the metals desired. But while technology keeps ahead of depletion, providing what appear to be ever-cheaper metals, they only appear cheap, because the stripped rainforest and the mountain of toxic tailings spilling into rivers, the impoverished villages and eroded indigenous cultures — all the consequences they leave in their wake — are not factored into the cost of production.

It is not the supplies of oil or copper that are beginning to limit our development but life itself. Today, our continuing progress is restricted not by the number of fishing boats but by the decreasing numbers of fish; not by the power of pumps but by the depletion of aquifers; not by the number of chainsaws but by the disappearance of primary forests. While living systems are the source of such desired materials as wood, fish, or food, of utmost importance are the *services* that they offer,[2] services that are far more critical to human prosperity than are nonrenewable resources. A forest provides not only the resource of wood but also the services of water storage and flood management. A healthy environment automatically supplies not only clean air and water, rainfall, ocean productivity, fertile soil, and watershed resilience but also such less-appreciated functions as waste processing (both natural and industrial), buffering against the extremes of weather, and regeneration of the atmosphere.

Humankind has inherited a 3.8-billion-year store of natural capital. At present rates of use and degradation, there will be little left by the end of the next century. This is not only a matter of aesthetics and morality, it is of the utmost practical concern to society and all people. Despite reams of press about the state of the environment and rafts of laws attempting to prevent further loss, the stock of natural capital is plummeting and the vital life-giving services that flow from it are critical to our prosperity.

Natural capitalism recognizes the critical interdependency between the production and use of human-made capital and the maintenance and supply of natural capital. The traditional definition of capital is accumulated wealth in the form of investments, factories, and equipment. Actually, an economy needs four types of capital to function properly:

- human capital, in the form of labor and intelligence, culture, and organization
- financial capital, consisting of cash, investments, and monetary instruments
- manufactured capital, including infrastructure, machines, tools, and factories
- natural capital, made up of resources, living systems, and ecosystem services

The industrial system uses the first three forms of capital to transform natural capital into the stuff of our daily lives: cars, highways, cities, bridges, houses, food, medicine, hospitals, and schools.

The climate debate is a public issue in which the assets at risk are not specific resources, like oil, fish, or timber, but a life-supporting system. One of nature's most critical cycles is the continual exchange of carbon dioxide and oxygen among plants and animals. This "recycling service" is provided by nature free of charge. But today carbon dioxide is building up in the atmosphere, due in part to combustion of fossil fuels. In effect, the capacity of the natural system to recycle carbon dioxide has been exceeded, just as overfishing can exceed the capacity of a fishery to replenish stocks. But what is especially important to realize is that there is no known alternative to nature's carbon cycle service.

Besides climate, the changes in the biosphere are widespread. In the past half century, the world has a lost a fourth of its topsoil and a third of its forest cover. At present rates of destruction, we will lose 70 percent of the world's coral reefs in our lifetime, host to 25 percent of marine life.[3] In the past three decades, one-third of the planet's resources, its "natural wealth," has been consumed. We are losing freshwater ecosystems at the rate of 6 percent a year, marine ecosystems by 4 percent a year.[4] There is no longer any serious scientific dispute that the decline in every living system in the world is reaching such levels that an increasing number of them are starting to lose, often at a pace accelerated by the interactions of their decline, their assured ability to sustain the continuity of the life process. We have reached an extraordinary threshold.

Recognition of this shadow side of the success of industrial production has triggered the second of the two great intellectual shifts of the late twentieth century. The end of the Cold War and the fall of communism was the first such shift; the second, now quietly emerging, is the end of the war against life on earth, and the eventual ascendance of what we call natural capitalism.

Capitalism, as practiced, is a financially profitable, nonsustainable aberration in human development. What might be called "industrial capitalism" does not fully conform to its own accounting principles. It liquidates its capital and calls it income. It neglects to assign any value to the largest stocks of capital it employs — the natural resources and living systems, as well as the social and cultural systems that are the basis of human capital.

But this deficiency in business operations cannot be corrected simply by assigning monetary values to natural capital, for three reasons. First, many of the services we receive from living systems have no known substitutes at any price; for example, oxygen production by green plants. This was demonstrated memorably in 1991–93 when the scientists operating the $200 million Biosphere 2 experiment in Arizona discovered that it was unable to maintain life-supporting oxygen levels for the eight people living inside. Biosphere 1, a.k.a. Planet Earth, performs this task daily at no charge for 6 billion people.

Second, valuing natural capital is a difficult and imprecise exercise at best. Nonetheless, several recent assessments have estimated that biological services flowing directly into society from the stock of natural capital are worth at least $36 trillion annually.[5] That figure is close to the annual gross world product of approximately $39 trillion — a striking measure of the value of natural capital to the economy. If natural capital stocks were given a monetary value, assuming the assets yielded "interest" of $36 trillion annually, the world's natural capital would be valued at somewhere between $400 and $500 trillion — tens of thousands of dollars for every person on the planet. That is undoubtedly a conservative figure given the fact that anything we can't live without and can't replace at any price could be said to have an infinite value.

Additionally, just as technology cannot replace the planet's life-support systems, so, too, are machines unable to provide a substitute for human intelligence, knowledge, wisdom, organizational abilities, and culture. The World Bank's 1995 *Wealth Index* found the sum value of human capital to be three times greater than all the financial and manufactured capital reflected on global balance sheets.[6] This, too, appears to be a conservative estimate, since it counts only the market value of human employment, not uncompensated effort or cultural resources.

It is not the aim of this book to assess how to determine value for such unaccounted-for forms of capital. It is clear, however, that behaving as though they are valueless has brought us to the verge of disaster. But if it is in practice difficult to tabulate the value of natural and human capital on balance sheets, how can governments and conscientious businesspersons make decisions about the responsible use of earth's living systems?

CONVENTIONAL CAPITALISM

Following Einstein's dictum that problems can't be solved within the mind-set that created them, the first step toward any comprehensive economic and ecological change is to understand the mental model that forms the basis of present economic thinking. The mind-set of the present capitalist system might be summarized as follows:

- Economic progress can best occur in free-market systems of production and distribution where reinvested profits make labor and capital increasingly productive.
- Competitive advantage is gained when bigger, more efficient plants manufacture more products for sale to expanding markets.
- Growth in total output (GDP) maximizes human well-being.
- Any resource shortages that do occur will elicit the development of substitutes.
- Concerns for a healthy environment are important but must be balanced against the requirements of economic growth, if a high standard of living is to be maintained.
- Free enterprise and market forces will allocate people and resources to their highest and best uses.

The origins of this worldview go back centuries, but it took the industrial revolution to establish it as the primary economic ideology. This sudden, almost violent, change in the means of production and distribution of goods, in sector after economic sector, introduced a new element that redefined the basic formula for the creation of material products: Machines powered by water, wood, charcoal, coal, oil, and eventually electricity accelerated or accomplished some or all of the work formerly performed by laborers. Human productive capabilities began to grow exponentially. What took two hundred workers in 1770 could be done by a single spinner in the British textile industry by 1812. With such astonishingly improved productivity, the labor force was able to manufacture a vastly larger volume of basic necessities like cloth at greatly reduced cost. This in turn rapidly raised standards of living and real wages, increasing demand for other products in other industries. Further technological breakthroughs proliferated, and as industry after industry became mechanized, leading to even lower prices and higher incomes, all of these factors fueled a self-sustaining and increasing demand for transportation, housing, education, clothing, and other goods, creating the foundation of modern commerce.[7]

The past two hundred years of massive growth in prosperity and manufactured capital have been accompanied by a prodigious body of economic theory analyzing it, all based on the fallacy that natural and human capital have little value as compared to final output. In the standard industrial model, the creation of value is portrayed as a linear sequence of extraction, production, and distribution: Raw materials are introduced. (Enter nature, stage left.) Labor uses technologies to transform these resources into products, which are sold to create profits. The wastes from production processes, and soon the products themselves, are somehow disposed of somewhere else. (Exit waste, stage right.) The "somewheres" in this scenario are not the concern of classical economics: Enough money can buy enough resources, so the theory goes, and enough "elsewheres" to dispose of them afterward.

This conventional view of value creation is not without its critics. Viewing the economic process as a disembodied, circular flow of value between production and consumption, argues economist Herman Daly, is like trying to understand an animal only in terms of its circulatory system, without taking into account the fact it also has a digestive tract that ties it firmly to its environment at both ends. But there is an even more fundamental critique to be applied here, and it is one based on simple logic. The evidence of our senses is sufficient to tell us that all economic activity — all that human beings are, all that they can ever accomplish — is embedded within the workings of a particular planet. That planet is not growing, so the somewheres and elsewheres are always with us. The increasing removal of resources, their transport and use, and their replacement with waste steadily erodes our stock of natural capital.

With nearly ten thousand new people arriving on earth every hour, a new and unfamiliar pattern of scarcity is now emerging. At the beginning of the industrial revolution, labor was overworked and relatively scarce (the population was about one-tenth of current totals), while global stocks of natural capital were abundant and unexploited. But today the situation has been reversed: After two centuries of rises in labor productivity, the liquidation of natural resources at their extraction cost rather than their replacement value, and the exploitation of living systems as if they were free, infinite, and in perpetual renewal, it is people who have become an abundant resource, while *nature* is becoming disturbingly scarce.

Applying the same economic logic that drove the industrial revolution to this newly emerging pattern of scarcity implies that, if there is to be prosperity in the future, society must make its use of *resources* vastly more productive — deriving four, ten, or even a hundred times as much benefit from each unit of energy, water, materials, or anything else borrowed from the planet and consumed. Achieving this degree of efficiency may not be as difficult as it might seem because from a materials and energy perspective, the economy is massively inefficient. In the United States, the materials used by the metabolism of industry amount to more than twenty times every citizen's weight per day — more than one million pounds per American per year. The global flow of matter, some 500 billion tons per year, most of it wasted, is largely invisible. Yet obtaining, moving, using, and disposing of it is steadily undermining the health of the planet, which is showing ever greater signs of stress, even of biological breakdown. Human beings already use over half the world's accessible surface freshwater, have transformed one-third to one-half of its land surface, fix more nitrogen than do all natural systems on land, and appropriate more than two-fifths of the planet's entire land-based primary biological productivity.[8] The doubling of these burdens with rising population will displace many of the millions of other species, undermining the very web of life.

The resulting ecological strains are also causing or exacerbating many forms of social distress and conflict. For example, grinding poverty, hunger, malnutrition, and rampant disease affect one-third of the world and are growing in absolute numbers; not surprisingly, crime, corruption, lawlessness, and anarchy are also on the rise (the fastest-growing industry in the world is security and private police protection); fleeing refugee populations have increased throughout the nineties to at least tens of millions; over a billion people in the world who need to work cannot find jobs, or toil at such menial work that they cannot support themselves or their families;[9] meanwhile, the loss of forests, topsoil, fisheries, and freshwater is, in some cases, exacerbating regional and national conflicts.

What would our economy look like if it fully valued *all* forms of capital, including human and natural capital? What if our economy were organized not around the lifeless abstractions of neoclassical economics and accountancy but around the biological realities of nature? What if Generally Accepted Accounting Practice booked natural and human capital not as a free amenity in putative inexhaustible supply but as a finite and integrally valuable factor of production? What if, in the absence of a rigorous way to practice such accounting, companies started to act *as if* such principles were in force? This choice is possible and such an economy would offer a stunning new set of opportunities for all of society, amounting to no less than the *next industrial revolution.*

CAPITALISM AS IF LIVING SYSTEMS MATTERED
Natural capitalism and the possibility of a new industrial system are based on a very different mind-set and set of values than conventional capitalism. Its fundamental assumptions include the following:

- The environment is not a minor factor of production but rather is "an envelope containing, provisioning, and sustaining the entire economy."[10]

- The limiting factor to future economic development is the availability and functionality of *natural capital,* in particular, life-supporting services that have no substitutes and currently have no market value.

- Misconceived or badly designed business systems, population growth, and wasteful patterns of consumption are the primary causes of the loss of natural capital, and all three must be addressed to achieve a sustainable economy.

- Future economic progress can best take place in democratic, market-based systems of production and distribution in which *all* forms of capital are fully valued, including human, manufactured, financial, and natural capital.

- One of the keys to the most beneficial employment of people, money, and the environment is radical increases in resource productivity.

- Human welfare is best served by improving the quality and flow of desired services delivered, rather than by merely increasing the total dollar flow.

- Economic and environmental sustainability depends on redressing global inequities of income and material well-being.

• The best long-term environment for commerce is provided by true democratic systems of governance that are based on the needs of people rather than business.

This book introduces four central strategies of natural capitalism that are a means to enable countries, companies, and communities to operate by behaving as if all forms of capital were valued. Ensuring a perpetual annuity of valuable social and natural processes to serve a growing population is not just a prudent investment but a critical need in the coming decades. Doing so can avert scarcity, perpetuate abundance, and provide a solid basis for social development; it is the basis of responsible stewardship and prosperity for the next century and beyond.

1. RADICAL RESOURCE PRODUCTIVITY. Radically increased resource productivity is the cornerstone of natural capitalism because using resources more effectively has three significant benefits: It slows resource depletion at one end of the value chain, lowers pollution at the other end, and provides a basis to increase worldwide employment with meaningful jobs. The result can be lower costs for business and society, which no longer has to pay for the chief causes of ecosystem and social disruption. Nearly all environmental and social harm is an artifact of the uneconomically wasteful use of human and natural resources, but radical resource productivity strategies can nearly halt the degradation of the biosphere, make it more profitable to employ people, and thus safeguard against the loss of vital living systems and social cohesion.

2. BIOMIMICRY. Reducing the wasteful throughput of materials — indeed, eliminating the very idea of waste — can be accomplished by redesigning industrial systems on biological lines that change the nature of industrial processes and materials, enabling the constant reuse of materials in continuous closed cycles, and often the elimination of toxicity.

3. SERVICE AND FLOW ECONOMY. This calls for a fundamental change in the relationship between producer and consumer, a shift from an economy of goods and purchases to one of *service* and *flow*. In essence, an economy that is based on a flow of economic services can better protect the ecosystem services upon which it depends. This will entail a new perception of value, a shift from the acquisition of goods as a measure of affluence to an economy where the continuous receipt of quality, utility, and performance promotes well-being. This concept offers incentives to put into practice the first two innovations of natural capi-

talism by restructuring the economy to focus on relationships that better meet customers' changing value needs and to reward automatically both resource productivity and closed-loop cycles of materials use.

4. INVESTING IN NATURAL CAPITAL. This works toward reversing worldwide planetary destruction through reinvestments in sustaining, restoring, and expanding stocks of natural capital, so that the biosphere can produce more abundant ecosystem services and natural resources.

All four changes are interrelated and interdependent; all four generate numerous benefits and opportunities in markets, finance, materials, distribution, and employment. Together, they can reduce environmental harm, create economic growth, and increase meaningful employment.

RESOURCE PRODUCTIVITY

Imagine giving a speech to Parliament in 1750 predicting that within seventy years human productivity would rise to the point that one person could do the work of two hundred. The speaker would have been branded as daft or worse. Imagine a similar scene today. Experts are testifying in Congress, predicting that we will increase the productivity of our resources in the next seventy years by a factor of four, ten, even one hundred. Just as it was impossible 250 years ago to conceive of an individual's doing two hundred times more work, it is equally difficult for us today to imagine a kilowatt-hour or board foot being ten or a hundred times more productive than it is now.

Although the movement toward radical resource productivity has been under way for decades, its clarion call came in the fall of 1994, when a group of sixteen scientists, economists, government officials, and businesspeople convened and, sponsored by Friedrich Schmidt-Bleek of the Wuppertal Institute for Climate, Environment, and Energy in Germany, published the "Carnoules Declaration." Participants had come from Europe, the United States, Japan, England, Canada, and India to the French village of Carnoules to discuss their belief that human activities were at risk from the ecological and social impact of materials and energy use. The Factor Ten Club, as the group came to call itself, called for a leap in resource productivity to reverse the growing damage. The declaration began with these prophetic words: "Within one generation, nations can achieve a ten-fold increase in the efficiency with which they use energy, natural resources and other materials."[11]

In the years since, Factor Ten (a 90 percent reduction in energy and materials intensity) and Factor Four (a 75 percent reduction) have entered the vocabulary of government officials, planners, academics, and businesspeople throughout the world.[12] The governments of Austria, the Netherlands, and Norway have publicly committed to pursuing Factor Four efficiencies. The same approach has been endorsed by the European Union as the new paradigm for sustainable development. Austria, Sweden, and OECD environment ministers have urged the adoption of Factor Ten goals, as have the World Business Council for Sustainable Development and the United Nations Environment Program (UNEP).[13] The concept is not only common parlance for most environmental ministers in the world, but such leading corporations as Dow Europe and Mitsubishi Electric see it as a powerful strategy to gain a competitive advantage. Among all major industrial nations, the United States probably has the least familiarity with and understanding of these ideas.

At its simplest, increasing resource productivity means obtaining the same amount of utility or work from a product or process while using less material and energy. In manufacturing, transportation, forestry, construction, energy, and other industrial sectors, mounting empirical evidence suggests that radical improvements in resource productivity are both practical and cost-effective, even in the most modern industries. Companies and designers are developing ways to make natural resources — energy, metals, water, and forests — work five, ten, even one hundred times harder than they do today. These efficiencies transcend the marginal gains in performance that industry constantly seeks as part of its evolution. Instead, *revolutionary* leaps in design and technology will alter industry itself as demonstrated in the following chapters. Investments in the productivity revolution are not only repaid over time by the saved resources but in many cases can *reduce* initial capital investments.

When engineers speak of "efficiency," they refer to the amount of output a process provides per unit of input. Higher efficiency thus means doing more with less, measuring both factors in physical terms. When economists refer to efficiency, however, their definition differs in two ways. First, they usually measure a process or outcome in terms of expenditure of money — how the market value of what was produced compares to the market cost of the labor and other inputs used to create it. Second, "economic efficiency" typically refers to how fully and perfectly market mechanisms are being harnessed to minimize the monetary total factor cost of production. Of course it's important to harness economically efficient market mechanisms, and we share economists' devotion to that goal. But to avoid confusion, when we suggest using market tools to achieve "resource productivity" and "resource efficiency," we use those terms in the engineering sense.

Resource productivity doesn't just save resources and money; it can also improve the quality of life. Listen to the din of daily existence — the city and freeway traffic, the airplanes, the garbage trucks outside urban windows — and consider this: The waste and the noise are signs of inefficiency, and they represent money being thrown away. They will disappear as surely as did manure from the nineteenth-century streets of London and New York. Inevitably, industry will redesign everything it makes and does, in order to participate in the coming productivity revolution. We will be able to see better with resource-efficient lighting systems, produce higher-quality goods in efficient factories, travel more safely and comfortably in efficient vehicles, feel more comfortable (and do substantially more and better work)[14] in efficient buildings, and be better nourished by efficiently grown food. An air-conditioning system that uses 90 percent less energy or a building so efficient that it needs no air-conditioning at all may not fascinate the average citizen, but the fact that they are quiet and produce greater comfort while reducing energy costs should appeal even to technophobes. That such options save money should interest everyone.

As subsequent chapters will show, the unexpectedly large improvements to be gained by resource productivity offer an entirely new terrain for business invention, growth, and development. Its advantages can also dispel the long-held belief that core business values and environmental responsibility are incompatible or at odds. In fact, the massive inefficiencies that are causing environmental degradation almost always cost more than the measures that would reverse them.

But even as Factor Ten goals are driving reductions in materials and energy flows, some governments are continuing to create and administer laws, policies, taxes, and subsidies that have quite the opposite effect. Hundreds of billions of dollars of taxpayers' money are annually diverted to promote inefficient and unproductive material and energy use. These include subsidies to mining, oil, coal, fishing, and forest industries as well as agricultural practices that degrade soil fertility and use wasteful amounts of water and chemicals. Many of these subsidies are vestigial, some dating as far back as the eighteenth century, when European powers provided entrepreneurs with incentives to find and exploit colonial resources. Taxes extracted from labor subsidize patterns of resource use that in turn displace workers, an ironic situation that is becoming increasingly apparent and unacceptable, particularly in Europe, where there is chronically high unemployment. Already, tax reforms aimed at increasing employment by shifting taxes away from people to the use of resources have started to be instituted in the Netherlands, Germany, Britain, Sweden, and Denmark, and are being seriously proposed across Europe.

In less developed countries, people need realistic and achievable means to better their lives. The world's growing population cannot attain a Western standard of living by following traditional industrial paths to development, for the resources required are too vast, too expensive, and too damaging to local and global systems. Instead, radical improvements in resource productivity expand their possibilities for growth, and can help to ameliorate the polarization of wealth between rich and poor segments of the globe. When the world's nations met in Brazil at the Earth Summit in 1992 to discuss the environment and human development, some treaties and proposals proved to be highly divisive because it appeared that they put a lid on the ability of nonindustrialized countries to pursue development. Natural capitalism provides a practical agenda for development wherein the actions of both developed and developing nations are mutually supportive.

BIOMIMICRY

To appreciate the potential of radical resource productivity, it is helpful to recognize that the present industrial system is, practically speaking, a couch potato: It eats too much junk food and gets insufficient exercise. In its late maturity, industrial society runs on life-support systems that require enormous heat and pressure, are petrochemically dependent and materials-intensive, and require large flows of toxic and hazardous chemicals. These industrial "empty calories" end up as pollution, acid rain, and greenhouse gases, harming environmental, social, and financial systems. Even though all the reengineering and downsizing trends of the past decade were supposed to sweep away corporate inefficiency, the U.S. economy remains astoundingly inefficient: It has been estimated that only 6 percent of its vast flows of materials actually end up in products.[15] Overall, the ratio of waste to the *durable* products that constitute material wealth may be closer to one hundred to one. The whole economy is less than 10 percent — probably only a few percent — as energy-efficient as the laws of physics permit.[16]

This waste is currently rewarded by deliberate distortions in the marketplace, in the form of policies like subsidies to industries that extract raw materials from the earth and damage the biosphere. As long as that damage goes unaccounted for, as long as virgin resource prices are maintained at artificially low levels, it makes sense to continue to use virgin materials rather than reuse resources discarded from previous products. As long as it is assumed that there are "free goods" in the world — pure water, clean air, hydrocarbon combustion, virgin forests, veins of minerals — large-scale, energy- and materials-intensive manufacturing methods will dominate, and labor will be increasingly marginalized.[17] In contrast, if the subsidies distorting resource prices were removed or reversed, it would be advantageous to employ more people and use fewer virgin materials.

Even without the removal of subsidies, the economics of resource productivity are already encouraging industry to reinvent itself to be more in accord with biological systems. Growing competitive pressures to save resources are opening up exciting frontiers for chemists, physicists, process engineers, biologists, and industrial designers. They are reexamining the energy, materials, and manufacturing systems required to provide the specific qualities (strength, warmth, structure, protection, function, speed, tension, motion, skin) required by products and end users and are turning away from mechanical systems requiring heavy metals, combustion, and petroleum to seek solutions that use minimal inputs, lower temperatures, and enzymatic reactions. Business is switching to imitating biological and ecosystem processes replicating natural methods of production and engineering to manufacture chemicals, materials, and compounds, and soon maybe even microprocessors. Some of the most exciting developments have resulted from emulating nature's life-temperature, low-pressure, solar-powered assembly techniques, whose products rival anything human-made. Science writer Janine Benyus points out that spiders make silk, strong as Kevlar but much tougher, from digested crickets and flies, without needing boiling sulfuric acid and high-temperature extruders. The abalone generates an inner shell twice as tough as our best ceramics, and diatoms make glass, both processes employing seawater with no furnaces. Trees turn sunlight, water, and air into cellulose, a sugar stiffer and stronger than nylon, and bind it into wood, a natural composite with a higher bending strength and stiffness than concrete or steel. We may never grow as skillful as spiders, abalone, diatoms, or trees, but smart designers are apprenticing themselves to nature to learn the benign chemistry of its processes.

Pharmaceutical companies are becoming microbial ranchers managing herds of enzymes. Biological farming manages soil ecosystems in order to increase the amount of biota and life per acre by keen knowledge of food chains, species interactions, and nutrient flows, minimizing crop losses and maximizing yields by fostering diversity. Meta-industrial engineers are creating "zero-emission" industrial parks whose tenants will constitute an industrial ecosystem in which one company will feed upon the nontoxic and useful wastes of another. Architects and builders are creating structures that process their own wastewater, capture light, create energy, and provide habitat for wildlife and wealth for the community, all the while improving worker productivity, morale, and health.[18] High-temperature, centralized power plants are starting to be replaced by smaller-scale, renewable power generation. In chemistry, we can look forward to the end of the witches' brew of dangerous substances invented this century, from DDT, PCB, CFCs, and Thalidomide to Dieldrin and xeno-estrogens. The eighty thousand different chemicals now manufactured end up everywhere, as Donella Meadows remarks, from our "stratosphere to our sperm." They were created to accomplish functions that can now be carried out far more efficiently with biodegradable and naturally occurring compounds.

SERVICE AND FLOW

Beginning in the mid-1980s, Swiss industry analyst Walter Stahel and German chemist Michael Braungart independently proposed a new industrial model that is now gradually taking shape. Rather than an economy in which *goods* are made and sold, these visionaries imagined a *service economy* wherein consumers obtain *services* by leasing or renting goods rather than buying them outright. (Their plan should not be confused with the conventional definition of a service economy, in which burger-flippers outnumber steelworkers.) Manufacturers cease thinking of themselves as sellers of products and become, instead, deliverers of service, provided by long-lasting, upgradeable durables. Their goal is selling results rather than equipment, performance and satisfaction rather than motors, fans, plastics, or condensers.

The system can be demonstrated by a familiar example. Instead of purchasing a washing machine, consumers could pay a monthly fee to obtain the *service* of having their clothes cleaned. The washer would have a counter on it, just like an office photocopier, and would be maintained by the manufacturer on a regular basis, much the way mainframe computers are. If the machine ceased to provide its specific service, the manufacturer would be responsible for replacing or repairing it at no charge to the customer, because the washing machine would remain the property of the manufacturer. The concept could likewise be applied to computers, cars, VCRs, refrigerators, and almost every other durable that people now buy, use up, and ultimately throw away. Because products would be returned to the manufacturer for continuous repair, reuse, and remanufacturing, Stahel called the process "cradle-to-cradle."[19]

Many companies are adopting Stahel's principles. Agfa Gaevert pioneered the leasing of copier services, which spread to the entire industry.[20] The Carrier Corporation, a division of United Technologies, is creating a program to sell coolth (the opposite of warmth) to companies while retaining ownership of the air-conditioning equipment. The Interface Corporation is beginning to lease the warmth, beauty, and comfort of its floor-covering services rather than selling carpets.

Braungart's model of a *service economy* focuses on the nature of material cycles. In this perspective, if a given product lasts a long time but its waste materials cannot be reincorporated into new manufacturing or biological cycles, then the producer must accept responsibility for the waste with all its attendant problems of toxicity, resource overuse, worker safety, and environmental damage. Braungart views the world as a series of metabolisms in which the creations of human beings, like the creations of nature, become "food" for interdependent systems, returning to either an industrial or a biological cycle after their useful life is completed. To some, especially frugal Scots and New Englanders, this might not sound a novel concept at all. Ralph Waldo Emerson once wrote, "Nothing in nature is exhausted in its first use. When a thing has served an end to the uttermost, it is wholly new for an ulterior service."[21] In simpler times, such proverbial wisdom had highly practical applications. Today, the complexity of modern materials makes this almost impossible. Thus, Braungart proposed an Intelligent Product System whereby those products that do not degrade back into natural nutrient cycles be designed so that they can be deconstructed and completely reincorporated into *technical nutrient cycles of industry.*[22]

Another way to conceive of this method is to imagine an industrial system that has no provision for landfills, outfalls, or smokestacks. If a company knew that nothing that came into its factory could be thrown away, and that everything it produced would eventually return, how would it design its components and products? The question is more than a theoretical construct, because the earth works under precisely these strictures.

In a *service economy,* the product is a means, not an end. The manufacturer's leasing and ultimate recovery of the product means that the product remains an asset. The minimization of materials use, the maximization of product durability, and enhanced ease of maintenance not only improve the customer's experience and value but also protect the manufacturer's investment and hence its bottom line. *Both* producer and customer have an incentive for continuously improving resource productivity, which in turn further protects ecosystems. Under this shared incentive, both parties form a relationship that continuously anticipates and meets the customer's evolving value needs — and meanwhile rewards both parties for reducing the burdens on the planet.

The service paradigm has other benefits as well: It increases employment, because when products are designed to be reincorporated into manufacturing cycles, waste declines, and demand for labor increases. In manufacturing, about one-fourth of the labor force is engaged in the fabrication of basic raw materials such as steel, glass, cement, silicon, and resins, while three-quarters are in the production phase. The reverse is true for energy inputs: Three times as much energy is used to extract virgin or primary materials as is used to manufacture products from those materials. Substituting reused or more durable manufactured goods for primary materials therefore uses less energy but provides more jobs.[23]

An economy based on a service-and-flow model could also help stabilize the business cycle, because customers would be purchasing flows of services, which they need continuously, rather than durable equipment that's affordable only in good years. Service providers would have an incentive to keep their assets productive for as long as possible, rather than prematurely scrapping them in order to sell replacements. Over- and undercapacity would largely disappear, as business would no longer have to be concerned about delivery or backlogs if it is contracting from a service provider. Gone would be end-of-year rebates to move excess automobile inventory, built for customers who never ordered them because managerial production quotas were increased in order to amortize expensive capital equipment that was never needed in the first place. As it stands now, durables manufacturers have a love-hate relationship with durability. But when they become service providers, their long- and short-term incentives become perfectly attuned to what customers want, the environment deserves, labor needs, and the economy can support.[24]

INVESTING IN NATURAL CAPITAL

When a manufacturer realizes that a supplier of key components is overextended and running behind on deliveries, it takes immediate action lest its own production lines come to a halt. Living systems are a supplier of key components for the life of the planet, and they are now falling behind on their orders. Until recently, business could ignore such shortages because they didn't affect production and didn't increase costs. That situation may be changing, however, as rising weather-related claims come to burden insurance companies and world agriculture. (In 1998, violent weather caused upward of $90 billion worth of damage worldwide, a figure that represented more weather-related losses than were accounted for through the entire decade of the 1980s. The losses were greatly compounded by deforestation and climate change, factors that increase the frequency and severity of disasters. In human terms, 300 million people were permanently or temporarily displaced from their homes; this figure includes the dislocations caused by Hurricane Mitch, the deadliest Atlantic storm in two centuries.)[25] If the flow of services from industrial systems is to be sustained or increased in the future for a growing population, the vital flow of life-supporting services from living systems will have to be maintained and increased. For this to be possible will require investments in natural capital.

As both globalization and Balkanization proceed, and as the per-capita availability of water, arable land, and fish continue to decline (as they have done since 1980), the world faces the danger of being torn apart by regional conflicts instigated at least in part by resource shortages or imbalances and associated income polarization.[26] Whether it involves oil[27] or water,[28] cobalt or fish, access to resources is playing an ever more prominent role in generating conflict. In addition, many social instabilities and refugee populations — tens of millions of refugees now wander the world — are created or worsened by ecological destruction, from Haiti to Somalia to Jordan. On April 9, 1996, Secretary of State Warren Christopher gave perhaps the first speech by an American cabinet officer that linked global security with the environment. His words may become prophetic for future foreign policy decisions: ". . . [E]nvironmental forces transcend borders and oceans to threaten directly the health, prosperity and jobs of American citizens. . . . [A]ddressing natural resource issues is frequently critical to achieving political and economic stability, and to pursuing our strategic goals around the world."

Societies need to adopt shared goals that enhance social welfare but that are not the prerogatives of specific value or belief systems. Natural capitalism is one such objective. It is neither conservative nor liberal in its ideology, but appeals to both constituencies. Since it is a means, and not an end, it doesn't advocate a particular social outcome but rather makes possible many different ends. Therefore, whatever the various visions different parties or factions espouse, society can work toward resource productivity now, without waiting to resolve disputes about policy.

The chapters that follow describe an array of opportunities and possibilities that are real, practical, measured, and documented. Engineers have already designed hydrogen-fuel-cell-powered cars to be plug-in electric generators that may become the power plants of the future. Buildings already exist that make oxygen, solar power, and drinking water and can help pay the mortgage while their tenants work inside them. Deprintable and reprintable papers and inks, together with other innovative ways to use fiber, could enable the world's supply of lumber and pulp to be grown in an area about the size of Iowa. Weeds can yield potent pharmaceuticals; cellulose-based plastics have been shown to be strong, reusable, and compostable; and luxurious carpets can be made from landfilled scrap. Roofs and windows, even roads, can do double duty as solar-electric collectors, and efficient car-free cities are being designed so that men and women no longer spend their days driving to obtain the goods and services of daily life. These are among the thousands of innovations that are resulting from natural capitalism.

This book is both an overview of the remarkable technologies that are already in practice and a call to action. Many of the techniques and methods described here can be used by individuals and small businesses. Other approaches are more suitable for corporations, even whole industrial sectors; still others better suit local or central governments. Collectively, these techniques offer a powerful menu of new ways to make resource productivity the foundation of a lasting and prosperous economy — from Main Street to Wall Street, from your house to the White House, and from the village to the globe.

Although there is an overwhelming emphasis in this book on what we do with our machines, manufacturing processes, and materials, its purpose is to support the human community and all life-support systems. There is a large body of literature that addresses the nature of specific living systems, from coral reefs to estuarine systems to worldwide topsoil formation. Our focus is to bring about those changes in the human side of the economy that can help preserve and reconstitute these systems, to try and show for now and all time to come that there is no true separation between how we support life economically and ecologically.

CHAPTER 2

Reinventing the Wheels
Hypercars and Neighborhoods

The first automobile industry — Changing the world's industrial struc-
ture — Ultralight, hybrid-drive Hypercars — Starting at one percent
efficiency — Making light cars safe — The hydrogen-fuel-cell revolu-
tion — The end of the Iron Age — Birth control for cars — From com-
muting to community

THE LARGEST INDUSTRY IN THE WORLD, AUTOMOTIVE TRANSPORTATION, IS
already well along the way to a Factor Four or greater breakthrough in
resource productivity. It is also beginning to close its materials loops by
adopting durable materials that can be continuously reused to make
new cars, and to reduce dramatically its pressure on air, climate, and
other key elements of natural capital by completely rethinking how to
make a car move. This restructuring of so well established a segment of
the economy is gaining its momentum not from regulatory mandates,
taxes, or subsidies but rather from newly unleashed forces of advanced
technology, customer demands, competition, and entrepreneurship.

Imagine a conversation taking place at the end of the nineteenth
century. A group of powerful and farseeing businessmen announce that
they want to create a giant new industry in the United States, one that
will employ millions of people, sell a copy of its product every two seconds, and provide undreamed-of levels of personal mobility for those
who use its products. However, this innovation will also have other
consequences so that at the end of one hundred years, it will have done
or be doing the following:

- paved an area equal to all the arable land in the states of Ohio, Indiana, and
  Pennsylvania, requiring maintenance costing more than $200 million per day;
- reshaped American communities and lives so as to restrict the mobility of most
  citizens who do not choose or are not able to own and operate the new product;
- maimed or injured 250 million people, and killed more Americans than have
  died in all wars in the country's history;

- be combusting 8 million barrels of oil every day (450 gallons per person annually);
- made the United States increasingly dependent on foreign oil at a cost of $60 billion a year;
- relied for an increasing percentage of that oil on an unstable and largely hostile region armed partly by American oil payments, requiring the United States to make large military expenditures there and maintain continual war-readiness;
- be killing a million wild animals per week, from deer and elk to birds, frogs, and opossums, plus tens of thousands of domestic pets;
- be creating a din of noise and a cloud of pollution in all metropolitan areas, affecting sleep, concentration, and intelligence, making the air in some cities so unbreathable that children and the elderly cannot venture outside on certain days;
- caused spectacular increases in asthma, emphysema, heart disease, and bronchial infections;
- be emitting one-fourth of U.S. greenhouse gases so as to threaten global climatic stability and agriculture;
- and be creating 7 billion pounds of unrecycled scrap and waste every year.

Now imagine they succeeded.

This is the automobile industry — a sector of commerce so massive that in 1998, five of the seven largest U.S. industrial firms produced either cars or their fuel. If this industry can fundamentally change, every industry can. And change it will. This chapter describes how the world's dominant business is transforming itself to become profoundly less harmful to the biosphere.

That transformation reflects, today partially and soon fully, the latest in a long string of automotive innovations. In 1991, a Rocky Mountain Institute design called the Hypercar[1] synthesized many of the emerging automobile technologies. To maximize competition and adoption, the design was put in the public domain (making it unpatentable), hoping this would trigger the biggest shift in the world's industrial structure since microchips. As revolutions go, it started quietly, with simple observations and heretical ideas.

The automobile industry of the late twentieth century is arguably the highest expression of the Iron Age. Complicated assemblages of some fifteen thousand parts, reliable across a vast range of conditions, and greatly improved in safety and cleanliness, cars now cost less per pound than a McDonald's Quarter Pounder. Yet the industry that makes them is overmature, and its central design concept is about to be overtaken. Its look-alike products fight for small niches in saturated core markets; they're now bought on price via the Internet like file cabinets, and most dealers sell new cars at a loss. Until the mid-1990s, the industry had become essentially moribund in introducing innovation. As author James Womack has remarked, "You know you are in a stagnant industry when the big product innovation of the past decade is more cup holders."[2] Virtually all its gains in efficiency, cleanliness, and safety have been incremental and responded to regulations sought by social activists. Its design process has made cars ever heavier, more complex, and usually costlier. These are all unmistakable signs that automaking had become ripe for change. By the 1990s, revolutions in electronics, software, materials, manufacturing, computing, and other techniques had made it possible to design an automobile that would leapfrog far beyond ordinary cars' limitations.

The contemporary automobile, after a century of engineering, is embarrassingly inefficient: Of the energy in the fuel it consumes, at least 80 percent is lost, mainly in the engine's heat and exhaust, so that at most only 20 percent is actually used to turn the wheels. Of the resulting force, 95 percent moves the car, while only 5 percent moves the driver, in proportion to their respective weights. Five percent of 20 percent is one percent — not a gratifying result from American cars that burn their own weight in gasoline every year.

The conventional car is heavy, made mostly of steel. It has many protrusions, edges, and seams that make air flow past it turbulently. Its great weight bears down on tires that waste energy by flexing and heating up. It is powered by an internal combustion engine mechanically coupled to the wheels. Completely redesigning cars by reconfiguring three key design elements could save at least 70 to 80 percent of the fuel it currently uses, while making it safer, sportier, and more comfortable. These three changes are:

1. making the vehicle ultralight, with a weight two to three times less than that of steel cars;

2. making it ultra-low-drag, so it can slip through the air and roll along the road several times more easily; and

3. after steps 1 and 2 have cut by one-half to two-thirds the power needed to move the vehicle, making its propulsion system "hybrid-electric."

In a hybrid-electric drive, the wheels are turned largely or wholly by one or more electric motors; but the electricity, rather than being stored in heavy batteries recharged by plugging into the utility grid when parked (as is true of battery-electric vehicles), is produced onboard from fuel as needed. This could be achieved in any of a wide range of ways: An electric generator could be driven by an efficient gasoline, diesel, Stirling (external-combustion) engine, or by a gas turbine. Alternatively the electricity could be made by a stack of fuel cells — solid-state, no-moving-parts, no-combustion devices that silently, efficiently, and reliably turn hydrogen and air into electricity, hot water, and nothing else.[3]

Electric propulsion offers many key advantages. It can convert upward of 90 percent of the electricity produced into traction. Electric propulsion uses no energy when a vehicle is idling or coasting. Electric motors are light, simple (they contain only one moving part), reliable, inexpensive in volume production, and able even at low speeds to provide high torque — several horsepower continuously, or about ten briefly, from a motor the size of a fist. Finally, a motor that uses electricity to accelerate a car can also act as a generator that recovers electricity by deceleration. Energy recovered by this "regenerative braking" can be reused, rather than wasted, as is the case with mechanical brakes.[4]

Ultralight hybrid-drive autos could be more durable, and could potentially cost less, than traditional cars. Blending today's best technologies can yield a family sedan, sport-utility, or pickup truck that combines Lexus comfort and refinement, Mercedes stiffness, Volvo safety, BMW acceleration, Taurus price, four- to eightfold improved fuel economy (that is, 80 to 200 miles per gallon), a 600 to 800 mile range between refuelings, and zero emissions. Such integration may require one or two decades to be achieved fully, but all the needed technologies exist today.[5]

Hypercars could also decrease by up to tenfold each of four key parameters of manufacturing. These are the time it takes to turn a conceptual design into a new car on the street, the investment required for production (which is the main barrier to new firms' or models' entering the market and the main source of automakers' financial risk), the space and time needed for assembly, and the number of parts in the autobody — perhaps even in the entire car. Together, such decisive advantages would give early adopters a significant economic edge in what is now a trillion-dollar industry.

To introduce Hypercars into the market successfully, new gasoline taxes or government standards are not required. Nor is it necessary to adopt many environmentalists' assumption, and oil drillers' hope, of sharply rising longer-term oil prices. (Such a price hike is unlikely for two reasons. First, there is intense competition from other ways to produce or save energy. Second, like any commodity, oil prices have been perfectly random for at least 118 years,[6] and no important social objective should be made to depend on a random variable.) Nor, finally, would Hypercars be small, sluggish, or unsafe; on the contrary, as an uncompromised and indeed superior product, they would sell for the same reason that people buy compact discs instead of vinyl phonograph records.

For these reasons, during the years 1993–98, the private sector committed roughly $5 billion to developments on the lines of the Hypercar concept — investments that produced an explosion of advances.[7] In April 1997, Daimler-Benz announced a $350 million joint effort with the Canadian firm Ballard to create hydrogen-fuel-cell engines. Daimler pledged annual production of 100,000 such vehicles per year by 2005, one-seventh of its total current production. Six months later, the president of Toyota said he'd beat that goal, and predicted hybrid-electric cars would capture one-third of the world car market by 2005.

In December 1997, a decade earlier than most analysts had expected, Toyota introduced its hybrid-electric Prius sedan. It dominated the innovation-driven Tokyo Motor Show, winning two Car of the Year Awards. Entering the Japanese market for just over $16,000, the Prius sold out two months' production on the first day. Ford meanwhile added more than $420 million to the Daimler/Ballard fuel-cell deal. The next month, GM riposted, unveiling at the Detroit Motor Show three experimental four-seat hybrid models (gas turbine–, diesel-, and fuel-cell-powered) of its EV-1 battery-electric car. GM promised production-ready hybrids by 2001 and fuel-cell versions by 2004. *Automotive News* reported that a marketable Ford P2000 — a 40 percent lighter aluminum sedan whose 60 to 70 mpg hybrid versions had been tested earlier that year — could be in dealerships by 2000. Chrysler showed lightweight, low-cost, molded-composite cars, one of them a 70 mpg hybrid.

In February 1998, Volkswagen's chairman, Ferdinand Piëch (whose grandfather Ferdinand Porsche had invented hybrid-electric propulsion in 1900), said that his company, about to start volume production of a 78 mpg car, would go on to make 118 and then 235 mpg models.

Indeed, by the spring of 1998, at least five automakers were planning imminent volume production of cars in the 80 mpg range.

By mid-1998, Toyota, still expanding Prius production to meet demand and prepare for its U.S. and European release in 2000, revealed plans to market fuel-cell cars "well before 2002" (later slipped to 2003). In October 1998, GM confirmed that the combination of fuel cells and electric drive has "more potential than any other known propulsion system." In November 1998, Honda announced that its 70-mpg hybrid would enter the U.S. market in autumn 1999, a year before the Prius.

These innovations are the forerunners of a technological, market, and cultural revolution[8] that could launch an upheaval not only in what and how much we drive but in how the global economy works. Such Hypercars could ultimately spell the end of today's car, oil, steel, aluminum, electricity, and coal industries — and herald the birth of successor industries that are more benign.

Eventually, Hypercars will embody the four different elements of natural capitalism. Their design reflects many forms of advanced resource productivity. Their materials would flow in closed loops, with toxicity carefully confined or designed out and longevity designed in. They are likely to be leased as a service, even as part of a diversified "mobility service," rather than sold as a product. Their direct and indirect transformation of the energy and materials sectors, as discussed below, makes them a powerful way to reverse the erosion of natural capital, particularly global warming — the more so if combined with sensible transportation and land-use policies that provide people mobility without having to own cars.

So what, precisely, is a Hypercar?

ON THE ROAD TO EFFICIENCY

To correct the loss of 99 percent of the car's energy in between filling its tank and moving its driver, one must address two fundamental design flaws: The vehicle is about twenty times heavier than the driver, and its engine is about ten times larger than average driving requires. Both these flaws are the result of the pioneering choice that Henry Ford made in order to make cars mass-producible and affordable, namely, making them mainly from steel. To accelerate such a heavy vehicle quickly requires a large engine. But the car then needs only one-sixth of its available power to cruise on the highway and severalfold less in the city. The result is a mismatch not unlike asking a three-hundred-pound weightlifter to run marathons: The disparity between the engine's large output capability and its modest normal loads cuts its efficiency in half. Steel is a splendid material if weight is an unimportant or advantageous factor, but in a car, weight is neither. An efficient car can't be made of steel, for the same reason that a good airplane can't. And when cars are designed less like tanks and more like aircraft, magical things start to happen, thanks to the laws of physics.

Detroit has long focused on improving the efficiency of the drive-line — the fraction of the fuel's energy that's converted by the engine into torque and then transmitted by the drivetrain to the wheels. But there is an even better approach. The Hypercar concept attacks the problem from the other end, by reducing the amount of power that is needed at the wheels in the first place. Because about five to seven gallons of fuel are required to deliver one gallon's worth of energy to the wheels of a conventional car, increasing energy efficiency *at* the wheels reverses those losses and hence offers immensely amplified savings in fuel.

The power required to move a car can be systematically reduced in three ways. In city driving on level roads, about a third of the power is used to accelerate the car, and hence ends up heating the brakes when the car stops. Another third heats the roughly six to seven tons of air that the car must push aside for each mile it travels — this is called "aerodynamic drag." The last third of the power heats the tires and road in the form of rolling resistance. The key to designing an efficient car, therefore, is to cut all these losses.

Autobodies molded from carbon-fiber composites can cut weight by two- to threefold. This proportionately reduces the losses from both braking and rolling resistance, as well as the size of the propulsion system required to achieve a given acceleration. Such simple streamlining details as making the car's underside as smooth as its top, and slightly smaller frontal area, can together cut air resistance by about 40 to 60-plus percent without restricting stylistic flexibility. The vehicle's lighter weight, combined with doubled-efficiency tires already on the market, can cut rolling resistance by about 66 to 80 percent.[9] Together, these changes can cut by half or more the power needed to move the car and its passengers — and can therefore cut by severalfold the amount of fuel needed to deliver that reduced power.

In the mid-1980s, many automakers demonstrated concept cars — handmade models for testing new ideas — that could carry four to five passengers but weighed as little as a thousand pounds, one-third as much as the average new U.S. car today. Conventionally powered, they were two to four times as efficient as today's average new car, but were made from light metals like aluminum and magnesium. The same results can now be achieved even better by replacing the stamped metal body with molded composite materials made by embedding carbon, Kevlar (polyaramid), glass, and other ultrastrong fibers in special moldable plastics. Such advanced-composite cars could weigh initially about 1,500 pounds for a six-seater comparable in volume to a 3,140-pound Ford Taurus, and could be trimmed to perhaps 1,300 pounds or less with further refinement. A typical four-to-five-seat sedan could weigh a few hundred pounds less.

Special attention devoted to making the car ultralight is important because saved weight multiplies. Making a heavy car one pound lighter actually makes it about a pound and a half lighter, because it needs lighter structure and suspension to support that weight, a smaller engine to move it, smaller brakes to stop it, and less fuel to run the engine. Saving a pound in an ultralight car saves even more weight, because the vehicle's components do not merely become smaller; some may even become unnecessary. For example, power steering and power brakes are not required for easy handling of such light vehicles. A hybrid-electric drive becomes small and cheap enough to be especially attractive in such a light car, and it can in turn eliminate the clutch, transmission, driveshaft, universal joints, axles, differentials, starter, alternator, et cetera. Special characteristics of the ultralight body and glazings can also combine with innovative techniques to reduce noise and to provide comfort, lights, and other accessory services with several-fold less energy and weight.

MAKING A LIGHT CAR SAFE

Henry Ford said that a light man can outrun a heavy man: Weight is not a prerequisite for strength. Today's advanced-composite materials make this especially true: Crash tests have proven that innovative ultralight designs are at least as safe as standard cars, even in high-speed collisions with bridge abutments or with heavy steel vehicles. Composites are so extraordinarily strong that they can absorb five times more energy per pound than steel. About ten pounds of hollow, crushable carbon-fiber-and-plastic cones can smoothly absorb the entire crash energy of a 1,200-pound car hitting a wall at 50 mph. Such properties permit novel safety designs that can more than offset ultralight cars' disadvantage in mass when colliding with heavy sport-utility vehicles.

Millions have watched news coverage of Indy 500 race cars crashing into walls. These are ultralight carbon-fiber cars whose parts are designed to dissipate crash energy by controlled buckling or breaking away. Despite being subjected to crash energies many times those of highway accidents, the car's structure and the driver's protective devices typically prevent serious injury. Hypercars would combine this materials performance with a design that copes with the full range of possible accidents. Metaphorically, the approach could be described as "people, cushioned in foam, surrounded by a superstrong nutshell, wrapped in bubblepack." Ultralight cars, while protecting their own occupants, also pose less danger to passengers in the vehicles they hit — reversing the senseless "mass arms race" of ever heavier juggernauts. Additional safety features, ranging from all-wheel traction to blind-spot sensors, from always-dry electronic rearview mirrors to nimble handling, could make accidents less likely to happen in the first place.

THE ECONOMICS OF ULTRALIGHTING

Hypercars gain much of their advantage by abandoning nearly a century of materials and manufacturing experience based on steel. This notion might at first appear quixotic. Steel is ubiquitous and familiar, and its fabrication highly evolved. The modern steel car expertly satisfies often conflicting demands — to be efficient yet relatively safe, powerful yet relatively clean. Most automakers still believe that only steel is cheap enough for affordable cars, and that alternatives like carbon fiber are prohibitively costly. Yet industrial history is filled with examples in which standard materials have been quickly displaced. U.S. autobodies switched from 85 percent wood in 1920 to over 70 percent steel in 1927. The same Detroit executives who think polymer composites will never gain much of a foothold in automaking may in fact spend their weekends zooming around in glass-and-polyester-composite boats: Synthetic materials already dominate boatbuilding and are making rapid gains in aerospace construction. Logically, cars are next, because new manufacturing methods, and new ways of thinking about the economics of producing an entire vehicle, suggest that steel is a cheap material but is costly to make into cars, while carbon fiber is a costly material but is cheap to make into cars.

Carbon fibers are black, shiny, stiff filaments finer than a human hair, and one-fourth as dense as steel but stiffer and stronger. In 1995, structural carbon fiber cost about twenty times as much per pound as did steel. By 2000, the ratio may fall to about twelve. But if fibers are aligned properly to match stress and interwoven to distribute it, the same strength and stiffness as steel can be achieved with two or three times fewer pounds of carbon fiber, embedded in a strong polymer "matrix" to form a composite material. Moreover, for many uses, such fibers as glass and Kevlar are as good as or better than carbon and are two to six times cheaper. Combinations of fibers offer vast design flexibility to match exactly the properties that a given part needs. Composites also make it possible to use the lightest-weight body designs, including truly frameless "monocoques" (like an egg, the body *is* the structure) whose extreme stiffness improves handling and safety. (If you doubt the strength of a thin, stiff, frameless monocoque, try eating a lobster or a crab claw with no tools.) Such designs economize on the use of costly materials, needing only about one hundred pounds of carbon fiber per car.

Carbon fiber, even if frugally used, still looks too costly per pound. But cost per pound is the wrong basis for comparison, because cars are sold by the car, not by the pound, and must be manufactured from their raw materials. Only about 15 percent of the cost of a typical steel car part is for the steel itself; the rest pays for pounding, welding, and finishing it. But composites and other molded synthetics emerge from a mold *already* shaped and finished. Even very large and complex units can be molded in a single piece. A composite autobody needs only about five to twenty parts instead of a steel unibody's two hundred to four hundred. Each of those hundreds of steel parts needs an average of four tool-steel dies, each costing an average of $1 million. Polymer composites, in contrast, are molded to the desired shape in a single step, using low-pressure molding dies that can even be made of coated epoxy, cutting tooling costs by up to 90 percent. More savings arise in the manufacturing steps after the autobody is formed, where assembly effort and the space to carry it out decrease by about 90 percent. The lightweight, easy-to-handle parts can be lifted without a hoist. They fit together precisely without rework, and are joined using superstrong glues instead of hundreds of robotized welds. Painting — the costliest, most difficult, and most polluting step in automaking, which accounts for one-fourth to one-half the total finished cost of painted steel body parts — can be eliminated by lay-in-the-mold color. Together, these features can make carbon-fiber autobodies competitive with steel ones.[10]

The differences between using steel and composites are profound at every level of manufacturing. For a conventional new car model, a thousand engineers spend a year designing and a year making more than a billion dollars' worth — a football field–full — of car-sized steel dies whose cost can take years, even decades, to recover. This inflexible tooling in turn demands huge production runs, and magnifies financial risks by making product cycles last far longer than markets can be reliably forecast. If the product fails, huge investments are effectively lost. Hypercars' soft tools, roughly shapable overnight, reverse these disadvantages. The Hypercar strategy exploits small design teams, low production runs, very low break-even volume per model, rapid experimentation and model diversification, and greater flexibility. The combination of low capital intensity and fast product cycles is less financially risky, combines processes that have been individually demonstrated, and should be cleaner and safer for workers.[11]

HYBRID-ELECTRIC PROPULSION
AND THE HYDROGEN-FUEL-CELL REVOLUTION

Hypercars share with battery-electric cars the use of very efficient electric motors to turn their wheels, and the ability to recover much of the braking energy for reuse. However, Hypercars differ from battery-electric cars not only in their much lighter weight but also in their source of electricity. Despite impressive recent progress, batteries recharged from the utility grid continue to be too heavy, costly, and short-lived a way to store enough energy for much driving range. Battery-electric vehicles, as Professor van den Koogh of the University of Delft put it, are "cars for carrying mainly batteries — but not very far and not very fast, or else they would have to carry even more batteries."

Since gasoline and other liquid fuels store a hundred times as much useful energy per pound as do batteries, a long driving range is best achieved by carrying energy in the form of fuel, then converting it into electricity as needed using a small onboard engine, turbine, or fuel cell. The hybrid drive system is small, can be sized closer to typical driving loads because the engine need not be directly coupled to the wheels, and runs very near its optimal conditions at all times. As a result, a modern hybrid-electric drive system weighs only about one-third as much as the half ton of batteries required for a battery-electric car, and its temporary energy storage capacity need be only a few percent as large. Hybrids thus offer all the advantages of electric propulsion sought and elicited by California's Zero Emission Vehicle requirement, but without the disadvantages of batteries.

Depending on the choice of onboard power plant, Hypercars could use gasoline or any clean alternative fuel, including liquids made from farm and forest wastes.[12] Enough such "biofuels" are available to run a very efficient U.S. transportation system without needing special crops or fossil hydrocarbons. Compressed natural gas or hydrogen would also become convenient fueling options in such efficient cars, because even a small, light, affordable tank can store enough gaseous fuel for long-range driving — especially if the fuel is hydrogen and it is used in a fuel cell whose very high efficiency further reduces the amount of fuel that must be carried for a given driving range.

But Hypercars' greatest impact may lie in their transformation not only of the automobile, oil, steel, and aluminum industries but also of the coal and electricity industries. If this takes place, it will be because the cleanest and most efficient known way to power a Hypercar is a hydrogen fuel cell — a technology invented in 1839 but only achieving in the 1990s the breakthroughs needed for widespread deployment.

You already know the principle of a fuel cell if in high-school chemistry class you did the experiment of passing an electric current through water in a test tube, splitting the water into bubbles of hydrogen and oxygen. That process is called "electrolysis." A fuel cell simply does the same thing backward: It uses a thin, platinum-dusted plastic membrane[13] to combine oxygen (typically supplied as air) with hydrogen to form electricity, pure hot water, and nothing else. There is no combustion. The electrochemical process, akin to a battery's but using a continuous flow of fuel, is silent, rugged, and the most efficient and reliable known way to turn fuel into electricity at any scale, from running a hearing aid[14] to a factory. Submariners and astronauts drink fuel cell's by-product water. Mayors are photographed drinking the water coming out the tailpipes of the fuel-cell buses being tested in Vancouver and Chicago.

To be competitively used in Hypercars, fuel cells need to become less expensive, which will occur if they are engineered for mass production and produced in sufficient quantities. The cells use a modest amount of relatively simple (though sophisticated) materials — and are potentially much easier to fabricate than, say, car engines, with their thousand-odd moving metal parts. It is a truism of modern manufacturing, verified across a wide range of products, that every doubling of cumulative production volume typically makes manufactured goods about 10 to 30 percent cheaper. There's every reason to believe fuel cells will be subject to the same trends. In 1998, fuel-cell prototypes handmade by PhDs cost around $3,000 per kilowatt. In early mass production — say, around 2000 to 2001 — a kilowatt will probably fall to $500 to $800, and over the following few years, to around $100 as production expands and design improves. That's only severalfold more than the cost of today's gasoline engine/generators (after more than a century of refinement), about tenfold cheaper than a coal-fired power station, and severalfold cheaper than just the *wires* to deliver that station's power to your building, where the fuel cell could already be located. When fuel cells are manufactured in very large volumes, they could become extremely cheap — probably less than $50 per kilowatt,[15] which is about a fifth to a tenth the cost of today's cheapest power stations. Most automakers assume they need to attain such low costs before fuel cells can compete with internal combustion engines. Hypercars, however, being so light and aerodynamic, need less power — fewer kilowatts — and so can tolerate costs around $100 per kilowatt, enabling them to start adopting fuel cells years earlier.[16]

A sufficient production volume to achieve $100 per kilowatt could readily come from using fuel cells first in buildings — a huge market that accounts for two-thirds of America's electricity use. The reason to start with buildings is that fuel cells can turn 50 to 60-odd percent of the hydrogen's energy into highly reliable, premium-quality electricity, and the remainder into water heated to about 170°F — ideal for the tasks of heating, cooling, and dehumidifying. In a typical structure, such services would help pay for natural gas and a fuel processor[17] to convert it into what a fuel cell needs — hydrogen. With the fuel expenses thus largely covered, electricity from early-production fuel cells should be cheap enough to undercut even the operating cost of existing coal and nuclear power stations, let alone the extra cost to *deliver* their power, which in 1996 averaged 2.4 cents per kilowatt-hour.[18] Electric or gas utilities could lease and operate the fuel cells most profitably if they initially placed them in buildings in those neighborhoods where the electrical distribution grid was fully loaded and needed costly expansions to meet growing demand, or where fuel cells' unmatched power quality and reliability are valued for special uses like powering computers.

Once fuel cells become cost-effective and are installed in a Hypercar, the vehicle becomes, in effect, a clean, silent power station on wheels, with a generating capacity of around 20 to 40 kilowatts. The average American car is parked about 96 percent of the time, usually in habitual places. Suppose you pay an annual lease fee of about $4,000 to $5,000 for the privilege of driving your "power plant" the other 4 percent of the time. When you are not using it, rather than plugging your car into the electric grid to recharge it — as battery cars require — you plug it in as a generating asset. While you sit at your desk, your power-plant-on-wheels is sending 20-plus kilowatts of electricity back to the grid. You're automatically credited for this production at the real-time price, which is highest in the daytime. Thus your second-largest, but previously idle, household asset is now repaying a significant fraction of its own lease fee. It wouldn't require many people's taking advantage of this deal to put all coal and nuclear power plants out of business, because ultimately the U.S. Hypercar fleet could have five to ten times the generating capacity of the national grid.

For fuel-cell cars, the often-expressed concerns about hydrogen safety are misplaced. Although no fuel is free from potential hazard, carrying compressed hydrogen around in an efficient car could actually be safer than carrying an equivalent-range tank of gasoline.[19] The car's modest inventory of hydrogen[20] would typically be stored in an extremely strong carbon-fiber tank. Unlike spilled gasoline, escaped hydrogen likes nothing better than to dissipate — it's very buoyant and diffuses rapidly. While it does ignite easily, ignition requires a fourfold richer mixture in air than gasoline fumes do. Making hydrogen explode requires an eighteenfold richer mixture plus an unusual geometry. Moreover, a hydrogen fire can't burn you unless you're practically inside it, in contrast to burning gasoline and other hydro*carbons* whose white-hot soot particles emit searing heat that can cause critical burns at a distance. (Because of the gas's unique burning properties, no one was directly killed by the hydrogen fire in the 1937 *Hindenburg* disaster. Some died in a diesel-oil fire or by jumping out of the airship, but all sixty-two passengers who rode the flaming dirigible back to earth, as the clear hydrogen flames swirled upward above them, escaped unharmed.)[21]

Another common objection to hydrogen-fueled cars — that the first such car can't be sold until the whole country is laced with hydrogen production plants, pipelines, and filling stations costing hundreds of billions of dollars — is equally misplaced. The fueling apparatus can instead be built up with existing methods and markets in a strategy that's profitable at each step, starting now. At first, fuel-cell cars could be leased to people who work in or near the buildings in which fuel cells have already been installed. Those cars can then refuel using surplus hydrogen that the buildings' fuel processors make in their spare time. Meanwhile, those same mass-produced fuel processors will start to be installed outside buildings too. Such "gas stations" can be more profitable than those that sell gasoline today, and they won't need a new distribution system because they'll exploit idle offpeak capacity in the existing natural-gas and electricity distribution systems. Competition between those energy sources will force hydrogen prices downward to levels Ford Motor Co. predicts will beat gasoline's present cost per mile.

Hydrogen production already uses 5 percent of U.S. natural gas, mainly in refineries and petrochemical plants.[22] As decentralized production expands the market for hydrogen to run fuel cells in buildings, factories, and vehicles, more centralized production methods and pipeline delivery will become attractive. An especially profitable opportunity will involve reforming natural gas at the wellhead, where a large plant can strip out the hydrogen for shipment to wholesale markets via new or existing pipelines. Professor Robert Williams of Princeton University points out[23] that the other product of the separation process, carbon dioxide, could then be reinjected into the gas field, adding pressure that would help recover about enough additional natural gas to pay for the reinjection. The carbon would then be safely "sequestered" in the gas field, which can typically hold about twice as much carbon in the form of CO_2 as it originally held in the form of natural gas. The abundant resources of natural gas — at least two centuries' worth — could thus be cleanly and efficiently used in fuel-cell vehicles, and in fuel-cell-powered buildings and factories, without harming the earth's climate. The hydrogen provider would be paid three times: for the shipped hydrogen, for the enhanced recovery of natural gas, and a third time, under future Kyoto Protocol trading, for sequestering the carbon. This opportunity is already leading several major oil and gas companies to move into the hydrogen business. Using electricity to split water to produce hydrogen can also be climatically benign if the electricity is derived from such renewable sources as solar cells or wind farms, which can often earn a far higher profit selling hydrogen than electricity.

The more widely hydrogen is used, the more its climatically benign production — from wind farms, natural-gas fields, biofuels, et cetera — will expand to meet the demand. Retail price competition will be strong, because the four main ways to generate hydrogen — upstream and downstream, from electricity and from natural gas — will all be vying for the same customers. The technology to accomplish this already exists; the main task remaining is to trigger this commercialization strategy by manufacturing enough fuel cells so they become cheap and ubiquitous. The companies aiming to do so over the next few years read like a *Who's Who* of formidable technological and manufacturing firms worldwide.

This combination of technologies can abate, at a profit, close to two-thirds of America's carbon-dioxide emissions while preserving the mobility, safety, performance, and comfort of traditional cars. But with or without fuel cells, successful Hypercars and their cousins, from superefficient buses and trucks[24] to hybrid-electric bicycles[25] and low-cost ultralight rail vehicles,[26] will ultimately save as much oil as OPEC now sells, making gasoline prices both low and irrelevant. Between Hypercars and other new ways to displace oil at lower cost in each of its main uses today, oil will most likely become uncompetitive even at low prices before it becomes unavailable even at high prices.[27] Like most of the coal and all of the uranium now in the ground, oil will eventually be good mainly for holding up the ground.

BEYOND THE IRON AGE

A Hypercar, weighing two to three times less than a conventional car, would require about 92 percent less iron and steel, one-third less aluminum, three-fifths less rubber, and up to four-fifths less platinum. It typically would need no platinum unless it was powered by fuel cells, in which case it would use less platinum than is now in a catalytic converter. Further refinements would eliminate about three-fifths of the remaining other metals except copper.[28] The Hypercar design would double each vehicle's polymer content, but even if every U.S.-made automobile were a Hypercar, America's total use of polymers would rise by only 3 percent — less than a year's average growth.[29]

Initially, the manufacturing of Hypercars would reduce the U.S. steel industry's tonnage by about a tenth and raise carbon-fiber production volume by about a hundredfold. This level of demand should turn carbon fiber from a specialty product into a normal commodity, and reduce its cost by two- or even threefold from the 1998 bulk price of seven to eight dollars a pound. A drop in price would, in turn, make carbon fiber competitive with steel in most other industrial applications as well, from beams and girders to refrigerator shells to rebar. Hypercars would require about a tenfold lesser flow of such consumable fluids as oil, antifreeze, and brake and transmission fluids (fourteen kinds in all are used in a standard automobile), and there would be a similarly decreased flow of the twenty-one most routinely replaced automotive parts.[30] The rust-free, fatigue-free, nonchipping, nearly undentable composite body would last for decades until it was eventually recycled.[31] Together with reduced materials flows in the processing industries upstream, each Hypercar could thus represent a total saving of materials dozens of times its own weight — a total of billions of tons per year.

Best of all for the owner, the complex mechanical systems of the traditional automobile would be largely replaced by solid-state electronics and software. The most immediate benefit would be that the twenty or so most frequent mechanical causes of breakdowns *would no longer be components of the car at all.* Instead, a wireless link with the factory could keep the car up-to-date, calibrated, and tuned, improving its reliability. An expanding range of intelligent software features would enhance safety, economy, security, convenience, and customizability.

HOW DO YOU GET THERE FROM HERE?

The inherent advantages of Hypercars should make them a rapid success with drivers. However, the additional strategic advantages they offer of saving oil, protecting the climate, and strengthening the economy may justify giving automakers strong incentives to pursue their introduction into the marketplace even more aggressively. One powerful stimulus adoptable at the state level would be "feebates":[32] Whenever a customer bought a new car, he or she'd either pay a fee or receive a rebate. Which alternative and how large an amount would be involved would depend on how efficient the vehicle was. Year by year, the fees would pay for the rebates.[33] An even better strategy would involve basing the rebate for a new car on how much more efficient it is than the old car that's scrapped rather than traded in.[34] This plan would encourage competition, reward automakers for bringing efficient cars to market, and open a market niche into which to sell them — a series of benefits that has lately led GM to express interest in the concept.

Because ultralight hybrids are not just another kind of car, they will probably be made and sold in completely novel ways. Car-industry jobs will shift, though their total number could well be sustained or increased.[35] The entire market structure will change, too. Today's cars are marked up an average of about 50 percent from their production cost; more Americans sell cars than make cars. But inexpensive tooling might make Hypercars' optimal production scale as small as that of a regional soft-drink bottling plant. Cars could be ordered directly from a local factory, made to order, and delivered to a customer's door in a day or two. Such just-in-time manufacturing would eliminate inventory, its carrying and selling costs, and the discounts and rebates needed to move premade stock that's mismatched to current demand. Being simple and reliable, Hypercars could be maintained automatically by supplementing their wireless remote diagnostics with technicians' housecalls, as Ford does in Britain today. Since this market structure makes sense today for a $1,500 mail-order personal computer, why should it not work for a $15,000 car?[36]

America leads — for now — both in startup-business dynamism and in all the required technical capabilities to assume leadership in the Hypercar industry. The main obstacles are no longer technical or economic but cultural. As energy analyst Lee Schipper remarked, big automakers start with two major disadvantages, namely that they're big, and that they're automakers. Hypercars will more resemble computers with wheels than they do cars with chips. They will be driven more by software than by hardware, and competition will favor not the most efficient steel-stampers but the fastest-learning systems integrators and simplifiers. Manufacturers like Dell and systems companies like Sun Microsystems or Intel may fare better in the business than companies like GM or Mitsubishi. As Professor Daniel Roos of MIT told the 1998 Paris Auto Show, "In the next 20 years, the world automotive industry will be facing radical change that will completely alter the nature of its companies and products. . . . In two decades today's major automakers may not be the drivers of the vehicle industry; there could be a radical shift in power to parts and system suppliers. Completely new players, such as electronics and software firms, may be the real competitors to automakers."

BEYOND EFFICIENCY: THE BEST ACCESS AT THE LEAST COST

One problem that Hypercars cannot solve is that of too much driving by too many people in too many cars: Hypercars could worsen traffic and road congestion by making driving even cheaper and more attractive. U.S. gasoline is now cheaper than bottled water. Dr. Paul Mac-Cready points out that in 1986 dollars, buying the fuel to drive an average new car 25 miles cost about $4 in 1929, $3 in 1949, $2 in 1969, and $1 in 1989. Extrapolation would reach zero in 2009. Hypercars could make that right within about a nickel. The fuel saved by the 1980s doubling of U.S. new-car efficiency was promptly offset by the greater number of cars and more driving: America has more licensed drivers than registered voters. Global car registrations are growing more than twice as fast as the population — 50 million cars in 1954, 350 million in 1989, 500 million in 1997.[37] Fifteen percent of the world's people own 76 percent of its motor vehicles, and many of the other 85 percent desire their own as well. Standard projections suggest that global travel (person-miles per year) will more than double from 1990 to 2020, then redouble by 2050, with world car travel tripling from 1990 to 2050.[38] The transportation sector is the fastest-growing and apparently most intractable source of carbon emissions (21 percent of the global energy-related total). In part this is because it is the most subsidized and centrally planned sector of the majority of the world's economies — at least for such favored modes as road transport and aviation. It has the least true competition among available modes, and the most untruthful prices.

For these reasons, it is even more important to extend Hypercars' gains in resource productivity by making any kind of car less necessary. This could multiply the cars' efficiency gains by reductions in cars and driving to yield Factor Ten or greater overall savings. The key is to promote effective community design to enable more access with less driving. You could still pile the family in the car whenever you wanted and drive from Los Angeles to a magnificent national park — but when you got there, you'd actually be able to see it.

With or without Hypercars, the problem of excessive automobility is pervasive.[39] Congestion is smothering mobility, and mobility is corroding community. People demand a lot of travel and have few non-automotive ways to do it. This effectively immobilizes everyone too old, young, infirm, or poor to drive — a group that includes one-third of all Americans, and whose numbers are rising. Street life and the public realm are sacrificed as we meet our neighbors only through wind-shields. As architect Andres Duany puts it, this stratification "reduces social interactions to aggressive competition for square feet of asphalt."

A fleet of 200 mpg, roomy, clean, safe, recyclable, renewably fueled cars might keep drivers from running out of oil, climate, or clean air, but they'd instead run out of roads, land, and patience — the new con-straints *du jour*. Many of the social costs of driving have less to do with fuel use than with congestion, traffic delays, accidents, roadway dam-age, land use, and other side effects of driving itself. Those social costs approach a trillion dollars a year — about an eighth of America's gross domestic product. Because that figure is not reflected in drivers' direct costs, the expenses are in effect subsidized by everyone.[40]

Cars cause extensive pollution-induced illness and social problems. Road accidents cost about $90 billion annually by killing over 40,000 Americans, about as many as diabetes or breast cancer, and injuring 5 million more. Globally, car accidents are the fifth- and will soon be the third-largest cause of death: They currently kill a half million people and injure 15 million more every year.[41] If automobility were a disease, vast international resources would be brought to bear to cure it.

In fact, a cure has already been broadly defined, but it is a complex solution made of many details that will take time to implement. Cre-ative public-policy instruments can introduce market mechanisms that would reconfigure a transportation system long dependent on subsi-dies and central planning. Three mutually supportive types of solutions are emerging that:

1. Make parking and driving bear their *true costs*.
2. Foster genuine *competition* between different modes of transportation.
3. Emphasize sensible *land use* over actual physical mobility — a symptom of being in the wrong place.

Ever since ancient Rome suffered from chariot congestion,[42] urban congestion has been abetted by the overprovision of apparently free roads and parking — that is, by underpricing or not pricing road and parking resources.[43] However, instead of today's nearly universal U.S. practice of providing "free" parking occupying up to several times as much area as workers' office space, employers could instead charge fair market value for parking and pay every employee a commuting allowance of equal after-tax value. Workers — a third of whose household driving miles are for commuting — could then use that sum to pay for parking, *or* find access to work by any cheaper method — living nearby, walking, biking, ridesharing, vanpooling, public transit, or telecommuting.[44] Users of alternatives could pocket the difference. This "parking cash-out" concept is now the law in California for firms of fifty-plus people in smoggy areas. Reportedly, many of the firms that have implemented it are extremely pleased with the results.[45] In 1997, Congress encouraged its wider use.

Most American building regulations require developers to provide as much parking for each shop, office, or apartment as people would demand *if parking were free*. This misconceived rule diverts investment from buildings into parking spaces, making affordable housing scarcer.[46] In contrast, a San Jose, California, city council member once proposed that developers of workplaces and multi-unit downtown housing be forbidden to provide a parking place but instead be required, at far lower cost, to provide a perpetual transit pass with each unit. In Frankfurt, Germany, an office cannot be built with associated parking: Workers must buy their own. Britain is authorizing local taxation of firms that provide free or below-market employee parking.[47] Metropolitan Sydney taxes many nonresidential parking spaces to fund suburban railway-station parking and other transit improvements. In Tokyo, you can't buy a car without proving that you own or rent a place to park it. Stockholm even proposed issuing a monthly permit to allow residents to drive downtown — but the same permit would also serve as a free pass to the regional transit system (which it funds). In many American cities, allowing residents to rent out their daytime parking spaces could yield enough income to pay their home property tax.[48]

Excessive Western automobility is analogous to the extravagantly wasteful use of energy in the former Soviet Union, where it was typically priced at less than one-third of its production cost. Of course, people used it lavishly. But once true social costs began to be reflected in prices, people began to consume energy far more efficiently and sensibly. Pretending that driving is free has imposed a comparable tide of unsupportable costs.[49] Slowly, citizens and governments at all levels are realizing that drivers must start to pay the costs they incur.

Singapore's prosperity could have turned it into another bumper-to-bumper Bangkok, whose congestion — gridlocking the average driver the equivalent of forty-four full days a year — is estimated to reduce Thailand's entire GDP by about one-sixth. Yet Singapore is rarely congested, because it taxes cars heavily, auctions the right to buy them, imposes a US$3 to 6 daily user fee on anyone driving downtown, *and* channels the proceeds into an excellent transit system. Just the morning-rush-hour $3 entry fee cut the number of cars entering the city by 44 percent and solo trips by 60 percent, helping traffic move up to 20 percent faster. London now hopes to follow suit, expecting twice the speed gain from a $1 charge.[50]

Charging more to use roads, tunnels, bridges, or parking areas when they're most crowded[51] is easy with the kinds of electronic passes that already debit drivers' accounts as they whiz through tollgates in roughly twenty states. Accurate price signals can then be effectively augmented by physical redesign of roadways. Converting existing highway lanes to high-occupancy-vehicle lanes — and thus enabling faster driving — is one of many incentives for moving the same amount of passengers in fewer cars. From Europe to Australia, "traffic calming" — slowing cars with narrow streets set with trees and planters — is emerging as an effective means of slowing and discouraging driving so people can reclaim their neighborhoods.[52] It repays its cost twice over in avoided accidents alone: Contrary to a traffic-engineering dogma now being belatedly abandoned, properly designed narrow streets are actually safer than wide ones.[53] In America, where most streets are wide and most driving on them is fast, "people are more likely to be killed in the suburbs by a car than in the inner city by a gun."[54] In contrast, safety and quality-of-life concerns spurred Amsterdam to ban cars gradually from its central district: The city has begun by introducing wider sidewalks and new bike lanes, much scarcer and costlier parking, and an eighteen-mile-an-hour urban speed limit. Four other Dutch cities are developing similar plans. Such initiatives tend to be self-reinforcing. In a country like Denmark, where bikes outnumber cars two to one (four to one in current sales) and where walking and buses are widely used, there's no need for "huge roads and parking lots. This keeps towns and villages walkable, bikeable and transit-reachable."[55] Danes are thus reversing the dynamics of more cars, more sprawl, and more driving — a vicious circle that increased the average U.S. commute by over 30 percent during the years 1983–90.[56]

Reducing traffic dangers and removing barriers to walking and biking can help these individual methods of "individual mass transit,"[57] which already account for as much as 30 to 40 percent of all trips in some major European cities.[58] Yet around 1990, although some 54 percent of working Americans lived within five miles of their workplace, only 3 percent biked to work and even fewer walked. The stakes are high: A Canadian analysis found that if only 5 percent of non-rush-hour mileage in North America were shifted from cars to bikes, the social savings could top $100 billion.[59] In pursuit of those benefits, some communities are becoming more bicycle-friendly. Pasadena, California, has even found it cost-effective to give free bicycles to city workers who promise to commute with them, and plans to expand this to the general public, imitating the heavily used 2,300-free-bike ($3 deposit) program in Copenhagen. Palo Alto, California, requires office buildings to offer lockers and showers for bike commuters. A big boost for U.S. bicycling may prove to be the police departments whose bike units are reporting greater policing effectiveness, better community relations, and 10- to 25-fold lower equipment costs.[60]

As land-use and transportation choices improve, alternatives to single-family car ownership also start to become attractive. Carsharing in Berlin, now spreading across Europe, cuts car ownership by three-fourths and car commuting by nearly 90 percent, yet retains full mobility options.[61] In Canton Zürich and in Leiden, collaboration between regional public transit and car rental firms guarantees unimpaired mobility at lower cost than owning a car if you drive fewer than about 6,000 miles a year. Internet bookings integrate rental city cars with Swiss railways. Even individual carsharing can be beneficial: One enterprising immigrant to the United States leased his car to a taxi company during the day while he was attending college classes, earning him enough to pay for a new car every two years plus the cost of his education.

Modern information systems can markedly improve even old transit modes, permitting conveniently dispatched paratransit and "dial-a-ride" services. The information superhighway can also help displace physical highways in an era when half of Americans work in the information economy.[62] Bringing optical fiber into every home in America would cost less than what we spend every two years building new roads. For those tasks and jobs that can be "virtualized," ever better and cheaper telecommunications can move just the information in the form of electrons and leave the heavy nuclei in the form of human beings at home. This would offer a welcome saving in time, fatigue, energy, and cost. For many office jobs, the main benefit of such "virtual mobility" is more likely to be the increase in personal freedom and flexibility than the major traffic reductions, but both are important. A world-class Canadian firm of consulting engineers, which has sustained steady growth since it was founded in 1960, maintains staff in more than 70 locations worldwide yet has no central headquarters and hence low overheads. Wholly owned by its 1,700 employees and managed by a nine-member team that meets only electronically across three continents, Golder Associates exemplifies the emerging "virtual company" that is both nowhere and everywhere.[63]

FROM COMMUTING TO COMMUNITY

In the 1970s, Portland, Oregon, estimated it could cut gasoline consumption 5 percent merely by resuscitating the concept of the neighborhood grocery store. Such concepts are the foundation for re-creating community. Zoning and land-use planning can provide comprehensive market-based incentives to reward the clustering of housing, jobs, and shopping, as is typical in Canada's denser, more homogeneous cities and towns. Density bonuses and penalties can be based on proximity to transit corridors, and since the 1950s have helped steer nearly all of Toronto's development to within a five-minute walk of subway or light-rail services. Recent California studies suggest that in little more than a decade, such incentives for clustering can so shift land-use patterns that every person-mile of mass transit in the form of buses or light rail can displace the need for four to eight person-miles of car travel.[64] Arlington, Virginia, has cut traffic by using Metro stations as development foci. Whenever a new Washington-area Metro station opens, its proximity boosts real estate values by 10 percent for blocks around, encouraging further private development — $650 million worth just in the system's first three years.

Sensible land use would make many trips unnecessary by clustering within walking distance the main places where people want to be. Developers who do this are actually succeeding in the marketplace. Many U.S. jurisdictions, however, prohibit clustering by enforcing obsolete zoning rules enacted, as the key 1927 Supreme Court decision put it, to "keep the pigs out of the parlor." Current zoning typically mandates land-use patterns that maximize distance and dispersion, forbid proximity and density, segregate uses and income levels, and require universal car traffic on wide, highly engineered roads. Such zoning, once designed to increase amenity and protect from pollution, now makes every place polluted, costly, and unlivable.

Mortgage and tax rules that subsidize dispersed suburbs are another long-standing cause of sprawl. Especially since 1945, when they were reinforced by subsidized cars and roads, such provisions have encouraged America's exodus to the suburbs. The suburbs thus have received roughly 86 percent of the nation's growth since 1970. Europe largely avoided this decentralization, and now has four times the central-city density.[65] In Europe, 40 to 50 percent of trips are taken by walking and biking, and about 10 percent by transit — versus America's 87 percent by car and 3 percent by transit.[66] U.S. sprawl imposes staggering costs. In 1992, Rutgers University's Center for Urban Studies found that if a half million new residents moved to New Jersey over the next twenty years, each new homeowner would have to pay $12–15,000 more because of such indirect costs of sprawl as roads and extended infrastructure than if development were more compact.[67] A recent Bank of America study warned of "enormous costs that California can no longer afford. Ironically, unchecked sprawl has shifted from an engine of California's growth to a force that now threatens to *inhibit* growth and degrade the quality of our life."[68]

A good start to correcting these costly distortions would be to make developers bear the expenses they impose on the community. Another would be "locationally efficient mortgages" that effectively allow homebuyers to capitalize the avoided costs of the car they no longer need in order to get to work. Existing Fannie Mae and Freddie Mac rules qualify energy-efficient American homes for a bigger mortgage on less income, because their low energy costs can support more debt service with less risk of default. Dr. David Goldstein, senior scientist at the Natural Resources Defense Council, suggested that including in the same formula a neighborhood's typical *commuting* costs (which are manyfold larger per household than direct energy bills) would make urban housing cheaper and suburban sprawl more expensive, better reflecting their relative social impact.[69] Fannie Mae launched a billion-dollar experiment in 1995 to see how this scheme worked; now it's being expanded nationwide. It may ultimately reduce driving dramatically, because studies in three cities have shown that, compared with sprawl, higher urban density reduces driving by up to two-fifths, proximity to transit by one-fifth.[70]

Making sprawl pay its way will further boost the market advantage of New Urbanist design, which seeks instead to put the places people live, work, shop, and play all within *five minutes' walk* of one another —

the pattern observed worldwide in human settlements that have grown organically. Pedestrian-friendly spatial arrangement in turn re-creates community. As Alan Durning of Northwest Environment Watch explains it, "Most people believe the alternative to cars is better transit — in truth, it's better neighborhoods."[71] That is the key to making the car "an accessory of life rather than its central organizing principle."[72]

In short, for personal mobility as also for freight, demand for traffic is akin to demand for energy or water or weapons: It's not fate but choice. Cost-minimizing methods are now emerging to enable us to select whether to invest more in cars, other modes of transport, substitutes for transport such as videoconferencing and satellite offices, or smarter land use and stronger neighborhoods. Meanwhile, the car is being reinvented faster than the implications of its reconception are being rethought. The recent history of computers, telecommunications, and other technological convergences suggests that the switch to Hypercars could come faster than the reconsideration of where people live, work, shop, and play or how people choose among means of mobility. Hypercars can buy time to address these issues but cannot resolve them. Unless basic transport and land-use reform evolve in parallel and in step with Hypercars, cars may become extremely clean and efficient before we've gotten good enough at not needing to drive them. This success might even undermine transport reform, because if the smog vanishes and struggles for oil control are no longer necessary, it may be hard to get excited about unbearable traffic and the more subtle and insidious effect of excessive automobility on equity, urban form, and social fabric.

Hypercars are quickly becoming a reality. If their technical and market advantages seemed speculative and controversial as late as 1995, by 1999 it's clear that one of the greatest adventures in industrial history is under way. Yet as in many other contexts, the powerful technologies of resource efficiency should coexist with a keen sense of social purpose: Means cannot satisfy without worthy ends. T. S. Eliot warned: "A thousand policemen directing the traffic / Cannot tell you why you come or where you go." Mobilizing the ingenuity to create a better car must be matched by finding the wisdom to create a society worth driving around in — but less often.

CHAPTER 3

Waste Not

Industrial metabolism — The amazing amount of waste — When employment disappears, one billion and counting — Overproductivity — $2 trillion in potential savings — Growth versus progress

CARS ARE A BIG COMPONENT OF THE MODERN INDUSTRIAL ECONOMY BUT only one part. Think of the material flows required to maintain the industrial production of the United States in biological terms as its metabolic flow. Industry ingests energy, metals and minerals, water, and forest, fisheries, and farm products. It excretes liquids and solid waste — variously degradable or persistent toxic pollutants — and exhales gases, which are a form of molecular garbage. The solid waste makes its way into landfills, backyards, junkyards, recyclers, and the ocean. The molecular waste goes into the atmosphere, oceans, rivers, streams, groundwater, soil, plants, and the flesh of wildlife and people. Like the human circulatory system, most industrial flows are invisible or only partly visible. People tend to take them for granted, much as they do their bodily functions. Some of the flow can be seen in Dumpsters, shopping malls, gas stations, truck stops, or in shipping containers stacked up along docks. While its most obvious manifestations are the goods people buy or use every day — soap, food, clothing, cars, et cetera — household items make up only a small fraction of the material required to maintain our standard of living. A greater amount is needed for buildings, roads, and infrastructure. But even these taken together are dwarfed by the greatest contributor to the daily flow of materials: waste in the form of tailings, gangue, fly ash, slurry, sludge, slag, flue gases, construction debris, methane, and the other wastes of the extractive and manufacturing processes.

A critical difference between industrial and biological processes is the nature of production. Living systems are regulated by such limiting factors as seasons, weather, sun, soil, and temperature, all of which are governed by feedback loops. Feedback in nature is continual. Such elements as carbon, sulfur, and nitrogen are constantly being recycled. If you could trace the history of the carbon, calcium, potassium, phosphorus, and water in your body, you would probably find that you are made up of bits of the Black Sea, extinct fish, eroded mountain ranges, and the exhalations of Jesus and Buddha. Industrial systems, in contrast, although they get feedback from society in the form of bosses, employees, Wall Street, and monitoring machines, have largely ignored environmental feedback. The materials cycle takes high-quality natural capital from nature in the form of oil, wood, minerals, or natural gas and returns them in the form of waste. Twenty centuries from now, our forests and descendants will not be built from pieces of polystyrene cups, Sony Walkmen, and Reebok cross-trainers. The components of these goods do not naturally recycle. This means, of course, that industrial waste is accumulating and it is accumulating in nature.

A striking case study of the complexity of industrial metabolism is provided by James Womack and Daniel Jones in their book *Lean Thinking*, where they trace the origins and pathways of a can of English cola. The can itself is more costly and complicated to manufacture than the beverage. Bauxite is mined in Australia and trucked to a chemical reduction mill where a half-hour process purifies each ton of bauxite into a half ton of aluminum oxide. When enough of that is stockpiled, it is loaded on a giant ore carrier and sent to Sweden or Norway, where hydroelectric dams provide cheap electricity. After a monthlong journey across two oceans, it usually sits at the smelter for as long as two months.

The smelter takes two hours to turn each half ton of aluminum oxide into a quarter ton of aluminum metal, in ingots ten meters long. These are cured for two weeks before being shipped to roller mills in Sweden or Germany. There each ingot is heated to nearly nine hundred degrees Fahrenheit and rolled down to a thickness of an eighth of an inch. The resulting sheets are wrapped in ten-ton coils and transported to a warehouse, and then to a cold rolling mill in the same or another country, where they are rolled tenfold thinner, ready for fabrication. The aluminum is then sent to England, where sheets are punched and formed into cans, which are then washed, dried, painted with a base coat, and then painted again with specific product information. The cans are next lacquered, flanged (they are still topless), sprayed inside with a protective coating to prevent the cola from corroding the can, and inspected.

The cans are palletized, forklifted, and warehoused until needed. They are then shipped to the bottler, where they are washed and cleaned once more, then filled with water mixed with flavored syrup, phosphorus, caffeine, and carbon dioxide gas. The sugar is harvested from beet fields in France and undergoes trucking, milling, refining, and shipping. The phosphorus comes from Idaho, where it is excavated from deep open-pit mines — a process that also unearths cadmium and radioactive thorium. Round-the-clock, the mining company uses the same amount of electricity as a city of 100,000 people in order to reduce the phosphate to food-grade quality. The caffeine is shipped from a chemical manufacturer to the syrup manufacturer in England.

The filled cans are sealed with an aluminum "pop-top" lid at the rate of fifteen hundred cans per minute, then inserted into cardboard cartons printed with matching color and promotional schemes. The cartons are made of forest pulp that may have originated anywhere from Sweden or Siberia to the old-growth, virgin forests of British Columbia that are the home of grizzly, wolverines, otters, and eagles. Palletized again, the cans are shipped to a regional distribution warehouse, and shortly thereafter to a supermarket where a typical can is purchased within three days. The consumer buys twelve ounces of the phosphate-tinged, caffeine-impregnated, caramel-flavored sugar water. Drinking the cola takes a few minutes; throwing the can away takes a second. In England, consumers discard 84 percent of all cans, which means that the overall rate of aluminum waste, after counting production losses, is 88 percent.[1] The United States still gets three-fifths of its aluminum from virgin ore, at twenty times the energy intensity of recycled aluminum, and throws away enough aluminum to replace its entire commercial aircraft fleet every three months.

Every product we consume has a similar hidden history, an unwritten inventory of its materials, resources, and impacts. It also has attendant waste generated by its use and disposition. In Germany, this hidden history is called "ecological rucksack." The amount of waste generated to make a semiconductor chip is over 100,000 times its weight; that of a laptop computer, close to 4,000 times its weight.[2] Two quarts of gasoline and a thousand quarts of water are required to produce a quart of Florida orange juice.[3] One ton of paper requires the use of 98 tons of various resources.[4]

In Canada and other parts of the world, there is growing use of a concept known as "the ecological footprint," put forth by Mathis Wackernagel and William Rees, which examines the ecological capacity required to support the consumption of products, even entire lifestyles. An ecological footprint is calculated by totaling the flows of material and energy required to support any economy or subset of an economy. Those flows are then converted to standard measures of production required from land and water areas. The total land surface required to support a given activity or product is the footprint. Worldwide, productive land available per capita since 1900 has declined from fourteen acres to 3.7 acres of which less than an acre is arable. On the other hand, the amount of land required to support populations in industrialized countries has risen from two and a half acres per person in 1900 to an average of ten acres today. From a surplus of eleven acres in developed countries in 1900, there is now a deficit of seven acres per person. For all the world to live as an American or Canadian, we would need two more earths to satisfy everyone, three more still if population should double, and twelve earths altogether if worldwide standards of living should double over the next forty years.[5]

HOW MUCH WASTE IS THERE?

Fresh Kills — the world's largest dumping ground, located in Staten Island, New York — provides a repository for the daily garbage of the five boroughs of New York City. Visitors to the site are awed by a landfill that receives 26 million pounds of commercial and household waste per day.[6] Covering four square miles and rising more than a hundred feet high, it contains 2.9 billion cubic feet of trash, consisting of 100 million tons of newspaper, paint cans, potato peels, polystyrene clamshells, chicken bones, soggy breakfast cereals, cigarette butts, Coke cans, dryer lint, and an occasional corpse.[7] By the time it is filled to capacity and closed in 2001, it will be the highest mountain on the eastern coastal plain. But as massive as Fresh Kills is, it takes in just 0.018 percent of the waste generated in the United States daily. Americans and American industry create or dispose of an additional 5,500 times as much solid waste elsewhere.

Industry moves, mines, extracts, shovels, burns, wastes, pumps, and disposes of 4 million pounds of material in order to provide one average middle-class American family's needs for a year. In 1990, the average American's economic and personal activities mobilized a flow of roughly 123 dry-weight pounds of material per day — equivalent to a quarter of a billion semitrailer loads per year. This amounts to 47 pounds of fuel, 46 of construction materials, 15 of farm and 6 of forest products, 6 of industrial minerals, and 3 of metals of which 90 percent is iron and steel. Net of 6 pounds of recycled materials, that average American's daily activities emitted 130 pounds of gaseous material into the air, created 45 pounds of material artifacts, generated 13 pounds of concentrated wastes, and dissipated 3.5 pounds of nongaseous wastes into the environment in such scattered forms as pesticides, fertilizers, and crumbs of material rubbed off tires. In addition, the person's daily activities required the consumption of about 2,000 pounds of water that after use is sufficiently contaminated that it cannot be reintroduced into marine or riparian systems, and produced 370 pounds of rock, tailings, overburden, and toxic water as a result of extracting oil, gas, coal, and minerals.[8]

In sum, Americans waste or cause to be wasted nearly 1 million pounds of materials per person per year. This figure includes: 3.5 billion pounds (920 million square yards) of carpet landfilled,[9] 3.3 trillion pounds of carbon in CO_2 gas emitted into the atmosphere,[10] 19 billion pounds of polystyrene peanuts, 28 billion pounds of food discarded at home, 360 billion pounds of organic and inorganic chemicals used for manufacturing and processing,[11] 710 billion pounds of hazardous waste generated by chemical production,[12] and 3.7 trillion pounds of construction debris. Furthermore, these are merely domestic figures for material flows, and do not account for wastes generated overseas on our behalf. For example, the Freeport-McMoRan gold mine in Irian Jaya, Indonesia, annually generates 400 pounds of tailings and toxic waste for every man, woman, and child in the United States. Only a tiny fraction of the 130,000 tons of daily material flow comes to the United States as gold; the rest remains behind in the form of toxic tailings from which leachates run off and destroy riparian areas of low-lying rainforest.

Total annual wastes in the United States, excluding wastewater, now exceed 50 trillion pounds a year. (A trillion is a large number: To count to 50 trillion at the rate of one per second would require the entire lifetimes of 24,000 people.) If wastewater is factored in, the total annual flow of waste in the American industrial system is 250 trillion pounds.[13, 14] Less than 2 percent of the total waste stream is actually recycled — primarily paper, glass, plastic, aluminum, and steel. Over the course of a decade, 500 trillion pounds of American resources will have been transformed into nonproductive solids and gases.

These are all American numbers. Developing nations generally aspire to an economy like America's, but many are growing and industrializing much faster. Britain required more than a century to double its income in the first industrial revolution. Korea took fewer than 25 years. After the United States began its industrialization, 50 years passed before income doubled; in China, it required only nine years. The staggering rate of waste in the United States could therefore be quickly overtaken by the rest of the world, which has 21 times as many people.

WASTING PEOPLE

In society, waste takes a different form: people's lives. According to the International Labor Organization in Geneva, nearly a billion people (about 30 percent of the world's labor force) either cannot work or have such marginal and menial jobs that they cannot support themselves or their families. In China, it is predicted that the number of un- and underemployed will top 200 million by the year 2000, a situation that is already leading to protests, addicted youth, heroin use, drug wars, violence, and rising criminality.[15] In the United States, in 1996, a year when the stock market hit new highs, the Fordham University "index of social health" did not. The index, which tracks problems like child abuse, teen suicide, drug abuse, high-school dropout rates, child poverty, the gap between rich and poor, infant mortality, unemployment, crime, and elder abuse and poverty, had fallen 44 percent below its 1973 best value.[16] Globally, rates of unemployment and disemployment have been rising faster than those for employment for more than 25 years. For example, unemployment in Europe in 1960 stood at 2 percent; in 1998 it was nearly 11 percent.[17] In many parts of the world, it has reached between 20 and 40 percent.

The United States is proud of its relatively low 4.2 percent unemployment rate (1999), and should be. Yet official U.S. figures mask a more complex picture. According to author Donella Meadows, of the 127 million people working in the United States in 1996, 38 million worked part-time, and another 35 million, though working, weren't paid enough to support a family. The official unemployed rolls of 7.3 million do not count an additional 7 million people who are discouraged, forcibly retired, or working as temps. Of those counted as employed, 19 million people worked in retail and earned less than $10,000 per year, usually without any type of health or retirement benefits.

Unemployment percentages also mask the truth about the lives of inner-city residents. In *When Work Disappears,* W. Julius Wilson cites fifteen predominantly black neighborhoods in Chicago, with an overall population of 425,000. Only 37 percent of the adults in these areas are employed. While there are many reasons for the high rates of unemployment, the dominant cause is the disappearance of jobs: Between 1967 and 1987 Chicago lost 360,000 manufacturing jobs, and New York over 500,000. When reporting corporate restructuring, the media focuses on jobs lost. When covering the inner city, the emphasis is more on welfare, crime, and drugs; the attrition of meaningful work is rarely mentioned.[18] The irony of urban America is that fifty years after World War II, parts of Detroit, Philadelphia, and Newark look as if they were bombed, while Dresden, London, and Berlin are livable and bustling.

People are often spoken of as being a resource — every large business has a "human resources" department — but apparently they are not a valuable one. The United States has quietly become the world's largest penal colony. (China ranks second — most Americans have probably bought or used something made in a Chinese prison.) Nearly 5 million men in the United States are awaiting trial, in prison, on probation, or on parole.[19] In 1997 alone, the number of inmates in county and city jails increased by 9 percent.[20] One out of every twenty-five men in America is involved with the penal or legal system in some way. Nearly one of every three black men in his twenties is in the correctional system.[21] Is there a connection between the fact that 51 percent of the prison population is black and that 44 percent of young black men grow up in poverty? While crime statistics have been dropping dramatically since 1992 due to a combination of economic growth, changing demographics, and more effective policing, we are still so inured to criminality that rural counties seek new prison construction under the rubric of "economic development." Indeed, despite the drop in crime, during the period 1990–94, the prison industry grew at an annual rate of 34 percent, while crime and crime-related expenses rose to constitute an estimated 7 percent of the United States economy.[22] Is this level of crime really caused by Colombian drug lords, TV violence, and lack of family values? Is there not something more fundamentally amiss in a society that stores so many people in concrete bunkers at astounding costs to society? (There is no cost difference between incarceration and an Ivy League education; the main difference is curriculum.) While we can reasonably place individual blame on each drug-user, felon, and mugger, or anyone who violates civil and criminal law, we should also ask whether a larger pattern of loss and waste may be affecting our nation. Our right to assign individual responsibility should not make us blind to a wider, more comprehensive social cause and effect.

In a world where a billion workers cannot find a decent job or any employment at all, it bears stating the obvious: We cannot by any means — monetarily, governmentally, or charitably — create a sense of value and dignity in people's lives when we are simultaneously creating a society that clearly has no need for them. If people do not feel valuable, they will act out society's dismissal of them in ways that are manifest and sometimes shocking. Robert Strickland, a pioneer in working with inner-city children, once said, "You can't teach algebra to someone who doesn't want to be here." By this he meant that his kids didn't want to be "here" at all, alive, anywhere on earth. They try to speak, and when we don't hear them, they raise the level of risk in their behavior — turning to unprotected sex, drugs, or violence — until we notice. By then a crime has usually been committed, and we respond by building more jails, and calling it economic growth.

Social wounds cannot be salved nor the environment "saved" as long as people cling to the outdated assumption of classical industrialism that the *summum bonum* of commercial enterprise is to use more natural capital and fewer people. When society lacked material well-being and the population was relatively small, such a strategy made sense. Today, with material conditions and population numbers substantially changed, it is counterproductive. With respect to meeting the needs of the future, contemporary business economics is the equivalent of pre-Copernican in its outlook. The true bottom line is this: A society that wastes its resources wastes its people and vice versa. And both kinds of waste are expensive.

But it is not only the poor who are being "wasted." In 1994, several hundred senior executives from Fortune 500 companies were asked for a show of hands based on the following questions: Do you want to work harder five years from now than you are today? Do you know anyone who wants to work harder than they are now? Do you know anyone who is or are you yourself spending too much time with your children? No one raised a hand.[23]

Just as overproduction can exhaust topsoil, so can overproductivity exhaust a workforce. The assumption that greater productivity would lead to greater leisure and well-being, while true for many decades, may no longer be valid. In the United States, those who are employed (and presumably becoming more productive) find they are working one hundred to two hundred hours more per year than people did twenty years ago.[24]

From an economist's point of view, labor productivity is a Holy Grail, and it is unthinkable that continued pursuit of taking it to ever greater levels might in fact be making the entire economic system less productive. We *are* working smarter, but carrying a laptop from airport to meeting to a red-eye flight home in an exhausting push for greater performance may now be a problem, not the solution. Between 1979 and 1995, there was no increase in real income for 80 percent of working Americans, yet people are working harder today than at any time since World War II.[25] While income rose 10 percent in the fifteen-year period beginning in 1979, 97 percent of that gain was captured by families in the top 20 percent of income earners. The majority of families, in fact, saw their income decline during that time. They're working more but getting less,[26] in part because a larger portion of our income is paying to remedy such costs of misdirected growth as crime, illiteracy, commuting, and the breakdown of the family. At the same time, we continue to overuse energy and resources — profligacy that will eventually take its toll in the form of even lower standards of living, higher costs, shrinking income, and social anxiety. While increasing human productivity is critical to maintaining income and economic well-being, productivity that corrodes society is tantamount to burning furniture to heat the house.

Resource productivity presents business and governments with an alternative scenario: making radical reductions in resource use but at the same time raising rates of employment. Or, phrased differently: Moving the economy toward resource productivity can increase overall levels and quality of employment, while drastically reducing the impact we have on the environment. Today companies are firing people, perfectly capable people, to add one more percentage point of profit to the bottom line. Some of the restructuring is necessary and overdue. But greater gains can come from firing the wasted kilowatt-hours, barrels of oil, and pulp from old-growth forests, and hiring more people to do so.

In a world that is crying out for environmental restoration, more jobs, universal health care, more educational opportunities, and better and affordable housing, there is no justification for this waste of people.

LOST WEALTH

Finally, in the reckoning of national waste, there is money. The United States, which prides itself on being the richest country in the world, cannot balance its budgets (the present federal budget is *not* balanced using conventional accounting methods), fund properly its educational system, repair its bridges, or take care of its infirm, aged, mentally ill, and homeless. Where, then, is all our wealth going?

The degree to which resources and people are wasted shows up, in fact, in overall gross domestic product. Of the $9 trillion spent every year in the United States, at least $2 trillion annually is wasted. What is meant by "waste" in this context? Simply stated, it represents money spent where the buyer gets no value. An example of waste familiar to everyone is sitting in a traffic jam on a congested freeway. Money is being expended on gas, time, and wear and tear on car and driver, but it produces zero value. Discretionary activities, cruising the streets in low riders or speeding across Lake Mead in a 600 hp cigar boat, aren't counted here as waste. Waste is a built-in feature of an outmoded industrial system and it saps our national strength. Here is a partial list of how money is wasted in the United States:

Highway accidents cost society more than $150 billion per year, including health care costs, lost productivity, lost tax revenue, property damage, and police, judicial, and social services costs. According to the World Resources Institute, highway congestion costs $100 billion per year in lost productivity; that figure does not include gasoline, increased accidents, and maintenance costs. In the United States alone, the total hidden social costs of driving, not paid by the motorist, total nearly $1 trillion, including such expenses as building and repairing roads, economic losses due to congestion, ill health caused by air pollution, and medical costs for the victims of the 2 million accidents each year.[27] We spend $50 billion a year for military forces that mainly guard Mideast oil sources we would not need if the Reagan administration had not gutted light-vehicle efficiency standards in 1986.[28] Nearly $200 billion a year in energy costs is wasted because we do not employ the same efficiency practices as Japan in businesses, homes, and transportation.

In health care, $65 billion is spent annually on nonessential or even fraudulent tests and procedures (including 420,000 unneeded caesareans).[29, 30] By some estimates, $250 billion of inflated and unnecessary medical overhead is generated by the current insurance system.[31] We spend $50 billion a year in health costs because of our dietary choices, and as much as $100 billion on costs related to the effects of polluted air.[32, 33] We spend $69 billion on obesity, $274 billion on heart disease and strokes,[34] and $52 billion on substance abuse. Health-care budgets are being increasingly burdened by such "old" diseases as staphylococcus and tuberculosis, now appearing in new drug-resistant forms thanks to shortcuts taken to save money in public health, prisons, homeless shelters, and medical treatment.

Legal, accounting, audit, bookkeeping, and recordkeeping expenditures that are required to comply with an unnecessarily complex and unenforceable tax code cost citizens at least $250 billion a year. What Americans fail to pay the IRS adds up to another $150 billion.

We pay criminals $40 billion a year for illegal drugs.[35] Crime costs $450 billion a year.[36] Another $300 billion is spent on lawsuits (how much of that amount is necessary can be gauged by the fact that the United States has 70 percent of the world's lawyers).

This inventory doesn't account for costs to clean or contain Superfund sites. It doesn't count cleanup of nuclear weapons facilities (estimated as high as $500 billion) or the annual expense of disposing of 25 billion tons of material waste. Also ignored are subsidies to such environmentally damaging industries as mining, nuclear utilities, unsound agriculture, and forestry. In various ways topsoil loss, loss of fisheries, damage from poor land management, water pollution, and potential losses due to climate change are all subsidized. Then there is government waste, consumer fraud, legal and illegal gambling, costs related to replacing shoddy products, and the social costs of unemployment. It is conceivable that as much as one-half of the entire GDP is attributable to some form of waste. If even a portion of these expenditures could be shifted to more productive uses, money would be available to balance the budget, raise superbly educated children, restore degraded environments, and help the less fortunate. If that seems an overly optimistic projection, consider that, had we adopted in 1974 the efficient energy practices of some other advanced industrial countries, and applied the savings to the national debt, we would not today have a national debt.

WASTE AS A SYSTEM

Because of the profligate nature of current industrial processes, the world thus faces three crises that threaten to cripple civilization in the twenty-first century: the deterioration of the natural environment; the ongoing dissolution of civil societies into lawlessness, despair, and apathy; and the lack of public will needed to address human suffering and social welfare. All three problems share waste as a common cause. Learning to deal responsibly with that waste is a common solution, one that is seldom acknowledged yet increasingly clear.

There is nothing original in this record of national waste; what is novel is that each of the three types of waste is presented as interlocking symptoms of one problem: using too many resources to make too few people more productive. This increasingly expensive industrial formula is a relic of a past that no longer serves a present or a future.

At this point, it is worth asking, do we have any reasons to be hopeful about the future? History has demonstrated that societies may act stupidly for periods of time, but eventually they move to the path of least economic resistance. The loss of natural capital services is already imposing severe costs. Despite the convoluted economic theories and accounting systems that have been devised to persuade ourselves that they aren't a significant problem, those costs are starting to become apparent, undeniable, and unavoidable, as evidenced above in the cost of waste.

Further, if the growth in human-made capital is genuinely being affected by the loss of natural capital, there should be economic and social indices of that fact, measures that can be recognized and acknowledged by businesspeople and policymakers alike. As it happens, the signs are there for us to see. Economic growth in the United States may not be as robust as we have been led to believe; in fact, the economy may not be growing at all. That assertion may sound preposterous, but more and more economists are taking this possibility seriously. Obviously, "growth" in this context does not refer to dollar-denominated GDP, which has increased at 2.5 percent per year since 1973. It is *net* growth that has come to a standstill: the growth in the quality of life, in leisure and family time, in higher real wages, in a better infrastructure, and in greater economic security. We can't say with any confidence that America is growing because the index relied upon, the GDP, only measures money spent, not value received. But there is a world of difference between the exchange of dollars and the creation of well-being. By current economic definitions, most industrial, environmental, and social waste is counted as gross domestic product right alongside TVs, bananas, cars, and Barbie dolls. The definition of economic growth includes *all* expenditures, regardless of whether society benefits or loses. Growth includes crime, emergency room charges, prison maintenance, dump fees, environmental cleanups, the costs of lung disease, oil spills, cancer treatment, divorce, shelters for battered women, every throwaway object along every highway, and liquor sold to the homeless. When accepted economic indices so wildly diverge from reality, we are witnessing the tottering end of a belief system. These beliefs become even more tenuous as the experts reassure us that more of this type of growth will save us from the very ills this type of growth creates.[37] In fact, an alternate term for what the country is now experiencing has been suggested: uneconomic growth.[38]

According to Jonathan Rowe of Redefining Progress, a public-policy think tank that is analyzing and reframing measures of progress: "The GDP is simply a gross measure of market activity, of money changing hands. It makes no distinction whatsoever between the desirable and the undesirable, or costs and gain. On top of that, it looks only at the portion of reality that economists choose to acknowledge — the part involved in monetary transactions. The crucial economic functions performed in the household and volunteer sectors go entirely unreckoned. As a result the GDP not only masks the breakdown of the social structure and the natural habitats upon which the economy — and life itself — ultimately depend; worse, it portrays such breakdown as economic gain."[39] Since growth as conventionally defined encompasses both decay and improvements, an honest accounting would subtract decline from revenue to determine if the result is a net credit or debit. Those calculations can't be done as long as the government is using a calculator with no minus signs. Then again, if you consider the fact that natural capital isn't even valued, and is theoretically worth as much as all the economic activity shown on the books, it almost doesn't matter what signs are on the calculator.

By masking impoverishment in society, the GDP sends signals to commerce that are as specious as those it conveys to the government and to citizens. While it is not business's responsibility to recalculate government indicators, business may have to get more involved in such debates to enable it to get the sort of feedback it will need to plan strategically for a viable future in which it has a role to play. Ironically, most economists don't like the GDP standard either. In 1972, economists William Nordhaus and James Tobin wrote, "Maximization of GNP is not a proper objective of policy." Economist Robert Repetto goes further: "Under the current system of national accounting, a country could exhaust its mineral resources, cut down its forests, erode its soils, pollute its aquifers, and hunt its wildlife and fisheries to extinction, but measured income would not be affected as these assets disappeared. . . . The result can be illusory gains in income and permanent losses in wealth."[40] Given the pressures that are being placed upon living systems, it is critical for companies to look at their own industrial metabolism and begin to change course. Early adopters and forward-looking competitors will soon stake out the high ground of how a corporation can profitably deliver what people will need yet with radical reductions in throughput.

By any measure, we are destroying the most productive systems ever seen on earth while statistically blinding ourselves to the problem. Economics cannot function as a reliable guide until natural capital is placed on the balance sheets of companies, countries, and the world. As it stands, the capitalist system is based on accounting principles that would bankrupt any company. A healthy economy needs, as any accounting student understands, an accurate balance sheet. In the meantime, acting as though natural and human capital *were* properly valued is critically important. When natural capital is no longer treated as free, unlimited, and inconsequential, but as an integral and indispensable part of the production process, our entire system of accounting will change. Prices, costs, and how we calculate value will alter dramatically.

The next four chapters show what can happen when biological and material limits are seen as an opportunity rather than a problem. In industry, the "waste" problem is being approached with ingenious methods and technologies. The advances in radical resource productivity that have been achieved in a relatively short time are more than surprising; they are revolutionary. Within these techniques and processes resides a whole new set of business and design principles.

CHAPTER 4

Making the World

Fewer calories, more energy — A new design mentality — No limits to innovation — Distributing control — Organizations that learn — Getting as smart as clams — Repurifying Swiss drinking water — Ephemeralization — Born-again materials

INDUSTRY MAKES THINGS. IT TAKES MATERIALS — GENERALLY OUT OF THE ground — and processes them into desired forms. These objects are distributed, sold, used, discarded, and then typically dumped back in or onto the ground. Because economic consumption doesn't create or destroy matter[1] but only changes its location, form, and value, the same tonnages that were mined from the ground as resources, treated, transported, made into goods, and distributed to customers are then hauled away again as waste or emitted as pollution.

For the average American, the daily flows of materials (other than water) total more than twenty times a person's body weight, nearly all of it waste. But that waste can be greatly reduced without compromising our well-being. Any improvement that provides the same or a better stream of *services* from a smaller flow of *stuff* can produce the same material wealth with less effort, transportation, waste, and cost.

MORE ENERGY-EFFICIENT MANUFACTURING

For centuries, even millennia, engineers have sought to reduce industry's use of energy and resources. The previous industrial revolution sped the transition from Newcomen's 0.5 percent efficient steam engine to today's better than 50 percent efficient diesel engines. For decades, the energy used to make a given product has been falling by typically a percent or two a year — faster when energy prices rise, slower when they fall. Yet at each stage of the industrial process, a host of opportunities still exists for doing more and better with much, much less. Even in the most efficient countries and industries, opportunities to wring out waste and improve product quality, as human ingenuity develops new technologies and finds better ways to apply them, are expanding faster than they're being used up. This is partly because technology improves faster than obsolete factories are replaced, but often it's just because people and firms aren't yet learning as fast as they could and should. The possible improvements will no doubt lose momentum at some point, but it's no more in sight than is the end of human creativity.

To look at only one example, chemical manufacturing uses heat and pressure, first to cause reactions that shift and shape molecules into desired forms, then to separate those products from undesired ones. Chemical engineers have been saving energy and materials costs for over a century, cutting U.S. chemical firms' energy intensity in half just since 1970. They've plugged steam leaks, installed thermal insulation, and recovered and reused heat. But there's still more to be saved — far more. "Pinch technology" helps deliver heat at just the temperature required for the process and then recover it. These two improvements can often save another half or more of the remaining energy, yet pay for themselves quickly — within six months in typical retrofits.[2] Meanwhile, designer catalysts are being tailored to help make specific chemical reactions take place faster and more efficiently, yielding less mass of the undesired products that in fine chemicals often weigh 5 to 50, and in pharmaceuticals 25 to 100-plus, times as much as the desired product.[3]

No industry lacks potential for radically better energy efficiency, not even the world's most advanced major business, the making of microchips — the highest-value-added sector of U.S. manufacturing,[4] and soon to be one of the world's largest employers. Chipmaking plants are consistently designed so poorly that most of their energy can be saved with 100-plus percent typical after-tax returns on retrofit investments, better operations, and faster, cheaper construction of new plants.[5] For example, a large Asian chip-assembly plant in 1997 cut its energy bills by 69 percent per chip in less than a year; a Singapore chipmaking plant between 1991 and 1997 cut its energy use per wafer by 60 percent with half the paybacks under twelve months and four-fifths under eighteen months; another saved $5.8 million per year from $0.7 million of retrofit projects.[6] Chipmakers, with $169 billion worth of new plants on the drawing boards worldwide,[7] are just discovering that highly efficient plants, and the design and management philosophy they reflect, will allow them to outcompete their rivals.

The potential for saving energy, resources, pollution, waste, and money in the industrial realm would take many specialized books to describe, because its range of activities is so diverse and complex. The U.S. chemical business alone comprises more than 30 industries producing over 70,000 distinct products in more than 12,000 factories.[8] However, if considered in sufficiently general terms, the methods to increase industry's energy and material productivity can be classified into at least six main categories, which often reinforce one another:

- design
- new technologies
- controls
- corporate culture
- new processes, and
- saving materials

DESIGN

The whole-system approach applied to Hypercars can be applied in the rest of industry, too: Virtually all the energy-using equipment now in use was designed using rules of thumb that are wrong. Asking different questions, much as the scientist Edwin Land did when he described invention as "a sudden cessation of stupidity," can suggest areas to be targeted for innovation. This can achieve large energy savings in such commonplace equipment as valves, ducts, fans, dampers, motors, wires, heat exchangers, insulation, and most other elements of technical design, in most of the technical systems that use energy, in most applications, in all sectors. This new efficiency revolution, much of it retrofittable, relies not so much on new technology as on the more intelligent application of existing technology, some of which dates back to the Victorian period.

Sometimes the best changes in design are the simplest. Enabling America's half million laboratory fume hoods to use 60–80 percent less fanpower yet become even safer is largely a matter of changing the position of one louver.[9] In the mundane but very costly task of removing contaminated air from cleanrooms, a new mechanical flow controller,[10] using a single moving part operated solely by gravity and airflow, can reduce energy use by around 50–80 percent, reduce total construction cost, and improve safety and performance. New geometries can double the efficiency of sewage pumps[11] and quintuple that of aerators.[12] Such simple but large opportunities abound in the heaviest industries, too. Steel slabs are normally cast far from the rolling mills that make them thinner, so by the time they arrive to be rolled, they need to be reheated; moving the two processes closer together saves about 18 percent of that reheat energy.[13] The U.S. glass industry's goal of halving its process energy consumption by 2020[14] will depend partly on losing less heat from regenerative furnaces. R&D so far has focused mainly on the smallest loss — the 23 percent that is dissipated up the stack. But why not first address cutting the biggest loss — the 40 percent escaping through the furnace wall, which can be superinsulated?

It may finally take a wakeup call to bring about a shift of design mentality in some entrenched industries. Few believed that Weiss, a Hamburg oil re-refinery, could eliminate its unlicensed discharge into the harbor until Greenpeace activists got impatient, plugged up the pipe, and announced that the plant had two hours to figure out how to clean up before its tanks started overflowing. The plant shut down for a half year, completely redesigned its refining process, and hasn't discharged effluent since.[15]

NEW TECHNOLOGIES

New materials, design and fabrication techniques, electronics, and software can fuse into unexpected patterns — technologies more powerful than the sum of their parts. From superefficient cooling coils to switched-reluctance motors (which can continuously adjust their software for peak efficiency under all operating conditions), smart materials to sophisticated sensors, rapid prototyping to ultraprecision fabrication, improved power-switching semiconductors to atomic-scale manipulation, microfluidics[16] and micromachines,[17] revolutions are under way in myriad technical arts and sciences.

Innovation seems in no danger of drying up. Technologies available today can save about twice as much electricity as was feasible five years ago, at only a third the real cost. That rate of progress has been consistent for the past fifteen to twenty years. Much of the continuing improvement in energy efficiency is due to ever better technologies for wringing more work out of each unit of energy and resources. Lately, though, the changes in design mentality — the ways to apply these established technologies — have become even more critical.

Each time practical limits to innovation seem to be approaching, or even limits imposed by the laws of physics, someone devises a way to evade those limits by redefining the problem. Generations of power engineers knew their generating plants couldn't ever be more than 40-odd percent efficient because of Carnot's Law, which first described the theoretical limits. Surprise: Now you can buy off-the-railcar combined-cycle gas turbines that are about 60 percent efficient, using a different thermodynamic cycle not subject to Carnot's Law. Fuel cells can do even better. And of course the rest, the "waste" heat, need not be wasted. Recovering it can raise the useful work extracted, mostly as electricity, to more than 90 percent of the original fuel energy.

CONTROLS

Information technologies provide large savings as various industries adopt them. A coal-fired power station that ran the old way — hard-hatted guys with big wrenches ran around adjusting valves as a supervisor scanned a wallful of hydraulic gauges — hired a couple of young engineers fresh out of Georgia Tech. They harried their boss into letting them buy a two-hundred-dollar Radio Shack portable computer on which they wrote a simple program to help optimize the plant's operations. Their initiative saved millions of dollars in the first year. The rookie engineers soon found themselves telling their story to the board of directors, launching a transformation in the culture of the Georgia Power Company.[18]

Most factories throughout the world still lack such simple, gross-scale optimization and controls. Moreover, many existing controls aren't properly used. Controls should measure what's happening now, not what happened an hour ago, because problems not discovered and fixed immediately cause waste. The Toyota empire was built on revenues garnered from Sakichi Toyoda's "self-monitoring" looms, which shut down instantly if a thread broke, before they could make defective cloth. This obvious principle is still often ignored in those industries where delayed feedback is the most costly. Distillation columns use 3 percent of total U.S. energy to separate chemical and oil products, but most operators, instead of continuously monitoring the purity of product as it emerges, test only occasionally to make sure samples meet specification. Between tests, the operators, flying blind, often feed the same material back through the column more times than necessary — using 30–50 percent excess energy — to be really sure the product will pass the test. Better controls that measure the purity actually coming out and keep fine-tuning the process for the desired results could cut that waste about in half.[19] A civilization that can robotically measure the composition of rocks on Mars should be able to measure the composition of chemicals in a pipe on Earth.

Measurement and control intelligence can be distributed into each piece of manufacturing equipment so that each part of the process governs itself. Reactions can be kept at the right temperature, machine tools fed to cut at the optimal rate, textiles heated until they're dry but not baked. The more localized the control and feedback, the more precise the levels of control. Ubiquitous microchips now permit not just such simple controls but also the construction of neural networks that learn, and the use of fuzzy logic that makes eerily smart decisions.

The emerging next step in distributed intelligence is self-organizing systems of all kinds. Hierarchical control systems have one centralized boss, human or computerized, telling everyone what to do and enforcing commands through layers of authority. Distributed intelligence, in contrast, uses many decentralized decision makers of comparable power, interpreting events under shared rules, interacting with and learning from each other, and controlling their collective behavior through the interaction of their diverse local decisions, much like an ecosystem works. Kevin Kelly, in his book *Out of Control*, describes how this ecosystem-like model, where many small parts join together to create a highly adaptive whole, is gradually taking over the world as complex systems organize and adapt in coevolution with their changing environments, just like life itself. Thus the "world of the made" will increasingly come to resemble the "world of the born": technical artifacts will start being organized and controlled more and more by biologic, because biological systems already have evolved successful design solutions.[20]

In these and other important ways, designers are beginning to incorporate the billions of years' design experience reflected in biological principles into industrial applications. These are being carried out not merely in process design but also in areas of system architecture and control. The plant whose operators rely on luck or intuition to optimize complex processes with hundreds of interacting variables is already losing out to the plant whose operators have turned to powerful computers equipped with artificial intelligence and "genetic algorithms," which evolve the fittest solutions by a mathematical version of Darwinian natural selection. The operator scanning endless tables of numbers won't understand what's happening as well as the operator whose computer graphics let her see at a glance what's happening in the plant, how to improve it, and how to design the next plant even better. Ultimately, if factories become really smart, they won't need special control systems. They'll guide even the most awesomely complex processes with the insouciant ease with which self-controlling cells make their myriad biochemicals, or self-controlling ecosystems adapt to their changing environments.

CORPORATE CULTURE

A business that functions as a learning organization — rewarding measurement, monitoring, critical thought, and continuous improvement — will always outpace a corporate culture peopled by dial-watchers and button-pushers. A business that takes advantage of powerful tools for measurement, simulation, emulation, and graphic display can turn the design and operating processes from linear — require, design, build, repeat — to cyclic — require, design, build, *measure, analyze, improve,* repeat. A business that ignores measurement will inevitably fall behind in making useful and cost-saving discoveries — like the chemical company that for decades had been unwittingly running a forty-kilowatt electric heater under its parking lot year-round to melt snow. Nobody remembered or noticed the device until measurement found that the energy books didn't balance, and the wiring was traced to track down the discrepancy.

Many manufacturing firms are unwittingly experiencing similar financial drains in their compressed-air systems: You can walk through their plants listening to the money hissing out of the leaks. Improved compressed-air maintenance and hardware typically yield savings approaching 50 percent with six-month paybacks.[21] But if nobody pays attention, bad housekeeping persists. It typically gets fixed only when someone wanders in on a weekend, notices the compressor turning on to replenish pressure being lost through leaks, and happens to wonder why the compressor is working at all when nobody else is.

Sometimes it's clear to everyone that something's wrong, but no one can figure out why. A southwestern adobe hotel, long passively cooled, suddenly started overheating. Just as the owner was about to buy a big air conditioner, a guest, who happened to be an Israeli solar expert, diagnosed the problem: the walls, originally whitewashed, had been painted brown.

You might think that such obvious answers should be easily worked out in modern factories full of smart engineers. But they aren't.[22] Sometimes equipment is improperly installed because it is mislabeled at the factory. In 1981, Pacific Gas and Electric Company built the Diablo Canyon nuclear power plant's major pipe supports the wrong way around, costing billions of dollars to fix, because someone had reversed the blueprint. The twenty-year, $2.5 billion Hubble Space Telescope project launched a misshapen mirror into space because of a sign error in an algebraic equation. Or to pick a mundane case, measurements on three thousand Southern California houses found one-fifth were miswired, with either no functional ground or ground and neutral interchanged. The electricians who wire factories are equally fallible.

For decades, even after computer memory had become so cheap that the original rationale had long since vanished, skilled computer programmers, often under direct orders from their superiors, saved money by writing dates with two year digits instead of four — snarling the world's software and hardwired chips into the Year 2000 bug. The costs of fixing that are so incalculable that they may erase much or all productivity gains from worldwide computerization. Fortunately, most mistakes are more farcical than economy-busting: To test a high-speed train design, British Rail borrowed the Federal Aviation Administration's gun that fires dead chickens at aircraft windshields to ensure they can withstand a bird strike. BR's engineers were horrified when the test chicken went through the windshield, through the driver's chair, and made a big mess on the back wall. The FAA checked the protocol and recommended a retest — "but this time, make sure the chicken has first been thawed."

NEW PROCESSES

Process innovations in manufacturing help cut out steps, materials, and costs. They achieve better results using simpler and cheaper inputs. In practically every industry, visionaries are improving processes and products by developing highly resource-efficient materials, techniques, and equipment. Even in iron- and steelmaking, one of the oldest, biggest, and most resource-intensive of the industrial arts, researchers have discovered ways to reduce energy use by about four-fifths with better output quality, less manufacturing time, less space, often less investment, and probably less total cost.

A particularly exciting area of leapfrog improvements is the potential to replace high-temperature processes with gentler, cheaper ones based on biological models that often involve using actual microorganisms or enzymes. Such discoveries come from observing and imitating nature. Ernie Robertson of Winnipeg's Biomass Institute remarked that there are three ways to turn limestone into a structural material. You can cut it into blocks (handsome but uninteresting), grind it up and calcine it at about 2,700°F[23] into Portland cement (inelegant), or feed it to a chicken and get it back hours later as even stronger eggshell. If we were as smart as chickens, he suggested, we might master this elegant near-ambient-temperature technology and expand its scale and speed. If we were as smart as clams and oysters, we might even do it slowly at about 40°F, or make that cold seawater into microstructures as impressive as the abalone's inner shell, which is tougher than missile-nosecone ceramics.[24]

Or consider the previously noted sophisticated chemical factory within every humble spider. Janine Benyus contrasts arachnid with industrial processes:

> The only thing we have that comes close to [spider] silk . . . is polyaramid Kevlar, a fiber so tough it can stop bullets. But to make Kevlar, we pour petroleum-derived molecules into a pressurized vat of concentrated sulfuric acid and boil it at several hundred degrees Fahrenheit in order to force it into a liquid crystal form. We then subject it to high pressures to force the fibers into alignment as we draw them out. The energy input is extreme and the toxic byproducts are odious.

> The spider manages to make an equally strong and much tougher fiber at body temperature, without high pressures, heat, or corrosive acids. . . . If we could learn to do what the spider does, we could take a soluble raw material that is infinitely renewable and make a superstrong water-insoluble fiber with negligible energy inputs and no toxic outputs.[25]

Nature's design lessons can often be turned to an unexpected purpose. Watching a TV report on sea otters soaked by the 1989 *Exxon Valdez* oil spill, Alabama hairdresser Philip McCrory noticed that otter fur soaked up oil extremely well. This was a good trait for keeping the otter dry in clean water, but for the same reason, fatal when the otter had to swim through oil. Could the characteristic be exploited to help pull oil *out* of the water? Could comparably oil-prone human hair do the same thing? McCrory took hair swept from his salon floor, stuffed it into a pair of tights to make a dummy otter, and threw it into a baby pool filled with water and a gallon of motor oil. In two minutes, he reported, "the water was crystal clear." Salon clients who worked for NASA put him in touch with an expert there who ran a larger-scale test. It found that "1.4 million pounds of hair contained in mesh pillows could have soaked up the entire *Exxon Valdez* oil spill in a week," saving much of the $2 billion Exxon spent to capture only 12 percent of the 11 million gallons spilled.[26]

In nature, nothing edible accumulates; all materials flow in loops that turn waste into food, and the loops are kept short enough that the waste can actually reach the mouth. Technologists should aim to do the same. One of most instructive of such loop-closings occurred in 1988 when the University of Zürich decided to revise the 1971-vintage elementary laboratory course accompanying the lectures in introductory inorganic, organic, and physical chemistry.[27] Each year, students' lab exercises turned $8,000 worth of pure, simple reagents into complex, nasty, toxic goop that cost $16,000 to dispose of. The course was also teaching the students once-through, linear thinking. So Professors Hanns Fischer and C. H. Eugster decided to *reverse the process* — redesigning some exercises to teach instead how to turn the toxic wastes back into pure, simple reagents. This would save costs at both ends and encourage "cycle thinking": "A few generations of science students trained in this domain," they suggested, "are the best investment for environmental protection by chemistry." Students volunteered vacation time for recovery, and by 1991, their demand for residues had outstripped the supply. Since then, the course has produced only a few kilograms of chemical waste annually — less than 100 grams per student per year, a 99 percent reduction — and cut net annual operating costs by around $20,000, or about $130 per student.

The chemical industry that will hire those students is already discovering multiple advantages from many other kinds of process innovations. For example, polyoxymetalates are emerging as a substitute for paper-bleaching chlorine, which can form dioxins. The new bleaching agents work as well, are easily regenerated, reduce pulp mills' effluent, increase the recycling of process water, and save half the electricity.[28] A small Oregon firm[29] developed a way to make foods like tomato paste using membranes instead of boiling; it's simpler, yields more product with higher quality, and uses 95 percent less energy. A molecular sieve, somewhat like Saran wrap with extremely tiny holes in it, concentrates food products *at room temperature* and retains the flavor, texture, and nutritional value destroyed by conventional boiling. A brine solution creates intense osmotic pressures — as much as four hundred pounds per square inch — that "suck" the water out of the food and across the membrane to dilute the brine. By not breaking up the large molecules that give tomato and other food purées their viscosity, direct osmosis retains texture with less water removal, yielding more of the intact food product, at higher value, per pound of input. Similar membranes are being applied to removing heavy metals and other toxic materials from landfill leachate. They can also remove 95 percent of the water from livestock manure, separating a lagoonful of toxic slurry into drinking-quality water plus a two-thirds-lighter fertilizer that's easier to transport.[30]

Some process innovations achieve many benefits at once. Architect William A. McDonough writes of an award-winning project for the DesignTex division of Steelcase, the largest American maker of office furniture:

> A few years ago we helped to conceive and create a compostable upholstery fabric — a biological nutrient . . . a fabric so safe one could literally eat it. . . . [European] government regulators had recently defined the trimmings of the [textile mills'] . . . fabric as hazardous waste. We sought a different end for our trimmings: mulch for the local garden club. . . . If the [naturally derived] fabric was to go back into the soil safely, it had to be free of mutagens, carcinogens, heavy metals, endocrine disruptors, persistent toxic substances, and bio-accumulative substances. Sixty chemical companies were approached about joining the project, and all declined. . . . Finally . . . Ciba-Geigy . . . agreed to join. With that company's help the project team considered more than 8,000 chemicals used in the chemical industry and eliminated 7,962. The fabric — in fact, an entire line of fabrics — was created using only thirty-eight chemicals. . . . When regulators came by to test the effluent, they thought their instruments were broken. After testing the influent as well, they realized that the equipment was fine — the water coming out of the factory was as clean as the [Swiss drinking] water going in. The manufacturing process itself was filtering the water.[31]

McDonough also reports a reduced production cost — no regulatory concerns, cheaper chemicals. The design concept, as he puts it, had "taken the filters out of the pipes and put them where they belong — *in the designers' heads.*" Everything that shouldn't be in the process had been eliminated by design. Design mentality can reshape production processes — and even the entire structure and logic of a business.

Ultimately, there's every indication that large-scale, specialized factories and equipment designed for product-specific processes may even be displaced by "desktop manufacturing." Flexible, computer-instructed "assemblers" will put individual atoms together at a molecular scale to produce exactly the things we want with almost zero waste and almost no energy expended. The technology is a feasible one, not violating any physical laws, because it is exactly what happens whenever nature turns soil and sunlight into trees, bugs into birds, grass into cows, or mothers' milk into babies. We are already beginning to figure out how to do this molecular alchemy ourselves: such "nanotechnologies" are doing surprisingly well in the laboratory.[32] When they take over at a commercial scale, factories as we know them will become a thing of the past, and so will about 99 percent of the energy and materials they use. The impact of that technology will dwarf that of any of the technical proposals in this book. Yet until nanotechnology is widely commercialized, industry should continue to explore how to reduce the massive flows of materials in its conventional production processes. Even if the nanotechnology revolution never arrives, savings nearly as great can still be achieved by focusing on the last and perhaps richest of our six near-term opportunities — materials efficiency.

Materials efficiency is just as much a lesson of biological design as the making of spider-silk: biomimicry can inform not just the design of specific manufacturing processes but also the structure and function of the entire economy. As Benyus notes, an ecologically redesigned economy will work less like an aggressive, early-colonizer sort of ecosystem and more like a mature one. Instead of a high-throughput, relatively wasteful and undiversified ecosystem, it will resemble what ecologists call a Type Three ecosystem, like a stable oak-hickory forest. Its economy sustains a high stock of diverse forms of biological wealth while consuming relatively little input. Instead, its myriad niches are all filled with organisms busily sopping up and remaking every crumb of detritus into new life. Ecosystem succession tends in this direction. So does the evolution of sustainable economies. Benyus reminds us, "We don't need to invent a sustainable world — that's been done already."[33] It's all around us. We need only to learn from its success in sustaining the maximum of wealth with the minimum of materials flow.

SAVING MATERIALS

If everybody in society is to have one widget, how many widgets must we make each year? Just enough to accommodate the number that break, wear out, or are sent away, plus however many we need to keep up with growth in the number of people. A key variable in production levels is clearly *how long* the widgets last. If the widgets are something to drink out of, we need a lot fewer ceramic mugs than paper or plastic cups, because the ceramic lasts almost forever unless we drop it, while the throwaways can be used only once or twice before they fall apart. If we make the ceramic mug unbreakable — especially if we also make it beautiful, so people enjoy having and using it — then it can last long enough to hand on to our great-grandchildren. Once enough such unbreakable mugs were manufactured to equip everybody with one, or with enough, relatively few would need to be made in each subsequent year to keep everyone perpetually supplied with the service that mugs provide.

Of course, if the ceramic mug is replacing disposable single-use paper or plastic cups, it keeps on saving those throwaway materials — made of forests and natural gas, birds and bayous — continually, for as long as the durable product is used instead. To be sure, half the fun of buying consumer goods is getting an ever-growing array of diverse items. But for most of what industry produces, this is hardly a consideration: Few of us collect washing machines, let alone steel billets or blast furnaces. In fact, washing machines not only cost money and take up space; they are used so relatively seldom, and repaired and remanufactured so little, that they are ten to eighty times more materials-intensive, per load of wash done, than are semicommercial machines, like those shared by the occupants of an apartment house.[34] Thus if even a modest fraction of people shared a washing machine, considerable materials flow could be avoided.

Items can be made even more economical if they're designed with the spare and elegant simplicity of a Shaker chair or a Ming vase. Good design needs less material to create a beautiful and functional object. Sculptural talent can be enhanced nowadays by computer-aided design, which calculates stresses and determines exactly how little material will make the object just as strong as we want — but no stronger. Often this requires severalfold less material. Strength can also be put only where it's needed: If an object will tend to break in one inherently weaker place, then it would be wasteful to make it excessively strong in another place. Conversely, small changes in design can produce vastly better function. Surgical bone screws used to pull out or break frequently, requiring further painful and costly operations. Then computer-aided engineering revealed that moving just a few percent of the metal from where it wasn't needed to where it was needed would make the screws hold tenaciously and hardly ever break.[35]

Another area for savings is the efficiency with which the raw material is converted into the finished object. That factor depends on the manufacturing process: Excess material needn't be removed to achieve the desired shape if all the material is *already* in the desired shape. "Net-shape" and "near-net-shape" manufacturing makes virtually every molecule of material fed into the process emerge as a useful product. (Pratt & Whitney used to scrap 90 percent of its costly ingots when making them into jet engine turbine blades, before it asked its alloy suppliers to cast the metal into bladelike shapes in the first place.)[36] Many processes implement scrap recovery to take back leftover material for reuse, but ideally, there will be no scrap because it will have been designed away at the outset.

Net-shape production unlocks a further way to save materials: consolidating many small parts, each individually fabricated, into a single large part molded to net shape. A toilet float/valve assembly, made mainly of cast or machined brass parts, was redesigned from 20 to 3 ounces, 14 parts to one molded plastic part, and $3.68 to $0.58 production cost. A 13-pound steel tricycle with 126 parts was redesigned to a 3-pound, 26-part plastic version at one-fourth the cost. A windshield-wiper arm was reengineered from 49 parts to one, at lower total cost, even though it was made of $68-a-pound carbon-fiber composites.[37] Since molded plastic parts produce a very low amount of manufacturing scrap compared to metals,[38] these examples actually saved far more input materials than they saved weight in the finished parts: The avoided scrap amplified the direct savings from parts consolidation. Moreover, not only plastics and clays can be molded to net shape, but also metal parts, through techniques like hydroforming, semiplastic forming, plasma spray, and powder metallurgy. These are increasingly eliminating machining scrap by eliminating machining.

Eliminating scrap takes many forms. In a sawmill, three-dimensional laser measuring devices can "visualize" how to slice up a log into the highest-value combination of lumber with the least sawdust, just as computers in clothing factories design complex cutting patterns to waste the least cloth. In Shimizu's advanced robotic system for high-rise building construction, precut and preassembled materials are computer-controlled and delivered on a just-in-time basis to the job site, eliminating on-site storage, with its associated pilferage, damage, and weather loss, and reducing packaging and construction waste by up to 70 percent.[39] The Swedish construction firm Skanska has a similar system for not delivering to the construction site anything that won't go into the building — thus saving not only materials waste but also, importantly, transportation in both directions.

A further key way to waste fewer materials is to improve production quality. The U.S. metal-casting industry[40] has only a 55 percent average yield; 45 percent of its castings are defective and must be melted down and recast. Nearly half the equipment, labor, and melting energy is thus wasted. However, available innovations could probably push yields to 80–90 percent, nearly doubling this industry's output per unit of capital, labor, and energy and cutting its waste of materials by two- to four-fold.[41]

Still another way to save materials is to make a given unit of product more *effective* in providing the desired service. In 1810, iron boilers for locomotives weighed 2,200 pounds per horsepower. Steel boilers cut this ratio by more than threefold by the mid-1800s. By 1900, it was 220 lb/hp; by 1950, with electric locomotives, about 55; and by 1980, with more advanced magnetic materials, about 31.[42] Much of this 71-fold increase in the mass-effectiveness of the iron came from the process change from steam to electric traction.

Other examples of substituting quality and innovation for mass abound in modern life. In the United States, aluminum cans weigh 40 percent less than they did a decade ago;[43] Anheuser-Busch just saved 21 million pounds of metal a year by making its beer-can rims an eighth of an inch smaller in diameter without reducing the contents.[44] A new Dow process that eliminates varnishing, spraying, and baking can save 99.7 percent of the wasted materials and 62 percent of the energy needed for preparing aluminum beverage cans for filling. The mass of the average European yogurt container dropped by 67 percent during the years 1960–90, that of a beer bottle by 28 percent during the years 1970–90, that of a Kodak film canister by 22 percent.[45] An office building that needed 100,000 tons of steel 30 years ago can now be built with no more than 35,000 tons because of better steel and smarter design.[46]

Interface's reduced-face-weight carpet, with lower pile height and higher density, is beautiful, *more* durable, and saves twice as much embodied energy as is needed to run the factory that makes it.[47]

Following its philosophy, stated with emphasis, that "sustainable growth has to be focused on a *functionality* not a product," and that "*the next major step toward sustainable growth is to improve the value of our products and services per unit of natural resources employed*" — that is, to raise resource productivity across the board[48] — DuPont is "down-gauging" its polyester film. Making it thinner, stronger, and more valuable lets the company "sell less material at a higher price. On average, for every 10 percent of material reduced there is a 10 percent increase in value and price." Says DuPont, "Our ability to continually improve the inherent properties enables this process to go on indefinitely."[49] The next step is to recycle used film and other polyester products by "unzipping" their molecules. A 100 million-pound-a-year methanolysis plant for this purpose is now being developed in order "to keep those molecules working indefinitely, reducing the need for new feedstocks from natural resources." The same loop-closing process is under way in the carpet industry, whose products, 95 percent petrochemical-based, are now ending up in American landfills at the rate of nearly 10 million pounds a day.[50]

Still another way to save materials is to improve the design not merely of the specific component but of the entire product or process that uses them — the essence of the design approach the designer Buckminster Fuller called "ephemeralization,"[51] doing the job with the merest wisps of material, optimally deployed. In J. Baldwin's words, "The less material used per function, the closer the design is to pure principle." Even less than Fulleresque versions can yield impressive results. For example, a Romanian-American engineer noticed that overhead cranes, a ubiquitous means of moving heavy objects around factories and dockyards, were made of very heavy-duty steel beams. This was necessary because the hoist-motor traveled along the whole length of the cross beam, so when it was in the middle, its great weight would buckle any but the stiffest beam. He redesigned the crane so the hoisting motor was at the end of the cross beam, where its force would be borne straight down the support frame or wall to the ground. A light pulley, not a heavy motor, moved along the cross beam to do the lifting. Result: same lifting capacity, six-sevenths less steel.

BORN-AGAIN MATERIALS

Ultimately, though, people get tired of even a well-designed and efficiently made object, or it gets irreparably destroyed or worn out. Repair, reuse, upgrading, remanufacturing, and recycling are then the five main ways to keep the gift of good materials and good work moving on to other users and other uses. Repair, which works better if the product was designed to facilitate it, returns failed goods to satisfactory service for the same or a thriftier owner. Reuse passes them to another user, or perhaps to a new life with a different purpose.

Industry is already rising to these opportunities. Remanufacturing worldwide is saving energy equivalent to the output of five giant power stations, and saving annually enough raw materials to fill a freight train 1,100 miles long.[52] More than 73,000 U.S. remanufacturing firms, directly employing 480,000 people, generated 1996 revenues of $53 billion, "a value greater than the entire consumer durables industry (appliances, furniture, audio and video, farm and garden equipment)."[53] The biggest remanufacturer in the United States, regularly rebuilding everything from radars to rifles to entire aircraft, is the Department of Defense.[54] The second-biggest U.S. maker of furniture, Herman Miller, has a special daylit factory devoted exclusively to remanufacturing into like-new condition every kind of furniture the company has ever made.[55] Its larger rival, Steelcase, is one of several large firms battling with independent remanufacturers to benefit from remaking its own products.[56]

Big benefits flow to both customers and manufacturers when products get reborn. "Disposable" cameras are affordable because Fuji and Kodak actually salvage them from photo finishers, remanufacture them, reload the film, and sell them again. IBM remanufactures its computers; by 1997 its 100,000-square-foot Asset Recovery Center in Endicott, New York, was recovering 35 million pounds of computers and computer parts per year.[57] The Italian firm Bibo shifted in 1993 from making throwaway plastic plates to charging for their use, then recycling them into new ones.[58] Xerox's worldwide remanufacturing operations boosted earnings by about $200 million over three recent years,[59] $700 million over its whole history; its latest green-designed photocopier, with every part reusable or recyclable, is expected to save it $1 billion via long-term remanufacturing.[60] The University of North Carolina's business school has even hired a professor of "reverse logistics" — "dedistributing" products back from customers for remanufacture.[61]

Obviously, it's much easier to disassemble a product for remanufacturing or reuse of its parts if it was designed with that end in mind. Personal-computer software can now help designers minimize disassembly time and compare the manufacture and disposal impacts of design alternatives.[62] For an increasing range of products in Germany, which pioneered the concept of "extended product responsibility" — you make it, you own it forever — factories producing everything from televisions to cars design them for easy disassembly and disposition, because otherwise the costs of assuming the post-user responsibility are prohibitive. The system, which is spreading across Europe and to Japan, raised the German rate of packaging recycling from 12 percent in 1992 to 86 percent in 1997, and during the years 1991–97, raised plastic collection by 1,790 percent and reduced households' and small businesses' use of packaging by 17 percent.[63] By the end of 1998, some 28 countries had implemented "takeback" laws for packaging, 16 for batteries, and 12 were planning takeback requirements for electronics.[64] Such life-cycle responsibility also creates unexpected benefits: BMW designed the Z-1 sports car's recyclable all-thermoplastic skin to be strippable from the metal chassis in 20 minutes on an "unassembly line" mainly for environmental reasons, but that configuration also made repairs much easier.[65] Or when Alpha-Fry Group in Germany felt burdened by the cleaning costs of returned jars for its solder paste, it switched to pure tin containers, which on return are remelted into new solder — 11 cents cheaper per jar.[66] Avoiding dissipation of materials that are costly to buy and toxic when dispersed is smart business: When Dow announced a $1 billion, 10-year environmental investment program, it was not just being socially responsible. It also anticipated a 30–40 percent annual return.[67]

What if an item's options for repair, reuse, and remanufacturing are exhausted? Then it can be recycled to reconstitute it into another, similar product. As a last resort, it can be downcycled — ground, melted, or dissolved so its basic materials can be reincarnated for a lower purpose, such as a filler material. (Thus do many recycled plastics, no longer pure or strong enough for their original purpose, end up as tent pegs and park benches.) Waste exchanges like the Internet regional exchange sponsored by Canberra (which aims to eliminate waste by 2010), or a private-sector initiative in the region around Brownsville, Texas, and Matamoros, Mexico, aim to match waste materials with potential buyers.[68] Hard-to-recycle materials, like tires, drywall, plastics, insulation, glass, and biosolids, can even be disintegrated by intense sound waves into fine powders for easier reprocessing.[69] Materials that don't now biodegrade can be replaced with compostable ones, like the 1.8 billion potato-starch-and-limestone containers that McDonald's is trying as replacements for polystyrene clamshells — replacements that also happen to cost no more and to need much less energy to make.[70]

These options can shift with improvements in technologies and prices as innovations turn trash into cash. Henry Ford's original car factories had an entire section devoted to reclaiming wooden crates and pallets, many of which were made into autobodies.[71] In 1994, Mitsubishi Motors in Japan, which ships about 2,800 cases of car parts each month to its German distributor, switched from throwaway cardboard and wooden boxes to steel cases that are emptied, folded down, sent back to Japan, reused for an expected ten years, then remanufactured or recycled.[72] Three-fourths of all fresh produce in Germany is now shipped in standard reusable crates sold or leased by the International Fruit Container Organization — another consequence of the 1991 take-back law.[73] DuPont's Petretec process can indefinitely regenerate throwaway polyester film (four-fifths of its billion-dollar films business) into new film with the same quality as that made from virgin materials but costing up to one-fourth less.[74] Recycling old car batteries, which every state requires to be turned in when buying a new one, now provides 93–98 percent of all the lead for U.S. lead-acid batteries.[75]

Some recycled materials, like old bricks, beams, and cobbles, can actually be worth more than new ones. Others can gain novel properties from reprocessing. "Environ" biocomposite, for example, is a decorative nonstructural surface-finish material, made from recycled paper and bioresin, that looks like stone, cuts like wood, is twice as hard as red oak, and has half the weight of granite but better abrasion resistance.[76] When you apply these closed-loop principles to everything from packaging[77] to the three billion tons of construction materials used each year,[78] a substantial amount of reclaiming is at stake — and every ton not extracted, treated, and moved means less harm to natural capital.

What is the potential effect, throughout the industrial system, of combining *all* of these steps — product effectiveness and longevity, minimum-materials design and manufacturing, scrap recovery, reuse, remanufacturing, recycling, and materials savings through better quality, greater product effectiveness, and smarter design? Nobody knows yet. But many experts now believe that if the entire spectrum of materials savings were systematically applied to every material object we make and use, and if enough time were allowed for all the indirect materials savings to work through the structure of the whole economy,[79] together they would reduce the total *flow* of materials needed to sustain a given *stock* of material artifacts or *flow* of services by a factor much nearer to one hundred, or even more, than to ten. This is in large part because smarter design can often wring more service from a given artifact, so all these savings won't just add; they'll multiply. And as each of those multiplying savings turns less green land into brown wasteland, less fossil fuel into climate change, less stuff into waste, it will accelerate the restoration and increase the abundance of natural capital.

In short, the whole concept of industry's dependence on ever faster once-through flow of materials from depletion to pollution is turning from a hallmark of progress into a nagging signal of uncompetitiveness. It's dismaying enough that, compared with their theoretical potential,[80] even the most energy-efficient countries are only a few percent energy-efficient. It's even worse that only one percent of the total North American materials flow ends up in, and is still being used within, products six months after their sale. That roughly one percent materials efficiency is looking more and more like a vast business opportunity. But this opportunity extends far beyond just recycling bottles and paper, for it involves nothing less than the fundamental redesign of industrial production and the myriad uses for its products. The next business frontier is rethinking everything we consume: what it does, where it comes from, where it goes, and how we can keep on getting its service from a net flow of very nearly nothing at all — but ideas.

CHAPTER 5

Building Blocks

A bank whose workers don't want to go home — A creek runs through it — Green buildings and bright workers — Just rewards and perverse incentives — Windows, light, and air — Every building a forecast — Harvesting bananas in the Rockies — Urban forests — Walkable cities

IN SOUTHEASTERN AMSTERDAM, AT A SITE CHOSEN BY THE WORKERS BE-cause of its proximity to their homes, stands the headquarters of a major bank.[1] Built in 1987, the 538,000-square-foot complex consists of ten sculptural towers linked by an undulating internal street. Inside, the sun reflects off colored metal — only one element in the extensive artwork that decorates the structure — to bathe the lower stories in ever-changing hues. Indoor and outdoor gardens are fed by rainwater captured from the bank's roof. Every office has natural air and natural light. Heating and ventilation are largely passive, and no conventional air conditioners are used. Conservatively attired bankers playfully trail their fingers in the water that splashes down flow-form sculptures in the bronze handrails along the staircases. The building's occupants are demonstrably pleased with their new quarters: Absenteeism is down 15 percent, productivity is up, and workers hold numerous evening and weekend cultural and social events there.

These results surpassed even the directors' vision of the features, qualities, and design process they had mandated for their bank. Their design prospectus had stipulated an "organic" building that would "integrate art, natural and local materials, sunlight, green plants, energy conservation, quiet, and water" — not to mention happy employees — and that would "not cost one guilder more per square meter" than the market average. In fact, the money spent to put the energy saving systems in place paid for itself in the first three months. Upon initial occupancy, the complex used 92 percent less energy than an adjacent bank constructed at the same time, representing a saving of

$2.9 million per year and making it one of the most energy-efficient buildings in Europe.

Architect Ton Alberts took three years to complete the design of the building. It took so long mainly because the bank board insisted that all participants in the project, including employees, understand its every detail: The air-handling design had to be explained to the landscape architect, for example, and the artwork to the mechanical engineers. In the end, it was this level of integration that contributed to making the building so comfortable, beautiful, and cost-effective. When it was done, the structure became the most readily recognized in all Holland after the Parliament House. Since the headquarters building was completed, the bank that was then called NMB has gained a dynamic new public image and corporate culture, though whether this is directly related to the new building's design is impossible to prove. It has grown from the fourth- to the second-largest bank in Holland, changed its name to ING, and bought the venerable English merchant bank Barings.

When Michael and Judy Corbett began Village Homes in Davis, California, in the 1970s, there was no housing development like it. It featured mixed housing types on narrower streets, greenbelts with fruit trees, agricultural zones among the houses, natural surface drainage, solar orientation, and abundant open space. By the 1980s it had grown to encompass 240 homes on 70 acres, and had become a dearly loved neighborhood with a delightful ambience, lower utility and food costs, and a strong community spirit.[2]

One example of its unique design philosophy was the use of natural drainage swales instead of costly underground concrete drains, a choice that saved eight hundred dollars of investment per house. Those savings paid for much of the landscaping of the extensive parks and greenbelts, while the swales allow enough water to soak in that the landscaping needs one-third to one-half less irrigation water. The drainage swales are themselves part of the greenways, which not only provide routes for pedestrian and bicycle circulation but are also a focus for community life. The houses — some nearly hidden behind grapevines, flowers, and shrubs — face one another across the greenways. Cars are parked discreetly around the back on narrow (twenty-four-foot-wide), tree-shaded streets.

The street and greenway networks enter the site from opposite directions, like interlocking fingers, so they don't cross. Safe from traffic, children can play in the heavily used and watched greenways. Thanks to the vibrant street life and the strong sense of community, the crime rate is only one-tenth that of adjacent subdivisions built in the usual car-dominated, "dead worm" layout. The average number of cars per household is 1.8 in Village Homes, compared to 2.1 elsewhere in Davis.

The narrower streets not only reduce the level and speed of traffic and save money and land but also require less paving material, which improves the summer microclimate: Because trees can shade the entire street, there's far less dark paving exposed to sunlight to absorb and reradiate solar heat. Combined with passive-solar design and proper site orientation, this feature raises comfort and cuts energy bills by half to two-thirds — an impressive achievement for 1970s design and materials.

Residents were also allowed to conduct business in their homes, an activity that was illegal in many American communities at that time. Community organic gardens and edible landscaping provide fresh fruit for breakfast. Village Homes is also able to help finance its parkland maintenance by selling its organic crops of vegetables and almonds — the fruits, so to speak, of investments originally paid for partly by eliminating those eight-hundred-dollar-per-lot storm drains.

Because it has proven to be so desirable a place to live, Village Homes, originally modest in its market positioning, now realizes some of the highest resale prices per square foot of floorspace in Davis. Units sell in less than one-third of the normal listing time (that is, when they are listed for sale — most are quickly snapped up by word of mouth) and fetch eleven dollars per square foot above normal market value. At first considered so quirky that agents wouldn't show it, Village Homes is now described by real estate brochures as "Davis's most desirable subdivision."

The Inn of the Anasazi is a fifty-nine-room luxury hotel located just off the Governor's Plaza in Santa Fe, New Mexico. The building began its life in the 1960s as an ugly steel-and-glass box — a sort of giant shipping container used as a juvenile detention center and penitentiary headquarters. In 1991, the developers of the inn transformed it into an adobe-style structure that looks centuries old.

The inn is extremely comfortable and fairly efficient. But the vision that inspired it reflected more than a simple desire to conserve physical resources. Its construction materials, furniture, and art are produced from local resources by traditional artisans. Its toiletries are made from traditional Native medicinal herbs, and, like the art in the rooms and lobby, are also sold by the hotel for the makers' benefit. Staff are drawn from all three local cultures — Native, Hispanic, and Anglo — and are not only trained in conflict resolution but often provide it to other community organizations as a free service. Staff members are also paid for two hours' volunteer work a week for local groups, and can choose to sign a "Right Livelihood" agreement authorizing them to undertake ecologically responsible work in the name of the hotel. Staff turnover is minimal — a source of wonderment to competing hostelries, whose management are now requesting seminars offered by the inn to learn how they can emulate this success.

The hotel's celebrated gourmet restaurant obtains 90 percent of its ingredients from local organic farmers, many of whom are Hispanic land-grant families. (Keeping their land in agricultural production protects them from losing it to taxation at development value.) Leftover food goes to homeless shelters, kitchen scraps to an organic pig farm, table scraps to compost. With time, ever more and deeper links integrate the hotel into its place and its peoples. Why isn't every building so organically rooted?

Or so profitable: Despite its high prices, the inn broke even in its second year of operation — a rarity for a new hotel. It has 83 percent average annual occupancy, unheard-of in Santa Fe's highly seasonal market, and gets a high 35 percent repeat traffic.

What do a Dutch bank, a California tract development, and a New Mexico hotel have in common? All three projects are archetypes of a successful fusion of resource efficiency, environmental sensitivity, attention to human well-being, and financial success that has been called "green development."[3]

Buildings, however much we take them for granted, are where Americans spend about 90 percent of their time. They use one-third of our total energy and two-thirds of our electricity. Their construction consumes one-fourth of all wood harvested; 3 *billion* tons of raw materials are used annually to construct buildings worldwide.[4]

In the recent past, most choices about building design and materials have been made carelessly, yielding low returns on human capital or actual losses to society. In the future, the design paradigm illustrated by these three examples can yield far greater benefits to people, their pocketbooks, and the earth. Green buildings compete in bottom-line terms as well as in aesthetics. They are relatively inexpensive to build, operate, and convert to their next use, as human needs inevitably evolve. Their mechanical systems to maintain comfort are small and well designed, or better still, eliminated by design. More buildings will be built around, within, or from recycled old ones. New materials are being supplemented by rediscovered ancient ones like rammed earth, straw bales, adobe, and caliche (a dense clay) — all nontoxic, safe, durable, and versatile. High technology will make its own contributions. Slender carbon-fiber-reinforced layers are already cost-effectively integrated into wood-frugal structural beams, creating a sense of lightness that extends through structural and seismic design. These innovations are part of a new design thinking that emulates the airy strength of spiderwebs and feathers, enclosing the most space with the least structural materials.

Such buildings' resource and economic efficiency and their environmental sensitivity spring not merely from a desire to save money and prevent pollution but from a deeper consciousness that integrates design arts and sensibilities too long sundered from architecture and engineering. At its best, green development fuses a biologically and culturally informed appreciation of what people are and want, and a tool kit of technologies to fulfill those needs. Their most extraordinary prototypes, like the three projects described in the preceding pages, occur when all these elements are integrated and their synergies captured. At first the results seem magical, in the sense of Sir Arthur Clarke's remark that "any sufficiently advanced technology is indistinguishable from magic." Yet now the practices that create that magic are starting to be widely valued and appreciated. They will drive a revolution in buildings and in how we inhabit them.

The benefits that can accrue from intelligent design extend far beyond the buildings themselves. The placement of structures on the land also affects our sense of community, for it determines both where we must go, and how we can do so, to travel between the places where we live, work, shop, and play. It also governs what land is available for farms, ranches, forests, wildlife, and wild places. Too few designers ask, as poet and farmer Wendell Berry has, "What does this place require us to do? What will it allow us to do? What will it help us to do?" Berry also said, "What I stand for is what I stand on" — reminding us that land must be measured not just in acres and dollars but in love and respect.

These three projects, and more described below, begin to redefine real estate development as more of an art — not simply one that does less harm but one that can actively rebuild community, restore pedestrian safety and access, and reduce the context for crime. And it's even more profitable.

GREEN BOTH WAYS

Fundamentally, green buildings are superior to ordinary structures as a result of the same sort of design integration that makes Hypercars better than ordinary cars. The shell, lighting, and internal machines, appliances, and equipment of the building are so energy efficient that indoor comfort can be maintained with little or no active heating or cooling. Energy savings can accumulate in green buildings in a way comparable to how weight savings increase in Hypercars. In both cases, a high level of design integration crossing traditional professional boundaries, and careful planning that takes the right steps in the right order, create synergies that both reduce cost and enhance performance: The better the design, the greater the benefits. The economic advantage of green design extends throughout and beyond the project's operating life, but it begins with the design, approvals, and construction process. Integrative design may also initially appear to be more costly, but that premium quickly vanishes as designers gain experience with it, and it is more than offset by the savings on hardware. Although many developers assume that green buildings must cost more to build, green design can actually *decrease* construction costs, chiefly by saving infrastructure expenses and by using passive heating and cooling techniques that make most costly mechanical equipment unnecessary.[5]

While efficient new buildings save around 70–90 percent of traditional energy use, and often several percent in capital cost, they offer three additional and even more valuable economic benefits:[6]

- Green projects typically sell or lease faster, and retain tenants better, because they combine superior amenity and comfort with lower operating costs and more competitive terms. The resulting gains in occupancies, rents, and residuals all enhance financial returns.

- The buildings' greater visual, thermal, and acoustic comfort creates a low-stress, high-performance environment that yields valuable gains in labor productivity, retail sales, and manufacturing quality and output. These improvements in turn create a key competitive advantage, and hence further improve real estate value and market performance.

• Better indoor air quality can improve health and productivity and reduce liability risks. The EPA estimates that building-related U.S. illnesses account for $60 billion of annual productivity lost nationwide, and a wider study valued that loss as high as over $400 billion.[7]

People are not simple, uniform entities that thrive in a box. They are, rather, complex living organisms that evolved in and still function best in a dynamic and diverse environment. The typical Western mechanical engineer strives to *eliminate* variability in human-made environments with thermostats and humidistats and photosensors, to maximize the conditions under which a statistical fraction of diverse people will feel "comfortable" according to a standard equation. In contrast, state-of-the-art Japanese buildings deliberately and constantly vary temperatures over a modest range. Their microchip controls deliver air not in a steady stream but in seemingly random gusts. They may even inject subliminal whiffs of jasmine or sandalwood scent into the ventilation system to stimulate the senses. This variability reflects the belief that people are healthier, happier, and more alert under subtly dynamic than under constant conditions. Western designers are starting to appreciate that this evolution-based view may offer a superior basis for design.

Few people have ever experienced real comfort — thermal, visual, or acoustic — but once they do, they tend to want more of it. Revolutions in technology, design, and consumer consciousness are already starting to create market conditions in which real estate developers and design professionals offer inferior products at their peril. Buildings that are alternately a solar oven or a walk-in refrigerator, with discomfort and energy bills to match, are coming to be seen as unacceptable. In the rapidly arriving era of green design, buildings that cost more than they should to construct and run and that work worse, look worse, and make informed customers feel worse than they demand will simply stand empty.

The theme of superior worker satisfaction and performance runs like a golden thread through the fabric of green development. Consider these examples:[8]

• Lockheed's Building 157 in Sunnyvale, California, used sophisticated daylighting to save three-fourths of its lighting energy and make the space more attractive and easier to work in. The owners expected to recover the cost of installation in four years. Yet a 15 percent drop in absenteeism and a 15 percent gain in labor productivity paid for the daylighting in the first year. Moreover, the lower overhead gave the company the edge in a tough contract competition, and the profits from that unexpected contract earned Lockheed more than it had paid for the whole building.

· When sorting speeds and accuracy at the main mail-sorting office in Reno, Nevada, suddenly shot up from unimpressive levels to the best performance in the western United States, managers realized that a lighting retrofit introduced to save energy had also enabled workers to see better. Accompanying changes in ceiling design had also reduced distracting and fatiguing noise.

· VeriFone renovated a 76,000-square-foot, tilt-up concrete warehouse in California into a new distribution headquarters.[9] The old building had few windows, and its air-handling system was inadequate to filter out pollutants from outside air. The retrofit included daylighting, a new filtration system, nontoxic materials, and improved energy efficiency, while meeting the low budget of $39 a square foot. The 65–75 percent energy saving was predicted to pay back in 7½ years — an after-tax annual return of 10 percent — but the 45 percent decrease in absenteeism was an unanticipated bonus.

· When Boeing Corporation retrofitted the lighting systems in its design and manufacturing areas, it not only cut the lighting energy by up to 90 percent (and recovered the investment in less than two years) but also helped workers to see defects in the aircraft they were constructing. The result was a valuable improvement in avoided rework, on-time delivery, and customer satisfaction.

· Wal-Mart's experimental "Eco-Store" in Lawrence, Kansas, installed a novel daylighting system in half the store and normal fluorescent lighting in the rest. Cash registers hardwired to corporate headquarters revealed significantly higher sales of merchandise on the daylit side as compared to sales in other stores. Workers preferred it, too. Now Wal-Mart is experimenting with daylighting in its other prototype stores.

Examples like these represent an untapped source of potential savings for many companies. These and other well-measured case studies now show consistent gains in labor productivity of around 6–16 percent when workers feel more comfortable thermally, when they can see what they're doing, and when they can hear themselves think.[10] Yet as shown in the graph on page 90, typical American offices spend about one hundred times as much per square foot for people (payroll, benefits, employer taxes, and individual equipment) as for energy. It may be that managers can't afford *not* to retrofit buildings to save energy, because doing so can also make workers more productive. If labor productivity goes up just one percent, that will produce the same bottom-line benefit as *eliminating* the entire energy bill. The gains in labor productivity that the case studies show would therefore be worth at least ten times as much as the direct energy savings, which themselves are worth tens of billions of dollars a year to businesses throughout the United States.

This might seem a commonsense sort of conclusion, yet it has been overlooked until now. For the past sixty years, business schools have been teaching the myth that only management — not working conditions — can substantially affect employee productivity.[11] Obviously, workers tend to do better when respected and paid attention to. But working conditions also matter, and have been too long neglected.

REWARDING WHAT WE WANT
Conventional buildings are typically designed by having each design specialist "toss the drawings over the transom" to the next specialist. Eventually, all the contributing specialists' recommendations are integrated, sometimes simply by using a stapler. Green builders, in contrast, are insisting on the sort of highly integrative design process that was used by the Amsterdam bank, a process that melds diverse skills and perspectives into a whole that is greater than the sum of its constituent parts. One of the best ways to ensure that this takes place is to have the architects, engineers, landscapers, hydrologists, artists, builders, commissioners (specialists who get the building working properly between construction and occupancy), occupants, maintenance staff, and others who have a stake in a particular building all design the building together. All these stakeholders collaborate in a "charrette" process — a

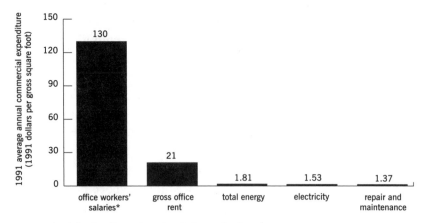

COMPARING PEOPLE, ENERGY, AND OTHER COSTS OF RUNNING AN OFFICE BUILDING

*excluding benefits, equipment, and other overhead

short, intensive, teamwork-oriented, multidisciplinary roundtable — to ensure that key synergies between design elements are captured and that those elements work together to yield big energy and resource savings at the lowest possible cost.

One reason that buildings are inefficient is that the compensation paid to architects and engineers is frequently based directly or indirectly on a percentage of the *cost* of the building itself or of the equipment they specify for it. Designers who attempt to eliminate costly equipment therefore end up with lower fees, or at best with the same fees for a greater amount of work. Energy engineer Eng Lock Lee irreverently describes the resulting mechanical-engineering standard operating practice typical of large building projects as follows:

- Take previous successful set of drawings.
- Change the box that indicates the name of the project.
- Submit drawings to client.
- Building is constructed.
- Client gripes about discomfort.
- Wait for client to stop griping.
- Repeat process.

This safe but uninspired procedure calls for mechanical equipment that is big, complex, and costly. It will work, after a fashion, and usually no one will sue because there is no liability for in*eff*iciency — only for in*suff*iciency. The engineer won't be held responsible for the capital or operating costs, even though the equipment is probably severalfold larger and less efficient than it should be. The engineering looks cheap to the owner; indeed, the engineer's one-time fee is less than *one-thousandth* as much as the tenant organization's long-term payroll costs for employees whose productivity, as noted above, depends significantly on the comfort produced by that engineer's handiwork. So by skimping on design, the owner gets costlier equipment, higher energy costs, and a less competitive and comfortable building; the tenants get lower productivity and higher rent and operating costs. Since World War II, such backward priorities and inverted incentives have led the United States to misallocate about $1 *trillion* of capital for the construction of about 200 million tons[12] of air-conditioning equipment, plus 200,000 megawatts of utility capacity to power them (two-fifths of the total national peak load) — neither of which would have been necessary had the same buildings been optimally designed to produce the same or better comfort at the least cost.[13]

An obvious remedy for this mess is for a developer to stipulate a positive incentive for achieving efficiency. Pilot projects launched by Rocky Mountain Institute in 1996–97 are now testing how much more efficient buildings can become if their designers are rewarded for what they save, not what they spend. Through simple supplementary contracts, designers would keep a portion of several years' measured energy savings as a bonus fee.[14] Rewards can also be balanced with penalties for poor performance. The incentive can also be paid partly up-front and partly several years later, trued up to measured savings, so the designers have the right inducement to see that their intentions are fully realized in construction, commissioning, training, and operation. Like a Chinese "wellness doctor," they could even be paid a small performance-based fee for attending to sustaining and improving the building's performance throughout its life.

But perverse incentives for design professionals are only one symptom of a much larger problem. In a typical large deal, the real estate value chain consists of twenty-five or so parties who conceive, approve, finance, design, build, commission, operate, maintain, sell, lease, occupy, renovate, and dispose of the property. Most if not all of these parties are systematically rewarded for inefficiency and penalized for efficiency.[15] Repairs to incentive structures are needed for the entire range of real estate practitioners, their professional societies, public-policy bodies, and other market actors.[16]

Encouragingly, productive tools are starting to emerge. For example, lease riders can stipulate a fair sharing of savings between landlords and tenants so both have an incentive to overcome the "split incentive" problem, in which one party selects the technology while another pays its energy costs. Savings commonly built into self-owned space are often missing from rented space. Tenants traditionally devote little attention to the efficiency of the office equipment, lights, and terminal air-handling equipment they install. They would be more conscientious if, when they were shopping for and negotiating a lease, a landlord showed them a graph of the extra direct and common-space utility bills, and the extra rent (for the capital cost of mechanical systems in a new building) that they would have to pay if they made those tenant-finish choices inefficiently — or the discounts they could earn if their designers collaborated with the landlords to minimize total building costs. Similar split incentives burden the manufacturers and consumers of all kinds of equipment used in buildings and factories. Much of this equipment is inefficient and designed for low initial cost alone, since its designers, builders, and vendors are not liable for the user's operating costs and since most buyers don't shop carefully. Indeed, for the majority of equipment, efficient models simply aren't available — at least until a big customer demands them, as Wal-Mart successfully did for daylighting and air-conditioning systems. It's remarkable how quickly "Sorry, we don't make that" changes to "When do you want it?" once the customer offers a huge order.

Because appraisers, too, rarely credit efficient buildings for their energy savings, the value of the efficiency cannot be capitalized, making financing and valuation more difficult. (A few appraisers are just beginning to capitalize savings in net operating income.) Leasing brokers typically base pro forma financials on average *assumed* operating costs, rather than on actual ones. Few buildings have efficiency labels and few renters have access to past energy bills with which to gauge expenses. In response, some jurisdictions have instituted right-to-know laws, while others obtain similar results by training renters and buyers to be inquisitive. Some leasing brokers have begun to distinguish their services by offering advice on minimizing occupancy costs. Home and commercial-building energy rating systems are emerging. A more transparent and accurate market is starting to recognize that buildings' energy efficiency is an important constituent of their financial value. The ability to upgrade America's inefficient building stock depends largely on creating better market-based information and accurate incentive structures for both tenants and owners. An important step will be the U.S. Green Building Council's release in 2000 of the Leadership in Energy and Environmental Design (LEED) rating system,[17] which provides a national standard for evaluating and comparing green building performance.

Another way to improve the efficiency of new buildings, even multi-family or multi-tenant structures, is for energy utilities to apply "feebates" for energy hookups, just as for efficient cars. Under the feebate system, you either pay a fee or receive a rebate when you connect to the gas or electric system, but which alternative and how large it is depends on how efficient your building is. Each year, the fees pay for the rebates, which makes for a politically attractive revenue-neutrality. Unlike building codes and appliance standards — which are better than nothing, but quickly become obsolete, and offer no incentive to improve upon the standards — feebates drive continuous improvement: The more efficient you are, the bigger rebate you get. You also get it up front, very close to when the design decisions are being made, so it is more likely to influence the design than are the long-term operating costs you may experience later.[18] Feebates to save energy have been tried only in small-scale U.S. experiments but are successfully used by some providers of water and wastewater services.

TRANSFORMING COMMERCIAL BUILDINGS

While design standards are continuing to improve, many successful projects prove that the current state of the art can make commercial buildings that synergistically achieve multiple goals.

For example, S. C. Johnson's 250,000-square-foot Worldwide Professional Headquarters, completed in 1997 in Racine, Wisconsin, sought to save half its energy, prevent pollution, reduce risk and waste, approach zero net water use, and restore biodiversity nearby. It's also a far more pleasant space to work in — and to eat in, since its dining facility is supported by on-site orchards and food gardens.

Equally impressive is the 15,704-square-foot Antioch, California, regional office of the California State Automobile Association.[19] This 1994 building combined better insulation and solar features with advanced windows, daylighting, and efficient artificial lighting to save 63 percent of the energy permitted by the state's strict and supposedly optimal Title 24 code. It's also the cheapest CSAA structure ever built, and its annual energy savings alone are worth twice their cost.

The characteristics that make these buildings superior are straightforward. First, a well-designed new commercial structure will have the physical shape, and will face in the direction, that takes the greatest advantage of solar gain and deflects unwanted heat or wind. These simple considerations alone generally save about a third of a building's energy use at no extra cost.[20] In fact, a carefully designed building will use not just its orientation and form but also its thermal mass, shading, surface finishes, landscaping, and other architectural elements to optimize its passive-solar heat gains and passive cooling.

Proper building alignment also provides glare-free natural light throughout the structure with the help of such techniques as curved light shelves, light pipes, light-colored surfaces, and glass-topped partitions. Whatever the weather, so long as the sun is above the horizon, artificial lighting is rarely required. The electric lights will automatically dim or turn themselves off according to daylight unless overridden. Less lighting puts less heat into the building, reducing the need for air-conditioning. Students even learn better in daylit schools, with better physical health and growth and sharply higher test scores.[21]

Modern electric lighting systems are designed to deliver light precisely in directions that wash the ceiling and walls, not flood the room's empty volume. Advanced light sources eliminate flicker, hum, and glare and produce pleasant and accurate color because the lamps are tuned to the way the eye sees red, green, and blue. Adjustable swing-arm task lights on desks combine with variable ambient lighting to control contrast and beautify the space. These features make visual tasks easier and less fatiguing. All the lighting and most of the daylighting options can be profitably retrofitted; available equipment can fit almost any use. Typical savings in lighting energy range from 80 to 90 percent at the same or lower cost in new buildings, or around 70 to 90 percent with one-to-three-year paybacks in most retrofits. Better lighting equipment often more than pays for itself just by costing less to maintain, before its electrical savings are counted.[22] It may even cost less up front to buy and install. Technology improves so rapidly that it may be worth re-retrofitting lighting systems every few years. A 1998 Malden Mills warehouse retrofit saved 93 percent of lighting energy, greatly improved visibility, and paid back in eight months (six after a utility rebate), even though the replaced system was of a type — metal halides — normally considered very efficient and hence traditionally used to improve on ancient incandescent and mercury-arc lamps.[23]

Good lighting is complemented by ergonomically designed and superefficient office equipment. For example, high-contrast, glare- and flicker-free flat-screen liquid-crystal displays adapted from portable to desktop computers are justified today by any one of the five advantages they offer — better visibility and reliability, saved energy, saved desk space, and avoidance of potential health concerns about electromagnetic fields. With all five advantages combined, the liquid-crystal screens are the best choice despite their higher price. New varieties of high-performance office equipment, including printers, faxes, and copiers, reduce their heat load to a total of as little as a fifth of a watt per square foot, about one-third of the norm.[24] Comparable gains can be achieved by carefully selecting everything from the watercooler to the coffeemaker.

Dramatic improvements can also be made in the building's shell or envelope that separates people from weather. Improved insulation and airtightness are important factors, but the key innovation in this area is "superwindows." These entered the market in the early 1980s and have become steadily more sophisticated, diverse, and widely available.[25] Superwindows, which keep people warm in the winter and cool in the summer, typically combine two or three invisibly thin coatings (which let light pass through but reflect heat) with heavy gas fillings such as krypton to block the flow of heat and noise. Mass-produced versions competitively priced at about 10–15 percent above double-glazed windows can insulate four and a half times better, or as well as eight sheets of glass. The most efficient units insulate as well as twelve sheets of glass, but look like double glazing and cost less than triple glazing. Superwindows have enabled experimental superinsulated eighties and nineties buildings to maintain comfort with no heating or cooling equipment in outdoor temperatures that range from about −47 to 115°F. They're often "tuned" so that on different sides of a building they all look the same but have different infrared properties, a feature that independently optimizes the flow of heat and of light across the building shell in each direction. This technique can make a building so passive that it needs few or none of the elaborate and unreliable active control systems that, in marketing parlance, define a "smart" building. A truly smart building keeps you comfortable without controls.

Even better windows will soon reach the market. Nearing commercialization are aerogel glazings whose almost invisible, lighter-than-air silica foam can insulate several times better than today's best superwindows. Next out of the lab will be glazings whose solar-powered microchips and sensors continuously vary their light- and heat-transmitting properties to maximize comfort with no external controls or intervention.

The building envelope does not simply keep out the weather and noise, let in light, and present an architectural face to the world. It should also integrate insulation, thermal mass (often incorporated into wall materials), and passive control functions. And in the newest structures, such as New York's Four Times Square and many European showcase buildings, it has one additional function: It's the power station. Photovoltaic power generation is now commercially available, at increasingly attractive prices, in such forms as opaque or clear glass, asphalt-like shingles, standing-seam metal roofing, and other elements that directly replace normal parts of the building shell. They look and work the same as ordinary building materials but produce electricity whenever struck by light, even through clouds. An efficient building surfaced with such materials can renewably produce more daytime electricity than it uses. The better of the world's half million solar-powered homes[26] do just that.

Thus the best mid-1990s efficiency achievements — buildings that save around 99 to 100 percent in heating energy and 97[27] to 100[28] percent in air-conditioning energy — can be bested by making the building a net *exporter* of energy. For example, the world's largest residential solar development, now being built at the Sydney (Australia) Olympic Village, will include a kilowatt of solar cells installed on the roof of each unit. Yet because of good passive design, the units will also maintain comfort with no air-conditioning, freeing most of the solar power for other uses. In 1998, the 350-room Mauna Lani Bay Hotel, a AAA Five-Diamond resort on the Kona-Kohala coast of the island of Hawai'i, turned its 10,000-square-foot roof into a hundred-kilowatt power station — the biggest on any hotel in the world — by retiling it with solar cells.

Smaller buildings can use photovoltaics that produce alternating current, the power that comes from a wall outlet but of higher quality and with no pollution. Such "AC-out" photovoltaics function like any plug-in appliance, except that when you plug them in and shine sunlight on them, they put electricity back into the building rather than drawing from it — say, 250 peak watts from a four-by-six-foot panel. This innovation makes on-site solar power convenient and increasingly affordable for unsophisticated users, for renters who prefer to take their solar units with them when they move, and for the 2 billion people who still lack electricity. As *The Economist* put it, "Just as villages that have never seen a telephone pole now never will because of cellular technology, others that have never seen an [electric transmission-line tower] . . . could be spared them in favor of solar panels. . . ."[29]

In buildings a lot of energy is used to blow air around. This can be reduced by using nontoxic materials for both construction and cleaning, and by ventilating during construction. Once toxicity is designed out, green buildings usually let occupants open nearby windows or vents. Further fresh air, if needed, can be introduced silently and unobtrusively at floor level, rising to displace stale air. Such "displacement ventilation" can often be controlled individually by each user, or automatically, or both. As the exhaust air flows passively up and out, its heat or coolness, moisture or dryness can be recovered. Many such designs use 100 percent fresh air, with none recirculated. Either way, the bonuses of advanced ventilation design include better health, blessed quiet, and major energy savings.

Other vital benefits emerge from *combining* many of these green-building features. For example, Rocky Mountain Institute has helped major firms to devise a new kind of speculative office building that melds under-floor displacement ventilation, under-floor wiring, super-windows, daylighting, superefficient lighting suspended from and bounced off the ceiling, and certain structural innovations. Costly ducts and, if desired, the suspended ceiling to hide them are virtually eliminated. This raises the ceilings, helping to distribute light, but reduces the height between floors, so six stories, not the usual five, can fit within building codes' seventy-five-foot high-rise limit. Comfort, beauty, and visual performance are much improved. Total construction cost is unchanged, and may even fall slightly. Energy cost falls by half, or by about three-fourths if tenants can be educated and incentivized to choose efficient equipment. The greatest benefit for fast-moving businesses, which tend to rearrange people every six to eighteen months, is that reconfiguration cost is greatly reduced. There's no need to rearrange the lighting or ventilation, and all the plug-in power and signal wiring is instantly accessible — just pop up a carpet tile and the raised-floor tile beneath it. This flexibility alone is so valuable that in the first year of occupancy it saved Owens-Corning $300 per worker per move, or $1.35 per square foot per year — equivalent to three-fourths of an average office building's total energy bill.

Some advanced buildings move air with highly efficient fans and low-friction ducts that cut fan energy to only a tenth of industry norms while reducing noise and capital cost. But the most innovative buildings have no fans at all. Instead, they design with computational fluid dynamics — simulations of airflow driven by natural buoyancy and calculated by supercomputers — to move the air passively and silently. Using this technique, the 107,000-square-foot Queens Building — a

1993 engineering teaching and laboratory structure at DeMontfort University in Leicester, England — eliminated all its chillers and fans, maintained comfort, and cut $1.4 million out of its construction cost. Sixty percent of the building's shell area consists of operable windows or vents. The mechanical engineering students have to learn about mechanical equipment from diagrams because the school has no such equipment to demonstrate; the electrical engineering students learn lighting design in daylit rooms with the lights off. The building had the lowest construction cost ($110 per square foot unfinished, or $184 finished and completely equipped) of any recent engineering building known to its architect. A follow-on design is expected to eliminate cooling, air-handling, *and* probably heating energy for the new EpiCenter materials-science research facility at Montana State University in Bozeman. It is also expected to cut capital cost.

In the few climates so extreme that some heating or cooling (more commonly just dehumidification) is still required, these functions will increasingly be performed not only with far greater efficiency (the demonstrated energy savings range from about 65 to 100 percent) but also without using electricity or fuel directly. Rather, these functions will be powered by waste heat from on-site fuel cells, microturbines, or all-weather solar devices. For example, a retrofit of a multimillion-square-foot corporate campus is currently being planned to use modular miniature gas turbines to make the required electricity. The turbines' waste heat will provide heating, cooling, and dehumidification. The system will be profitable against the utility's electricity prices, which are near the national average.

RECYCLED BUILDINGS, MATERIALS, AND LAND

Design innovations are not confined to new buildings. Green design will slowly replace or retrofit nearly all the old structures too. For example, in 1992 the National Audubon Society recycled a century-old, 98,000-square-foot building at a cost roughly 27 percent below that of building anew, and toward the lower end of the market range. Yet the retrofit not only achieved two-thirds energy savings but also created a superior working environment with excellent daylighting and 30 percent more fresh air, established 70 percent efficient recycling of office wastes, and greatly reduced if not eliminated toxic hazards. Accomplishing all this repaid its cost in five years — three years counting utility rebates. Similarly, in 1996, when the City of San Diego retrofitted the

73,000-square-foot, 13-year-old Ridgehaven municipal office building to be the most efficient commercial structure in town, the 60 percent reduction in energy cost yielded a four-year payback. The retrofit also used low- or no-toxicity, sustainably sourced, high-recycled-content materials for greater durability, recycled over 40 tons of construction debris, and improved indoor air quality.[30] Combining technical with *financial* innovations can yield even more impressive results.

Today buildings are frequently "reincarnated," becoming a new element of community life and gaining commercial value. Stewart Brand's sound 1994 advice in *How Buildings Learn* — "Every building is a forecast. Every forecast is wrong" — is already leading to such flexibility-enhancing innovations as walls, pipes, and other interior elements that can be easily moved. Some of the recently built outstanding green buildings, such as the Audubon and Natural Resources Defense Council headquarters buildings in New York or the Inn of the Anasazi in Santa Fe, are recycled buildings. This saves the energy and landfill space embodied in construction materials, which are responsible for 40 percent of all materials flows and mainly end up as waste whose disposal typically costs 2–5 percent of construction budgets. Depending on the region, between 15 percent and 40 percent of the content of American landfills is construction waste — seven tons per typical 1,800-square-foot house.[31]

If an entire building can't be recycled, the next best approach is often to reuse wood, bricks, and other materials from prior structures. This is preferable to sourcing new materials from sustainably harvested wood and other natural materials, because the materials were already produced and needn't be produced afresh. The energy required to create the materials (wood, Sheetrock, wiring, plumbing, masonry, et cetera) in an energy-efficient building can exceed the heating and cooling energy it will use in a half century.[32] Reusing that embodied energy saves both energy and capital costs. Southern California Gas Company's Energy Resource Center was built at about 31 percent lower cost by recycling an old building and using 80 percent recycled materials.[33] Dismantling buildings and selling their materials can also be profitable.[34] British Columbia Building Corporation's 1991 prison demolition cost 26 percent less and reduced landfilling by 95 percent, because selling recovered materials more than paid for the dismantling crew's welcome extra six weeks' work. Regional and local marketplaces are springing up on the Internet to hook up providers and users of recycled building materials, both conventional and imaginative. (In Audubon House, the only incandescent lamps in use are those that were crushed and recycled into nonslip floor tiles.) Vermont's largest construction firm, when converting an IBM office complex, had to remove 5,500 4-by-10-foot sheets of drywall. Landfilling them would have cost about $20,000. Because there wasn't a drywall-remanufacturing plant close by, they were advertised as free take-aways and quickly snapped up.[35] While building the Rose Garden arena in Portland, Oregon, Turner Construction rerouted 45,000 tons of concrete, steel, gypsum, paper, and other construction waste to recyclers, reducing its volume of waste sent for disposal by 95 percent, and turning what would have been disposal costs into $190,000 of income.

Sites can be recycled as effectively as materials. Many military bases, such large tracts as Denver's former Stapleton Airport, and numerous infill sites are being creatively reused. The U.S. Environmental Protection Agency is helping private developers mitigate any remaining toxic materials so they can build on the nearly half million abandoned or underused industrial "brownfield" sites throughout the United States. For example, Portland, Oregon, recycled a heavy industrial site into a bustling and financially successful ten-acre mixed-use development called RiverPlace after a public-private partnership assessed, and the developers paid for, the toxic-waste cleanup. The main obstacle to such redevelopment is fear of liability, but both the EPA and some states are changing the rules to encourage safe reuse of these mostly urban sites, whose good access to transit, infrastructure, and workers gives them a market advantage over greenfield sites.

HOMEBUILDING JOINS THE REVOLUTION

Most Americans go home to buildings as inefficient and uncomfortable as those in which they work and shop. Most U.S. houses, compared with those built in line with today's best practice, are drafty, poorly insulated boxes designed with most of the same deficiencies as commercial buildings, plus a few new ones. For example, typical Pacific Northwest homes have hot-air ducts so leaky that 25–30 percent of gas heating energy, or 40–50-plus percent of electric heating energy, is lost before it ever reaches the rooms. This wastes energy and money, makes temperatures uneven, and can even threaten the occupants by sucking in toxic furnace exhaust.[36] Similarly, a typical three-kilowatt California central air conditioner delivers only two kilowatts of cool air; the rest leaks out of the ducts.[37] Such faults are easily fixed, the latest method being to spray into the ducts a sort of nontoxic aerosolized chewing gum called Aeroseal that automatically lodges in the cracks (up to dime-sized) and seals them up. This eliminates over 90 percent of the duct leakage. It can yield a typical internal rate of return around 30 percent per year, an annual U.S. saving upward of $1 billion, and a displacement of ten giant power plants.[38] Ducts shouldn't leak in the first place, but many are carelessly installed.

Although homebuilding is an extremely fragmented sector of the U.S. economy — its unit of production is often the pickup truck — encouraging progress is being made. As with commercial buildings, these advances embrace integrated design processes, new technologies, and a more biological and adaptive understanding of human needs.

Archetypes of today's most efficient houses, in climates ranging from subarctic to fully tropical, have existed since the 1980s, and some much earlier.[39] American superinsulation techniques have adopted and adapted the best from Scandinavian and Canadian practices. Superwindows marketed as early as 1983 could gain net heat in the winter, even facing north. For example, Rocky Mountain Institute's 4,000-square-foot headquarters[40] stands at an elevation of 7,100 feet in western Colorado in a climate that occasionally gets as cold as −47°F. There is only a 52-day nominal growing season between hard frosts here, and midwinter cloudy spells last as long as 39 days. Still, the building has no heating system aside from two small woodstoves. Yet its 99 percent space-heating savings made it cost *less* than normal to build in 1982–84, because its superinsulation, superwindows, and 92 percent efficient heat-recovering ventilators added less cost than was saved up front by eliminating the furnace and ductwork. Moreover, the structure was able to save half the water usage, about 99 percent of the water-heating energy, and 90 percent of the household electricity — for which the bill, if the building were only a house, would be about five dollars a month, before taking credit for its manyfold larger photovoltaic power production. The energy savings repaid all the costs of those efficiency improvements in ten months. That was achieved with 1983 technologies; today's are better and cheaper.

Such a building can also keep its occupants more alert, happy, and healthy. It features curving forms, natural light, and waterfall sounds. It lacks mechanical noise (because there are no mechanical systems) and most electromagnetic fields. It has low air temperature, high radiant temperature, ample winter humidity in a high-desert climate, good indoor air quality, and a central semitropical garden offering the sight, smell, ions, oxygen, and occasional taste of the plants. Bougainvillea blooms over ponds in which frogs jump while turtles, carp, and catfish swirl below. You can come in out of a blizzard to the scent of night-blooming jasmine and the blur of a miniature hedgehog running silently about eating bugs. In December 1997, RMI harvested its twenty-sixth indoor banana crop — perhaps the world's altitude record for passive-solar bananas.

Comparable results have been achieved in many different climates. In cloudy Darmstadt, Germany, Dr. Wolfgang Feist's no-furnace "Passivhaus" uses less than 10 percent the normal amount of heat (all produced by its water heater) and 25 percent the normal amount of electricity. It uses about as much energy for all its needs as a typical German house uses just for small appliances. In 1996, one of its architects, Folkmer Rasch, designed equally efficient public housing at competitive prices; by the Expo 2000 exposition in Hannover, a whole city called the Kronsberg Siedlung is to be built with quadrupled energy efficiency but at no extra cost. Forty similarly "hyperinsulated" homes needing no heating are being built in 1999 in two cold and cloudy Swedish cities.[41] Conversely, in muggy Bangkok, Thailand, where people feel comfortable outdoors for only 15 percent of the year, architect Professor Soontorn Boonyatikarn built an elegant and comfortable three-story, 3,750-square-foot house whose superwindows, overhangs, and other design features reduce its air-conditioning requirements by 90 percent, to a system so small that he couldn't find an engineer willing to work on it. The house cost no more to build than a standard model.[42]

Capital costs can even go *down*. A Pacific Gas and Electric Company experiment eliminated cooling equipment in two normal-looking tract houses. The first, in Davis, California, where peak temperatures can reach 113°F, was a mid-range ($249,500), 1,656-square-foot speculative home, completed in 1993. During three-day, 104°-plus heat storms, the indoor temperature didn't top 82°, and the neighbors came into the house with no air conditioner to take refuge from their own inefficient houses, whose big air conditioners couldn't cope. Yet if routinely built, rather than as a one-off experiment, the Davis house would cost about $1,800 *less* to build, and $1,600 *less* to maintain over its life than a comparable but normally inefficient home, because it had no heating or cooling equipment to buy or maintain. A later model did even better.[43]

Proving that such efficient houses are feasible is only the first step. Builders must still cope with fragmented regulatory jurisdictions, obsolete building codes and other standards, uninformed building inspectors, homebuyers, appraisers, and real estate agents who ascribe no market value to energy efficiency, split incentives between landlords and tenants, and myriad other forms of market failure. Such hurdles can be cleared, however, and passive-solar heating is now becoming common in some regions.

Novelty can even be turned to marketing advantage. Some innovative builders offer guaranteed maximum heating bills of, say, $100–200 a year — a technique used by speculative builder Perry Bigelow of Palatine, Illinois, to sell more than a thousand comfortable no-furnace houses over more than a decade. In these homes a water heater provides all the space-heating backup needed, even without superwindows. (Of course, you don't *call* it a no-furnace house; instead, you market its advanced hydronic radiant heat.)

Most of the American houses that will exist a few decades from now have already been built. But fortunately, basic improvements can be made to the air- and heat-leaking shells of these structures. Thanks to the pioneering efforts of Canadian and Scandinavian engineers from the 1970s onward, innovative techniques for retrofitting superinsulation and "outsulation" onto existing homes, for sealing air leaks, and for using stick-on selective coatings and add-on selective glazings to make every window a near-superwindow are now fairly mature. Their widespread adoption can be coordinated with normal facade renovations or furnace or air-conditioner replacements to cut costs — or can even be combined with "gut rehabs" of derelict masonry row houses.[44]

APPLIANCES

Heat-tight homes can be complemented by a wide range of efficient appliances. The Environmental Protection Agency is working with hundreds of voluntary manufacturer partners to provide more efficient appliances with special Energy Star labels. These models can save the typical U.S. household about 30 percent of its energy bills with a 30 percent internal rate of return. Over the next 15 years, full adoption of Energy Star appliances could save American households as much as $100 billion.[45] (A similar effort now dominates the U.S. market for office equipment.) Another EPA/industry voluntary initiative will eliminate the need for about ten giant power plants and save U.S.

households $3 billion a year, by saving most of the "standby" energy used by equipment that's supposedly turned off.

But these devices represent only the beginning of a revolution in efficient appliances. Prototype washing machines have dirt and grease sensors to control fuzzy-logic chips that add fresh water and soap only until the water comes out clean. New induction cooktops save energy and have no hot element to burn an inquisitive child. Heat-pump clothes dryers are emerging. Twenty-odd innovations can save two-thirds of a typical house's water-heating energy yet repay their cost in about a year.[46] Appliances will also become better integrated with one another. A washing machine using a new kind of smart motor can perform a high-speed spin that wrings out almost all the water, then shakes out the wrinkles, using only a few percent as much energy for this form of drying as hot-air dryers require. Then, because the washing machine is made of polymers, it can become a microwave dryer — fast, easy on clothes, and efficient.[47]

Refrigerators use a sixth of U.S. households' electricity — the output of about thirty giant power stations. Most in-service refrigerators are poorly insulated boxes with their inefficient compressor mounted at the bottom, so its heat rises up into the food compartment. They typically have an undersized, dust-clogged, and hence fan-cooled condenser on the back, leaky air seals, internal heaters to prevent "sweating" caused by the thin insulation, and inefficient lights, fans, and defroster coils inside that generate still more heat. Each such refrigerator uses so much electricity that the coal burned to generate it would about fill up the whole inside of the refrigerator every year.

But again, recent improvements in design have dramatically improved the energy efficiency of refrigerators. If an average model sold in the United States in 1972, adjusting for the mix of refrigerator and freezer space, used what we might call a hundred "units" of electricity to cool a given volume, then:[48]

- By 1987, when California introduced efficiency standards, the average new refrigerator used only 56 units.

- In 1990, a new federal standard forbade the sale of models using more than 45 units. The best mass-produced model used only 39 units but was not as expensive as the less efficient models that preceded it.

- In 1993, the federal standard was tightened to 35 units, and in 1997, to 25 units so as to adopt cost-effective new technologies.[49]

• In 1994, Whirlpool won a Swedish design competition with a 32-unit model, which the major U.S. makers agreed to cut to no more than 26 units by 1998.

• Since 1988, the Danish firm Gram has been mass-producing a 13-unit model, improvable readily to only 8 units — and with the best 1997 superinsulation, compressor, and other technologies to 1–2 units.[50]

Thus refrigerators that are available now can save about 87 percent — and with the best available technology could save 98–99 percent — of the normal 1972 amount of refrigerator energy. Yet they keep food just as cold — indeed, thanks to better controls, fresher for longer — and they look the same, make less noise, can be more reliable, and in mass production would cost about the same or less.

Cooking, too, can combine efficient pots and kettles that save about a third of the time and energy to heat food or water, efficient heating methods such as induction, and microprocessor controls to achieve and maintain just the desired temperature and no more. Thus a milk-based dessert that formerly required an hour of constant stirring to prevent scorching can simply be put on the chip-controlled cooker and left alone until done. These technologies for combining efficiency with convenience and better food quality also already exist.

The Technical University of Denmark found that combining all the appliance improvements demonstrated by 1989 could save three-fourths of appliances' total electricity while providing the same or better services. The extra cost involved would be recouped in fewer than four years — the equivalent of a bank account paying about 22 percent annual interest tax-free.[51] A decade later, the technologies are even better.

REDESIGNING COMMUNITY

Rethinking design is not only a matter of improving hardware but of looking at the larger context in which we live and work every day. For example, the amenity and land-use lessons of New Urbanism — integrating housing and other land uses within walking distance in compact communities — may soon combine with changing demographics, more flexible zoning, and fast-changing real estate attitudes to introduce further innovations. For example, clustering houses around mini-greens preserves privacy but offers shared pocket parks and gardens and fosters neighborliness. This in turn could make time-sharing of major capital items more attractive. Shared equipment, in tandem with the usual reforms from product longevity, design for takeback and remanufacturing, and minimum-materials design and manufacturing, could greatly decrease the net flow of materials through the household. Shared laundry facilities in apartment buildings could displace less efficient, less fully loaded, and less durable individual household washing machines, improving energy efficiency by about fourfold and materials efficiency by about tenfold.[52] New kinds of businesses may also emerge, like an experimental amalgam of a community center, indoor garden, child-care center, laundry facility, and Internet café.

The new village-style layouts with "granny flats" can also encourage a return to three- and even four-generation families. Indeed, despite the diverse and shifting conditions of contemporary family life, aspects of many of the best values and attitudes of the first half of the twentieth century, according to some sociohistorians, may reemerge with the help of ubiquitous wireless information and telecommunications systems that encourage both home-based and lifelong learning.

As in the commercial sector, progressive designers and developers are discovering many other ways to improve the quality of community life. In 1996–97, historical sleuthing disclosed that standard American street widths were generally enormous because of some 1950s civil-defense planners' notion that heavy equipment would need the space to be able to clear up rubble after a nuclear attack.[53] Returning to sensible widths, as developers and jurisdictions are starting to do,[54] enables the streets to be tree-shaded and encourages safer driving (as noted in Chapter 2, people are more likely to be killed by a car in the suburbs than by crime in the inner city),[55] pedestrian use, and pleasant microclimates. It also creates vibrant street life, local "third places"[56] (like the English pub, neither home nor work) for friendly local association, real front porches, and houses that front onto and engage the street rather than blankly walling it off — all of which can reduce crime.

Better understanding of urban heat islands and vegetative shading is encouraging efforts in urban forestry and the use of lighter-colored paving and building surfaces. By helping bounce solar heat away, such measures could cool Los Angeles by about 6F°, a temperature drop that would cut the city's cooling loads by about 20 percent and smog by about 12 percent, saving more than a half billion dollars per year.[57] By 2015, as trees mature and roofs are replaced, the nationwide savings could include $4 billion a year on air-conditioning costs, 7 million metric tons of annual carbon emissions, and numerous deaths from air pollution and heat emergencies.[58] An urban tree keeps about nine times as much carbon out of the air as the same tree planted in a forest, and it also saves air-conditioning energy by keeping people and buildings cooled and shaded.[59] Making streets both narrower and tree-shaded in California's hot Central Valley communities could lower larger areas' summer temperatures by 10–15F°, greatly reducing air-conditioning energy costs.[60]

Urban hydrology meanwhile is launching a porous-surface, watershed-restoration movement that helps land absorb rainwater quickly and release it slowly. An important technique is helping plants to grow on and over buildings, not just near them. "Green" roofs growing grass, moss, or flowers are now so popular, sophisticated, and competitive in the German-speaking countries of central Europe that it's hard to get a permit for a flat-roofed building in Stuttgart without making the roof green. Even a major building at Amsterdam's international airport has a grass roof. These systems are encouraged and even subsidized because they reduce both flooding risks and cooling needs.[61] Following the lead of Village Homes, such cities as Scottsdale, Arizona, are replacing the civil-engineering tradition of costly concrete storm drains with natural drainage swales. These allow rainwater to flow where it has naturally gone, through the arteries of the earth.

This hydrological reform is part of a broader design movement that takes unnecessary infrastructure dollars out of the ground and invests them in houses, neighborhood support systems, and landscapes.[62] In 1974 a federally sponsored industry study called *The Costs of Sprawl*[63] found that on a given land area, a high-density planned development could leave over half its land area as open space, *and* significantly reduce road and utility investments, compared with a traditional suburban layout. Reducing the amount of paving would also reduce storm runoff. Shorter distances would lower automotive fuel use and air pollution. Clustering and attaching some homes so as to decrease the area of exterior walls would help too. This ensemble could reduce the cost for site preparation[64] by an estimated 35 percent, or $4,600 (1987 dollars), per house. Adopting a New Urbanist plan instead of large-lot sprawl for Haymount, a new town in Virginia, reduced projected infrastructure costs by 40 percent.[65]

Recently, developers started trying out these concepts — and discovered they could get lower costs *and* higher market value. In 1994, Prairie Crossing, a 667-acre residential development near Chicago, broke ground on infrastructure designed to minimize environmental harm. The developer made the streets 8–12 feet narrower than the suburban norm, minimized the area of impervious sidewalks, and installed vegetated swales and detention ponds instead of storm sewers. These measures saved $4,400 per lot, which was reinvested in common areas and other project amenities, increasing property values. Sacramento's 1,000-acre Laguna West development, which opened in 1991, invested $1,500 per house in a lake and street trees — and thereby raised its property values by $15,000 per house. Even more strikingly, in an Alabama project, waterfront lots laid out in standard suburban fashion recently sold for $7 a square foot, while lots across the street, in a traditional neighborhood layout that had no shoreline, sold for $22 per square foot.[66]

Such neotraditional projects are beginning to challenge the American habit of ceding community design to traffic engineering. Their popular acceptance and favorable economics show that the opportunities they create for "negacars" and "negatrips," for convivial communities, and for safer and better places to raise children can be welcome both to the yearnings of those who live there and to developers' bottom lines.

The unexpected and outstanding success of such integrated-design projects in real estate markets is starting to persuade developers to rethink many of their basic assumptions and to reimagine development as a tool for restoring nature and communities. Where these still-evolving trends will lead is not yet clear. But what is evident is that the isolation, car dependency, and social pathologies that afflict late-twentieth-century American suburbanism are an aberration.

Towns and cities are also starting to prevent unnecessary leaks of dollars out of the local economy through more productive use of local resources. They are finding that the most powerful form of local economic development, as the BBC's Malcolm MacEwan once remarked of a bathtub whose water keeps draining out, is to get not a bigger water heater but a plug. The plugs offered by advanced resource efficiency are turning out to be ever cheaper, simpler and more powerful engines for creating sustainable local economies from the bottom up.[67]

Designing great buildings and projects is not simply a way to earn a profit. It is about creating the spaces in which we live, grow, and learn. At first, Winston Churchill said, we shape our buildings, and then our buildings shape our lives. This high purpose requires designs that celebrate life over sterility, restraint over extravagance, beauty over tawdriness. Green buildings do not poison the air with fumes nor the soul with artificiality. Instead, they create delight when entered, serenity and health when occupied, and regret when departed. They grow organically in and from their place, integrating people within the rest of the natural world; do no harm to their occupants or to the earth; foster more diverse and abundant life than they borrow; take less than they give back. Achieving all this hand in hand with functionality and profitability requires a level of design integration that is not merely a technical task but an aesthetic and spiritual challenge.

There is a name for this challenge. Years ago, biologist Bill McLarney was inventing some advanced aquaculture at the New Alchemy Institute in Costa Rica. He was stirring a tank of algae one day when a brassy lady from North America strode in and demanded, "Why are you standing there stirring that green goop, when what really matters in the world is *love?*"

Bill thought for a minute and replied, "Well, there's *theoretical* love; and then there's *applied* love" — and kept on stirring. Today's best real estate developments, and the reasons we create them, are that application.

Tunneling Through the Cost Barrier

Improving mindware — Optimize without compromise — More costs less — Seeing the obvious sooner — Big pipes, small pumps — Optimizing the system — Like eating a lobster — Thinking backward — Doing things in the right order — Solving for pattern

THE EXAMPLES OF THE HYPERCAR, ADVANCED INDUSTRIAL AND MATERIALS techniques, and green buildings all demonstrate that design is really just applied foresight. It's what you do now carefully and responsibly to achieve what you want later.

By the time the design for most human artifacts is completed but before they have actually been built, about 80–90 percent of their life-cycle economic and ecological costs have already been made inevitable.[1] In a typical building, efficiency expert Joseph Romm explains, "Although up-front building and design costs may represent only a fraction of the building's life-cycle costs, when just 1 percent of a project's up-front costs are spent, up to 70 percent of its life-cycle costs may already be committed. When 7 percent of project costs are spent, up to 85 percent of life-cycle costs have been committed."[2] That first one percent is critical because, as the design adage has it, "All the really important mistakes are made on the first day." This chapter presents ways to think differently — to use a different design mentality — on that first day.

We can make no better higher-leverage investments for the future than improving the quality of designers' "mindware" — assets that, unlike physical ones, don't depreciate but, rather, ripen with age and experience. Senior mechanical engineer Eng Lock Lee offers the following example. A typical colleague may specify nearly $3 million worth of heating, ventilating, and air-conditioning (HVAC) equipment every year — enough to raise a utility's summer peak load by a megawatt. Producing and delivering that extra megawatt conventionally requires the utility to invest several million dollars in infrastructure. If better engineering education were ultimately responsible for the equipment's being made 20–50 percent more efficient (a reasonably attainable and usually conservative goal), then over a 30-year engineering career, the utility would avoid about $6–15 million in present-valued investments *per brain*, without taking into account any of the savings in operating energy or pollution. This returns at least a hundred to a thousand times the extra cost of that better education. The savings would cost even less if good practitioners disseminated their improved practices through professional discourse, mentoring, or competition, so that educating just one engineer could influence many more. In addition, a good engineer's lifetime designs can improve comfort for perhaps 65,000 office workers, whose 30-year present-valued salary totals about $36 billion. If increasing their comfort will increase their productivity on the lines suggested by the evidence mentioned in chapter 5,[3] then society can gain perhaps a million times more benefit than the additional cost of the better engineering education.

Many architects, engineers, and other designers, however, are not being well taught. J. Baldwin, long the technology editor of *Whole Earth Review*, was told on his first day in design school that "design is the art of compromise." Design, he was instructed, means choosing the least unsatisfactory trade-offs between many desirable but incompatible goals. He believed that this formulation described "a political technique masquerading as a design process," and he realized it was wrong. His inspiration came as he gazed out the classroom window and saw a pelican catching a fish. For the past 3.8 billion years or so, nature has been running a successful design laboratory in which everything is continually improved and rigorously retested. The result, life, is what works. Whatever doesn't work gets recalled by the Manufacturer. Every naturalist knows from observation that nature does not compromise; nature optimizes. A pelican, nearing perfection (for now) after some 90 million years of development, is not a compromise between a seagull and a crow. It is the best possible pelican.

A pelican, however, is not optimized within a vacuum. It exists in an ecosystem, and each part of that ecosystem, in turn, is optimized in coevolution with the pelican. A change in the pelican or in any aspect of its ecosystem could have widespread ramifications throughout the system, because all its elements are coevolving to work optimally together. For the same reason, an engineer can't design an optimal fan except as an integral part of its surrounding cooling system, nor an optimal cooling system without integration into the building around it, nor an optimal building without integration into its site, neighborhood, climate, and culture. The greater the degree to which the components of a system are optimized together, the more the trade-offs and compromises that seem inevitable at the individual component level becomes unnecessary. These processes create synergies and felicities for the entire system. And this in turn exposes a core economic assumption as a myth.

TUNNELING THROUGH THE COST BARRIER

Economic dogma holds that the more of a resource you save, the more you will have to pay for each increment of saving. That may be true if each increment is achieved in the same way as the last. However, if done well, saving a large amount of energy or resources often costs *less* than saving a small amount.[4] This assertion sounds impossible, and indeed, most economic theorists can "prove" it won't work. Blissfully unaware of economic theory, however, intelligent engineers put it into practice every working day as part of an approach called *whole-system engineering.*

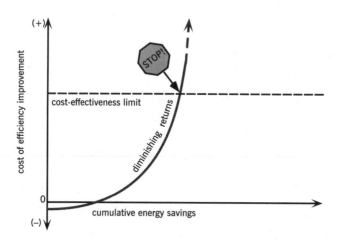

If you build a house, you'll be told that thicker insulation, better windows, and more efficient appliances all cost more than the normal, less efficient versions. If you build a car, you'll be told that lighter materials and more efficient propulsion systems are more expensive options.

These statements are often true — but at the level of single components considered in isolation. On the cost-versus-savings graph shown on page 113, as you save more energy (that is, as you move from the lower left end of the curve toward the right), the cost of saving the next unit of energy initially rises more and more steeply. This is called "diminishing returns." When you've struggled up to the limit of cost-effectiveness, you should stop additional outlays of money, because they're no longer justified by their results. This part of the curve illustrates the common principle that better usually costs more, a principle that has taken a death grip on our consciousness.

Actual engineering practice, however, presents a different possibility. Only recently noticed is an additional part of the curve further to the right (see the graph below): There, saving even more energy can often "tunnel through the cost barrier," making the cost come *down* and the return on investment go up. When intelligent engineering and design are brought into play, big savings often cost even less *up front* than small or zero savings. Thick enough insulation and good enough windows can eliminate the need for a furnace, which represents an investment of more capital than those efficiency measures cost. Better appliances help eliminate the cooling system, too, saving even more capital cost. Similarly, a lighter, more aerodynamic car and a more efficient drive system work together to launch a spiral of decreasing weight, complexity, and cost. The only moderately more efficient house and car do cost more to build, but when designed as whole systems, the *super*efficient house and car can often cost less than the original, unimproved versions.

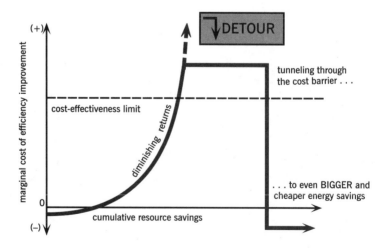

There are two main ways to achieve this more-for-less result. The first is to integrate the design of an entire package of measures, so that each measure achieves multiple benefits, such as savings on both energy *and* equipment costs.[5] The second method is to piggyback on improvements being made anyway for other reasons, such as renovation of aging equipment, renewal of deteriorating building facades, or removal of such hazards as CFCs, asbestos, and PCBs. These two practices, which can also be combined, rely not on some arcane new technology but on well-known engineering fundamentals rigorously applied. A well-trained engineer will be guided by the following three precepts:

- The whole system should be optimized.
- All measurable benefits should be counted.
- The right steps should be taken at the right time and in the right sequence.

Most engineers would agree with these principles in the abstract but have actually been trained to do something different. Perhaps the scheme is too *simple*. (As broadcaster Edward R. Murrow once remarked, "The obscure we always see sooner or later; the obvious always seems to take a little longer.") Tunneling through the cost barrier requires not a change in what we know but a shift of what we already know into new patterns — patterns that can lead to innovations as rich and diverse as the Hypercar, the superefficient passive building, the New Urbanist neighborhood. That shift can ultimately reach the scale of an industry, city, or society, but it must start at a more immediate and fine-grained level: at the building or factory, and even earlier, at their constituent systems and subsystems. This chapter addresses design at the latter level, the realm of machinery and infrastructure, while the following chapter considers the broader implications of this approach for manufacturing and industrial development.

INTEGRATING DESIGN TO CAPTURE MULTIPLE BENEFITS

Motors use three-fifths of the world's electricity. Their largest use, at least a fifth of their total output, is pumping. Almost every factory or major building is full of huge pumps, often running around the clock. In industrial pumping, most of the motor's energy is actually spent in fighting against friction. But friction can be reduced — indeed, nearly eliminated — at a profit by looking beyond the individual pump to the whole pumping *system* of which it is a part.

In 1997, leading American carpet maker Interface was building a factory in Shanghai. One of its industrial processes required 14 pumps. In optimizing the design, the top Western specialist firm sized those pumps to total 95 horsepower. But a fresh look by Interface/Holland's engineer Jan Schilham, applying methods learned from Singaporean efficiency expert Eng Lock Lee,[6] cut the design's pumping power to only 7 horsepower — a 92 percent or 12-fold energy saving — while *reducing* its capital cost and improving its performance in every respect.

The new specifications required two changes in design. First, Schilham chose to deploy big pipes and small pumps instead of the original design's small pipes and big pumps. Friction falls as nearly the fifth power of pipe diameter, so making the pipes 50 percent fatter reduces their friction by 86 percent. The system then needs less pumping energy — *and* smaller pumps and motors to push against the friction. If the solution is this easy, why weren't the pipes originally specified to be big enough? Because of a small but important blind spot: Traditional optimization compares the cost of fatter pipe with only the value of the saved *pumping energy*. This comparison ignores the size, and hence the capital cost, of the *equipment* — pump, motor, motor-drive circuits, and electrical supply components — needed to combat the pipe friction. Schilham found he needn't calculate how quickly the savings could repay the extra up-front cost of the fatter pipe, because capital cost would fall more for the pumping and drive equipment than it would rise for the pipe, making the efficient system as a whole cheaper to construct.

Second, Schilham laid out the pipes first and *then* installed the equipment, in reverse order from how pumping systems are conventionally installed. Normally, equipment is put in some convenient and arbitrary spot, and the pipe fitter is then instructed to connect point A to point B. The pipe often has to go through all sorts of twists and turns to hook up equipment that's too far apart, turned the wrong way, mounted at the wrong height, and separated by other devices installed in between. The extra bends and the extra length make friction in the system about three- to sixfold higher than it should be. The pipe fitters don't mind the extra work: They're paid by the hour, they mark up the pipe and fittings, and they won't have to pay the pumps' capital or operating costs.

By laying out the pipes before placing the equipment that the pipes connect, Schilham was able to make the pipes short and straight rather than long and crooked. That enabled him to exploit their lower friction by making the pumps, motors, inverters, and electricals even smaller and cheaper.

The fatter pipes and cleaner layout yielded not only 92 percent lower pumping energy at a lower total capital cost but also simpler and faster construction, less use of floor space, more reliable operation, easier maintenance, and better performance. As an added bonus, easier thermal insulation of the straighter pipes saved an additional 70 kilowatts of heat loss, enough to avoid burning about a pound of coal every two minutes, with a three-month payback.

Schilham marveled at how he and his colleagues could have overlooked such simple opportunities for decades. His redesign required, as inventor Edwin Land used to say, "not so much having a new idea as stopping having an old idea." The old idea was to "optimize" only part of the system — the pipes — against only one parameter — pumping energy. Schilham, in contrast, optimized the *whole* system for *multiple* benefits — pumping energy expended plus capital cost saved. (He didn't bother to value explicitly the indirect benefits mentioned, but he could have.)

Such whole-system life-cycle costing, in which all benefits are properly taken into account over the long run, is widely accepted in principle but almost always ignored in practice. Instead, single components are usually considered in isolation. Designing a window without the building, a light without the room, or a motor without the machine it drives works as badly as designing a pelican without the fish. *Optimizing components in isolation tends to pessimize the whole system* — and hence the bottom line. You can actually make a system less efficient while making each of its parts more efficient, simply by not properly linking up those components. If they're not designed to work with one another, they'll tend to work against one another.

A charrette improving the design of a chemical plant noticed a big pump whose function was to send fluid up a pipe. Because it had such an important task, the pump required an adjacent, identical spare pump. The designer had drawn two identical rectangles, side by side, representing the two pumps. Up out of each rectangle came a line, representing a pipe. The two lines bent at right angles, came together and joined, bent upward again, and continued on together as the common exit pipe, with a valve on each of the three sides of the T-junction. As a drawing, it was a clear enough design intention. The trouble was that it had been built exactly as drawn.

What's wrong with this picture? The primary flow, coming from the first pump 99-plus percent of the time, must nevertheless always pass through two right-angle bends and two valves. To combat that added friction, the pump, motor, motor-drive controller, and electric supply must all be larger and hence costlier, and will use more energy forever after. Instead, the designer should have drawn (and the contractor installed) the pipe from the primary pump going directly to its destination *with no bends and* (usually) *no valves.* The pipe from the backup pump, in turn, should have come up and joined the main pipe at a shallow angle, using probably just one valve. This layout may look less orderly, but it works better, makes less noise, has fewer parts to fail, offers better maintenance access, and costs less both to build and to run. It also requires less space, one or two fewer valves to buy, install, and mend when they jam or leak, and less pipe fitting.

This novel pipe layout, like Schilham's rethinking of his pumping system, requires a *change of design mentality.* Once that change happens, it tends to be irreversible. An engineer exposed to so simple and adhesive an idea is unlikely ever again to use the traditional right-angle-bends layout and skinny, twisting pipes — at least not without squirming. And that transformation in design mentality opens the mental door to others: Layout is only the first step in reducing the friction in piping systems, and friction is only one of the forces that pumps must overcome.

Traditionally poor designs often persist for generations, even centuries, because they're known to work, are convenient, are easily copied, and are seldom questioned. One story traces the standard fifty-six-and-a-half-inch U.S. rail gauge back through British railways, trams, and wagons, back for two millennia to the spacing of ruts in ancient roads built by the Romans. So if, the story concludes, you look at some modern specification and wonder what horse's ass designed it, you may be exactly right in your assessment — because those ruts were made by chariots designed to fit the back ends of two Imperial Roman Army warhorses.

Saving a lot of energy, or any other resource, at low cost is like eating a lobster. To do it successfully requires both a grasp of system anatomy and attention to detail. There are big, obvious chunks of meat in the tail and the front claws. There's also a roughly equal quantity of tasty morsels hidden in crevices, requiring skill and persistence to extract but worth the effort. It was this "whole-lobster" approach, as described in chapter 5, that eliminated heating and cooling systems both in the Davis house and in Rocky Mountain Institute's headquarters. Both structures, in climatic extremes ranging over 160 Fahrenheit degrees, perform as well as or better than conventional houses but cost less to build.[7] Their success resulted from combining the right details with an important underlying principle that ignored practically every text-book's description of how to select the basic design elements for energy-efficient buildings. That description instructs you to add more insulation, buy more heat-tight windows, and purchase more efficient appliances only to the point justified by the value of how much energy *each of those individual components* will save over time. But this is an instruction for designing a wall or a window by itself, not a house that combines them. For the whole house, it gives the wrong answer. America has $6 trillion worth of houses whose thermal efficiency rests on a methodological design error.

The fallacy is the same one that Schilham found in pipe-diameter selection: Counting saved energy costs as the only benefit ignores the additional savings available in *capital* equipment, such as heating and cooling systems, that can be reduced or eliminated if efficiency is sufficiently increased. This avoided capital expense made the far more efficient houses cheaper to build, by reducing construction cost more than the efficiency measures increased it. In the RMI building, this involved simply a substitution of superinsulation, superwindows, and ventilation heat recovery for a heating system, including associated fuel and power supplies, vent, ductwork, plumbing, wiring, and controls.[8] The Davis house used a more complex series of substitutions, but the net effect was the same — tunneling through the cost barrier to achieve much larger savings at negative cost.[9] In short, neither house had heating or cooling equipment for the simplest possible reason: Each cost less to build that way.

PIGGYBACK ONTO RENOVATIONS ALREADY PLANNED
A 200,000-square-foot all-glass-and-no-windows[10] curtainwall office tower near Chicago needed its twenty-year-old windows replaced because they were starting to leak as the seals failed, and its large air-conditioning systems needed renovation to renew the moving parts and replace their ozone-eating CFC refrigerant. Analysis revealed that

changing the renovation design to a whole-systems approach could dramatically improve comfort, quadruple energy efficiency, and cost about the same as normal renovations. Superwindows, deep daylighting, and efficient lights and office equipment could reduce the cooling load (except that caused by the occupants) by 85 percent. This in turn could make the replacement cooling equipment three-fourths smaller than the original system, four times as efficient, *and* $200,000 cheaper — a sum large enough to pay for the other improvements. The annual energy bill would then fall by 75 percent, or by $1.10 per square foot per year — at least ten times the competitive rent difference in the local market. The fourfold energy efficiency improvement would cost essentially the same as the standard renovation that was about to be done anyway (its extra cost would pay for itself in between minus five and plus nine *months*), with far better amenity, aesthetics, and rentability.[11] By the time America's 100,000 or so glass office buildings now ripe for such renovation have been retrofitted, another generation of roughly as many similar structures will have reached the age of rehabilitation. If the building discussed above was typical in all respects (not too bad an approximation), then redesigning the routine renovation of all big U.S. office towers in similar fashion could save about $45 billion a year.

Reducing this project's total capital cost depended on spending the renovation money in different places than a standard rehabilitation would have — more on windows and daylighting and efficient lights, less on the downsized air-conditioning system. This required *optimizing the entire building as a system,* not value-engineering its individual components. Normal "value engineering," which is about neither value nor engineering, would have cut out the costlier windows and any other component that wasn't the cheapest possible commodity, considered in isolation. But like a squeezed balloon, the costs would then have bulged out elsewhere — in this case, as fourfold bigger air-conditioning equipment.

The key is whole-system engineering with meticulous attention to detail. Close enough attention often reveals more than just two benefits per technology. Not surprisingly, superwindows have ten engineering-economic benefits. These include radiant comfort, no under-window radiators, smaller ducts, better blocking of noise and ultraviolet rays, no condensation, better daylighting, and simpler controls. Some common technologies have even more benefits: eighteen each for premium-efficiency motors and dimming electronic ballasts, for example. Those multiple benefits have been demonstrated in a wide range of applications.[12] They are the key to extraordinary economic performance. They make superwindows often the most important single technology for highly efficient, comfortable, and cheaper-to-construct buildings. They also make possible comprehensive motor- and lighting-system retrofits that, applied nationwide, could inexpensively save upward of half of all U.S. electricity used.[13]

TO LEAP FORWARD, THINK BACKWARD

Much of the art of engineering for advanced resource efficiency involves harnessing helpful interactions between specific measures so that, like loaves and fishes, the savings keep on multiplying. The most basic way to do this is to "think backward," from downstream to upstream in a system. A typical industrial pumping system, for example (as illustrated below), contains so many compounding losses that about a hundred units of fossil fuel at a typical power station will deliver enough electricity to the controls and motor to deliver enough torque to the pump to deliver only ten units of flow out of the pipe — a loss factor of about tenfold.

But turn those ten-to-one compounding losses around backward, as in the drivetrain of the Hypercar, and they generate a one-to-ten compounding *saving*. That is, saving one unit of energy furthest downstream (such as by reducing flow or friction in pipes) avoids enough compounding losses from power plant to end use to save about *ten* units of fuel, cost, and pollution back at the power plant.

A TYPICAL INDUSTRIAL PUMPING SYSTEM

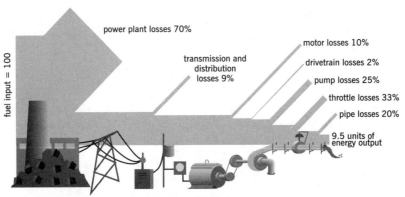

fuel input = 100

power plant losses 70%

transmission and distribution losses 9%

motor losses 10%

drivetrain losses 2%

pump losses 25%

throttle losses 33%

pipe losses 20%

9.5 units of energy output

From the *Drivepower Technology Atlas.* Courtesy of E SOURCE, www.esource.com.

Those compounding savings represent significant economic and environmental leverage — the same principle that a Hypercar uses to multiply its reduced air and rolling resistance into big fuel savings. This compounding effect also enables each successive component, as you go back upstream, to become smaller, simpler, and cheaper. This in turn means that *downstream savings merit the greatest emphasis.* The reason is simple. In a chain of successive improvements, all the savings will multiply, so they appear all to have equal *arithmetic* importance. However, the *economic* importance of an energy-saving measure will depend on its position in the chain. Savings furthest downstream will have the greatest leverage in making the upstream *equipment* smaller, and this saves not just energy but also capital cost. Downstream savings should therefore be done first in order to save the most money.

Downstream-to-upstream thinking is thus a special case of a more general rule: Do the right things *in the right order.* For example, if you're going to retrofit your lights and your air conditioner, do the lights first so you can make the air conditioner smaller. If you did the opposite, you'd pay for more cooling capacity than you'd need after the lighting retrofit, and you'd also make the air conditioner less efficient because it would either run at part-load or cycle on and off too much. There is a similarly logical sequence for such common efficiency improvements as improving office lighting[14] or providing hot-weather comfort.[15] Once you've done the right things in the right order, so as to maximize their favorable interactions, you'll have very little energy use left: Successive steps will have nibbled away at it a piece at a time, with each improvement saving part of what's left after the previous steps. The arithmetic of these multiplying terms is powerful.

Efficient distribution of ventilation air, generally from the floor toward the ceiling, is another system that captures this multiple benefit of "thinking backward." Indeed, properly designed, such an air system offers many additional advantages:

- It enables people to stay happier and healthier by eliminating toxic materials, improving thermal comfort, providing the options of individual ventilation control and even of operable windows or vents, and helping air to flow without fans by means of gravity, breezes, and other natural forces.

- It distributes the delivered fresh air more effectively to the people's bodies, and particularly to their noses.

- It minimizes friction, from downstream (grilles) to upstream (ducts, filters, silencers, fans).
- It makes the resulting smaller fans, and their controls and power supplies, more efficient, and it reoptimizes them for their new operating conditions.

Air-handling, in turn, interacts with other systems in the building: superwindows, lighting, daylighting, cooling, and a whole range of design elements. For example, smaller fans heat the air less, requiring less cooling and hence smaller fans.

The world's master of the new design mentality in fluid-handling and air-conditioning systems — the Singaporean engineer Eng Lock Lee — was trained in the same engineering principles as everyone else. He buys hardware from the same companies and looks up data in the same handbooks. Yet his designs are typically about three to ten times more efficient, deliver better services, and cost less to build. The trick is all in how he *thinks*. He wrings out friction and waste of every kind, downstream to upstream, end to end. To save land (very costly in Singapore), he untangles and compacts plant layouts so they take up less space, yet are easier to maintain. Space, money, metal, energy, time, words — he uses just the right amount of every resource, in the right place and time and manner. Every input and result is measured, nothing is guessed. Energy is used frugally, then recaptured and reused until almost nothing is left. When he was once congratulated on devising an especially clever way to use a building's outgoing air to pre-dry its incoming fresh air, using no energy and no moving parts, Mr. Lee replied: "Like Chinese cooking. Use everything. Eat the feet."

Inevitably, great engineering like Lee's is elegantly simple. Simplicity and elegant frugality are natural partners. Using less material means there is less to go wrong, less work involved, less cost, and better performance. All are products of the same design mentality. All reflect what farmer-poet Wendell Berry calls "solving for pattern" — finding solutions that are "good in all respects," solutions that improve not just the part that seems to be the problem but all parts of the system that contains it.[16] As Village Homes developer Michael Corbett put it, "You know you are on the right track when your solution for one problem accidentally solves several others. You decide to minimize automobile use to conserve fossil fuels, for example, and realize that this will reduce noise, conserve land by minimizing streets and parking, multiply opportunities for social contact, beautify the neighborhood, and make it safer for children." Corbett was solving for pattern as Christopher Alexander teaches in his famous design text, *A Pattern Language:*[17] "When you build a thing, you cannot merely build that thing in isolation, but must also repair the world around it, and within it, so that the large world at that one place becomes more coherent, and more whole; and the thing which you make takes its place in the web of nature, as you make it."

CHAPTER 7

Muda, Service, and Flow

Mental muda *spectacles — A continuous flow of value — Eddies and
undertows of waste — Simple now and always — Allowing value to
flow — Making money the same way — Leasing carpets, color, and
chemicals — Ending the business cycle*

PERHAPS "THE MOST FEROCIOUS FOE OF WASTE HUMAN HISTORY HAS PRODUCED"[1]
was Taiichi Ohno (1912–90). Ohno-sensei was the father of the Toyota
Production System, which is the conceptual foundation of the world's
premier manufacturing organization, and one of the pivotal innovators
in industrial history. His approach, though adopted successfully by
Toyota, remains rare in Japan. However, it has shown remarkable
results in America and elsewhere in the West, and is poised for rapid
expansion now that it has been systematized by industrial experts Dr.
James Womack and Professor Daniel Jones. With their kind permission, we gratefully quote and paraphrase their book, *Lean Thinking,* in
the hope that more business leaders will read it in full.[2]

Ohno created an intellectual and cultural framework for eliminating waste — which he defined as "any human activity which absorbs
resources but creates no value." He opposed every form of waste.[3]
Womack and Jones restated thus his classification of the forms of waste:
"mistakes which require rectification, production of items no one
wants so that inventories and remaindered goods pile up, processing
steps which aren't actually needed, movement of employees and transport of goods from one place to another without any purpose, groups
of people in a downstream activity standing around waiting because an
upstream activity has not delivered on time, and goods and services
which don't meet the needs of the customer." Ohno called these *muda,*
which is Japanese for "waste," "futility," or "purposelessness." Each of
these classes of *muda* involves a whole family of blunders, which range
from activities like having to inspect a product to see if it has the quality
it should have had in the first place (an unneeded process step) to filling
a new-car lot with vehicles that meet no specific demand — if the cars

were wanted, customers would have bought them already — and then discounting them enough to sell them. Ohno's and his students' vast practical experience helped them to develop penetrating modes of perception — mental "*muda* spectacles" — that reveal the previously invisible waste all around us.

So where is all this *muda?* Start, say, by visiting a job site where builders are constructing a custom house. You'll notice periods of recurrent inactivity. But these lags aren't taking place because the workers are lazy. Builder Doyle Wilson discovered that five-sixths of the typical custom-house construction schedule is spent in *waiting* for specialized activities to be completed and fitted into a complex schedule, or in *reworking* — tearing out and redoing work that was technically wrong or that failed to meet the customer's needs and expectations. Eliminating even part of that wasted time can create a huge competitive advantage for a savvy construction firm.

Or take a much more familiar experience: air travel. Often you can't get a direct flight to where you want to go. Instead, you must somehow get to a major airport, fly in a large airplane to a transfer point quite different from your actual destination, become "self-sorting cargo" in a huge terminal complex once you arrive there, and board another large plane going to the destination you originally wanted. Most travelers tolerate this because they are told that it's a highly efficient system that fully utilizes expensive airplanes and airports. Wrong. It looks efficient only for the tautological reason that the airplanes are sized for those large hubs, which are designed less for efficiency than to monopolize gates and air-traffic slots, thus *reducing* competition and economic efficiency as well as convenience.

Much if not most air travel would cost less, use less fuel, produce less total noise, and be about twice as fast point-to-point by using much smaller and more numerous planes that go directly from a departure city to a destination. That concept, reinforced by turning around planes in fifteen instead of thirty minutes, is the secret of Southwest Airlines' profits. In contrast, most other airlines have established systems designed to transfer idleness from capital to customers. These systems are so riddled with waste that Jones once found nearly half the door-to-door time of a typical intra-European air trip to have been spent in waiting in ten different lines, seven baggage-handling operations, eight inspections asking the same questions, and twenty-three processing steps performed by nineteen organizations. Each was specialized to perform its own narrowly defined task "efficiently" — in a way that ultimately added up to dreadful inefficiency for the customer. Removing inefficiencies like these through whole-system engineering of the firm is the next great frontier of business redesign.

The nearly universal antidote to such wasteful practices is what Womack and Jones call "lean thinking," a method that has four interlinked elements: the *continuous flow* of value, as *defined* by the customer, at the *pull* of the customer, in search of *perfection* (which is in the end the elimination of *muda*). All four elements are essential to lean thinking: For example, "if an organization adopts lean techniques but only to make unwanted goods flow faster, *muda* is still the result."[4] The parts of the definition also functionally reinforce one another. "Getting value to flow faster always exposes hidden *muda* in the value stream. And the harder you pull, the more the impediments to flow are revealed so they can be removed. Dedicated product teams in direct dialogue with customers always find ways to specify value more accurately[,] and often learn of ways to enhance flow and pull as well."

Value that flows continuously at the pull of the customer — that is, nothing is produced upstream until someone downstream requests it — is the opposite of "batch-and-queue" thinking, which mass-produces large inventories in advance based on forecast demand. Yet so ingrained is batch-and-queue — and so deeply embedded is the habit of organizing by functional departments with specialized tasks — that Womack and Jones caution: "[P]lease be warned that [lean thinking] requires a complete rearrangement of your mental furniture." Their basic conclusion, from scores of practical case studies, is that specialized, large-scale, high-speed, highly efficient production departments and equipment are the key to *in*efficiency and *un*competitiveness, and that maximizing the utilization of productive capacity, the pride of MBAs, is nearly always a mistake.[5]

Consider the typical production of glass windshields for cars. Economies-of-scale thinking says that the giant float-glass furnace should be as large as possible: a theoretically ideal situation would be if all the flat glass in the world could be made in a single plant. Big, flat sheets of glass emerge from the furnace and are cut into pieces somewhat larger than a windshield. The glass is cooled, packed, crated, and shipped 500 miles to the fabricator. There, 47 days later, it's unpacked and cut to shape, losing 25 percent in the process. It is then reheated and drooped or pressed into the right curving shape. (Because each car model has different specifications, huge batches of windshields are shaped at once while a given set of dies is installed.) Then the glass is cooled, repackaged, and shipped 430 miles to the glass encapsulator. There, 41 days later, it's unpacked, fitted with the right edge seals and other refinements, repacked, and shipped another 560 miles to the car factory. There, 12 days later, it's unpacked and installed in the car. Over 100 days have elapsed and the glass has traveled nearly 1,500 miles, almost none of which contributes to customer value.

Each part of this sequence may look efficient to its proprietor, but in fact the cooling, reheating, unpacking, repacking, shipping, and associated breakage is all *muda*. An efficient system for manufacturing windshields would build a small plant at the same place as the car factory, and carry out all the steps in the production process in immediate succession under one roof, even though several machines and companies might be involved. The machinery would be sized to deliver windshields only as fast as the automotive assembly line "pulls" them in.

Traditional substitutions of complex machines for people can backfire, as Pratt & Whitney discovered. The world's largest maker of jet engines for aircraft had paid $80 million for a "monument" — state-of-the-art German robotic grinders to make turbine blades. The grinders were wonderfully fast, but their complex computer controls required about as many technicians as the old manual production system had required machinists. Moreover, the fast grinders required supporting processes that were costly and polluting. Since the fast grinders were meant to produce big, uniform batches of product, but Pratt & Whitney needed agile production of small, diverse batches, the twelve fancy grinders were replaced with eight simple ones costing one-fourth as much. Grinding time increased from 3 to 75 minutes, but the throughput time for the entire process *decreased* from 10 days to 75 minutes because the nasty supporting processes were eliminated. Viewed from the whole-system perspective of the complete production process, not just the grinding step, the big machines had been so fast that they slowed down the process too much, and so automated that they required too many workers. The revised production system, using a high-wage traditional workforce and simple machines, produced $1 billion of annual value in a single room easily surveyable from a doorway. It cost half as much, worked 100 times faster, cut changeover time from 8 hours to 100 seconds, and would have repaid its conversion costs in a year even if the sophisticated grinders were simply scrapped.

Just as unwanted weight in a car or unwanted heat in a building is prone to compound and multiply, *muda* tends to amplify itself, because excessive scale or speed at any stage of production turns the smooth flow of materials into turbulent eddies and undertows that suck down earnings and submerge whole industries. Remember chapter 3's saga of the aluminum cola can? It takes 319 days in production to get to the customer's hand, then minutes to reach the trash bin. This is 99 and $^{96}/_{100}$ths percent pure *muda*. For such a massive batch-and-queue system to produce what the customer perceives as an uninterrupted supply of cola requires huge inventories at every upstream stage to deal with unforeseen fluctuations in demand or delays in supply. Wherever there's a bottleneck, the supplier adds buffer stocks to try to overcome it — thereby counterintuitively making the stop-and-go traffic of the materials flow even worse.

All this results from the mismatch between a very small-scale operation — drinking a can of cola — and a very large-scale one, producing it. The production process is designed to run in enormous batches, at very high speeds, with very high changeover costs. But that logic is the result of applying to business organization precisely the same design flaw — discussed in the previous chapter at the level of components — namely, optimizing one element in isolation from others and thereby pessimizing the entire system. Buying the world's fastest canning machine to achieve the world's lowest fill cost per can presumably looks like an efficient strategy to the canner. But it doesn't create customer value at least cost, because of such expenses as indirect labor (in such forms as technical support), the inventories throughout the value chain, and the pervasive costs and losses of handling, transport, and storage between all the elephantine parts of the production process. Just as Pratt & Whitney's grinders looked fast and cheap per grind but were slow and costly per finished blade, from a whole-system perspective, the giant cola-canning machine may well cost *more* per delivered can than a small, slow, unsophisticated machine that produces the cans of cola locally and immediately on receiving an order from the retailer.

The essence of the lean approach is that in almost all modern manufacturing, the combined and often synergistic benefits of the lower capital investment, greater flexibility, often higher reliability, lower inventory cost, and lower shipping cost of much smaller and more localized production equipment will far outweigh any modest decreases in its narrowly defined "efficiency" per process step. It's more efficient overall, in resources and time and money, to scale production properly, using flexible machines that can quickly shift between products. By doing so, all the different processing steps can be carried out immediately adjacent to one another with the product kept in continuous flow. The goal is to have no stops, no delays, no backflows, no inventories, no expediting, no bottlenecks, no buffer stocks, and no *muda*. Surprisingly, this is as true for small- as for large-scale production.

SIMPLIFICATION AND SCALE

One of the keys to lean thinking is simplification. In the previous chapter, simplification was a design opportunity for components and products. Enlarged to the context of the whole process or plant, it gains the wider ability to save simultaneously such resources as space, materials, energy, transportation, and time.

The VW Golf's mirrors have four completely different designs, each containing 18–19 elaborately engineered parts, and each available in 17 colors. The exterior rearview mirrors designed by Nissan for British-assembled Micra cars have one design, with four parts, and come in four colors. As a result, Nissan's production system involves only four mirror specifications while VW deals with sixty-eight, each with more than four times as many parts.[6] While it's not obvious that VW is providing premium value in offering customers more choices — choices they neither necessarily want nor are willing to take the trouble to decide about — it *is* obvious that multiplying product variety times product complexity bears heavy costs.

Another key question is: What's the right size for the task? As the case studies earlier in this chapter illustrate, matching the scale of production equipment to the rate of pull by the next step downstream is another key theme of lean thinking. *Every* tool, machine, or process should be the right size for the job. Too big is at least as bad as too small — and it is often worse, because it allows for less flexibility and creates many indirect forms of *muda*. However, right-sizing doesn't mean making everything small. E. F. Schumacher, whose classic *Small Is Beautiful* (1973) first questioned the cult of gigantism in business, emphasized that it would be just as pointless to run an aluminum smelter with little wind machines as it would be to heat houses with a fast breeder reactor; they're both a mismatch of scale. Moreover, both Schumacher and lean thinking teach that right-sizing is a *system* attribute.[7]

The right size for a soda-canning machine or a blade-grinding machine or a windshield-making machine depends on the entire production process viewed in the context of a whole market structure and business logic. Again, optimizing a machine's size in isolation pessimizes the system of which it is a part: The right size *depends on the rate and location of customer pull.*

History has strongly confirmed this conclusion with regard to electric power systems, the most capital-intensive sector of the economy. The proper size for a power station can't be determined in isolation from the system that supplies its fuel, delivers its electricity to customers, and creates its competitive business context. The U.S. utility industry, and most of its counterparts abroad, will take decades to recover from the financial consequences of doctrinaire gigantism. From that chastening experience, a compelling literature on the economics of power-plant scale emerged during the 1970s and early 1980s, then reemerged in the 1990s. By combining the rigorous analytic tools of portfolio theory, electrical engineering, and other disciplines, a recent synthesis found[8] that approximately seventy-five uncounted effects of scale on economics typically make decentralized power sources about tenfold more valuable than traditionally supposed. That is enough to make even solar cells cost-effective, *now,* in most applications.

While many details differ, the same whole-system design imperative applies, and analogous critiques are starting to emerge, in water and wastewater systems. The whole system that comprises classical central sewage-treatment plants and their farflung collection sewers — each piece optimized in isolation — is far costlier than such local or even on-site solutions as biological treatment. That is the case because even if the smaller plants cost more per unit of capacity (which they generally don't), they'd need far less investment in pipes and pumps — often 90 percent of system investment — to collect sewage from a greater area to serve the larger plant. They'd also recover valuable nutrients and water more thoroughly, with better quality, and closer to where they're needed, saving more distribution costs.

Comparable whole-system scale economics should apply to most technical systems, including transportation, communications, and even manufacturing — whose flow of materials between different production steps is somewhat analogous to the flow of power, water, or wastewater. The exploration of such applications has barely begun. Yet the conceptual lessons of the power-system synthesis have revealed surprises that resonate with lean thinking's matching of production scale to the rate of demand pull.

LEAN THINKING IN ACTION

How does Ohno's theory actually work in practice? Across a vast range of industries, many in America, the empirical results of applying lean thinking are dramatic. Approximately fifty companies that have tried this approach have typically found that, using the same workers and the same capital, over a period of five to ten years, production increases by two- to fourfold, while inventories, delays, defects, errors, accidents, scrap, and other unwanted outcomes fall by about four- to tenfold. Much of the improvement is immediate and dramatic: Womack and Jones conclude, "If you can't quickly take throughput times down by half in product development, 75 percent in order processing, and 90 percent in physical production, you are doing something wrong."[9] Shifting to a continuous-value-flow, demand-pull system unleashes the sorts of incremental improvements that redouble success again, and then both together set the stage for virtually endless further improvement. Two of Womack and Jones's examples offer impressive case studies of lean thinking in action:

· The biggest North American maker of seals and gaskets, Freudenberg-NOK General Partnership, tracked the February 1992– August 1995 production of a particular part at one factory in Indiana following the introduction of lean thinking there. The number of workers needed to make the part decreased from 21 to 3; pieces made per worker rose from 55 to 600; and space used fell by 48 percent. However, such huge (in this case, 76-fold) gains in labor productivity typically don't lead to workers' losing their jobs. Instead, the same workforce generally produces far more, and more diverse, products with the same capital and facilities, greatly expanding the company's markets — albeit at the expense of workers unfortunate enough to work for firms that don't follow suit. In fact, the specific process of adopting lean thinking often begins with a company-wide or factory-wide guarantee of no job loss on the shop floor, and then delivers on that promise.

· Lantech, a Louisville, Kentucky, firm, reorganized its development and manufacturing of stretch-wrapping machines from batch-and-queue in 1991 to continuous flow in 1995. This cut development time for a new product family from 3–4 years to 1 year. It halved work time and nearly halved the space occupied per machine. It also cut delivered defects by tenfold, in-process inventory (idle money) by 27 percent, production throughput time from 16 weeks to 0.6–5 days, and lead time for product delivery from 4–20 weeks to 1–4 weeks. In 1991, most of that lead time was needed for production. By 1995, any delay was caused by waiting for a production slot as workers struggled to keep up with soaring sales. Market share rose from 38 percent to 50 percent, and large operating losses turned into industry-leading financial performance.

Gains this dramatic usually demand a cataclysmic shift in thinking. Under the guidance of a changemaster trained by Ohno, a massive Pratt & Whitney plant cut its effort, space, and tooling per unit of product by fourfold in one *week*. In Danaher Corporation's Jacobs Vehicle Manufacturing Company, at 1:00 A.M., the Japanese sensei took a crowbar and uprooted machines that had stood in place for decades, then jockeyed them into new locations for continuous-flow production. The message and the method are stark: Don't study it, just do it, keep trying. If you've fixed it, fix it again.

Lean thinking fundamentally reduces waste at the level not only of the firm but of the whole society, because, as the *Financial Times* put it, "only what is needed will actually be made." It even changes the standards for measuring corporate success. Having performed only six years earlier a pathfinding global comparison[10] of numerous aspects of automakers' performance, Womack and Jones now think such benchmarking is a waste of time for managers who understand lean thinking and a dangerous distraction for those who don't. As they express it: "Our earnest advice to lean firms today is simple. To hell with your competitors; compete against *perfection* by identifying all activities that are *muda* and eliminating them. This is an absolute rather than a relative standard which can provide the essential North Star for any organization."

Charlie Eitel, then president and COO of commercial interior materials maker Interface, introduced the same concept several years earlier when, as part of Chairman Ray Anderson's response to the book *The Ecology of Commerce,* he called for a "zero-based waste budget." Waste, Eitel explained (unknowingly echoing Ohno-sensei), was "every measurable input that does not create customer value" — and he insisted that every input had to be presumed waste until shown otherwise. Once Interface started measuring its inputs, it discovered that most of them were indeed waste. The more the company learned about the potential for radically simpler processes, the larger the fraction of apparent waste became. Workers throughout the company started mining the newly visible waste. What can genuinely be considered "waste" is a moving target, but erring on the side of examining how *every* input can be eliminated is a powerful stimulus to resource productivity, and a source of continuing challenge and satisfaction.

That satisfaction is a hidden benefit: Lean production makes people happier, and not only because workers like to see waste eliminated. The University of Chicago psychologist Mihaly Csikszentmihalyi has found[11] that people all over the world feel best when their activity involves a clear objective, intense concentration, no distractions, immediate feedback on their progress, and a sense of challenge. Skiing just in control, or high-standard rock climbing or kayaking, or hunting something that can eat you, or writing or reading a good book are obvious examples. By creating, as Womack and Jones put it, "a highly satisfying psychological condition of *flow*," these tasks become the end in themselves, not a means of accomplishing something else. In contrast, traditional batch-and-queue production work fails every one of these criteria, which is why so few people enjoy it. But organizations where value flows continuously also create "the conditions for psychological flow. Every employee has immediate knowledge of whether the job has been done right and can see the status of the entire system."

SERVICE AND FLOW

The logic of lean thinking, with its emphasis on eliminating all forms of waste, combines with the work of such analysts as Walter Stahel, father of cradle-to-cradle production, to give rise to the third principle of natural capitalism: *service and flow.*

Resource productivity and closed loops provide better services, for longer periods, with less material, cost, and hassle. Lean thinking makes customer-defined value flow continuously with the aim of producing zero waste. Together, these practices offer the foundation for a powerful new business logic: Instead of selling the customer a *product* that you hope she'll be able to use to derive the service she really wants, provide her that service directly at the rate and in the manner in which she desires it, deliver it as efficiently as possible, share as much of the resulting savings as you must to compete, and pocket the rest.

This isn't an entirely new idea. Ten million buildings in metropolitan France have long been heated by *chauffagistes*; in 1995, 160 firms in this business employed 28,000 professionals.[12] Rather than selling raw energy in the form of oil, gas, or electricity — none of which is what the customer really wants, namely warmth — these firms contract to keep a client's floorspace within a certain temperature range during certain hours at a certain cost. The rate is normally set to be somewhat below that of traditional heating methods like oil furnaces; *how* it's achieved is the contractors' business. They can convert your furnace to gas, make your heating system more efficient, or even insulate your building. They're paid for results — warmth — not for how they do it or how much of what inputs they use to do it. The less energy and materials they use — the more efficient they are — the more money they make. Competition between *chauffagistes* pushes down the market price of that "warmth service." Some major utilities, chiefly in Europe, provide heating on a similar basis, and some, like Sweden's Göteborg Energi, have recently made it the centerpiece of their growth strategy.

Some American firms are now beginning to test this concept. Carrier, the world's leading maker of air-conditioning equipment, decided that it might as well capture that very efficient and reliable equipment's operating benefits by offering "coolth services." Carrier's new "comfort lease" is just like a *chauffagiste*'s contract, only it focuses on maintaining comfort in hot rather than in cold weather. Customers, Carrier reasoned, don't want what an air-conditioning system *is;* they only want what it *does.* How does one lease coolth? At first, the plan was merely to provide cooling as a commodity. But now Carrier is starting to team up with other service providers so it can not only deliver cooling but also do lighting retrofits, install superwindows, and otherwise upgrade customers' buildings so they'll ultimately need less air-conditioning to provide better comfort — and then Carrier can provide not the coolth but the comfort.

While at first glance it is tempting to regard this company as crazy for striving to sell less of its product, Carrier is in fact in the process of redefining the "product" it's selling. The firm's leaders understand that making comfort flow at the pull of the customer means that Carrier can develop relationships, not just conduct transactions. The system also offers important new opportunities to deliver and capture ever-increasing value. The less equipment Carrier has to install to deliver comfort, the more money Carrier makes. The longer the equipment lasts and the less energy and maintenance it requires, the more money Carrier makes. If Carrier retrofits a building so it no longer needs a lot, or even any, of its air-conditioning capacity, Carrier can remove those modules and reinstall them elsewhere. Not installing air conditioners is all right, so long as there's an even cheaper way to provide the desired comfort, and Carrier can capture the difference in cost before its competitors do.

The business logic of offering such continuous, customized, decreasing-cost solutions to an individual customer's problems is compelling because the provider and the customer *both make money in the same way* — by increasing resource productivity. This is not the case when selling equipment, where the vendor tries to convince you to buy a device bigger or costlier than you need, while you try to pay less. Nor is it like a traditional capital lease of equipment, which is often based on the hope of "churning" — re-leasing new and improved equipment once the first term expires (or even earlier). Again, this leaves the parties with opposing interests.[13] Rather, a relationship that provides a continuous flow of services to meet the customer's ever-changing needs automatically aligns the parties' interests, creating mutual advantage.

The form of compensation for the flow of service can be a sale (for a given term of service flow, the product's lifetime, or whatever), or a lease with a fixed or continuing term, or perhaps some other arrangement. But whatever its contractual form, such a relationship, by focusing on ends rather than means, can reward both parties for cost-minimizing choices of means. Where this logically leads is a world, not far in the future, where mere product-sellers will become suspect. Why — a prospective buyer may ask — if your product delivers its service with all the operational advantages you claim, don't you want to capture those advantages for yourself by owning the product and just providing me with its service? If you want to sell it to me and leave me to pay its operating costs, there must be something wrong with it!

Some utilities and third parties have been offering "torque services" that turn the shafts of your factory or pumping station for a set fee; the more efficiently they do so, the more they can earn. The same concept is emerging in transportation, which is now moving beyond mere car leases (which cover one-third of U.S. cars today) and short-term drive-it-yourself rentals toward concepts like those pioneered by Schindler. This leading Swiss maker of elevators makes 70 percent of its earnings by leasing vertical transportation services rather than by selling (or leasing) elevators. The logic is impeccable: Schindler's lifts are more efficient and reliable than many competing brands,[14] so by leasing their services, the company can capture the operational savings. As better ways of vertically moving people become available, Schindler can adopt them to provide better service at still lower cost;[15] its lease provides the service, not the specific equipment.

Dow Chemical Company does an extensive business leasing organic solvents, many of which are toxic or flammable or both. A consumer who purchases them is left with the responsibility of safely handling and disposing of them. But through the lease provisions of Dow or its competitor SafetyKleen, that chemical company's experts will deliver the solvent, help with its application, work with the client to recover the solvent again, and take it away. The customer never owns it and is never liable for it; it belongs to the provider of the "dissolving services" but is always available to do your job. Dow's German affiliate SafeChem, which has increased some solvents' life above one hundred uses, plans to take the next logical step — charging by the square inch degreased rather than by the gallon used — thereby incentivizing itself to use fewer rather than more gallons. It's in a good position to do this, having developed special airtight shipping containers to eliminate evaporative losses.[16] (Even better would be to use benign or no solvents.)[17]

This concept is rapidly spreading in the chemical industry: A Dutch firm, for example, has made a success of leasing photographic chemicals, cycling them many times, and recovering valuable silver en route.[18] (Again, there's a benign competitor: Imation's DryView eliminates the chemicals.) Ciba's Pigment Division is moving to provide "color services" rather than merely selling dyes and pigments.[19] Cookson in England leases the insulating service of refractory liners for steel furnaces, helping to close their materials loop.[20] The service concept has also become standard practice in the fast-moving world of information services. Xerox runs document distribution centers instead of just leasing copiers (they collect the original and you get it back with your copies).[21] Pitney Bowes handles your firm's mail instead of just leasing postage meters. In data processing, revenues from bundled service provision are growing faster than either hardware or software sales.[22] Again, what the customer wants and gets is the function; what equipment the provider uses, and how it does the job, is immaterial.

A NEW LEASE ON LIFE
Service leasing can be combined with other aspects of natural capitalism described earlier, especially since the provider retains ownership of the equipment.[23] This supports natural capitalism's goal of protecting

vital ecosystem services. For example, it fits perfectly with the manufacturer's life-cycle responsibility for ultimate remanufacturing or other disposition as a technical nutrient for industrial metabolism. Xerox's 95 percent recyclable, virtually 100 percent remanufacturable DocuCenter digital photocopier family, mentioned in chapter 4, was developed with these "zero to landfill" goals. It exceeds all North American and European standards for environmental and energy efficiency, and emits less noise, ozone, heat, and dirt than any other comparable machine on the market. It's designed to use 100 percent recycled paper, which causes some other copiers to jam. But similar thinking also went into its value chain. The machine is manufactured with lean techniques, built to order, and directly delivered from factory to customer in order to eliminate the *muda* (and the cost) of time and haulage to and from a distributor. It's even designed with few parts. Its upkeep will largely be done by the customer, reducing the *muda* of service calls.

Even more far-reaching advances are emerging from Electrolux in Sweden.[24] For example, Electrolux has developed the concept of providing its Swedish customers, with a guarantee of quality and reliability, the *service* provided by its professional floor-cleaning equipment, medical refrigeration, and vending machines. It is also experimenting with similar concepts for such commercial food-related services as refrigeration and cooking. The services are billed monthly as long as the customer needs them — but no longer, so the customer isn't bound to the term of a lease or to a period of ownership. There are no hidden costs, so the customer's costs are completely predictable. Besides ensuring optimal use of the resource-efficient machines, this concept "allows used machines and parts to be reused since the supplier always guarantees the performance and the appearance of the products used" and hence gives Electrolux a strong incentive to keep refurbishing them. The operators are also guaranteed to be properly trained. The service is turnkey and comprehensive: A single dedicated partner handles all equipment-related issues and provides continuous innovation and improvement.

Electrolux gains competitive advantage in four main ways: providing better equipment, being able to extend its life through optimal use and maintenance, knowing how to package the offer and control its costs, and sharing a diverse fleet of equipment among many users so as to keep it well matched to their changing uses and well occupied overall with a minimum of financial risk. This approach is clearly moving beyond traditional service provision. Indeed, it transcends distinctions between "products" and "services," as both "meld into one to become an offer."[25] Its focus is on the *relationship* that continuously provides and improves, for mutual benefit, what Womack calls "solutions to value needs." The acceleration of business makes that relationship ever more central to success. With shorter product life-cycles, as the Ernst & Young Center for Business Innovation notes, "There's no such thing as selling a product to a customer and then forgetting about him. The people who are your customers today will be customers again in six months — if not yours then someone else's. When you're dealing with the same customers with that frequency, doesn't it begin to qualify as a service business?"[26]

The solutions-providing relationship also has important psychological dimensions. Leasing formerly carried the stigma of being too poor to buy, and a corresponding interest penalty; now it is gaining a cachet as the shrewd purchase of a total solution underpinned by mutually beneficial incentives. Taking capital off the balance sheet, because you value "flow and change rather than . . . stock and stasis," is becoming a sign of astute and agile management.[27] And because the relationship requires mutual confidence and focuses on customer solutions rather than on provider products, it also takes "the customer is always right" to new levels.[28]

Perhaps the most novel and exciting application of the service-flow concept is emerging at Interface in Atlanta, the leading innovator in what used to be called the carpet business. Traditionally, old-fashioned broadloom carpet is replaced every decade because it develops worn spots. An office must be shut down, furniture removed, carpet torn up and sent to landfill, new carpet laid down, the office restored, operations resumed, and workers perhaps exposed to carpet-glue fumes. It takes two pounds of fossil fuel to turn one pound of mainly petro-based feedstock into carpet, plus an additional amount to transport it to the customer and back to the landfill, where it resides for the next 20,000 years or so. Over 5 billion pounds of the carpet now in landfills has Interface's name on it. Chairman Ray Anderson realized that not throwing more energy and money into holes in the ground represents a major business opportunity.

Interface therefore launched a transition from selling carpet to leasing floor-covering services. People want to walk on and look at carpet, not own it. They can obtain those services at much lower cost if Interface owns the carpet and remains responsible for keeping it clean and fresh in return for a monthly fee under the company's Evergreen Lease. Whenever indicated by monthly inspections, Interface replaces overnight the 10–20 percent of the carpet tiles that show 80–90 percent of the wear. This reduces the amount of carpet material required by about 80 percent because the unworn part of the carpet is left in place. It also provides better service at reduced life-cycle cost, increases net employment (less manufacturing but more upkeep), and eliminates disruption, since worn tiles are seldom under furniture. Because the carpet is laid in the form of tiles, glue fumes are also significantly reduced or possibly eliminated.[29] The customer's former capital investment becomes a lease expense.

So far so good: a Factor Five saving in materials, plus considerable energy and money. But Interface's latest technical innovation goes much further in turning waste into savings. Other manufacturers are starting to "downcycle" nylon-and-PVC-based carpet into a lower-quality use — backing — thus losing the embodied energy value of the nylon. Interface has instead made a novel polymeric material into a new kind of floor-covering service, called Solenium, that can be completely remanufactured back into itself. All worn materials can and will be completely separated into their components, fiber and backing, and each component remade into an identical fresh product. The production process is also simpler (several key steps become unnecessary) and less wasteful: Manufacturing the upper surface produces 99.7 percent less waste than making normal carpet, and the other 0.3 percent gets reused. The new product also provides markedly better service. It's highly stain-resistant, and does not mildew. It is easily cleaned with water, is 35 percent less materials-intensive, and yet is four times as durable, so it uses sevenfold less massflow per unit of service. It is suited to renewable feedstocks, and is acoustically and aesthetically improved — so superior in every respect that it won't even be marketed as an environmental product. In fact, it creates a new category of flooring, combining the durability of resilient flooring with the acoustics and aesthetics of soft flooring. It also comes installed, maintained, and reclaimed under a service lease. Compared with standard nylon broadloom carpet, Solenium's *combination* of improved physical attributes (Factor Seven less massflow from dematerialization and greater durability) *and* the service lease (a further Factor Five less massflow from replacing only the worn parts) multiplies to a reduction in the net flow of materials and embodied energy by 97 percent — Factor 31. Manufacturing cost is also substantially reduced and margin increased. Its net climate impact is zero.

This higher performance and competitive advantage did not evolve through incremental improvement. Rather, they emerged from a deliberate effort to redesign the flooring business from scratch so as to close all loops, take nothing from the earth's crust, and add nothing harmful to the biosphere. Product development began with seeking "new ways of directly satisfying customers' needs rather than finding new ways of selling what we wanted to make," explains Interface Research's Senior Vice President, Jim Hartzfeld. "'Ecological thinking' led to radically expanding the possibilities we found to meet these needs rather than [to] a new list of constraints that narrowed the design or creative space."[30] Indeed, the philosophical framework is even broader: Solenium reflects Interface's ambition to become the world's first truly sustainable enterprise.[31] In energy, for example, Ray Anderson has lately added all fossil-fuel inputs to his list of "waste" to be eliminated. By substituting process redesign, energy productivity gains, and renewable sources, Interface will avoid fuel costs, increase supply reliability, generate carbon credits for eventual trading, and gain a marketing edge. Ultimately, the firm aims not to use another drop of oil.

Providing a flow of services has other advantages, too. If a satisfactory quality of service isn't being delivered, the problem can be addressed directly and immediately. Service flows can often be structured as an operating lease whose cost can be fully deducted from taxable business income, just like any other normal operating expense. The product's value doesn't have to be capitalized, for its capital cost is entirely off your balance sheet and onto that of the firm that leases it — giving that firm in turn an incentive to minimize capital requirements per unit of service flow.

A client's relationship with a leasing company may also lead in new directions. It would be reasonable, for example, for Interface to lease not only carpet tile but the raised-floor system beneath it. That in turn can be linked to the displacement ventilation that's part of a Carrier comfort lease, which in turn can be part of, say, a Carrier or Enron or Trigen lease of a given site's entire set of energy services. Ideally, such service providers might even help you design your building so it takes no energy or special equipment to provide comfort. That design service could be leased — unbundled or as part of the cost of leasing the space.

Someday businesses will lease their office furniture, office equipment, manufacturing equipment, and even a whole building, just as they may be outsourcing their manufacturing, marketing, order-taking, and delivery services to create a weblike virtual company. These trends, already notable as more and more firms make their daily make-buy-or-lease decisions, are creating a competitive and productive economy defined not by the sporadic sale of objects but by the continuous flow of services.

Such an economy has important macroeconomic implications. The concept of *service and flow* goes to the heart of the business cycle, the periodic booms and busts in capital investments and inventories. Durable goods wear out and need replacement, whether they be metal lathes or trucks. Statistically, capital goods wear out evenly year after year, but you would never know that from observing the strong ebbs and flows in how individuals and businesses purchase. Small changes in economic growth or recession cause larger shifts in behavior, because the surplus funds available for investing in capital goods represent the small difference between two large numbers — total revenue and total cost. Modest fluctuations in revenues are thus magnified into big swings in purchasing, whether of new home starts or machine tools, cars or computers. In economic downturns, the small difference is squeezed, so more products are repaired and fewer bought. If the economy is strong, older goods are scrapped and replacements purchased. When revenues fluctuate moderately, purchasing gyrates vigorously along with such economy-moving figures as manufacturing, auto production, employment, money supply, and GDP growth.

For example,[32] while global passenger-miles traveled have steadily increased by 3 percent a year going back more than a decade, orders for commercial aircraft have soared and plummeted repeatedly. In 1989, 1,650 airframes were ordered. In 1993, netting out cancelations, orders were minus 100. In 1997, orders soared back to 1,200. Such buying frenzies exaggerate the business cycle's peaks and troughs. The leasing of services, on the other hand, "dampens" volatility. Volatility causes worker layoffs and anxiety. It also reinforces the "buy-in-the-good-times" mentality, and the need for enough extra capacity to meet boom-year demands, that help cause the volatility. In 1997, Boeing scrambled to manufacture faster, and when it couldn't speed up enough, had to post huge writeoffs, because aircraft orders were *too good*. The next year, Boeing laid off workers because orders had slumped again. Converting from this volatile "goods economy," with its inherent feast-and-famine risks for long-lead-time producers, to a continuous-flow "solutions economy," as Womack calls it,[33] would reduce fluctuations by shortening lead times: Fewer customers would order too soon in an effort to beat the peak. More important, it would place assets in the hands of capable "solution provider" entities with a strong interest in maximizing the life-cycle potential of their assets and no interest in churning. If this route can lead us to a "post-cyclical economy," then "producing firms can stop lugging around all the excess capacity they maintain on average through the cycle so as to make sure they don't [lose market] . . . share and long-time customers during the peaks. This permanent average excess capacity . . . is one last bit of *muda* to be squeezed from the lean, solution-focused economy."[34]

In an economy of service and flow, an entire company may end up owning little or nothing but accomplishing more, while being located nowhere to sell everywhere. The more that the services customers want can be met by efficiency, dematerialization, simplification, and lean manufacturing, the more enthusiastically those customers will be willing to pay teams of service providers. For the first time, we can plausibly and practically imagine a more rewarding and less risky economy whose health, prospects, and metrics reverse age-old assumptions about growth: an economy where we grow by using less and less, and become stronger by being leaner.

CHAPTER 8

Capital Gains

*How we ignore living systems — The resource riddle — Original qual-
ity provider — One teaspoon of good grassland — Nature's workers
out of business — $33 trillion and counting — Substitutes or com-
plements — When the limiting factor changes — Subsidizing global
loss — Taxing waste, not work — The first sustainable corporation*

WASTE ELIMINATION IN INDUSTRY LEADS TO A CHAIN OF EVENTS AND PRO-
cesses that can form the basis for startling innovation in the business
sphere. Ultimately, however, the chain leads back to biological systems,
the sphere of life from which all prosperity is derived.

So far, the connection between industry and living systems has
largely been ignored. The *Wall Street Journal* doesn't have a column
devoted to the latest news about natural capital, because natural capital has been for the most part irrelevant to business planning. The
exclusion of natural capital from balance sheets has been an under-
standable omission. There was so much of it available that it didn't
seem worth taking into account. Throughout the Industrial Revolution, manufactured capital — money, factories, machinery — was the
principal factor in industrial production, and natural capital was considered only a marginal input, one that rarely affected the economy
save for during periods of war or famine, when scarcity could become
a critical issue.

In 1972, a book commissioned by the Club of Rome entitled *The
Limits to Growth* investigated the long-term consequences of existing
patterns of consumption and production on factors like population
growth, industrial capacity, food production, and pollution.[1] Using the
system dynamics model created by engineer Dr. Jay Forrester, professor
at the Sloan School of Management at MIT, the authors predicted that,
sometime in the next hundred years, if then-current trends in population growth, industrialization, and resource depletion continued
unchanged, the world would face actual physical limits to growth. The

shortages we would face would be tantamount to pouring sand into the gears of the industrial machine. Prosperity could be preserved, but only by changing the trends. Shortly after the publication of the book, it seemed as if its cautionary warnings were already coming true as the 1973 Arab oil embargo and subsequent energy crisis gripped the nation. Drivers fought to secure places in six-mile-long gas lines, while food prices rocketed. Overanxious survivalists hoarded toilet paper, light-bulbs, and nitrogen-packed containers of wheat and beans.

Nine million copies of *The Limits to Growth* were eventually sold in a total of thirteen languages. The book represents the very first system-atic application of a comprehensive model to global futures. Although the methodology and terms used were not well understood, the book caused a furor. Businesspeople attacked it, arguing that the world had successfully adapted to previous shortages and that any future crises would be no exception. Robert Ayres, the inventor of the term "indus-trial metabolism," criticized the model because he thought it did not take into account the role prices would play in signaling shortages far enough in advance to precipitate innovation.[2] Energy analysts like Daniel Yergin said that such innovations, especially energy efficiency measures, would offset shortages and correctly foresaw that the price of oil, over time, would come down instead of going up.

Twenty-seven years later, what many observers most remember of *The Limits to Growth* is that some of the more specific predictions of resource shortages that it was thought (wrongly) to have made have not occurred.[3] Further, although the book described "present known reserves,"[4] and how they increase over time through fuller exploration and better technology, it didn't explicitly state that mining and oil com-panies have no financial incentive to prove out reserves much beyond the next thirty-odd years. Some readers therefore got the incorrect impression that the authors thought the reserves known in 1972 equaled the entire geological resource base. The authors didn't think that. Sure enough, reserves in 1972 turned out to be only a part of the resource base, so exploration and discoveries continued routinely to expand them. In 1970, estimated proven world reserves of oil were 455 billion barrels; by 1996, the proven figure had risen to 1,160 billion bar-rels.[5] For natural gas, the figures are even more dramatic. In 1970, reserves were 1,140 trillion cubic feet; by 1996, they had increased to 5,177 trillion cubic feet.[6] Most important, the annual compound growth in world demand for oil, which in 1972 was projected to stay around 4 percent a year indefinitely, turned negative in 1974 and then averaged only 0.9 percent for the next 20 years, greatly extending the reserves' useful life. In what will continue to be a durable equilibrium between price, availability, perception of scarcity, and energy efficiency, prices fell and stabilized. People now believe that there is no energy crisis, and Detroit now makes 8,000-pound-plus sport-utility vehicles for upper-middle-class suburbanites to pick their kids up at school. In other words, in the two and half decades that have passed since the publication of *The Limits to Growth*, we seem to have more "more" rather than less.

Because the book was widely perceived as an unfulfilled prediction of doom[7] — which was emphatically not the intent of the authors, who sought rather to point out that using resources at a rate greater than they could be replenished would lead to trouble and could be advantageously avoided — the idea of resource limits is scoffed at today in many business and political circles and has fallen into disrepute. What has been lost, however, in that simplistic dismissal is the genuine understanding of what a resource really is. The word comes from the Latin *resurgere*, to rise *again*. A true resource, in other words, is something that returns over and over again, because it is part of a cyclical process. Of course, the definition has changed with time and now describes such nonrenewables as coal and oil. But even they could be recreated in a billion years or so, if we had the time to wait.

ECOSYSTEM SERVICES

Another way to assess the worth of ecosystem services is to consider the $200-million Biosphere 2 experiment. In 1991, eight scientists entered a sealed, glass-enclosed, 3.15-acre structure near Oracle, Arizona, where they remained for two years. Inside was a diversity of ecosystems, each built from scratch, including a desert, a tropical rainforest, a savanna, a wetland, a field for farming, and an ocean with a coral reef. The "bionauts" were accompanied into their habitat by insects, pollinators, fish, reptiles, and mammals that were selected to maintain ecosystem functions. They were to live entirely off the land inside the dome. All air, water, and nutrient recycling took place within the structure.

Biosphere 2 was the most ambitious project ever undertaken to study life within a closed system. Never before had so many living organisms been placed in a tightly sealed structure. Inside the dome, air quality steadily declined. While a rise in carbon dioxide was expected, scientists were surprised at the drop in oxygen levels. While the ecosystems maintained life and, in some cases, flourished, there were many ecological surprises. Cockroaches multiplied greatly but fortunately took on the role of *de facto* pollinators as many other insects died off. Of the original 25 small vertebrate species in the Biosphere 2 population, 19 became extinct. At the end of 17 months, because of the drops in oxygen levels, the humans were living in air whose composition was equivalent to a 17,500-foot altitude.[8] The lesson for nonscientists is that it required $200 million and some of the best scientific minds in the world to construct a functioning ecosystem that had difficulty keeping eight people alive for 24 months. We are adding eight people to the planet every three seconds.

One of the primary lessons of Biosphere 2 is that there are some resources that no amount of money can buy.[9] Few if any human-made substitutes can truly supply the diverse array of benefits that flow from nature. We can't manufacture watersheds, gene pools, topsoil, wetlands, riverine systems, pollinators, or tropospheres, let alone create an entire ecosystem. Aldo Leopold's famous dictum to "think like a mountain" was not just a poetic device but a plea to think in terms of the integrity of systems, because we cannot interrupt or replace the complex interrelationships in ecosystems with good results. What we *do* know about nonlinear systems is that they can maintain dynamic equilibrium in the face of disruptions — but only up to a point. Then, even small shifts in their balance can cause critical changes that throw the system into disequilibrium and rapid perturbation from which it may never return to its original pattern.

For example, a slight global warming may actually precipitate a sudden ice age rather than, as one would expect, a hothouse. At present, the North Atlantic Current, a flow of warm water equivalent to the mass of one hundred Amazon Rivers, maintains Europe and its farms at temperatures nine to eighteen Fahrenheit degrees higher than would otherwise be the case. London is at the same latitude as Calgary, but thanks to the way the Atlantic organizes itself, there are no snowmobiles or sled dogs in Hyde Park. Increased flows of freshwater melting off the Greenland icecap, however, could simply stop the North Atlantic

Current in a matter of only a few years. When mixed with the current, the sweeter water of melted ice could prevent a downwelling, the process whereby the heavier North Atlantic Current sinks and returns eventually to the Equator. Such an event would be the equivalent of turning off the heat in Europe.[10]

The real possibility of sudden, dramatic system changes is something we should be able to understand. Our lives are full of mechanisms for which a slight nudge or force can cause rapid changes or "flip-flops," from light switches to thermostats to fire sprinklers to gun triggers.[11] Experience has taught us that ecosystems are laced with similar trigger mechanisms, and before our fingers get too itchy, we would do well to heed science's warnings about the possible outcomes of our actions.[12]

ENVIRONMENT AS SOURCE OF QUALITY

Science provides a necessary basis for business to comprehend the emerging economics of living systems and ecosystem services. In scientific terms, there is no phenomenon called production, only transformation. No matter how energy or resources are used, scattered, or dispersed, their sum remains essentially the same, as dictated by the Law of Conservation of Matter and Energy. This law is of more than passing interest because it means that the term "consumption" is the abstract figment of economists' imagination — that it is physically impossible in all processes or transformations.[13] What is consumed from the environment is not matter or energy but order or quality — the structure, concentration, or purity of matter.[14] This is a critically important concept, because it is "quality" that business draws upon to create economic value. Instead of focusing on whether physical resources will run out, it is more useful to be concerned about the specific aspects of the quality that natural capital produces: clean water and air; healthy soil, food, animals, forests, pollination, oceans, rivers; available and affordable sources of energy; and more. If industry removes concentrated and structured matter from the system faster than it can be replaced, and at the same time destroys the means of its creation, namely ecosystems and habitats, it introduces a fundamental problem in production.

Humankind has a long history of destroying its environs, especially soil and forest cover. The entire Mediterranean region shows the effects of siltation, overgrazing, deforestation, and erosion or salinization caused by irrigation.[15] In Roman times, one could walk North Africa's coast from end to end without leaving the shade of trees; now it is a blazing desert.[16] Today human activities are causing global decline in all living systems. The loss of 750 metric tons of topsoil per second world-wide and 5,000 acres of forest cover per hour becomes critical. Turning 40,000 acres a day into barren land — the present rate of desertifica-tion[17] — is not sustainable either. In 1997, more than 5 million acres of forest were destroyed by "slash-and-burn" industrialists in the Indone-sian archipelago. The Amazon basin, which contains 20 percent of the world's freshwater and the greatest number of plant and animal species of any region on earth, saw 19,115 fires in a six-week period in 1998, five times as many as in 1995.[18] In the oceans, the losses are similar. Our abil-ity to overfish oceans with 30-mile-long lines results in 20 million tons of annual bycatch — dead or entangled swordfish, turtles, dolphins, marlin, and other fish that are discarded, pushed overboard, tossed back, or definned for soup in the case of sharks. This bycatch that is thrown overboard is the equivalent of ten pounds of fish for everyone on Earth.[19] By now almost all the world's fisheries are being exploited at or beyond their capacity, and one-third of all fish species (compared with one-fourth of all mammal species) are threatened with extinc-tion.[20] A 7,000-square-mile "dead zone" — that's the size of New Jersey — is growing off the coast of Louisiana. No marine life can live there because nitrate runoff in the form of agricultural fertilizers borne by the Mississippi River has depleted supplies of oxygen. The growing marine desert threatens a $26 billion-a-year fishing indus-try.[21] Each fire, every degraded hectare of crop- and rangeland, and each sullied river or fishery reduces the productivity and integrity of our living planet. Each of them diminishes the capacity of natural capital systems to process waste, purify air and water, and produce new materials.

In the face of this relentless loss of living systems, fractious political conflicts over laws, regulations, and business economics appear petty and small. It is not that these issues are unimportant but that they ignore the larger context. Are we or are we not systematically reducing life and the capacity to re-create order on earth? This is the level on which our discourse should take place, for it is there that a framework for both understanding and action can be formulated. In spite of what such signals as the GDP or the Dow Jones Industrial Average indicate, it is ultimately the capacity of the photosynthetic world and its nutrient flows that determine the quality and the quantity of life on earth.

With human population doubling sometime in the next century, and per-capita availability of ecosystem services dropping significantly over that same period, no one can accurately predict when a limitation in a given resource or ecosystem service will affect commerce and society. Nevertheless, in the coming years and decades, it is clear that the value of natural capital will shift accordingly. Business does not need to reach a consensus on specific environmental problems, or regulatory analyses, to acknowledge that a basic shift in capital availability — scarcer natural capital — is inexorable.

NATURAL CAPITAL

Natural capital comes about not by singular miracles but as the product of yeoman work carried out by thousands upon thousands of species in complex interactions. While scientists can identify the organisms that provide such things as food, pharmaceuticals, spices, or fiber, no one fully understands their roles in the health of the ecosystem. The best example of this is the most complex ecosystem on earth — soil. Soil fertility is maintained by conversion processes carried out by an extremely large number of organisms, some of which are poorly understood and some of which are unknown. Fertilizers notwithstanding, nutrient flows cannot be maintained without these processes. Stanford University biologist Gretchen Daily calls the profusion of life forms in the soil "staggering." "One teaspoon of good grassland soil," explains gardener/biologist Evan Eisenberg, "may contain 5 billion bacteria, 20 million fungi, and 1 million protoctists."[22] Expand the census to a square meter and you will find, besides unthinkable numbers of the creatures already mentioned, perhaps 1,000 each of ants, spiders, wood lice, beetles and their larvae, and fly larvae; 2,000 each of earthworms[23] and large myriapods (millipedes and centipedes); 8,000 slugs and snails; 20,000 pot worms, 40,000 springtails, 120,000 mites, and 12 million nematodes.[24] These life forms belowground weigh more than those aboveground — the equivalent of a dozen horses per acre.[25]

Besides providing fertility, the soil stores water, holding rain and runoff for later release, feeding streams while preventing flooding. The fine particles in a pound of clay-rich soil contain about 100 acres of surface area[26] on which to host biological and physicochemical interactions including buffering acidity from rain. Soils decompose waste and remove litter, transforming animal, plant, and many types of human waste to nutrients and growing mediums. Soils cleanse and filter pathogens and toxins. Antibiotics were discovered in soil. Soil and soil organisms play an integral role in the cycling of nitrogen, carbon, and sulfur — the grand cycles that affect every aspect of climate.

The interaction between plants and animals, in conjunction with the natural rhythms of weather, water, and tides, provides the basis for the cycle of life, a cycle that is ancient, complex, and highly interconnected. When one of its components — say, the carbon cycle — is disrupted, it in turn affects oceans, soils, rainfall, heat, wind, disease, and tundras to name but some other components. Today, every part of the earth is influenced by human activity, and the consequences are unknowable. Since it may not be possible to determine precisely which species are needed to maintain soil or other living systems, there is no way to state with any confidence which organisms we can do without (if any). Charles Darwin both foretold and appreciated what biologists would discover when he wrote: "We cannot fathom the marvelous complexity of an organic being. . . . Each living creature must be looked at as a microorganism — a little universe, formed of a host of self-propagating organisms, inconceivably minute and as numerous as the stars in heaven."[27] As biologist E. O. Wilson has commented, the multitudinous diversity of obscure species don't need us. Can we say with certainty the same about them?[28]

Natural capital can be viewed as the sum total of the ecological systems that support life, different from human-made capital in that natural capital cannot be produced by human activity. It is easy to overlook because it is the pond in which we swim, and, like fish, we are not aware we're in the water. One can live perfectly well without ever giving a thought to the sulfur cycle, mycorrhizal formation, alleles, wetland functions, or why giant sequoia trees can't reproduce without chattering squirrels. We need not know that 80 percent of the 1,330 cultivated species of plants that supply our food are pollinated by wild or semi-wild pollinators,[29] but we should be aware that we are losing many of those pollinators including half of our honeybee colonies in the past 50 years in the United States, one-fourth since 1990. As biologists Gary Paul Nabhan and Steven Buchmann write in their book *Forgotten Pollinators*, "Nature's most productive workers [are] slowly being put out of business."[30]

Only when the services provided by ecosystem functions are unmistakably disrupted do we step back and reconsider. Virtually every fish caught and consumed in the Great Lakes region comes with some amount of industrially produced contamination. When rain disappears and soil blows away in the Midwest, when towns are flooded downstream by clear-cutting upstream, the absence of natural capital services becomes more apparent. Sometimes we mourn the loss much later. Kelp has become an increasingly valuable commodity, producing a wide range of products from food additives to nutritional supplements and pharmaceuticals. But Russian trappers critically injured Pacific Coast kelp beds in the eighteenth and nineteenth centuries, when sea otters from Alaska to Baja were hunted to near extinction. The otters ate urchins that eat kelp. Without the otters, the urchin population soared, and the beds, described by early explorers as vast underwater forests, were decimated. The Russians wanted the otter because after the invention of the samovar, Russian appetite for Chinese tea soared and otter furs were the only currency the Chinese would accept. Worth as much as precious metals, the fur was desired as trim for ornate robes.[31]

Compared to the rest of the world, North Americans have been fortunate in not having suffered debilitating degradation of their ecosystem services. Many countries and regions, more densely and historically populated, face far more severe effects of natural capital depletion. Yet American ecosystems cannot long endure without the health of their counterparts around the world. The atmosphere does not distinguish whether CO_2 comes from U.S. oil or Chinese coal, nor do the record-breaking 240 mph winds recorded in Guam in 1997 lose force if you don't happen to believe in climate change.[32]

SUBSTITUTES OR COMPLEMENTS?

Many economists continue to insist that natural and manufactured capital are interchangeable, that one can replace the other. While they may acknowledge some loss of living systems, they contend that market forces will combine with human ingenuity to bring about the necessary technological adaptations to compensate for that loss. The effort of creating substitutes, they argue, will drive research, promote spending, increase jobs, and create more economic prosperity. Hydroponics, for example, could theoretically replace farms, creating potential benefits. There are substitutes for many resource commodities, as is the case with copper, coal, and metals. And there may be other beneficial substitutes on the drawing boards or not yet invented. Nevertheless, look at this very human-oriented list and try to imagine the technologies that could replace these services:

- production of oxygen
- maintenance of biological and genetic diversity
- purification of water and air
- storage, cycling, and global distribution of freshwater
- regulation of the chemical composition of the atmosphere
- maintenance of migration and nursery habitats for wildlife
- decomposition of organic wastes
- sequestration and detoxification of human and industrial waste
- natural pest and disease control by insects, birds, bats, and other organisms
- production of genetic library for food, fibers, pharmaceuticals, and materials
- fixation of solar energy and conversion into raw materials
- management of soil erosion and sediment control
- flood prevention and regulation of runoff
- protection against harmful cosmic radiation
- regulation of the chemical composition of the oceans
- regulation of the local and global climate
- formation of topsoil and maintenance of soil fertility
- production of grasslands, fertilizers, and food
- storage and recycling of nutrients[33]

Thus far there are precious few if any substitutes for the services that natural capital invisibly provides. If it took a $200 million investment to minimally keep eight people alive for two years in Biosphere 2, how much would it cost to replicate functions in the preceding list?

In 1997 a group of highly respected scientists, primarily biologists, wrote a consensus paper on ecosystem services in an attempt to raise public awareness of their concern about this issue. Published in the Spring 1997 *Issues in Ecology,* it noted:

Based on available scientific evidence, we are certain that:

- Ecosystem services are essential to civilization.
- Ecosystem services operate on such a grand scale and in such intricate and little-explored ways that most could not be replaced by technology.
- Human activities are already impairing the flow of ecosystem services on a large scale.
- If current trends continue, humanity will dramatically alter or destroy virtually all of Earth's remaining natural ecosystems within a few decades.

That the public does not understand the economic implications of declining ecosystem services has been frustrating to scientists. But in 1994, a group of Pew Scholars gathered in Arizona. Out of this meeting came the book *Nature's Services,* edited by Gretchen Daily, and a paper, whose lead author was economist Robert Costanza, entitled "The Value of the World's Ecosystem Services and Natural Capital," published in the British journal *Nature* on May 15, 1997. Both publications occasioned headlines, press conferences, and follow-up stories. The issues finally received proper attention because the scientists shrewdly put a price tag on the annual value of seventeen ecosystem services: $36 trillion on average, with a high estimate of $58 trillion (1998 dollars). Given that in 1998 the Gross World Product was $39 trillion, the figures were surprising.[34]

Most of the ecosystem values the scientists identified had never been economically measured. They included $1.3 trillion a year for atmospheric regulation of gases, $2.3 trillion for the assimilation and processing of waste, $17 trillion for nutrient flows, and $2.8 trillion for the storage and purification of water. The greatest contribution, $20.9 trillion, was from marine systems, especially coastal environments. Terrestrial systems added $12.3 trillion, with forests and wetlands each responsible for about $4.7 trillion. The value of all terrestrial systems averaged just over $466 per acre per year. Marine systems were lower, averaging $234 per acre, but more highly concentrated in coastal environments, including the Continental Shelf, where the yield was $1,640 per acre. The highest annual value per acre recorded was for estuaries, at $9,240. The primary value of coastal estuaries is not as a food source but in their capacity to provide nutrient recycling services for 40 trillion cubic meters of river water every year. On land, the highest valued environments were wetlands and floodplains, at $7,924 per acre per year. The greatest benefits derived from these systems are flood control, storm protection, waste treatment and recycling, and water storage.

At first glance, these numbers may seem unduly high. After all, many farmers have much more modest incomes per acre; U.S. annual gross farm income averages about $200 per acre per year. But bear in mind that the values measured do not simply record resources extracted and sold. An acre of ocean or chaparral can't be conventionally monetized according to the standard economic point of view, which counts only what's taken away to market, not the service of supporting life itself.

In the United States, the decline in ecosystem services can be gauged in part by the loss of major ecosystems. These habitats or ecological communities, and many more, are all unique and are all under threat of destruction:

- California wetlands and riparian communities
- tallgrass prairies (which once nurtured nearly 100 million buffalo, elk, and antelope)
- Hawai'ian dry forests
- longleaf pine forests and savannas
- forest wetlands in the South
- ancient ponderosa pine forests
- ancient eastern deciduous forests
- California native grasslands
- southern Appalachian spruce-fir forests
- midwestern wetlands
- marine coastal communities in all lower forty-eight states and Hawai'i
- ancient redwood forests
- ancient cedar forests of the Northwest
- ancient pine forests of the Great Lakes
- eastern grasslands and savannas
- Southern California coastal sage scrub[35]

If we capitalized the annual income of $36 trillion for ecosystem services, using the going rate for U.S. Treasuries, it would mean that nature is roughly worth a little more than $500 trillion — an absurdly low figure, as it is comparable to the next thirteen years of economic output.[36] What prices can do, however, is to illustrate vividly and concretely a relationship that is breaking down. Establishing values for natural capital stocks and flows, as rough as they may be, or — as natural capitalism does — *behaving as if* we were doing so, is a first step toward incorporating the value of ecosystem services into planning, policy, and public behavior. When a Philippine fisherman tosses a stick of dynamite into coral reefs, harvesting stunned fish for local markets and broken pieces of coral for the pharmaceutical industry, he pockets cash at market prices. He does not pay for the loss of the coral reef, but it should be obvious that the net present value of the coral reef habitat as a future home of fish far outweighs the few pesos garnered by its destruction. Nevertheless, governments from developed and developing nations still use accounting methods that register the fish and coral harvest as net gains rather than net losses.

If the services provided by natural capital provide in effect annual "subsidies" to production worth tens of trillions of dollars, and these subsidies are declining while affluence and population growth are accelerating their depletion, at what point will civilization be affected? How will businesses all reliant on natural capital, and some especially so, prosper in the future? Given that all of the biomes studied in the *Nature* article are declining in area, viability, and productivity, perhaps a revision in economics is overdue. A reassessment of national and international balance sheets is needed in which the stock and flow of services from natural capital are at least partially if not fully valued.

Biologist Peter Raven, Director of the Missouri Botanical Garden and one of the world's foremost experts in biodiversity, writes that ecosystem services are not merely "a series of factors lying on the side of industrial processes, which added up could cause trouble, but rather an expression of the functioning of a healthy Earth. . . . [W]e're disrupting that functioning to an incredible degree." The cash estimate of their value commodifies the living world and says

> nothing about our real place in nature, morality, or the simple joy of living in a richly diverse, interesting, living world. As a biologist, I always think about such broad subjects in the way the world functions, as if there were no people there; and then I think about the flow of energy from the Sun, and the activities of all the photosynthetic organisms, the food chains and communities that regulate the flow of the stored energy here on Earth, and the ways in which human beings impact or break that flow, or divert it for their own purposes — what are the actual biological limits. For me, it is always the centrality of those functions, within which we evolved and which are so essential to our continued existence, that keeps looming so large.[37]

LIMITING FACTORS

Former World Bank economist Herman Daly believes that humankind is facing a historic juncture: For the first time, the limits to increased prosperity are due to the lack not of human-made capital but rather of natural capital.

Historically, economic development has periodically faced one or another limiting factor, including the availability of labor, energy resources, and financial capital. A limiting factor is one that prevents a system from surviving or growing if it is absent. If marooned in a mountain snowstorm, you need water, food, and warmth to survive; the resource in shortest supply limits your ability to survive. One factor does not compensate for the lack of another. Drinking more water will not make up for lack of clothing if you are freezing, just as having more clothing will not satisfy hunger. Because limiting factors in a complementary system cannot be substituted one for the other, the complement in shortest supply is what must be increased if the enterprise is to continue. Increasingly, the limiting factor for humanity is the decline of the living systems, quintessentially complements. Remove any of the ecosystem services listed previously, and others start to break down and eventually disappear.

The knowledge that shortages of ecosystem services will not lead to substitutions causes a different kind of anguish on both sides of the environmental debate. Eminent scientists and economists including Peter Raven, Herman Daly, J. Peterson Myers, Paul Ehrlich, Norman Myers, Gretchen Daily, Robert Costanza, Jane Lubchenco, and thousands more are trying to reach business, academic, and political audiences with this message. On the other hand, business acts as if scientists have either been unduly pessimistic or simply wrong in the past, and, in the case of climate change, will buy full-page ads in the *Wall Street Journal* arguing for, ironically, more studies and science, little of which they offer to fund. In the meantime, the loss of living systems is accelerating worldwide, despite huge capital spending on environmental cleanup by industrial nations and responsible corporations. The gap in understanding would be comical were it not potentially tragic. It's as if you are intent on cleaning your house, which is situated on a floodplain whose river is rising. Cleaning house is an admirable activity, but it's not an appropriate response to the immediate problem.

Whenever the economy has faced limiting factors to development in the past, industrial countries were able to continue to grow by maximizing the productivity or increasing the supply of the limiting factor. These measures sometimes came at a high cost to society. "From this foul drain the greatest stream of human industry flows out to fertilize the whole world," as de Tocqueville wrote.[38] Labor shortages were "satisfied" shamefully by slavery, as well as by immigration and high birthrates. Labor-saving machinery was supplied by the industrial revolution. New energy sources came from the discovery and extraction of coal, oil, and gas. Tinkerers and inventors created steam engines, spinning jennies, cotton gins, and telegraphy. Financial capital became universally accessible through central banks, credit, stock exchanges, and currency exchange mechanisms. Typically, whenever new limiting factors emerged, a profound restructuring of the economy was the response. Herman Daly believes we are once more in such a period of restructuring, because the relationship between natural and human-made capital is changing so rapidly.

As natural capital becomes a limiting factor, we ought to take into consideration what we mean by the concept of "income." In 1946, economist J. R. Hicks defined income as the "maximum amount that a community can consume over some time period and still be as well off at the end of the period as at the beginning."[39] Being well-off at the end of a given year requires that some part of the capital stock is used to produce income, whether that capital is a soybean farm, semiconductor factory, or truck fleet. In order to continue to allow people to be well-off, year after year, that capital must either increase or remain in place. In the past, this definition of income was applied only to human-made capital, because natural capital was abundant. Today, the same definition should also apply to natural capital. This means that in order to keep our levels of income stable, much less increase them, we must sustain the original stocks of both types of capital. The less able we are to substitute artificial for natural capital, the more *both* forms of capital must be safeguarded from liquidation.

To maintain income, we need not only to maintain our stock of natural capital but to increase it dramatically in preparation for the possible doubling of population that may occur in the next century. This fourth principle of natural capitalism, investing in natural capital, is a matter of common sense. The only way to maximize natural capital's productivity in the near term is by changing consumption and production patterns. Since today 80 percent of the world receives only about 20 percent of the resource flow, it is obvious that this majority will require more consumption, not less. The industrialized world will need radically improved resource productivity, both at home and abroad, and then begin to reverse the loss of natural capital and increase its supply. This is the only way to improve the quality of life everywhere in the world at once, rather than merely redistributing scarcity.

As economist Herman Daly explains, "[W]hen the limiting factor changes, then behavior that used to be economic becomes uneconomic.

Economic logic remains the same, but the pattern of scarcity in the world changes, with the result that behavior must change if it is to remain economic."[40] This proposition explains the despair and excitement on both sides of the issue of resource management. On the environmental side, scientists are frustrated that many businesspeople do not yet understand the basic dynamics involved in the degradation of biological systems. For business, it seems unthinkable if not ludicrous that you shouldn't be able to create the future by using the same methods that have been successful in the present and past. In this transitional phase, however, business is gradually coming to realize that economic activities that were once lucrative may no longer lead to a prosperous future. That realization is already fueling the next industrial revolution.

INVESTING IN NATURAL CAPITAL

The most fundamental policy implication of the resource productivity revolution is simple to envision but difficult to execute. We need, incrementally but firmly, to transform the sticks and carrots that guide and motivate business. That means, in essence, revising the tax and subsidy system — the mechanism that is most responsible for the constant rearrangement of monetary flows and that determines social, economic, and ecological outcomes by applying politically selected subsidies and penalties. In the world today, there are powerful incentives to "disinvest" in natural capital. While governments, NGOs, land trusts, and other agencies strive mightily to conserve and restore living systems, they are not keeping up with the rate of destruction. It is our belief that we already know how to "invest" in natural capital — thousands of groups are doing it around the world. What we haven't learned is how to conduct our economy so that degradation first stops, and then reverses.

Today, abusers of ecosystem services are imposing costs on the rest of society, because everyone depends on those services and is harmed by their decrease. Drivers of cars pollute everyone's air; paper mills pollute rivers that flow for miles into the surrounding countryside; chemical companies' pesticides are found in creatures large and small from the Arctic to remote Pacific atolls. The minority is profiting at the expense of the majority. Not only do users of ecosystem services get a free ride, but everyone else is forced to subsidize the resulting resource depletion and loss, at an estimated expense to taxpayers, as we shall see in a moment, of around $1.5 trillion per year.[41] A very large, money-saving, cost-free investment in natural capital can be made by eliminating both the perverse subsidies now doled out regularly by governments to industries and the practices, encouraged by those subsidies, that are heedless of the environment.

In a groundbreaking work of research and collaborative sleuthing, Dr. Norman Myers undertook an approximate accounting of the world's perverse subsidies in six sectors: agriculture, energy, transportation, water, forestry, and fisheries. Ideally, subsidies are supposed to exert a positive outcome by helping people, industries, regions, or products that need to overcome cost, pricing, or market disadvantages. For example, education is subsidized so that parents don't have to pay the full cost of their children's schooling. Microprocessor development was heavily subsidized by the U.S. Defense Department for over a decade, and still is in specialized areas. Today, that looks like a brilliant investment.

Perverse subsidies do the opposite. They function as disinvestments, leaving the environment and the economy *worse* off than if the subsidy had never been granted. They inflate the costs of government, add to deficits that in turn raise taxes, and drive out scarce capital from markets where it is needed. They confuse investors by sending distorting signals to markets; they suppress innovation and technological change; they provide incentives for inefficiency and consumption rather than productivity and conservation. They are a powerful form of corporate welfare that benefits the rich and disadvantages the poor.

For example, Germany pays $6.7 billion, or $73,000 per worker, every year to subsidize the Ruhr Valley coal regions.[42] The high-sulfur coal produced there contributes to air pollution, acid rain, lung disease, the die-off of European forests (*Waldsterben*), and global warming. For less money, the German government could pay all workers their full wages for the rest of their lives and shutter every coal company. In the mid-1990s, Bulgaria was still spending over 7 percent of its entire GDP on subsidies to make energy look cheaper than it really was so people would be encouraged to use it even more wastefully.[43] Perverse subsidies can also be involuntary. In past decades, the Swedes indirectly subsidized the electrical industry in the U.K. because their forests are unintentionally but heavily damaged by the sulfur-dioxide emissions of British coal-burning power plants. Perverse subsidies can even be embedded in taxes. For example, by taxing drivers for ownership of vehicles rather than their use, governments reduce the owner's marginal cost of driving while raising it for society as the number of people driving increases.

Dr. Myers found that governments are loath to cooperate to reveal their transfer payments to protected industries. Oligarchies, corruption, and/or lobbying can all contribute to discouraging full disclosure, much less interference. Subsidies are not regularly and officially tallied by any government in the world, including that of the United States.[44] They are euphemized, concealed, or brazenly defended as pro-growth and pro-jobs by the powerful interests who benefit but are seldom revealed clearly or directly to the taxpayers who finance them. That concealment is not surprising, since the sums of money are enormous: $1.5 trillion a year represents twice the money spent on defense and weapons, and is a sum larger than the GDP of all but five countries in the world — larger, indeed, than the total GDP of the world's seventy-four smallest countries. If even a third of these subsidies were transfer payments to the world's poor, the income of 1.3 billion people with the lowest incomes could double.

In the United States, automobile companies and related industries have effectively been on welfare for most of the twentieth century. Hidden automobile costs total nearly $464 billion annually, from the expense of taxpayer-funded road construction to the cost of Persian Gulf forces earmarked to protect America's access to "its" oil. But roads may be the most insidious of these beneficiaries because they are so often seen as vital for growth and jobs. Subsidizing them has led to suburban sprawl, urban decay, and highways to nowhere. Even a publication as conservative as *The Economist* has acknowledged the perversity of subsidies in this realm, perhaps influenced by the fact that in one-third of all European cities, traffic moves at less than nine miles per hour at peak times, and even slower in London:

> If roads continue to be operated as one of the last relics of a Soviet-style command economy, then the consequence will be worsening traffic jams and eventual Bangkok-style gridlock. If, on the other hand, roads were priced like any other scarce commodity, better use would be made of existing space and the revenues raised would be used to improve public transport. The mere fact of making motorists pay their way would free capacity to such an extent that bus travel would become easier and faster, and subsidies could be reduced.[45]

Not only did the magazine's editorial come out squarely for road pricing and taxes for road use, but it suggested that governments could borrow against the stream of future revenue from such taxes, thus accelerating financing to improve public transportation. This is a useful and practical principle and one that can be applied elsewhere: Once perverse subsidies are eliminated, the stream of income from realized savings can be reinvested in further savings. Tunneling through the subsidy barrier creates a multiplier effect that starts to compound the investment and finance the restoration of natural capital.

In some cases, the word "perverse" is too innocuous a description for the ways that various businesses are underwritten. Take, for example, the subsidies for agriculture provided by the twenty-nine member nations of the Organization for Economic Cooperation and Development (OECD). They total $300 billion per year, and are designed to suppress or restrain surplus production. In contrast, raising agriculture to Western standards in developing countries where food is not in surplus would cost only $40 billion per year. Similarly bizarre, while U.S. gasoline prices fall to their lowest levels in history, American subsidies to fossil-fuel industries exceed $20 billion per year.[46] Between May 1994 and September 1996, the U.S. government honored an 1872 mining law by transferring land containing $16 billion worth of minerals to private parties for the sum of $19,190 — nearly a millionfold less. Any downstream damage to streams and rivers will be paid by taxpayers, who will not receive a single penny of royalties. Already, an estimated $33–72 billion of cleanup at abandoned mining sites must be underwritten by those same taxpayers.[47] In all, polluting American industries, according to the Congressional Joint Committee on Taxation, will get $17.8 billion *more* in tax breaks over the next five years.[48] Fifteen direct subsidies to virgin resource extraction and waste disposal industries will account for another $13 billion in the same period.[49]

In farming, the U.S. government has set up a veritable universal sprinkler system for subsidies. It subsidizes agricultural production, agricultural nonproduction, agricultural destruction, and agricultural restoration, and for good measure, it subsidizes crops that cause death and disease, by giving over $800 million a year to tobacco farmers. American taxpayers heavily subsidize the 3,400 gallons of water it takes to produce one dollar's worth of California sugar beet.[50] Taxpayers paid to drain the Everglades, subsidize sugar producers with price supports, and cover the damage to wetlands and the Gulf from phosphate runoff and pesticide poisoning — and are now spending $1.5 billion to buy back some of the 700,000 acres that they had paid to drain and sell at below-market prices in the first place.[51] We subsidize cattle grazing on public lands ($200 million), and then pay for soil conservation services to try to repair the damage. And most notoriously, even wealthy landowners are paid to keep their land out of production. (The Conservation Reserve Program pays out $1.7 billion a year, meant to reduce soil loss but apparently structured partly to subsidize the rich.)[52]

The irrationality of agricultural subsidies is confirmed by many World Bank studies. Three examples suffice. Indonesia heavily subsidized pesticides, resulting in massive use and equally serious side effects. Starting in 1986, the government banned many pesticides and adopted Integrated Pest Management as official policy. By 1989, the subsidies were gone; pesticide production plummeted nearly to zero and imports by two-thirds; yet rice production *rose* by another 11 percent during the years 1986–90, thanks to the ecosystem's recovering health. Bangladesh's removal of fertilizer subsidies, which had amounted to 4 percent of the national budget, made food prices *drop* through increased competition. Throughout the developing countries that subsidize irrigation with some $22 billion a year, "massive underpricing of irrigation water has resulted in substantial overuse" and is a "major factor behind the waterlogging and salinization problems being experienced in many countries," yet has benefited mainly medium-sized and rich farmers.[53] U.S. agricultural subsidies teach precisely the same lessons.

While Americans subsidize environmental degradation, cars, the wealthy, corporations, and any number of technological boondoggles, the clean technologies that will lead to more jobs and innovation are often left to the "market." Free markets for sound investments are advocated in the same breath as corporate socialism for unsound investments — if they benefit the advocates. Between 1946 and 1961, the Atomic Energy Commission spent $1.5 billion to develop a plutonium-powered airplane; it was so laden with lead shielding that the vehicle could not get off the ground.[54] Tax-free bonds enrich owners of sports franchises who build stadiums, and then build the requisite roads and highways so that fans can leave games quickly ($9.1 billion a year is the lost federal revenue from tax-free municipal bonds).[55]

Then there is the money donated to dying industries, federal insurance provided to floodplain developers, cheap land leases to ski resorts, bailouts to felons controlling savings and loans ($32 billion a year for 30 years),[56] roads into National Forests so private forest-products companies can buy wood at a fraction of its replacement cost ($427 million a year) while taxpayers make up the losses to the Forest Service, long the world's largest socialist road builder.[57]

Those are some of the activities that our tax policies encourage. What they discourage, apparently, is jobs and well-being. In 1996, the federal government raised $1.587 trillion in taxes, over 80 percent of which came from taxes on individuals, in the form of either personal income taxes or Social Security levies. Another 11 percent was from corporate income tax.[58] Two-thirds of personal income tax is derived from the sale of labor, while one-third is from taxing dividends, capital gains, and interest. By taxing labor heavily in the United States (and even more in Europe), the system encourages businesses not to employ people. The system works, and taxpayers then have to pay the social costs for unemployment. German businesses are especially adept at not employing people because German social taxation nearly doubles the cost of each worker. Taxpayers then have to pay the social costs for unemployment, further raising taxes. Germany has just begun to reduce employment taxes by raising gasoline taxes.

Taxes and subsidies are, in essence, a form of information. At the most basic level, they cause change. Everybody in the world, whether rich or poor, acts on price information every day. Taxes make something more expensive to buy, subsidies artificially lower prices. Thus, when something is taxed, you tend to buy less of it, and when you subsidize, you reduce prices and stimulate consumption. A practical step in moving toward radical resource productivity would be to shift taxes away from labor and income, and toward pollution, waste, carbon fuels, and resource exploitation, all of which are presently subsidized. For every dollar of taxation that is added to the cost of resources or waste, one dollar is removed from taxes on labor and capital formation.

A tax shift is not intended to redefine *who* pays the taxes but only *what* is taxed. Work is freed from taxation as is business and personal income. Waste, toxins, and primary resources make up the difference. As the cost of waste and resources increases, business can save money by hiring now-less-expensive labor and capital to save now-more-expensive resources. As business saves by increasing resource productivity, higher resource taxes may ensue, because there will be a smaller base of resources and waste to tax. That, in turn, will spur further research and innovation in resource productivity. A positive feedback loop develops that incrementally generates more demand for labor while reducing demand for resources — and, importantly, less need for taxes in the first place, because the tax shift will reduce many of the environmental and social problems that government budgets seek to address. Economist Robert Ayres writes:

> I believe many of the problems with slow economic growth, growing inequity, unemployment, and environmental degradation in the western world could be solved, in principle, by restructuring the tax system. The fundamental cause of under-employment is that labor has become too productive, mostly as a result of substituting machines and energy for human labor. The underlying basic idea of the change would be to reduce the tax burden on labor, so as to reduce its market price — relative to capital and resources — and thus encourage more employment of labor vis-à-vis capital and especially fossil fuels and other resources. If there is any implication of neo-classical economics that seems to be beyond challenge it is that shifting the relative prices of factors of production (i.e. labor, capital resources) will eventually induce the economy to substitute the cheaper factor (labor) for the more expensive one (resources). For the same reason, I want to increase the tax burden on activities that damage the social or natural environment, so as to discourage such activities and reduce the resulting damage.[59]

A tax shift of this nature has to be steadily implemented over time, so that business has a clear horizon over which to make strategic investments. Further, the time span must be long enough — at least fifteen to twenty years — so that existing capital investments can continue to be depreciated over their useful lives. This provides a window wherein gradual changes can occur (such as reducing the use of and reliance on fossil fuels) but also a clear long-term signal that allows for acceleration of progress through innovation. In the end, the goal is to achieve zero taxation on employees, whether on wages, income, or employer contribution. Except for lower-income workers, a tax shift should leave the tax burden on different income groups roughly where it is now, and there are numerous means to accomplish this. (The Social Security tax is the most regressive and punitive tax of all, requiring the lowest-income worker to pay the highest rate as a proportion of total income.) Though it sounds elitist if not outlandish to shift taxes away from personal investments or corporate income, the purpose is to lower the rate of return required to make an investment worthy. When there are high taxes on investment income, the rate of return must be correspondingly higher to justify investment. In part, that is why more money can be made by rapidly exploiting resources rather than by conserving them. The higher the rate of return demanded on investments, the greater the likelihood of natural capital's liquidation. When lower rates of return are coupled with higher resource taxes, incentives shift dramatically toward restoration and regeneration of natural capital.[60] The important element to change is the purpose of the tax system, because the Internal Revenue Code, with its more than nine thousand sections, has no mission or goal.

It is easier, as the saying goes, to ride a horse in the direction it is going. The inevitable increases in the costs of natural capital should motivate us to get ahead of the curve. Shifting taxes toward resources creates powerful incentives to use fewer of them now. Simultaneously removing personal and employer taxes on labor creates new arenas of employment opportunity, since the cost of employment is reduced without lowering income. This in turn encourages many resource-saving activities, like closing the loops on material flows, disassembling products, and remanufacturing and repairing products, that currently look costlier than virgin resource use. This illusion is caused by keeping labor artificially expensive and raw materials artificially cheap.[61]

Many economists would say, let the markets dictate costs; taxation is interventionist. True, tax systems are by their very nature interventionist, but unless we abolish government, the question for society is *how* to intervene. A tax shift attempts to match price to cost. The present system is dissociative. People now know the price of everything but the true cost of nothing. Price is what the person pays. Cost is what society pays, here, now, elsewhere, and into the future. A pesticide may sell for thirty-five dollars a gallon, but what does it cost society as it makes its way into wells, rivers, and bloodstreams? Just because markets do not address value, goodness, justice, and morals does not mean that such concerns can be safely ignored.

To be clear, let's look at what would *not* be taxed. You would receive your whole paycheck. The only deductions would be discretionary contributions to a retirement plan such as a 401(k) or to a charity. If you were an independent contractor, such as a plumber, graphic designer, or consultant, you would pocket all billable income. Small businesses would not pay income taxes, nor would corporations. And there would be no taxes on interest received on savings or bonds, or on retirement plans, or on savings for college tuition.

What *would* be taxed? For starters, gases that cause climatic change. The atmosphere is not "free" when there are 6 billion other people who have to share it in the near term, and untold generations after them. If you want to put gases there, you have to pay. Nuclear power would be heavily taxed, as would all forms of electricity nonrenewably generated. Diesel fuels, gasoline, motor oils, nitrogen oxides, and chlorine would all pay their share. Air traffic of all kinds, from commercial to light aircraft, would be taxed (their fuel is now tax-exempt worldwide), along with all vehicular use and public roads. Motor vehicle insurance premiums would be collected at the gas pump, eliminating government subsidies of uninsured drivers. Pesticides, synthetic fertilizers, and phosphorus would join tobacco and alcohol as heavily taxed commodities. Piped-in water would be taxed, as would old-growth timber, harvests of free-run salmon and other wild fisheries, grazing "rights," irrigation water from public lands, and depletion of topsoil and aquifers. From the ground, coal, silver, gold, chromium, molybdenum, bauxite, sulfur, and many other minerals. Any waste sent to a landfill or incinerator would be taxed ("pay-as-you-throw"), at such interesting rates that most landfills would cease to exist. Some, like those in Japan, may even be excavated for "resources."[62]

The result of the partial listing is that every individual and business can "avoid" taxes by changing behavior, designs, processes, and purchases. This works. Many a municipality has greatly extended the life of a nearly full landfill by taxing unnecessary inputs to it and using the proceeds to reward reduction, reuse, and recycling. Denmark's landfill taxes increased the reuse of construction debris from 12 to 82 percent in less than a decade, twenty times greater than the 4 percent average rate seen in most industrial countries.[63] Holland's green taxes have cut heavy-metal leaks into lakes and canals by up to 97 percent since 1976.[64]

Thermal insulation and superwindows in such a world will have a bigger payout than Microsoft stock. You will be able to make Warren Buffet returns by simple investments in hardware-store technologies. When you save money, you will also be saving the environment for yourself and your children. For those who say that such a shift is regressive, bear in mind that it is the poor who bear the greatest burdens from environmental degradation. They cannot afford water filters, to live in the clean suburbs, to vacation in the mountains, or to obtain military deferments from Persian Gulf oil wars. They get the low-wage, high-risk jobs in solvent-laden dry cleaners, pesticide-laced farms, and dust-filled coal mines. In addition, the $1.5 trillion in annual subsidies previously outlined go almost entirely to business and the rich.

The intellectual inevitability of such a tax shift increases with time. Jacques Delors, former chairman of the European Commission, is urging its adoption there. Inquiries and small trial shifts are already under way in Sweden, Britain, Germany, the Netherlands, and Norway. Europe will lead because the solution offered by a tax shift addresses two key problems: environmental degradation and high structural unemployment coupled with jobless growth. The tax issue is alive in the United States, but the arguments are primarily ideological ones, chiefly conservative and libertarian, rather than constructive ones about aligning tax signals with social needs. Regardless, as Europe and other countries move toward tax shifting, it will force the United States to follow, for the very simple reason that it will lower our competitors' labor costs while spurring their innovation.[65] It will also help to ensure that the economic vitality stimulated will moderate, not worsen, the burden on natural capital.

These concepts are a startling reversal from the response to the environment that has been offered by the thousands of trade organizations, 60,000 lawyers, and 90,000 lobbyists clustered in Washington, D.C., who spend $100 million a month in direct lobbying expenses.[66] Not liquidating natural capital means that business will not only have to conserve existing natural capital but will have to forgo corporate welfare and find ways to invest in increasing the supply of its limiting factor. The good news is that one of the most economical ways to do that is to reduce the amount of materials required by industry to provide the services needed by its customers. Is it possible? Ray Anderson, the CEO of Interface, Inc., believes so. In a message to his customers and employees published in the *Interface Sustainability Report* in 1997, he offered the following:

> As I write this, there is not an industrial company on earth that is sustainable in the sense of meeting its current needs without, in some measure, depriving future generations of the means of meeting their needs. When Earth runs out of finite, exhaustible resources or ecosystems collapse, our descendants will be left holding the empty bag. But, maybe, just maybe, we can change this.
>
> At Interface, we are on a quest to become the first sustainable corporation in the world, and then we want to keep going and become the first restorative company. We know, broadly, what that means for us. It's daunting. It's a moun-

tain to climb that's higher than Everest. It means creating the technologies of the future — kinder, gentler technologies that emulate nature. That's where I think we will find the model. For example, when we understand how a forest works and apply its myriad of symbiotic relationships analogously to the design of industrial systems, we'll be on the right track. A tree operates on solar energy. The right track will lead us to technologies that will enable us to operate our factories on renewable energy. A half-way house for us may be fuel cell or gas turbine technologies; but ultimately, I believe we have to learn to operate off current income the way a forest does, and, for that matter, the way we do in our businesses, not off of capital — stored natural capital — but off current income; *i.e.*, the sun.

The technologies of the future will enable us to feed our factories with closed loop, recycled raw materials that come from harvesting the billions of square yards of carpets and textiles that have already been made — nylon face pile recycled into new nylon yarn to be made into new carpet; backing material recycled into new backing materials for new carpet; and in our textile business, Guilford of Maine, polyester fabrics recycled into polyester fiber, then to be made into new fabrics — closing the loop; using those precious organic molecules over and over in cyclical fashion, rather than sending them to landfills or downcycling them (into lower value forms) by the linear processes of the first industrial revolution. Linear must go; cyclical must replace it. That's nature's way. In nature, there is no waste; one organism's waste is another's food. For our industrial process, so dependent on petro-chemical, man-made raw materials, this means technical "food" to be reincarnated by recycling into the product's next life cycle. Of course, the recycling operations will have to be driven by solar energy, too. Otherwise we will consume more petro-material for the energy to recycle than we will save in virgin raw materials by recycling in the first place.

We look forward to the day when our factories have no smokestacks and no effluents. If successful, we'll spend the rest of our days harvesting yesteryear's carpets, recycling old petro-chemicals into new materials, and converting sunlight into energy. There will be zero scrap going into landfills and zero emissions into the ecosystem. Literally, it is a company that will grow by cleaning up the world, not by polluting or degrading it.[67]

Impractical? Four years after Interface began this quest in 1994, its revenues had doubled, its employment had nearly doubled, and its profits had tripled.[68]

CHAPTER 9

Nature's Filaments

The roots of technology — Forests and cultural memory — Bytes and brains — The biggest leverage is downstream — Multiplying savings — A factor 26 gain — Small trees, big beams — 400 million pallets a year — Field-grown paper

IT IS APPROPRIATE THAT A TEXTILE COMPANY LIKE INTERFACE SHOULD BE in the vanguard of the next industrial revolution. As late as 1830, the words "industry" or "factory" applied only to one endeavor: cotton mills. Industrialism was propelled by textile technologies: James Hargreaves's spinning jenny, Sir Richard Arkwright's spinning mill, and later the water frame and the power loom. Among the first applications of the coal-fired English steam engine, besides pumping out the coal mines, was running the "dark satanic mills" that produced textiles. The spinning jenny and mill together increased the output of a spinner by a factor of eight, then sixteen, and eventually by a factor of two hundred. A jenny with forty spindles cost £6, less than wages for one worker for one year. The advantages to the British from these productivity advances were enormous. The lower costs increased sales at home, displacing imports from India. Conversely, where Indian hand-spun calicoes were once cheaper and of higher quality than their English counterpart, English textiles made on mechanized equipment gained the upper hand, devastating India's industry. In other colonies, English textile imports reigned supreme, and if they couldn't, naval battles and wars were fought (usually with the French) to ensure they did. After Hargreaves's and Arkwright's inventions were commercialized in the 1760s, cotton manufacturing quadrupled in twenty years. By 1800, production increased another tenfold; fifteen years later, at the end of the Napoleonic Wars, production had tripled again. In just fifty-one years, English textile production increased 120 times over.[1]

The history of textiles is intimately linked to child labor and slavery, to colonialism, and to world trade and conquest. Slaves, often taken from Africa in exchange for European textiles, were imported to the American South in vast numbers to pick cotton once Eli Whitney's cotton gin made large-scale cotton farming cost-effective.[2] The West Indies got rapidly colonized to increase cotton exports to England. The modern organic chemistry industry, and many of the chemical companies like BASF that dominate the industry today, got started making aniline dyes for cloth. The very root of "technology," the Greek *technē*, refers to "weaving." The misery and suffering that textile mills occasioned became the seeds of social discontent, spawning the then radical political ideas of democracy, republicanism, and eventually the proletariat-based theories of Karl Marx.

Fibers stretch not only through the history of industry but through cultural and biological evolution: Biologist Peter Warshall describes fibers as the "longish, tough, flexible filaments that connect nature to itself and to human life."[3] The history of the use of fibers is in many ways the history of human development. Early in their cultural evolution, humans began to rig remarkably strong[4] natural fibers, often a coproduct of food production, to create clothes, baskets, ropes, sinews, houses, and many other artifacts. Over time, inventors figured out how to break the chemical bonds of wood to create paper, and then how to turn cellulose into resin and thence into many industrial products.

Fiber comes from many sources. The fiber products of forests include paper, lumber, tire-cord, rayon, and cigarette filters. Non-tree plants give us fiber in the form of cotton, flax, vegetable plastics, fabrics, ropes, et cetera. Livestock provide wool, skins, silk, and so on, while even minerals supply fibers of metal, asbestos, and glass. The oceans and tidal zones give chitosan and wound-healing chitin-based fabrics. All these natural products combine and compete with the vast range of fiber products derived from petroleum, natural gas, and asphalt. As Warshall states, "The market system for fibers is now global with petrochemical fibers (hydrocarbons) supplying the majority of textile, upholstery and industrial cloth, cordage, and related products. Only paper and, in some places, building materials remain somewhat immune from hydrocarbon competition."[5]

Producing any fiber has consequences. Most "natural" fibers are grown in unsustainable ways. Half of all textile fibers come from cotton, whose cultivation uses one-fourth of all agrochemicals[6] and of all insecticides.[7] Conventionally producing a pound of cotton fiber takes about two and a half tons of water, and in rainy areas, causes the erosion of about forty-four pounds of topsoil.[8] From the American South to Kazakhistan, intensive chemical-based cotton-growing has done serious and lasting harm to regions and societies. Similarly, unsound ways of raising sheep and goats have left millions of acres desertified around the world. Sustainable ways of growing wool, flax, hemp (the strongest plant fiber), and even cotton are both familiar and practical. Since 1996, Patagonia, a $165 million-a-year outdoor clothing company, has used only organic cotton for its merchandise,[9] but despite increasing usage by such larger firms as Nike and Levi Strauss, such practices are still far smaller-scale than the soil-mining, subsidized, chemically dependent methods.[10]

The petrochemical industry, which makes the building blocks for synthetic fibers, is also a notable polluter and uses a nonrenewable resource. However, its environmental performance can be (and often is being) considerably improved. Also, as Warshall points out, the advent of "petrochemical fibers undoubtedly postponed the cutting of huge acreage of trees, as well as the clearing of land for cotton." A 300-acre petrochemical plant, plus a rather small acreage of natural-gas facilities, can match the fiber production of 600,000 acres of cotton.[11]

A detailed comparison or even description of the impacts of all fibers, and the opportunities available to offset those impacts, is beyond the scope of this book, but it is worth looking at one form of fiber production, forests, as an example. The forests that produce wood fiber illustrate the issues well, and they form a significant part of the economy: The annual forest harvest is more than twice the weight of all U.S. purchases of metals.[12] While sustainable harvesting and forest management practices are known and often commercially viable, they are not yet widely practiced,[13] so conventional forestry remains a prominent cause of widespread harm to natural capital, degrading natural forests' more valuable ecosystem services.

Forests are cut primarily to produce paper products and lumber in roughly equal volumes, although the former is growing faster while the latter use fetches two to five times higher prices per unit of wood volume (and even more for veneer logs).[14] From the early 1960s to the mid-1990s, as per-capita U.S. consumption of timber products held constant or even sagged a bit, per-capita paper-product consumption nearly doubled. The world consumes five times more paper now than in 1950.[15] U.S. offices' paper use soared from 0.85 to 1.4 trillion sheets (about 4.2 to 7 million tons) just between 1981 and 1984, as early desktop computers and laser printers were being introduced.[16]

Other countries did not lag far behind America's wasteful ways. From 1970 to 1990, paper production rose 4 percent a year in Japan, and in Southeast Asia, 8 percent, compared with 2.5 percent in the United States. To keep up with the vast volumes demanded, papermaking, like logging, has changed in many regions from a handicraft to an industrial commodity enterprise of almost unimaginable scale.

A traditional rural Nepalese paper factory is an outdoor area the size of a living room with a production process that is simple, labor-intensive, and cheap. The fibrous inner bark of a certain tree — analogous to the Chinese mulberry tree from which paper was developed nineteen centuries ago — is stripped, soaked, and pounded in wood-ash lye. The resulting slurry of fibers is treated and washed in a series of small ponds. Pieces of cloth stretched on wooden frames are dipped into and raised up through the slurry so they are coated with a thin layer of fiber, then are propped up to dry in the sun. The resultant rice-paper-like sheet sells for about a dime in Nepal or a dollar in New York art-supply stores. In the almost cashless rural Nepali economy, the paper is a precious product, reserved largely for religious and ceremonial purposes.

Modern Western paper factories are gigantic operations costing upward of a billion dollars. A big paper mill uses energy at the same rate as a small city. Paper mills turn entire forests — a seventy-five-acre clear-cut per mill per day[17] — into hundreds of different high-performance products by the freight-train-load. The logs are chipped and boiled in gigantic kettles of acid, or ground between huge plates run by thousands-of-horsepower motors, to release the cellulose fibers from the surrounding lignin and hemicellulose. Papermaking machines bigger than a house echo the Nepali hand-run process, but at a vast scale, forming a web of fibers that thunders through steam-heated driers and onto shipping rolls with the speed of a locomotive. All this supports a culture in which paper is universally available, priced at perhaps a penny a sheet, and rarely paid for or thought about by its users.

Paper accounts for about 2 percent of world trade and 2.5 percent of world industrial production;[18] its U.S. shipments, over $132 billion a year, are comparable in value to primary metals and minerals, or to 90 percent of petrochemicals.[19] Yet much of the paper produced is used only for a short time and then discarded: Only about a tenth of the global paper stream goes into "cultural memory" — long-term storage in such forms as files, records, and books.[20] Much of the rest of printing and writing paper, which represented 28 percent of 1992 paper and paperboard consumption, finds its way into the office paper chase. The average American officeworker is estimated to use a sheet every 12 minutes — a ream per person every two and a half working weeks — and to dispose of 100–200 pounds of paper per person every year.[21] This paper accounts for as much as 70 percent of typical office waste. During the years 1972–87, America's discarded office printing and writing paper grew almost five times as fast as the human population, miscellaneous office paper over five times, and copier paper almost ten times — a 150 percent absolute increase.[22]

SUBSTITUTING BYTES AND BRAINS FOR PAPER

The elusive goal of substituting "electrons for fiber and pixels for paper"[23] is a worthy challenge. Multi-gigabyte hard disks that can search an entire library's worth of data in the blink of an eye are priced at the equivalent of pennies per ream of double-sided paper information. Some pioneering businesses have almost achieved a paperless, all-electronic office. But the initial cultural, financial, and practical barriers are often daunting.

Dan Caulfield, the CEO of Hire Quality, a Chicago job-placement service, decided to make his company all-electronic.[24] The transition was traumatic: At one point, Caulfield, an ex-Marine, seized and burned every scrap of paper he could find around the office, even important work products, in order to dramatize what a complete cultural change was needed. The firm had to spend nearly $400,000 on equipment and setup before it could do virtually everything onscreen and nothing on paper (all incoming paper is immediately scanned into data files). This investment, however, laid the foundations for durable competitive advantage. More than 200,000 candidates' files can be instantly searched by over 150 data fields. A single keystroke E-mails job descriptions from clients to job banks. The cost to process a job application has been cut by about three-fourths, the number of calls to pin down a referral by about half, and the time to fax ten resumes to a client by nine-tenths. (Nine-tenths of the paper previously used for that operation was also saved, but the saved time proved to be far more valuable.) More precious still are the better service quality, and the faster and smarter information flow, decisions, and teamwork that come from redesigning the business around people, not paper. The Danish firm Oticon found this when its electronics revolution, intended to yield sounder and quicker decisions, had the side effect of reducing its paper use by roughly 30–50 percent.[25]

Dutch business therapist Eric Poll[26] sought to take advantage of ubiquitous computers without having to redesign an entire business around them. A few years ago, he decided that his workplace — Dow's European headquarters at Horgen, Switzerland — had too much paper flying around, so he introduced three new practices as an experiment:

- Any paper or electronic message (many of which are subsequently printed) would automatically return an electronic reply saying whether the recipient had wanted it. This created a polite way to say, "It's ever so kind of you to think of me in this way, but I really don't think I should have received this information."
- Distribution lists were abolished, so multiple addressees had to be manually listed each time, discouraging unnecessary transmissions.
- Any long paper or book had to be sent with a short summary — easy for the sender if she had read the publication, and convenient for the recipient, but if the sender hadn't read it, why was she passing it along?

These innovations cut paper flow by about 30 percent in six weeks — and the "nega-information" improved labor productivity by even more, because now people had more time to read the things that really merited their attention. This was all the more impressive because a big potential source of further savings was left untapped — rewarding administrative assistants, who are most burdened by excess paperflow, with a share of the savings achieved by reducing it.

Electronic communications can save paper, time, and money in the most complex commercial transactions normally requiring very voluminous documents. BankAmerica Securities arranged a $4 billion syndication for Compaq Computer Corporation, for example, using a secure website to provide information to the lender group and distribute the draft loan documents. This saved over 11,000 pieces of paper — nearly 5 million a year when extended to all the syndications led by that one bank.[27]

Some short-term paperflow, like junk mail and handbills, is completely ephemeral, and can easily be dispensed with. A significant fraction, though, goes to such temporary but useful periodic reference works as telephone directories and catalogs. Both face competition from electronic media. A single CD-ROM, costing pennies to press, can contain every telephone directory in the United States — a quarter million pages. Even denser media like DVD-ROMs are becoming popular; a world phone book on a disk is practical today. Better still, anyone with Internet access can simply look up white, yellow, and other specialized kinds of phone book pages on various websites for free. This service is no slower or less up-to-date than today's decaying U.S. phone-company directory information service, and is often more informative. The new electronic media are also starting to come with convenient handheld readers. A physician can get the 3,000-page *Merck Manual,* plus the *Physician's Desk Reference,* on a single CD-ROM that's portable to the bedside, and retrieve any information in seconds. Mail-order catalogs, too, are increasingly threatened by much cheaper and handier Internet commerce.

Even greater gains in productivity and effectiveness are available to architects and engineers who replace roomsful of heavy paper parts catalogs with electronic versions. Instead of laboriously copying and scaling drawings from books for insertion into electronic drawings, they can do so with a keystroke from a CD-ROM. InPart Design, Inc., a startup company in Saratoga, California, claims that downloading digital drawings for fewer than ten parts from its more than 150,000-part online library (for $20 each) saves more than enough redrawing labor to pay its one-time $1,000 software license fee; after that it's pure gravy.[28] This option is gradually becoming popular in all kinds of design, and is being linked with Web-based commerce so that having decided what to specify, you can have an intelligent software agent find the best buy and order it. Hundreds of newspapers and magazines, too, are already published on the Internet; most are available free and with powerful search engines. At this point, these are still viewed as complements to print media. Should that change, the displacement of physical with virtual newspapers would be no small matter, since newsprint is a sixth of all U.S. paper production: The Sunday *New York Times* alone uses some 75,000 trees per edition.[29]

COMBINING SAVINGS SYSTEMATICALLY

At the heart of this chapter, and, for that matter, the entire book, is the thesis that 90 to 95 percent reductions in material and energy are possible in developed nations without diminishing the quantity or quality of the services that people want. Sometimes such a large saving can come from a single conceptual or technological leap, like Schilham's pumps at Interface in Shanghai, or a state-of-the-art building. More often, however, it comes from systematically combining a series of successive savings. Often the savings come in different parts of the value chain that stretches from the extraction of a raw resource, through every intermediate step of processing and transportation, to the final delivery of the service (and even beyond to the ultimate recovery of leftover energy and materials). The secret to achieving large savings in such a chain of successive steps is to multiply the savings together, capturing the magic of compounding arithmetic. For example, if a process has ten steps, and you can save 20 percent in each step without interfering with the others, then you will be left using only 11 percent of what you started with — an 89 percent saving overall. Wood fibers, because there are many separate steps in their production and use, offer many kinds of successive savings to be multiplied. They nicely illustrate the feasibility of radical reduction in the harvest required from forests — a key element of natural capitalism.

The best way to save resources is to emphasize the savings that occur closest to the customer, all the way downstream. The logic is precisely that of the "To Leap Forward, Think Backward" section of chapter 6. There we found that in a pumping system, ten units of fuel must be burned in a power station to deliver one unit flow from a pipe. The opposite is therefore also true — saving one unit of flow in the pipe can save ten units of fuel at the power station. Likewise, if (say) three pounds of trees must be cut in a forest in order to deliver one pound of paper, then saving that one pound of paper will avoid cutting three pounds of trees. The many compounding losses from tree to paper can be turned around backward into compounding savings. The savings with the greatest leverage are thus those furthest downstream.

The biggest savings can come from asking how much ultimate satisfaction a consumer obtains from each unit of end-use service delivered. No matter how wonderfully efficiently we convert forests to logs to pulp to paper, it's all for naught if the result is junk mail that nobody wants and that is thrown away unread and sent to landfill (as most of it seems to be). Every unit of such unwanted or despised "service" that can be avoided will in turn avoid the entire chain of compounding losses all the way back to the forest, saving the largest possible number of trees — and amount of forest damaged by cutting them down.

A good candidate for such elimination is overdesigned[30] or needless packaging.[31] Most industrial and some food packaging can be promptly cut by 20 to 50 percent.[32] A major German retailer found that 98 percent of all "secondary" packaging — boxes around toothpaste tubes, plastic wrap around ice-cream cartons — is simply unnecessary.[33]

The use of paper and lumber worldwide, for services wanted and unwanted, has shown an unbroken pattern of growth for the past fifty years. The consumption of wood fiber correlates strongly with overall affluence, leading analysts to believe that demand for forest products will greatly expand in the next century as population and living standards increase. Naturally, most analysts have assumed that the only way to meet growing demand for wood fiber is to produce more of it. But of course customers aren't demanding railcar-loads of raw wood fiber; rather, they're demanding the end-use services that the fiber ultimately provides to them, like support for a wall or for reading a book. To provide the same services with less fiber, therefore, we need to look more carefully at each step along the journey from forest to customer service. A helpful approach is summarized by a formula that combines the various factors that cause extraction of trees from forests. The formula then divides the product of those factors by the various ways to make the whole process more efficient. The result reveals the total potential for savings.[34]

The formula starts with:

- **Human Population,** which is multiplied by
- **Affluence:** the average amount of a given service each person consumes, which is multiplied by
- **Unsubstituted Fiber:** how much of the demand for the services provided by forest products is being met by wood fiber rather than by substituting non-wood materials, which is multiplied by
- **New-Materials Dependence:** what fraction of the items that provide those desired services is made from new fibers rather than from recycled fibers, new items rather than repaired or remanufactured, throwaway instead of durable goods, et cetera.

The product of those terms represents how much wood fiber would be needed if all the efficiencies in harvesting, processing, and using that fiber stayed constant. But these efficiencies can be improved. To identify where more service can be provided with less fiber, the result calculated above (the supposed need for fiber) must next be divided by the product of four kinds of efficiency improvements:

- **Field Efficiency:** how efficiently forests are turned into such primary products as logs or pulp, multiplied by

- **Conversion Efficiency:** how efficiently those intermediate forest products are turned into such intermediate goods as paper or lumber, multiplied by

- **End-Use Efficiency:** how efficiently those finished goods are turned into such delivered uses or services as a building or a presented document, multiplied by

- **Functional Efficiency:** how efficiently those uses increase human satisfaction by creating happiness or meeting objectives.

Population and Affluence are obviously important, but it may be difficult to establish how much flexibility they offer. Functional Efficiency and New-Materials Dependence, while potentially very significant, are also hard to define. However, even focusing on just the other four of the eight terms — on Fiber Substitutions, Field Efficiency, Conversion Efficiency, and End-Use Efficiency — reveals a potential (in five case studies and many anecdotal examples) for a roughly 75–80 percent reduction in the new wood fiber needed to provide popular services, from new homes to the morning newspaper.[35] The more detailed the assessment, the more opportunities for savings emerge.

It is possible to eschew needless messages, get off junk-mail and unwanted distribution lists, adopt E-mail (and learn not to print it out), edit with groupware, and preview documents on the computer screen before printing them. All these things increase Functional Efficiency — the class of savings that are furthest downstream and therefore most valuable. How about the paperflow that is required after that? The next step, also offering big paper savings with the same or better services, is to maximize End-Use Efficiency. (Being the next-to-furthest-downstream opportunity, it, too, has high leverage for savings.) End-Use Efficiency offers many important ways to save paper and money. Most photocopied or laser-printed documents would be easier to read, carry, and file if automatically printed double-sided. The modest extra cost of adding a duplexer is quickly recovered from the saved paper, file and supplies-inventory space, et cetera. If the duplexer is already a feature, it costs nothing to activate it as the default option.[36] Drafts can be printed with smaller-than-final margins and fonts, within reason; or better still, they can be edited only electronically. Fax cover sheets are seldom necessary. Two-way returnable envelopes are handy for bills and save 60–70 percent of envelope paper. Barcoding, especially the information-rich two-dimensional variety, can displace production- and shipping-tracking paperflow by containing details about a product's life history, customer information, legal documents, et cetera all on one small label. E-mail, by which this book was largely written and edited, already transmits over ten *trillion* words a year,[37] and it's a lot easier to find an old message by a computer search than by rummaging through a file cabinet.

These examples only cover the stages of Functional- and End-Use-Efficiency savings. Further upstream there are such steps as reducing New-Materials Dependence. This means reusing the back of used or spoiled paper for internal drafts and notes; recycling paper into new paper (or into lower-quality products that displace other wood fiber); or using lighter-basis-weight paper (less fiber per ream but with the same printing and viewing qualities). Then there are Substitutions that make paper from nonwood fiber, some of which is actually of higher quality than wood fiber.[38] There are Conversion Efficiency improvements that wring more paper from each ton of pulp or more pulp from each log. Finally, there are Field Efficiency improvements that get more volume of pulp logs per year from each acre of forest without damaging or destroying surrounding trees.

In the end, how much logging can be avoided through worthwhile improvements in practice at every stage of the office-paper value chain, treating it, for simplicity's sake, as one homogeneous process and market? If we use "nega-information," or convert to a truly paperless office (an unfulfilled dream so far), then a full 100 percent of the logging now done for making office paper becomes unnecessary. Tree-free paper is another option, though that may simply shift the harvest from forests to other crops or "wastes" grown in other places. In that case, the relative fragility or value of each crop or feedstock would have to be considered. What if changes were not so drastic but were more invisible and incremental? The results can still be surprising. Consider the possibilities of combining the following reasonable assumptions about downstream-to-upstream opportunities in a hypothetical office printing and copying paper value chain:

- **Functional Efficiency:** 10 percent reduction in paper use due to E-mail and procedures that curb unwanted printouts[39] = Factor 1.11 savings (that is, 1.11 times more service is obtained from the same resource use)[40]

- **End-Use Efficiency:** 50 percent reduction in paper use by instituting double-sided printing and copying, scratch-paper reuse, et cetera = Factor 2.0

- **Conversion Efficiency:** Pulp-mill conversion efficiency increase of 5 percent via process and equipment upgrades = Factor 1.05

- **Field Efficiency:** 400 percent increase in pulpwood yield per acre by specifying softwood plantations[41] rather than unmanaged natural forest = Factor 5.0

- **Materials Cycle:** 25 percent reduction in fiber required per sheet of paper by switching from 60-pound to 45-pound basis weight[42] = Factor 1.33

- **Unsubstituted Fraction:** 10 percent reduction in wood fiber use with supplemental nonwood (for example, straw) fiber plus 30 percent net reduction from paper recycling[43] = Factor 1.67

Assuming there are no economic "boomerangs" (for example, savings reduce or shift relative prices so much that more wood is used), these improvement factors would multiply out to a Factor 26 saving, or a 96 percent reduction in demand for acres of pulpwood forest harvest. Much of that saving is due to the switch to higher-yield plantations. Without that switch, the potential savings are still an impressive Factor 5.2 — quintupled resource efficiency, or an 81 percent reduction in extractive demand. With less growth (or even some shrinkage) in human population or affluence, or counting more technical opportunities, we could do even better.

Naturally, *combining* several kinds of improvements multiplies their savings even further. In Pará, Brazil, for example, improving harvesting practice by a straightforward 28 percent *and* sawmill efficiency from 35 percent to 50 percent means that a given net lumber yield could be achieved by harvesting 45 percent less forest. Comparably simple improvements already being achieved by one major Brazilian firm could improve harvest and mill productivity by 30–50 percent. If Brazil's sawmills became as efficient as their best Japanese counterparts, if field practice improved, and if the expected Brazilian tree-growth improvements of up to two- or threefold occurred, then 60–83 percent fewer harvested acres would deliver the same forest products at the mill gate.

NEW MATERIALS, NEW DESIGNS

Another area where wood fiber can be used more productively is in structural elements. The same concept as lighter-basis-weight paper can be applied to the construction trade. "Engineered wood products" like TrusJoist MacMillan's "Parallam" have about 1.8–2.4 times conventional lumber's product yield per unit of fiber, and can use younger, softer, lower-quality trees. With careful design, such "synthetic hardwood" products can achieve even greater efficiencies in converting raw timber into structural performance, albeit with additional inputs of energy and adhesives (which can be wood-derived). For example, a house floor would be just as strong and solid using engineered-wood-product I-joists weighing 44 percent less than traditional solid lumber. (The floor also won't squeak.) These savings compound because I-beams manufactured from engineered wood can also make houses' roof and floor supports so stiff that no internal load-bearing walls are needed. This allows layouts to be completely flexible, yields more useful living space per unit of external walls, and reduces the lumber needed for the internal walls, which need no longer be structural.

Designing from scratch with engineered wood products can yield even larger savings and many side benefits. For example, artfully designing an engineered wall framing (EWF) system has been demonstrated to save 70–74 percent of the wood in a wall, or about 50 percent in the entire house.[44] The wall used Timberstrand oriented strandwood studs made by pressing together small-diameter, low-grade hardwoods. The synthetic studs were so much stronger and more predictable than commodity-grade studs, and so free from knots, defects, or other irregularities, that they could provide about four times as much service per unit volume of delivered wood. To be sure, the compressive manufacturing process involved here meant that more than one cubic foot of (younger, lower-quality) raw wood had to go into each cubic foot of engineered wood products, along with a good deal of energy, typically derived from wood wastes. But such a dramatic saving, if widely practiced, would be highly cost-effective. The total materials-plus-labor mature-market cost of the wall was $433 *lower*, it was stronger and more durable and stable, and it could be built more quickly and easily.

Moreover, the wall accommodated almost twice the thickness of insulation (paid for by saved wood and labor), and the engineered studs, being thinner than lumber studs, reduced heat leakage through the wood. This doubled insulating value was the key to eliminating the house's heating and cooling equipment in an extreme climate (temperatures as high as 113°F), while improving comfort and reducing mature-market capital cost by about $1,800 and life-cycle maintenance cost by about $1,600.[45] With such inherent advantages, it's not surprising that sales of engineered wood products have lately been expanding by about 25 percent a year. They are now used by most U.S. builders, and are even traded as Chicago Board of Trade futures.

New ways to assemble small pieces of lumber into larger sections have begun to make it profitable to substitute small trees, little-used species, and "waste wood" for premium and old-growth timber.[46] Scrap wood, even if green, can be "fingerjointed" together to recover 500–700 board-feet of good dimensional lumber from each ton of what was previously wood waste. Thick boards can be made by gluing together edgewise a series of trapezoidal-section blocks cut in pairs from logs only about 4 to 5 inches in diameter. Alternatively, logs of this size can be squared and sawn into quarters; rotated so that their beveled outside corners are now placed facing the middle; and then glued together into a hollow-core square beam substantially larger than could have been cut from the original log. I-beam joists can be made by inserting a sheet of flakeboard between two peeled pine poles, in effect edging the sheet with a stiff beam on each side. The resulting structure can offer the stiffness of far more massive beams.

Another example of saving fiber through clever structural design is the Bellcomb[47] system of cardboard-like honeycombs sandwiched between sheets of cheap strandwood (pressed like chipboard, but using tough fibrous strands of wood). The sandwiches are prefabricated in many precisely cut shapes that fit tightly together like a child's miniature house kit — only this kit can be full-sized. Two unskilled adults could assemble a snug cottage from such components in a half hour and then, if the joints haven't been glued together, disassemble it even faster. The resulting structure is airtight, fire-resistant, optionally recyclable, and easy to superinsulate by adding foam layers into the sandwich. Its early versions saved 75–85 percent of the fiber but offered the same strength as conventional wood structures. Another firm, Gridcore (of Long Beach, California), makes honeycomb panels from 100 percent recycled agricultural fibers for furniture, cabinets, stage sets, and other items needing light weight.

Still another important wood-saving development is modern Glulam beams, which glue together many layers of wood to replace massive solid beams. This plywood-like principle achieves greater strength per unit of cross-sectional area than solid wood, especially if the layers are tailored to provide the type and direction of strength that the application will require. This strategy reduces the total amount of wood needed to span a long distance, which in modern European practice can be astonishingly large, and it substitutes younger for old-growth trees. A recent innovation achieves even better results by sandwiching carbon-fiber, aramid, or other superstrong synthetic fibers in between layers of wood. This combination can save two-thirds of the wood previously required, cut total costs, and make light, airy beams attractive for large structures.[48]

CLOSING MATERIALS LOOPS

Wood recycling is also an increasingly competitive area, as was noted in chapter 5's discussion of profitably recycled building materials. Another example of a product that can be substantially rethought is wooden shipping pallets, whose manufacture uses about 11 percent of the total lumber and an astonishing two-fifths of the hardwood cut in the United States.[49] There are now some 1.5 billion pallets in the United States — six pallets per American. Another 400 million are made every year. And Henry Ford's devotion to pallets' reuse, repair, and remanufacturing is now rare: Broken pallets are seldom mended, and even sound pallets are usually discarded; this wastes each year as much wood as would frame 300,000 average houses. Some firms are finding that minor changes in packaging patterns can greatly reduce pallet requirements per ton shipped.[50] Others are eliminating pallets or using rugged, easily recycled ones made of waste plastic. Others have realized that discarded pallets — which cost New York City businesses alone about $130 million a year to dispose of — are a better-than-free raw material for community-based remanufacturing. One such recent startup, Big City Forest in New York's Bronx,[51] produced 50,000 recovered pallets and some furniture from 54,000 input pallets in its 20-month pilot phase. This saved 1,500 tons of wood (over 1 million board-feet), and $500,000 for area firms. Rainforest Action Network estimates that reclaiming even half the discarded pallets from the largest 50 U.S. metropolises could provide 2,500 inner-city jobs and 765 million board-feet of annual lumber, equivalent to 152,000 acres of timberland.[52] Changing commercial incentives can help make this happen: Some German pallets, designed to be uniform, durable, and reparable, are even barcoded so the original maker gets a royalty-like credit each time it's reused and a charge each time it needs mending — a lifetime incentive to build it well.

The most familiar method of fiber recovery recycles not wood but paper. Encouragingly, each year since 1993, the United States has recycled more paper than it has landfilled (excluding incineration), and despite frequent imbalances between supply and demand, the market for recycled paper is gradually both growing and stabilizing. Paper recycling, which in 1994 was of a volume sufficient to fill a 15-mile train of boxcars daily,[53] is expected to contribute about 47 percent of fiber inputs to U.S. papermaking by 2000,[54] compared with 1996 figures of 96 percent in Holland and 52 percent in Japan.[55] Some potentially recyclable streams also remain untapped. Twenty million tons of urban wastewood, equivalent to 7 percent of the forest harvest, enters municipal waste dumps every year.[56] In the late 1970s, Los Angeles County logged daily landfilling of 4,000–5,000 tons of pure, separated tree trimmings and similar material. Now, 2,500 tons a day go to soil improvement, community gardens, and landfill cover — helping hold landfill tonnages constant despite population growth.[57]

Simple process innovations can make recycling an even more attractive option. Green Bay Packaging Company in Green Bay, Wisconsin — a state that banned all paper from its landfills in 1995 — improved its manufacturing processes enough by 1992 to be able to eliminate all the effluent discharge that had been a waste product from making all-recycled containerboard. This progress means that paper-recycling plants can be built far from any waterway or treatment plant, reducing the cost of fiber, water, solid-waste disposal, energy, labor, investment, and transportation. The company began exploring a nationwide network of such regional minimills that it hoped would take market share from large virgin-materials mills much as steel minimills had done. Moreover, during its first year, while recycling 200,000 tons of wastepaper, the firm's zero-discharge mill raised the normal-best-practice fiber recovery rate from 85–90 percent to 97–98 percent — equivalent to saving another 20,000 tons of wastepaper from going to landfill annually — and thus became the industry's low-cost producer.[58]

Even more fundamental technical innovations are on the horizon. Japanese firms are reportedly developing "recycle copiers" that strip off old toner so a sheet of paper can be reused up to ten times. In the United States, Decopier Technologies[59] is launching the Decopier, which is expected in a few years to remove toner with so little harm that paper could be used up to five times and transparency film up to ten times. (The current version doesn't yet permit reuse but can substitute recycling for shredding.) Other coming innovations in polymeric ink technology would allow ink to "float" off paper when immersed in 130°F water. The ink is collected, shipped to a local manufacturer to add more aqueous bonding agents, and then reshipped to the printer to be used continuously in closed loops. Although such ink would be expensive, it would never be thrown away. And because the paper fibers need not be chemically scalded to remove the ink, they can last ten to thirteen times longer than conventionally recycled paper fibers.[60] This single technique, if universally adopted, could reduce forest pulp use by 90 percent. It would also reduce the amount of hazardous and toxic ink residues that end up in landfills. Another candidate for such major paper savings is E-paper, a flexible and cordless computer screen that looks like a sheet of paper, uses no energy for storing images or for viewing, and can be electronically written and rewritten at least a million times. A million sheets of ordinary paper "would cost thousands of dollars and make a stack more than 300 feet tall." Nick Sheridon, its inventor at the Xerox Palo Alto Research Center, thinks it could be economical to produce and could be available by 2000.[61]

Recovered and nonwood fiber can also be supplemented or replaced by wood or nonwood fiber harvested from special plantations. For both structural and pulp uses, input-intensive temperate or tropical "fiber farms" show promise as a way to relieve pressure on primary or legacy forests. One plausible estimate indicates that the entire world demand for industrial wood fiber for all uses (excluding fuelwood, which is slightly larger) could be supplied by plantations on "good forest land" equivalent to only 5 percent of the currently forested global land area,[62] or about 490 million acres.[63] *Very*-high-yield plantations covering the equivalent of one half to one percent of current forest area — 57–99 million acres, no more than the area *currently* supporting industrial forest plantations[64] — could in principle meet today's world demand for wood fiber for all purposes at present efficiencies of use. Improving downstream efficiency by a total of, say, three- to fivefold in the long run could reduce the land needed to only a tenth to a third of one percent of current forest area. This is a land area as small as New Hampshire and Vermont or as large as Louisiana or Iowa. This means that existing high-yield industrial plantations (which already occupy 35 million acres), if cultivated more intensively, could in principle provide for the world's entire *efficient* wood-fiber needs. Those plantations' area is comparable to the amount of tropical forest *lost each year* in the early 1990s.[65]

Whether to encourage the use of genetic engineering for high-yield plantations is a complex issue with trade-offs not yet well understood. Today about a third of all wood-fiber and pulp production takes place on industrial plantations (with stocks consisting of one-third exotic and two-thirds native species); somewhat more from second-growth forests (which are nearly all under management); and only about one-fourth from dwindling old-growth forests.[66] Dependence on plantations, notably high-yield ones, would not automatically mean protection for primary forests, but it would surely help undercut the argument that it is necessary to cut mature, ecologically diverse forests. Those forests are part of a dwindling natural capital that provides benefits beyond the extraction of board-feet and tons of pulp. Old-growth forests support indigenous people, fish, and wildlife. They protect biodiversity, hold water,[67] provide recreation, beauty, and spiritual renewal. They also clean the air, and potentially sequester enough carbon to offset one-fourth of worldwide CO_2 emissions.[68] Most assessments find that these functions are many times more valuable than the commodity value of wood fiber,[69] especially if that fiber is to become a throwaway wrapper for a hamburger or an envelope for an unwanted credit-card solicitation.

Many societies are becoming increasingly aware that fiber value is a poor surrogate for the entire value of a forest, especially if the former destroys the latter. For example, in early 1998 China announced a decades-long, more than $30 billion program to try to reforest the watersheds of its two largest river systems. An immediate $12 billion commitment was underlined by the massive Yangtze River floods that killed 3,700 people, dislocated 233 million, and inundated 60 million acres of cropland later that year. All logging in the relevant watersheds has now been prohibited (though actually stopping it may prove more difficult). In China as in America, proper management of the forest resource for *all* its social values would have avoided the need for such costly remedial investments.[70]

ALTERNATIVE FIBERS AND FURTHER INNOVATIONS

Some nonwood fibers are already widely employed for structural uses. For example, bamboo, which is stronger per unit mass than steel and constitutes 6 percent of global fiber production[71] (an amount second only to wood fiber), is widely used in Asia for scaffolding even in high-rise construction. It also makes excellent small to medium-sized structures, and in some circumstances can even replace rebar.

Kenaf, an East Indian hibiscus akin to okra and cotton, is beginning to emerge as a viable wood substitute. Kenaf grows quickly, with low inputs, in a wide range of conditions, and can yield several times as much fiber per acre as wood — possibly at lower cost if produced and processed at industrial volumes. Although it is inconveniently seasonal, requiring storage for year-round paper production, its fiber, like that from many varieties of alternative crops, is markedly superior to that of wood. Another alternative is industrial (nonpsychoactive) hemp, which yields 20–30 tons of dry fiber per acre annually, exceeding the output of most tree species. It has many remarkable properties that led the U.S. government to promote its production in an earlier era. Its potential is now starting to be revived by Canada, Hungary, and such states as Kentucky, Vermont, and Colorado. Such other alternative fibers as elephant grass, canary grass, and bagasse (sugarcane waste) are also more productive fiber sources than any but the fastest-growing hardwood plantations.

Most important, agricultural residues *currently available* in the United States exceeded 280 million tons a year in 1994[72] — essentially the same, uncorrected for moisture differences, as *the entire world consumption of paper or the total U.S. wood harvest.* A substantial part of those residues is being wasted — burned, rotted, or landfilled — rather than used for products or for building soil fertility. However, the resulting business opportunity is starting to be grasped. Since 1980, nonwood paper production has grown more than three times as fast as wood-based paper, and now represents about 8 percent of world paper fiber input.[73] It provides less than one percent of America's paper, but as much as 80 percent of China's. By 1998, tree-free paper was made in 45 countries and provided 11 percent of the world's paper.[74] Both recycled and alternative-fiber paper typically can be produced with "minimill" technology at a much smaller scale than classical virgin-fiber paper, potentially reducing transportation energy. Many of these alternative fibers can also be well integrated with sustainable farming and forestry practices. For example, certain farmers' cooperatives in Oregon leave 90 percent of their formerly burned straw as stubble mulch to improve tilth and prevent soil erosion, and sell the other 10 percent to the Canadian firm Arbokem. The company turns it into chlorine-free agropulp plus effluent sold as fertilizer. The farmers' earnings from even this small portion of their straw can raise their income per acre by 25–50 percent.[75]

The innovations illustrated by these anecdotal examples, and the far larger potential still unexploited, provide good reason to believe that efficiency and substitution throughout the value chains of forest prod-ucts can displace most or all cutting of natural forests — freeing them for more valuable roles such as habitats and wellsprings of spiritual renewal — while providing the same or better services. Similar oppor-tunities for protecting and restoring natural capital apply to essentially all the other kinds of fiber, too. Obtaining the fibers we need to carry out the tasks of everyday life need not cost the earth.

CHAPTER 10

Food for Life

What we are undoing — Chemically dependent exhaustion — Wholly made of oil — Sustainable food and fiber — Productivity of place — When food needs passports — Rice and ducks — Dirt and climate — Unfarming — Chock-full of life

BY ONE MEASURE — THAT OF RAW OUTPUT — THE INDUSTRIALIZATION OF farming has been a triumph of technology. In the past half century, production of major crops has more than doubled; that of cereals has tripled. In the past thirty years, the number of food calories available (even if not provided) to each person on earth has risen 13 percent, despite a rapidly growing population. Almost all of the world's increase in food output has been the result of higher-yielding, faster-maturing crops, rather than from farming more land, because essentially all good land is already being cultivated. Although 1 to 4 billion more acres are potentially arable worldwide, mainly in developing countries, that land would cost more to irrigate, drain, and link to markets than crop prices now justify. Intensification is therefore conventionally considered the only feasible way to continue expanding world food production to feed the growing population.[1]

Intensive agriculture came to America in stages. It began with a mixture of brash and courageous persistence and ecological ignorance. As Wendell Berry put it, "When we came across the continent cutting the forests and plowing the prairies, we have never known what we were doing because we have never known what we were undoing." With pride and without misgivings, vast and complex native ecosystems were converted to equally vast expanses of wheat and sorghum, corn and soybeans.

People first filled and then departed the landscape. Engine-driven machines had essentially finished replacing draft-horse and human labor by the 1950s. Hybrid corn and other highly bred crops requiring synthetic fertilizers and pesticides replaced well-established varieties.

Increasingly, farmers' traditional knowledge and agrarian culture were displaced by a managerial and industrial culture — a profound shift in the foundations of society.[2] Today only one percent of Americans grow food for the rest; 87 percent of the food comes from 18 percent of the farms. Most farms have in effect become factories owned by absentee interests;[3] and ownership not only of farms but of such upstream and downstream enterprises as seed and chemical suppliers, meat-packers and grain merchants, is becoming rapidly more concentrated, leading to all the abuses that one might expect. Farmers represent about 0.9 percent of GDP, but those who sell to and buy from farmers — the entire food-supplying system, directly and indirectly — have a share about 14 times as large, and their market power tends to squeeze out small, independent, and diversified farmers.

A similar pattern of development is transforming agriculture around the world. Experts in this "Green Revolution" emphasize high-yield seeds, biocides, irrigation, and nitrogen fertilizers. Irrigation by itself accounted for more than half the increase in world food production from the mid-1960s to the mid-1980s. During the years 1961–96, nitrogen fertilizer use also rose 645 percent.[4] By 1991, the resulting level of artificial nitrogen fixation exceeded the low estimates and approximated half the midrange estimates of total natural nitrogen fixation on earth.[5]

Almost unnoticed in the figures charting the rise of agricultural output is that actual returns on agricultural intensification are diminishing. The president of the Rockefeller Foundation, among the world's leading authorities on the green revolution, warns that at least in developing countries, "Recent data on crop yields and production . . . suggest a degree of stagnation which is worrying."[6] Equally disquieting findings indicate more volatile yields and "increasing production problems in those places where yield growth has been most marked." The effects of any shortfalls in yield, and of all the increased inputs needed to sustain or increase yield, are being greatly amplified because of rapid growth in the fraction of the world's cereals (currently one-third) being fed to livestock, an inefficient use of grain. Animals turn only about 10–45 percent of grain inputs into meat — 5 percent or less in some cases.

Modern American agriculture has certain features uncomfortably similar to those of the Soviet economy. That system generated the outputs that planners considered necessary by rewarding participants for how much they manufactured (or, often, *consumed*), not how efficiently they produced. Similar distortion is caused in the United States by input subsidies, price supports, production quotas, and use-it-or-lose-it western water laws. Mechanisms like peanut permits, milk price supports (which were in force until 1999), sugar quotas, and similar schemes are attributes of overcentralized planning and unadaptive bureaucracies. Although U.S. agricultural and water systems are slowly becoming less rigid, almost all conventional sources of farm information, including Extension services and the land-grant universities, still offer the conventional party line — promoting intensive, chemically dependent production, which is profitable mainly for the input suppliers.

Industrialization, and developments like the heavily subsidized interstate highway system, enable food to be transported great distances — averaging 1,300 miles in the United States — and processed in ever more elaborate and costly ways. The food sector uses about 10–15 percent of all energy in the industrialized countries, and somewhat more in the United States. Despite improving efficiencies, about two-fifths of that energy goes to food processing, packaging, and distribution, and another two-fifths to refrigeration and cooking by final users. Only one-fifth is actually used on the farm — half of that in the form of chemicals applied to the land.[7]

American farms have doubled their direct and indirect energy efficiency since 1978. They use more efficiently manufactured fertilizer, diesel engines, bigger and multifunction farm machinery, better drying and irrigation processes and controls, and herbicides instead of plowing to control weeds. Yet U.S. farming still uses many — perhaps ten — times as much fossil-fueled energy in producing food as it returns in food energy. Our food, as ecologist Howard Odum remarked, is made wholly of oil with oil left over.

The superficial success of America's farms masks other underlying problems. A third of the original topsoil in the United States is gone, and much of the rest is degraded. Soil productivity in the semiarid Great Plains fell by 71 percent just during the 28 years after sodbusting.[8] Notwithstanding some recent progress in reviving soil conservation efforts,[9] topsoil is eroding very much faster than it is being formed. Growing a bushel of corn in conventional ways can erode two to five bushels of topsoil. In the 1980s a dumptruck-load of topsoil per second was passing New Orleans in the Mississippi River.[10] A decade later, 90 percent of American farmland was still losing topsoil faster — on average, 17 times faster — than new topsoil was being formed, incurring costs projected at $44 billion over the next 20 years.[11] In many developing countries, matters are even worse.

A more subtle decline than physical soil loss, but no less dangerous, is the invisible loss of the soil's organic richness. The ability of soil bacteria, fungi, and other tiny organisms to cycle nutrients, fight disease, and create the proper soil texture and composition to protect roots and hold water is essential to soil health. Texture matters: Coarse particles are needed for air spaces, fine ones for water retention and surface chemistry. So does humus: Of a good soil's 50 percent that is solid matter, the one-tenth that is organic content can hold about as much water and nutrients as the mineral nine-tenths.[12] Long-term experiments in wheat/fallow systems in the semiarid Northwest found that except when manure was applied, the soil's levels of organic carbon and nitrogen have been declining steadily since the early 1930s, even in fallow seasons.[13] Perhaps a tenth of on-farm energy use is already required to offset such soil problems as the degradation of nutrients, water-holding capacity, and hence crop productivity caused by erosion. As more soil quantity and quality are lost, that penalty — perhaps already reducing U.S. farm output by about 8 percent in the short term and 20 percent over the next 20 years[14] — will rise. Most ancient civilizations collapsed because they destroyed their topsoil,[15] but few policymakers seem mindful of that history. After a century of farming in Iowa, the place with the world's highest concentration of prime farmland, the millennia-old prairie soil, laments Evan Eisenberg, "is half gone. What is left is half dead, the roiling, crawling life burned out of it by herbicides, pesticides, and relentless monocropping. Petrochemicals feed its zombie productivity. Hospitable Iowans assure their guests that the coffee is made from 'reverse-osmosis' water, since agricultural runoff has made the tap water undrinkable."[16]

Agriculture uses about two-thirds of all the water drawn from the world's rivers, lakes, and aquifers. Irrigation waters only 16 percent of the earth's cropland, three-fourths of it in developing countries, but produces 40 percent of the world's food. In many key areas, groundwater is being overpumped and depleted — mined out just like oilfields. In the United States, about one-fourth of the groundwater pumped for irrigation (which is a third of the total withdrawal) is overdrafted. Salting and other side effects of poor irrigation and drainage management have already damaged more than a tenth of the earth's irrigated cropland, some irretrievably. Since 1945, moderate, severe, or extreme degradation of these and other kinds has already affected nearly 3 billion acres, roughly the area of China plus India. Four-fifths of those acres are in developing countries, where even governments, let alone farmers, lack capital to repair the damage, and nearly half the acres have too little water for ready restoration methods to work.[17] Of the one-ninth of the earth's land that was considered arable in 1990, little remains really healthy, most is stressed, and losses are generally accelerating.

Degradation of the natural capital that is the foundation for farming has been found to be decreasing overall farm productivity in almost all farm systems studied worldwide, including every irrigated Asian rice system. This loss continues regardless of the technological inputs that have been applied to alleviate it.[18] In many areas, tripled fertilizer use and new crop breeds have been necessary just to hold modern rice varieties' yields constant. The situation is analogous to what happened in U.S. forestry during the years 1970–94. Logging increased its labor productivity by 50 percent, but overall (total factor) productivity fell by 30 percent, because technological improvements in harvesting trees couldn't compensate for reduced accessibility and quality of the forest resources.[19]

Clear-cutting at the microscopic level of DNA may be creating the gravest problem of all. The world's farming rests on an extraordinarily narrow genetic base. Of the 200,000 species of wild plants, notes biogeographer Jared Diamond, "only a few thousands are eaten by humans, and just a few hundred of those have been more or less domesticated."[20] Three-quarters of the world's food comes from only seven crop species — wheat, rice, corn, potatoes, barley, cassava (manioc), and sorghum. Nearly half the world's calorie and protein intake eaten as food, not as feed, comes from only the first three of these crops.[21] Adding one pulse (soybeans), one tuber (sweet potato), two sugar sources (sugarcane and sugar beet), and one fruit (banana) to the list of seven would account for over 80 percent of total crop tonnage. In every one of these key crops, genetic diversity is rapidly disappearing as native habitats are destroyed. In this industrialized farming system, the most productive and narrowly specialized varieties typically become mass-produced and crowd out their diverse cousins. India, for example, is in the final process of replacing its 30,000 native varieties of rice with one super variety that will do away with centuries of botanical knowledge and breeding.[22]

Perhaps worse, seed banks that store and preserve thousands of different varieties of common and rare plants are being neglected — a consequence of government budget cuts — so their irreplaceable germ plasm is becoming nonviable.[23] Most seed companies have been bought by agrichemical companies. Not surprisingly, these companies are seeking to make themselves the sole lawful proprietors of the world's legacy of plant diversity — if not by purchase, then by manipulation of intellectual-property laws to include the traditional "free goods" of nature, or by increasingly frank grabs for legal monopoly. Such efforts to ensure that food cannot be grown without commercial control might be attractive to investors, but may not be a good long-term strategy for anyone's survival.

Crops are becoming more specialized for other reasons, too. Prospective income from single cash crops is overwhelming local subsistence traditions, which favored varied local production to meet balanced nutritional needs. Agricultural professionals tend to encourage producers to focus on single commodities rather than pursuing a wide range of goods. Farmers, having no safety margin for experimentation, are conservative about trying new products or techniques. Land-tenure practices and complex sociological issues may create further artificial incentives for cash crops, ecological simplification, intensive production, and short-term thinking. Only the increasing need to farm in such diverse and marginal conditions as dry regions may create pressure to diversify into such promising crops as the neglected major grains (quinoa, amaranth, triticale, millet, and buckwheat) and beans (winged, rice, fava, and adzuki).[24] These are only the beginning: Subsaharan Africa alone contains over 100 such forgotten grains and more than 2,000 forgotten crops; only a handful are receiving significant research.[25] In hindsight, it will seem odd that such attractive crops were so long neglected.

The single-crop mentality both ignores nature's tendency to foster diversity and worsens the ancient battle against pests. Monocultures are rare in nature, in part because they create paradises for plant diseases and insects — as science writer Janine Benyus puts it, they are like equipping a burglar with the keys to every house in the neighborhood; they're an all-you-can-eat restaurant for pests. Disease already damages or destroys 13 percent of the world's crops, insects 15 percent, and weeds 12 percent; in all, two-fifths of the world's harvest is lost in the fields,[26] and after some more spoils, nearly half never reaches a human mouth.[27] The conventional response of dousing infested plants and soil with biocides seemed promising at first, but using technology to combat natural processes hasn't worked. Around 1948, at the start of the era of synthetic pesticides, the United States used 50 million pounds of insecticides a year and lost 7 percent of the preharvest crop to insects. Today, with nearly 20-fold greater insecticide use — almost a billion pounds a year, two-fifths more than when Rachel Carson published *Silent Spring* in 1962 — the insects get 13 percent, and total U.S. crop losses are 20 percent higher than they were before we got on the pesticide treadmill.

To be sure, pesticides can be used more rationally. In the former East Germany, pesticide applications were reduced by about tenfold, with better results and about tenfold lower costs and risks, by nationwide installation of insect traps. Frequent inspections to see what pests were actually present replaced spraying for everything that might be. But the problem is more fundamental than one of mere measurement and management. The whole concept of pesticides has a basic flaw: In this game of "crops and robbers,"[28] the house always wins. Insects' huge gene pool, quick evolution, and very short reproductive cycles enable them to adapt and become resistant to our most powerful poisons — as more than 500 species have already done[29] — faster than we can invent new ones. Worse, by disrupting competition between species and by killing their natural predators, pesticides often transform previously innocuous insects into nasty pests.

Monocultures also leave most of the rich diversity of soil biota unemployed. Nature doesn't waste resources supporting underutilized organisms, so if they have nothing to do, they die. Treating soil like dirt — not as a living community but as a sterile medium on which to spread out leaves in the sun — makes the soil barren and unable to provide its natural services. Pathogens and insects with free habitat and no competition then flourish. California vintners have suffered phylloxera infestations on sprayed vineyards but generally not to date on organically grown ones. Some growers believe that phylloxera may not be an inevitable grapevine pest so much as a symptom of unhealthy soil.

Organic farmers, in contrast, rely on healthy soil, careful observation, and controllable levels of pests to raise their crops. In the organic, ecosystem-based view, the complete eradication of pests is a tactical blunder, because a healthy system needs enough pests to provide enough food to support predators so they can hang around and keep the pests in balance.[30] Some organic farmers also use biologically derived substances to cope with their pest problems. But the best-known of these compounds, the insect-specific family of natural *Bacillus thuringiensis* toxins, may become ineffective because agrichemical companies are putting Bt-making genes into common crops for universal use. This may appear to be a sound strategy — genes instead of pesticides, information instead of mass. But over time, and maybe sooner than expected,[31] the prevalence of Bt in the ecosystem will select for insects resistant to it and make the compound useless or, worse, begin to affect nontarget species. By 1997, eight insect pests in the United States had become resistant to Bt,[32] for the same reason that penicillin is now impotent against 90 percent of the staphylococcus infections and many of the other germs that it used to control. A coalition of organic farmers, consumers, and public-interest groups has sued the EPA to rescind all Bt-toxin transgenic crop registrations.

Monocultures' chemical dependence requires enormous amounts of fertilizers to make up for the free ecological services that the soil biota, other plants, and manure provide in natural systems. Healthy soil biota can provide about tenfold better uptake of nutrients, permitting the same or better crop yields with a tenth the application of soluble nutrients.[33] But having become dependent on ever-greater amounts of synthetic inputs, Americans consume more than 60 million metric tons a year of such agriculturally applied minerals as phosphorus and potash.[34] Alongside the average American's daily food sits the ghostly presence of nearly a half pound of synthetic nitrogen fertilizer used to grow it. Most of those chemicals are wasted, running off the soil to flow onto other land or into surface and groundwaters. Agriculture is America's largest, most diffuse, and most anonymous water polluter. In other respects as well, industrialized agriculture is increasingly presenting threats to public health.[35]

The growing volatility of weather and the potential for shifts in climate will only worsen the pressure on overspecialized crops. Finely tuned by a half century of breeding and lately by genetic engineering, they cope poorly with changes in such conditions as temperature, sun, and moisture. Genetically diverse natural populations in healthy ecosystems, in contrast, have millions of years' design experience in coping with surprises. The brittleness caused by shifting from resilient natural systems to specialized artificial ones could prove catastrophic as crops encounter conditions quite different from the stable ones assumed by their breeders and genetic engineers.

For economic, health, and environmental reasons, a major overhaul of current agricultural production methods[36] is needed to achieve adequate, acceptable, and sustainable food and fiber supplies.[37] Many practitioners in both developed and developing countries are therefore adopting new or modernizing old methods of agriculture that are more clearly based on natural models. Their overhaul doesn't involve just doing the same things differently, because the problem of agriculture cannot be solved within the mentality that created it. Rather, the new solutions are the result of whole-systems thinking and the science of ecology; they embody the principles of natural capitalism; they follow the logic not of Bacon and Descartes but of Darwin.

The innovations now emerging in agriculture are taking two complementary and interwoven paths. The less fundamental but more familiar path applies the first three principles of natural capitalism: It increases the resource and ecological efficiency of all kinds of farming, seeking new ways to wring more and better food from fewer resources, both through direct increases in resource productivity and through biomimetic, closed-loop, nontoxic practices. These are both encouraged by community-supported agriculture — an application of the third principle, whereby customers subscribe in advance to a particular farm's or cooperative's flow of food, typically organically grown. But in a deeper and even more promising break with industrial agriculture, some pioneers are also redesigning agriculture from scratch as an embodiment of the fourth principle — restoring, sustaining, and expanding natural capital. Their innovations go beyond conventional organic practices to create diverse forms of agriculture that are based, as geneticist Dr. Wes Jackson of the Land Institute in Salina, Kansas, says, "on nature's wisdom, not on people's cleverness"; that follow ecologist Aldo Leopold's dictum of tending "to preserve the integrity, stability, and beauty of the biotic community."

FARM-GROWN EFFICIENCY

Resource productivity on the farm — the first principle of natural capitalism, and the easiest to apply — comes from many small, simple applications of farmers' native inventiveness, as a few examples show. For instance, crop-drying, which is often needed to keep crops from mildewing, uses about 5 percent of direct U.S. on-farm energy. But in Kansas City, Kansas, in the 1980s the late Bill Ward invented a zero-energy way to dry grain in the silo.[38] He simply bored a hole in the top of the structure, atop which a hollow shaft connects into the hollow blades of a small windmill. As the prairie wind spins the blades, centrifugal force slings the air out the holes at the ends of them. The resulting vacuum pulls a slow, steady draft of air up through the grain from small, screened vents at the bottom of the silo. This gradually dries the grain — and evaporatively cools it, making any insects infesting it too sluggish to move and eat. This in turn means that no chemicals are needed to prevent mold or kill bugs.[39] Ward's process not only saves chemical costs but also keeps organically grown grain uncontaminated so it can fetch a premium price.

Many do-it-yourselfers have built effective solar hot-air dryers for fruits and vegetables, grains, herbs, and even lumber. But since crops are mostly water and often perishable, it may make more sense to bring the solar dryer directly to the fields. In the 1980s, Marcello Cabus, a Hispanic entrepreneur in Delta, Colorado, developed a semitrailer that unfolded into a complete fruit- and vegetable-processing and -drying plant. He'd drive it to any farm that had a distressed crop — perhaps ripe fruit that couldn't be gotten to market quite in time or couldn't command the desired price. The crop would be washed, peeled, sliced, and given any other necessary preparation. Spread on shallow racks and bathed in solar-heated rising air, the produce would dry to an exceptional quality. Backpackers, snackers, families who want to store food at home for emergencies, and people allergic to common sulfur-based preservatives — solar-air-dried food needs none — would pay high prices for such quality produce. And in countries like Korea, challenged to preserve nourishing food for the harsh winters, the method could greatly improve both farm income and public health.

The same innovations that save energy in houses can often be applied to livestock barns, too. The physical principles are the same; only the architecture and the occupants differ. Lighting chicken houses with compact fluorescent lamps instead of incandescents can increase a North Carolina chicken farmer's income by one-fourth. It even slightly increases egg production, perhaps by reducing overheating. Using big, slow fans instead of small, fast ones makes less noise, saves most of the fans' energy, and improves their reliability. Air-to-air heat exchangers can cleanly recover into fresh air 90-plus percent of the heat or coolth that would otherwise be lost in ventilation air. Insulation, weatherstripping, building orientation, and even simply making the roof the right color can greatly improve indoor comfort in a barn just as in a passive-solar house. Comfort, in turn, means healthier and more productive livestock.

Better buildings offer special advantages when crops are being grown under artificial conditions. The Netherlands uses seemingly cheap natural gas to grow about $0.7 billion worth of tomatoes per year — over 700,000 tons — in more than 3,800 acres of greenhouses.[40] Cold, cloudy Holland is not an obvious place to grow tomatoes. It takes over 100 times as much energy to produce them as the tomatoes actually contain. Over three-quarters of the fuel heats the greenhouse, and 18 percent goes toward processing, mainly canning. About two-thirds less energy would be needed to grow the tomatoes in, say, Sicily and *airfreight* them to Holland. Instead, Dutch tomatoes, most of which are not actually consumed there, are loaded into giant trucks that rumble across the continent to exploit slightly lower labor costs or laxer regulations, before being eaten or winding up in a tube of tomato paste.

If one really *did* want to grow tomatoes in Holland, it would surely make more sense to do so in passive-solar greenhouses so efficient that they burn no gas for heating. They would instead use not ordinary glass, through which heat rapidly escapes, but superwindows, like the passive-solar bananas grown at RMI's headquarters high in the Rockies. Individuals could even grow the tomatoes in a lean-to, a glorified cold-frame, or a big live-in "greenhome" like the New Alchemy Institute's "Ark" that grew crops year-round on Canada's cloudy Prince Edward Island, or, as at RMI, in their own living rooms. Some 15 percent of global food is already grown in cities. In China, urban farming in back gardens, on little plots, and on rooftops provides 85-plus percent of urban vegetables — more in Beijing and Shanghai — plus large amounts of meat and treecrops.[41]

Producing food more locally, whether indoors or outdoors, can greatly reduce the expenditures of transportation energy. A few years ago, frugal Germans were taken aback when Wuppertal Institute researcher Stephanie Böge revealed[42] that producing a cup of strawberry yogurt — a popular snack of which Germans eat 3 billion cups each year — typically entailed about 5,650 miles of transportation. The manufacturing process involved trucks crisscrossing all over the country to deliver the ingredients, glass cup, and finished product to, say, Stuttgart. Shipments from suppliers to processors to suppliers added a further 7,250 miles of transport — enough in all to bring the yogurt to Germany from New Zealand. There's nothing exotic about strawberry yogurt; it can be made in any kitchen from milk, strawberries, sugar, and a few other common ingredients. It's not obvious what advantage is gained by such extreme specialization and dispersion, which might not exist if transportation were unsubsidized. More localized production could enormously reduce transportation and probably yield a superior product.

As in industrial processes, better measurement and control systems are an inexpensive way to increase efficiency in farming. Substituting information for resources permits more intelligent management, results in more and better crops, and saves soil, time, water (as we'll see in the next chapter), and money. Instead of guessing how moist the soil is, what nutrients the crops have or need, how fast they're growing, or how many of what sorts of pests they have, farmers are beginning to use measuring devices to guide their day-to-day decisions. Some do this by remote sensing and satellite navigation equipment, monitoring and computer-controlling inputs to each part of their vast fields as they ride high in air-conditioned combines; others do it with the keen observation of a naturalist, focusing on leaves and soil from a distance of inches.

Because farms are (or used to be) natural systems, they offer major opportunities to combine the resource-productivity first principle of natural capitalism with the loop-closing second principle. Loop-closing design-integration strategies are the agricultural equivalent of industrial ecology or of a natural food web. The best of these systems reuse wastes in closed loops to improve the efficiency and resilience of the entire operation.

The most basic way to close loops is to reuse the wastes produced both on the farm and downstream in the food-processing industries. A typical Nebraska harvest season results in an accumulation of distressed grain — damp or otherwise below-grade. This waste could make enough ethanol to run a sixth of the state's cars for an entire year, if those vehicles were efficient enough to get 90 mpg, probably less than a first-generation Hypercar. With equally efficient cars, the straw burned in the fields of France or Denmark would run those countries' entire car fleets year-round. Similar waste exists in the form of nutshells in California, peach pits in Georgia, cotton-gin trash in Texas — that latter of a quantity adequate in the early 1980s to fuel with alcohol every vehicle in Texas. Most other organic wastes can also be usefully recovered and converted. Inedible vegetable oils can be cooked in a solar-heated catalytic device with wet or dirty ethanol or methanol to make esters that are better diesel fuels than petroleum diesel. Altogether, the diverse streams of farm and forestry wastes can probably provide enough sustainably grown liquid fuels to run an efficient U.S. transportation sector, without any further reliance on special fuel crops or fossil fuels. Across the United States today, more than 85 million tons of bio-based products and materials, valued at about $22–45 billion, are produced annually,[43] yet now most of these farm and forestry residues are wasted, benefiting neither the economy nor the soil.

When livestock wandered around in the manner for which evolution fitted them, they deposited their dung back on the land. But modern intensive raising of confined livestock turns those valuable nutrients into waste and their free redistribution into a gigantic disposal headache. Enter a Canadian building innovation — "hoop structures" within which contented pigs run around freely and nest on deep, absorbent beds of straw or cornstalks. This design is a pig shelter, not a pig jail. Unlike standard rigid barns, which cost ten times as much, the lightweight fabric cylinders are thermally passive: cooled by breezes through their open ends, heated even through northern winters by the composting bedding and the hogs' body heat. Even more important, instead of huge, foul-smelling, anaerobic lagoons of liquid manure, hoop structures yield dry manure ready to spread on the fields. The valuable nutrients are shielded from rain and runoff. In Iowa alone, more than one thousand covered "hoop houses" producing 3 percent of Iowa's hogs were successfully built just during the years 1995–98 — a little-noticed but important counterrevolution to gigantic concrete hog factories, much better both for the animals and for the farmers' bottom line.[44]

What if agricultural systems are redesigned to be even more like their wild cousins? An ecological success story rapidly influencing the course of much of the American rice industry is the California Rice Industry Association's creative response to the air pollution caused by the widespread practice of burning rice straw each winter. Silica in the straw was suspected of causing lung disease downwind. Some growers stopped burning and instead flooded their fields after harvest, turning them into habitat for millions of migrating ducks and other wild birds. The decomposing rice stubble rebuilt the soil. The ducks aerated and fertilized the fields. The ducks' favorite food animals — worms, little arthropods, minnows — came to live in the seasonal wetlands. Hunters paid to visit. Farm inputs could be reduced thanks to the natural fertilizers. Crop yields and net incomes rose. Now those farmers, with 30 percent of California's rice acreage, consider rice a coproduct of new businesses — providing water management, wildlife habitat, straw production, and other services.

The ultimate loop-closers, the basis of planetary metabolism, are the soil microorganisms that turn back into nutrient flows everything that falls on or grows within the ground. In Evan Eisenberg's metaphor:

> The soil is less a factory than a souk, a Casbah, a flea market, an economic free-for-all in which each buyer and seller pursues his or her own interest, and in which every scrap of merchandise — second-hand, seventh-hand, busted, salvaged, patched — is mined for its last ounce of value. Decay is good business because there are nutrients to be extracted and energy to be gained from the breaking of chemical bonds. If the net effect of the activity of the soil biota is overwhelmingly helpful — in fact, vital — to life on street level, it is not because nature has ordained it so, but because the various forms of life above and below ground have coevolved.[45]

Perhaps before long the companies now directing their sophisticated resources to the dubious goal of producing genetically engineered crops and their uninsurable risks[46] will use those skills instead to make soil-biota test kits. Such kits could tell the farmer what organisms are missing, whether their absence matters, and what, if anything, to do in order to restore the soil to healthy biodiversity. Farmers could then start to count their wealth in bacteria and fungi, roundworms and springtails, rather than in acres and bushels. But this will require major advances in knowledge: Soil biology is a vast and growing mystery. A recent RNA assay disclosed four thousand distinct genomes in each gram of soil, and they varied from place to place. Some appeared to represent major new taxonomic categories. Of each ten microbes observed on plant roots by microscopy, at most one could be cultured in nutrient media (the standard lab technique for determining what's living there); of each thousand in bulk soil, only one. The rest represent "a vast diversity of microbes . . . that we know nothing about."[47] Soils, in short, have recently been discovered to "harbor a complex and largely unknown microflora" implying "many unknown ecological and biochemical processes. . . ."[48] Science can't understand how plants grow until it understands the ecology of what they grow from: as Donald Worster put it,[49] "We can no more manufacture a soil with a tank of chemicals than we can invent a rain forest or produce a single bird." And understanding soil, the ultimate natural capital[50] (the Chinese call it the mother of all things), is in turn the key to changing agriculture from part of the climate problem into part of the solution.

SOIL AND CLIMATE

Farming, as presently practiced, contributes about one-fourth of the risk of altering the earth's climate.[51] Temperate farmland typically has about 20 to 30 times as much biomass below the surface as above-ground.[52] This hidden carbon stock, often upward of 44 tons of carbon per acre, is at risk of mobilization into the air if insensitive farming practices defeat living systems' tendency to fix carbon into soil biota. Turning land that hosted the prairie's hundreds of varieties of grasses and other plants into fields where just corn and soybeans are grown, and substituting synthetic for natural nutrient cycles, puts the huge standing biomass of soil bacteria, fungi, and other biota out of work. When they subsequently die, they oxidize or rot, releasing their carbon to the air. Breaking the sod also opens the soil not only to biological erosion via sterilizing air, heat, and ultraviolet light but also to physical erosion that strips it of its organisms and other organic constituents. The resulting "finely pulverized young coal" — carbon-bearing but ecologically destroyed — makes its way into riverbeds and deltas, where it decays into methane, a greenhouse gas twenty-one times as potent per molecule as carbon dioxide. Ever greater inputs of agri-chemicals must be used to substitute for the degraded services of the natural ecosystem. Making these chemicals, notably fertilizers, requires about 2 percent of all industrial energy.[53] None of these measures is really necessary to grow crops or make money; all are instead artifacts of an obsolete, mechanistic, abiotic practice.

Agriculture based more on natural models would feature reduced land clearance, tillage, and fertilization, higher energy efficiency, and greater reliance on renewable energy. These measures could probably eliminate most human releases of nitrous oxide, much of which is produced by the reactions of synthetic fertilizer with soil bacteria. Very large carbon-dioxide savings would undoubtedly result from building up organic matter in soil humus by accumulating a richly diverse soil biota. Soil loss — especially the physical loss or biological impoverishment, hence carbon depletion, of humus — is currently far outpacing soil and humus formation and enrichment worldwide. This net loss of soil carbon has contributed about 7 percent of the carbon now in the atmosphere.[54] Yet successful conversions to organic or low-input practices, chiefly in the United States and Germany, have demonstrated that after a few years' reequilibration, these carbon losses can actually be *reversed* — protecting the earth's climate and the farmer's soil simultaneously. U.S. cropland alone (8 percent of the cropland on earth) could thereby offset about 8–17 percent of U.S. carbon emissions.[55] If the carbon removed from the air could be traded for, say, $25 per metric ton — manyfold less than climate skeptics expect — it could earn $9–20 per acre per year[56] for the average U.S. farmer. Net farm income in 1996 was only $55 per acre and falling. Moreover, the organic content's extra nutrient- and water-holding power could have a natural-capital value of about $200 per metric ton of carbon, to say nothing of its other ecological functions.[57]

Worldwide, the potential is far greater. The world's cultivated soils contain about twice as much carbon as the atmosphere, whose carbon content is rising by half a percent per year. The earth's 5 billion acres of degraded soils are particularly low in carbon and in need of carbon-absorbing vegetative cover. Increasing degraded soil's carbon content at plausible rates[58] could absorb about as much carbon as all human activity emits.[59] This would also improve soil, water and air quality, agricultural productivity, and human prosperity. Especially important is the opportunity to use modern grazing management techniques, described below, and to refrain from plowing and burning in "brittle" environments, so as to diversify and densify the grasses that cover much of the earth. This can often reverse desertification, restore soils and water tables, increase livestock-carrying capacity, and put large amounts of carbon back into the grassland and savanna soils. It may seem farfetched to rebuild the deep black soils and abundant water that Herodotus noted around Libya, or restore the hippos that aboriginal peoples painted in what is now the interior of the Sahara Desert, but it may well be possible for the processes that built these flexible ecosystems over the ages to be set back into motion by applying today's understanding of how grasslands coevolved with grazers.

There are also many techniques for reducing the use of nitrogen fertilizer[60] in conventional farming practice: Overapplication is so common that in the early 1990s, U.S. farmers were applying 56 percent more nitrogen than their harvested crops removed.[61] Most reductions are cost-effective because they lower chemical and application costs and nitrate-runoff pollution without cutting yields. Better nitrogen management also decreases climate-altering emissions. In many developing countries, additional measures to cut methane emissions are available and desirable.

Changes in farming that have the highest potential climatic leverage involve livestock. Six billion people keep nearly 1.3 billion cattle, 900 million pigs, and 1.3 billion chickens. These animals' metabolisms are substantially larger than those of the people.[62] Just as saving electricity reduces carbon-dioxide emissions severalfold more than saving other forms of energy, because it takes several units of fuel to make one unit of electricity, so changing the numbers and rearing methods of livestock offers similar but even greater climatic (and food-supply) benefits. As mentioned earlier, under conventional practice, livestock converts from 2.2 to more than 20 pounds of grain into just one pound of meat. Beef averages 7 but can reach the least efficient end of that range in the later stages of grain-finishing, while fish, poultry, and pork are at or near the most efficient end.

High-priority actions for reconfiguring livestock raising include:[63]

- Desubsidizing livestock production, especially for cattle, which emit approximately 72 percent of all livestock methane:[64] Dairy and beef cattle would be grown differently and probably in considerably smaller numbers without their various subsidies, especially in rich countries;[65]

- Reducing the rich countries' dairy output to match demand rather than propping up demand with subsidies. Dairy cows emit extra methane because they're fed at about three times maintenance level to make them produce more milk;

- Improving livestock breeding, especially in developing countries, to increase meat or milk output per animal, consistent with humane practices;

- Regulating or taxing methane emissions from manure to encourage manure-to-biogas conversion for useful combustion;

- Reforming U.S. beef grading standards to reduce the inefficient conversion of costly, topsoil-intensive grains into feedlot fat that's then largely discarded;[66]

- Encouraging ultralean, organic range beef as a replacement for feedlot beef. The organically raised cattle then feed only on natural grass, need no antibiotics, taste better, can be just as tender, are more healthful, can cost less, and may produce less methane than equivalent feedlot beef;[67] and

- To the extent that cattle are still to be grown in feedlots, shifting some meat consumption to less feed- and methane-intensive animals and to aquaculture, preferably integrated with agriculture — a highly flexible and productive approach that may also help cut rice-paddy methane.

Several of these options would have important side benefits. For example, many cattle herds in the industrialized countries are fed at conversion ratios of 8:1 or worse, with grain grown in developing countries. The Western European herd consumes two-thirds of Europe's grain crop, and that continent imports over 40 percent of its feed grain from developing countries,[68] which need grain for human food. More grain nutrients are consumed by American livestock than by Americans or by people in other countries.[69] If the rich countries replaced part of their feedlot beef consumption with range beef and lamb, white meats, aquaculture, marine fish, or vegetable proteins, then Central and South America might feel less pressure to convert rainforest to pasture. Many developing countries could free up arable land. There could be less displacement of the rural poor onto marginal land, less soil erosion, and renewed emphasis on traditional food crops rather than on export cash crops. This one action could save enough grain, if properly distributed, to feed the world's half billion hungry people.[70]

NATURE AS MODEL AND MENTOR

An important alternative to intensive feedlot production of livestock, especially cattle, is to let them graze as their forebears were designed to do. Grazing has often been carried out in such a destructive way that growing crops for feeding confined animals is widely considered a normal and preferable alternative (and an even more profitable one if sufficiently subsidized). But pioneers of ecologically based grazing are showing that it is far better to restore and maintain grazing by cattle and other animals on grasslands that typically coevolved with grazing animals and cannot remain healthy without them.

When Allan Savory was a Zimbabwean wildlife biologist,[71] he became curious about why the huge herds of native ungulates grazing Africa's grasslands seemed to do no harm to the land, while cattle herded by tribal people did moderate damage to the grass and cattle herded by white ranchers destroyed it. He observed that the grazing of the native animals, hemmed in and agitated by prowling predators, is very concentrated in time and space. The herd quickly moves on, leaving in the churned-up ground deep hoofprints that catch dung, water, and seed to make next year's grass crop. The animals don't return until the following year, when the grass has regrown. Savory mimicked these patterns by establishing analogous grazing patterns with cattle in dry climates, notably in the western United States. He proved that much of the rangeland commonly considered overgrazed is actually *under*-grazed but grazed the wrong way. Range management based on an understanding of the ecology of each piece of land, often using more cattle, *more* intensely resident for shorter and less frequent periods, can improve carrying capacity for both livestock and wild grazers, while producing a premium product — the ultralean, organic range beef mentioned above. Though ecosystem-specific, and not a panacea, this approach has reportedly been successfully applied by thousands of ranchers in dry regions where beef is the traditional product. Criticized by some, Savory's approach clearly merits greater attention.

More recently, such management-intensive rotational grazing (MIRG) has spread through beef, pork, and especially dairy farming in the humid American Midwest, where it is now "the most innovative and fastest growing farming practice."[72] Just between 1993 and 1997, as Wisconsin lost 18 percent of its dairy farms, MIRG operations grew by three-fifths to about 15 percent of all the dairies in the state.[73] The grazing cows yield slightly less milk than confined animals but at far lower capital and operating cost, hence higher income per cow. The technique is simple in principle. The cows walk around fetching their own food (grass) and depositing their own manure within a paddock, moving on to another area about every day, so the grass can recover. But this practice isn't simplistic. It draws on attentive management and new knowledge of forage ecology to harvest the grass at its nutritional peak and then let it recover for the optimal period. It also ensures adequate time for the manure to return to the soil, closing the nutrient loop without producing toxic runoff. (About thirty-five times less nitrogen runs off perennial grass pastures than the corn-and-bean fields otherwise used to make cattle feed[74] — the main source of the nitrogen runoff that's asphyxiating that New Jersey–sized patch in the Gulf of Mexico.)[75] If MIRG's economic logic keeps driving its rapid expansion, it could displace enormous quantities of expensive feed grains. It could return soil to its original erosion-resistant grassland structure and restore groundwater. It could improve the habitat and wildlife (such as insect-eating songbirds),[76] the health of the cattle, the purity of the milk, and the waters now contaminated by sediments, agrichemicals, and manures (equivalent to the waste output of twenty-four people per cow). Careful rotational grazing can even heal and improve highly erosive soils in hill country: As veteran grazier Charles Opitz put it, "Your land is the canvas, the grass the paint and the cattle the brush."[77]

The naturalist's keen eye can reshape farming and gardening as well as ranching. In both the North and the South, ordinary organic farming practices modeled on complex ecosystems generally produce comparable or only slightly lower yields than chemical farming but at even lower costs. They therefore earn comparable or higher farm incomes[78] — without taking into consideration the premium many buyers are willing to pay for food free of unwelcome biocide, hormone, and antibiotic residues. The organic practices' economic advantage has been demonstrated in large commercial operations over a wide range of crops, climates, and soil types.[79] That advantage tends to increase at family-farm scale, which brings further social benefits.[80] It can also be successfully facilitated worldwide by a "farmer first" model that honors, empowers, learns from, and supplements local knowledge to achieve complex, individually tailored results, rather than trying to impose a uniform set of simplified techniques by top-down "technology transfer."[81]

Organic farming goes a long way toward providing better food from far smaller and more sustainable inputs. It is gaining market access, customers, and practitioners: In Vermont in 1995–98 alone, the number of certified organic farms doubled and their total acreage tripled. But conventional organic farming isn't the last word in the evolution of modern agriculture. Biointensive minifarming, for example, is a newer technique that combines four commonsense gardening principles: deep cultivation to aid root growth, compost crops, closely spaced plants in wide beds to optimize microclimates, and interplanting of mixed species to foil pests. Since nature does most of the work after the initial bed preparation, the upkeep is quite small and the yield can be high for crops and much higher for nutrients — the true measure of yield, as "bioneer" Kenny Ausubel rightly notes. The results are startling.

Standard U.S. agricultural practice today requires at least 45,000 square feet of land to feed a person on a high-meat diet, or about 10,000 for a vegetarian. Developing nations aspiring to similar diets have only about 9,000 square feet of land per person available for cultivation, and that amount will probably shrink with further urbanization, desertification, erosion, soil salinization, and other stresses. However, biointensive gardening can provide for a vegetarian's entire diet, plus the compost crops needed to sustain the system indefinitely, on only 2,000 to 4,000 square feet, even starting with low-quality land. Compared with conventional farming, water used per unit of food produced decreases by up to 88 percent. Off-farm energy inputs are reduced by up to 99 percent, land per unit of food produced by 60–80 percent, and land per dollar of net farm income by half. Except for the land and a few locally manufacturable hand tools, essentially no capital or any chemical inputs are required.[82] This works so well that biointensive agriculture is being practiced in 107 countries worldwide.

One of the models for biointensive techniques, yet an even less labor-intensive one in the right conditions, is Masanobu Fukuoka's "do-nothing" system of organic farming. On some of the highest-altitude fields in Japan, his system of "crops that look after themselves" reportedly yields 22 bushels of rice and 22 bushels of winter grains on a quarter acre. That's impressively productive, enough to feed 5 to 10 individuals, but it takes only one or two people a few days of work to hand-sow and harvest a crop, because an elegantly conceived sequence of plantings provides the weed control, composting, and other services automatically, just by doing the right few things at the right time and in the right sequence.[83] Science writer Janine Benyus states that Fukuoka-sensei's method has spread widely in Japan and to about a million acres in China.

Some of the most productive kinds of biofarming integrate livestock with crops, and garden and tree crops with field crops. They involve often tens and sometimes hundreds of cultivars instead of just one or a few. A typical Javanese kitchen garden, for example, looks like a miniature forest, growing over fifty cultivars in four layers on scarcely more than an acre. Its intricate diversity renders it highly and stably productive, providing food both equitably and sustainably.[84] In Asia, there is also a rich tradition of integrating many kinds of food production — vegetables, fish, rice, pigs, ducks, et cetera — in a sophisticated quasi-ecosystem that efficiently recycles its own nutrients through plant-animal interactions. A recent Bangladeshi adaptation stopped applying pesticides to rice in order to grow fish in the wet paddy fields — whereupon the fish flourished and the rice yields increased by one-fourth, because without interference, both crops could benefit each other.[85]

Biological farming principles can also be adapted to the vast areas now planted to grains. Its many variants can simultaneously reduce farmland's emissions of methane and nitrous oxide, and can reverse agricultural CO_2 emissions. These techniques can and often do use standard farm machinery but require it less often. They can work well on any scale but do not inherently disadvantage the small-scale farmer. They substitute natural for synthetic nutrients (for example, legumes, composted manure, or certain microorganisms[86] for synthetic nitrogen), mulches, compost, and cover crops for bare ground, and natural predators and rotations for biocides. Dr. Christine Jones's team at New South Wales's Land and Water Conservation Agency are even developing a new "pasture cropping" technique with controlled grazing on perennial grass cover but also annual grains sown into the grass in its dormant season. This yields the grain crop and livestock while protecting the soil and holding water.

High-yielding seeds developed for the green revolution and artificial fertilizers have often been assumed to be essential to growing enough food in land-short developing countries. Yet diverse African field studies have demonstrated that "ecoagriculture," by substituting good husbandry and local seed for otherwise purchased inputs, yields nearly as much of crops like corn and sorghum even in the short term. The small yield difference probably narrows with time, given the accelerated degradation of soils that is usually the result of chemical agriculture. Such results suggest that restorative and biological farming, often organized on the traditional family or village scale, could increase both in industrialized and developing countries without jeopardizing the goal of increasing Third World agricultural yields. Without this conversion, current trends suggest that arable land will continue to disappear, especially the thin soils of the tropics.[87] Research is revealing an even more far-reaching potential for what geneticist Wes Jackson, Janine Benyus, and others call Natural Systems Agriculture. This approach is based on the endurance, efficiency, and self-reliance of wildness. Reflecting on how much worse Minnesota cropland is damaged by a severe hailstorm than a natural grassland would be, Benyus notes that, in the prairie,

Some of the grasses suffer, but most survive quite well, thanks to a perennial root system that ensures next year's resurrection. There's a hardiness about the plants in a wild setting. When you look at a prairie, you don't see complete losses from anything — you don't see net soil erosion or devastating pest epidemics. You don't see the need for fertilizers or pesticides. You see a system that runs on sun and rain, year after year, with no one to cultivate the soil or plant the seeds. It drinks in no excess inputs and excretes no damaging wastes. It recycles all its nutrients, it conserves water, it produces abundantly, and because it's chock-full of genetic information and local know-how, it adapts.

What if we were to remake agriculture using crops that had that same kind of self-sufficiency, that ability to live amiably with their fieldmates, stay in sync with their surroundings, build soil beneath them, and handle pests with aplomb? What would agriculture look like?[88]

Experiments in rethinking agriculture are under way in biomes ranging from tropical forests to deserts, from temperate hardwood forests to prairies.[89] For example, Dr. Wes Jackson and his colleagues at the Land Institute in Salina, Kansas, are now seeking one long-term answer. They believe that, in the Great Plains of North America, it may be feasible to replace annual monocultures with perennial polycultures to form a diverse ecosystem that looks rather like native prairie, is closely modeled on it, doesn't erode (prairie soaks up rain eight times as well as a wheatfield does),[90] builds topsoil (a prairie contains about as much living matter per acre as a forest, mostly underground), and requires virtually no inputs.[91] Its efficiencies come from natural integration. Its rewards, as Jackson puts it, go "to the farmer and the landscape, not to the suppliers of inputs."

Such a replacement of annual grains with perennial cereals that do not require annual tilling and replanting could eliminate up to half the soil erosion in the United States, saving nearly $20 billion worth of U.S. soil and $9 billion worth of fuel for farm equipment every year.[92] If Jackson's ambitious research goal can be widely commercialized, a bigger and more daunting step, then at least in the earth's great grasslands, farming may ultimately come to look as if nothing at all is happening. The domestic prairie will occasionally be harvested by combines, or indirectly by harvesting various grazing animals. Such a system would require attention, but no chemicals, no cultivation, no irrigation. The efficiency of this method in turning sunlight into food will by its very nature be the highest possible, because if there were a more efficient way to do it, nature would have found it.

CHAPTER 11

Aqueous Solutions

Drilling to China — More water than rivers — Saving the aquifer — Drying with Xeriscapes — Everywhere in the house — Rainwater and graywater — Creating urban watersheds — Wastewater equals food — Watering the community

WE LIVE ON THE WATER PLANET. THREE-FOURTHS OF THE EARTH'S SURFACE is covered by water. Yet fresh, clean water is scarce and getting more so. Of all the water on earth, less than 3 percent is fresh, and all but three-thousandths[1] of that is locked up in glaciers and icecaps or is too deep in the earth to retrieve. The freshwater available in rivers, lakes, and accessible groundwater is increasingly polluted.[2] Despite nearly 200,000 square miles of reservoirs to store more than 1,400 cubic miles of water — a redistribution of natural flows that has measurably changed the orbital characteristics of the planet[3] — even whole cities the size of Mexico City are steadily becoming shorter of water, and water scarcity has changed global patterns of grain trade.[4] As the land's water-holding green skin changes to water-losing brown scabs, water tables are retreating on every continent, with 70 percent of the pumping to irrigate crops.[5] Tucson's water table is retreating toward the People's Republic, while Beijing's water table is getting closer to the United States.[6] The consequences are not merely local. Water is becoming a significant cause of international conflict.[7] To make matters worse, global climate change could intensify the droughts that have sporadically devastated and desertified subcontinental areas.

The answer to decreasing supplies of freshwater is not to try to supply more.[8] Human beings already use one-fourth of the earth's total water in natural circulation, and over half of the accessible runoff.[9] New dams might modestly increase available runoff but are costly and environmentally damaging. Even if most of the good sites had not already been taken long ago, no supply strategy could keep pace with the present rate of population growth and demand.[10] While population will probably increase 45 percent in the next thirty years, increases in accessible runoff are projected to be only 10 percent. Even after investing some $400 billion in water supply over the past century,[11] the United States, with all its wealth and technical prowess, faces shortages that have no easy remedies. As one authority put it in 1984, "The water supply of the West is nearly fully utilized. It is difficult to see major construction projects which will add significantly to the current supply."[12] Moreover, America's eighty thousand dams and reservoirs were not entirely benign: During the boom years of water-capturing projects, the United States lost over 60 percent of its inland wetlands, polluted half its stream-miles, and lost or badly degraded many major fish runs.[13] At home and abroad, with water as with energy, the only practical, large-scale solution is to use what we have far more efficiently.

Most, especially industrialized, countries, still make all the same mistakes with water that they made with energy.[14] They deplete nonrenewable supplies and seek more water instead of using inexhaustible sources more productively and enhancing their capture by restorative grazing, farming, and forestry. They rely on the highest-quality water for every task, flushing toilets and washing driveways with drinking water. They build big dams and water projects by reflex, rather than asking what's the best solution and the right size for the job.

Fortunately, this mind-set is changing. A host of available and emerging techniques is making it possible to increase radically the productivity of water directly where it's used. These technologies and management methods, and new ways to implement and reward them, can enable countries to deliver worldwide on South Africa's water-policy promise, "Some, for all, for ever." These breakthroughs come none too soon. All the water that can reasonably be obtained will be needed to feed the world in the coming century while protecting the natural capital on which all life depends.[15]

RUNNING DRY

Agriculture is responsible for about twice as much of total U.S. water withdrawals as all buildings, industry, and mining combined. It accounted for 81 percent of all 1995 consumptive use. Eighty-eight percent of the nation's 1995 irrigation water went to 17 western states, where the great majority of all water districts were mining groundwater faster than it was being recharged. This is a long-standing pattern. Freshwater flows from rivers are provided to agriculture under a program of federal subsidies that go back to the nineteenth century. California has built a vast agribusiness sector on water so heavily subsidized that 57 percent of its agricultural water grows four crops that produce only 17 percent of its agricultural revenue.[16] Arizona has long used subsidized water to flood-irrigate cotton and alfalfa in a desert. The states along the Colorado River, including five of the ten fastest-growing states in the United States, have already allocated on paper more water than is actually in the river, and in many years, the river never reaches the sea.

Many gargantuan water projects have failed to pass the giggle test. The Army Corps of Engineers wanted to pump the Missouri River uphill to recharge aquifers in and beyond west Kansas, even though there was no legal crop that farmers could grow with that water to earn enough to afford the pumping energy.[17] The 1968 Texas Water Plan would have needed seven Chernobyl-sized power plants to pump water about 3,000 feet up from the Mississippi River to a region of west Texas. The ultimate wet dream, the North American Water and Power Alliance, would have replumbed western North America. It proposed to dam the 500-mile-long Rocky Mountain Trench near Banff and Jasper National Parks, and to divert the major rivers of Alaska, the Yukon, and British Columbia to supply water to all of Canada, the western and mid-western United States (pumping over the Rockies as needed), and northern Mexico. This massive project, which was ultimately killed, would have cost the best part of a trillion dollars. Proposed with a straight face, this plan was the ultimate expression of how far some people are willing to go to put water where it isn't.

Under America's High Plains, extending from north Texas to the Dakotas, lies the Ogallala Aquifer, a deposit of Pleistocene groundwater spanning an area larger than California. By 1990, it was being drawn down at a rate of 3 to 10 feet a year to provide 30 percent of America's groundwater-based irrigation.[18] Recharged at a rate of less than a half inch per year, parts of the aquifer were getting badly depleted; half to two-thirds of the economically recoverable Texas portion was already drained by 1980.[19] Nevertheless, two-fifths of America's feedlot cattle were being fed grain made of Ogallala groundwater. Growing enough of that grain to add sufficient weight on a feedlot steer to put an extra pound of beef on the table consumed up to a hundred pounds of lost, eroded topsoil and over eight thousand pounds of Ice Age–vintage groundwater.[20]

The initial "water rush" that dotted the High Plains with center-pivot irrigation (those are the circular areas of irrigated land you see when flying across the country) from the 1950s to the 1980s presumed that water resources were inexhaustible. A study of High Plains farmers and ranchers found that only half had adopted as many as three of thirty-nine available irrigation-efficiency practices.[21] By the early 1990s, depletion and pumping costs had forced hard-hit towns to rediscover dryland farming. Some, like Hays, Kansas, where water was considered abundant twenty years ago, are now turning toward water efficiency for their very survival.[22] Often the problem is not just whether the groundwater exists but also whether one can afford to pump it to the surface.

Dependence on increasingly scarce supplies is not limited to agriculture: Providing water to Las Vegas has become a regional obsession. Every drop that can be saved, bought, borrowed, or otherwise appropriated from other areas in Nevada or the rest of the West is used to fuel the city's subsidized sprawl, creating, in effect, a second Los Angeles in a country that has one too many. Even in the rainy eastern states, most cities, even those with relatively static populations, have recently suffered water shortages.

THE EFFICIENCY SOLUTION

The combination of dwindling federal water subsidies, the end of the big-dam era, energy and environmental constraints, and growing population and economic-growth pressures is creating a future of scarcer and costlier water, even in a country as rich in available water, money, and technology as the United States. Fortunately, demand-side solutions are emerging that can not only avert most water shortages but, as in the case of energy, turn deficits into abundance.

Almost unnoticed by nonspecialists, and in a radical deviation from the beliefs and experiences of water planners,[23] American farmers, landscapers, building operators, industrial engineers, and communities are making impressive progress in using water more productively. The graph opposite[24] shows that in all sectors — especially agriculture, industry, and power generation — the overall efficiency of water use has been improving since about 1980. Even as the population and the economy grew, the amount of freshwater withdrawn per American fell by 21 percent during the years 1980–95, and water withdrawn per dollar of real GDP fell by a startling 38 percent — over twice as fast as energy efficiency improved.

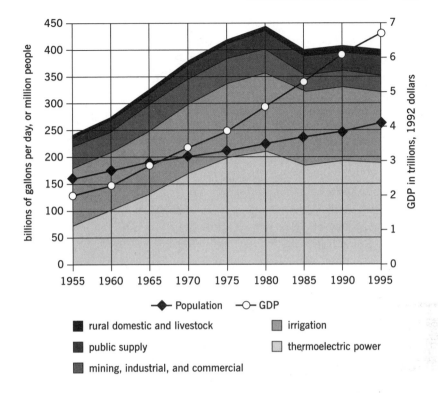

This success is starting to be mirrored worldwide: 1995 world water withdrawals were only about half what planners had predicted thirty years earlier by extrapolating historical trends.[25] And this is only the beginning. In every sector and every society, far larger opportunities beckon for saving water, money, and natural capital.[26]

AGRICULTURE

Nobody is more cost-conscious than an informed farmer. As Wayne Wyatt, manager of the High Plains Underground Water Conservation District in Lubbock, Texas, said, "The nerve to the hip pocket is mighty sensitive." Farmers in his district are starting to water their crops only when they need it, rather than on a regular schedule. A common technique uses a one-dollar block of gypsum, the size of a lump of sugar, buried at the root zone. Wires embedded in the gypsum run back up to the surface to a clip-on meter that indicates soil moisture. In many areas, such readings are saving one-third to two-thirds of the water with no change in crop yields, and are allowing farmers both to distribute water more evenly across a field and to schedule irrigation more efficiently. This technique also cuts pumping costs and reduces runoff of soil salts and agrichemicals.

Education in water-saving techniques is a powerful tool. A 1990–91 survey in Oregon showed that a typical three-hour visit by a consultant quickly saved a tenth to a fifth of farmers' water, and sometimes twice that amount, just through better management.[27] After making those "good housekeeping" improvements, farmers had available to them a longer list of other refinements worth investing in. In Lubbock, a decade of applying these methods saved a quarter to nearly half of the water and nearly halted aquifer depletion.[28]

Better pricing structures can provide rational incentives to invest in savings that cost less than new supplies. In California's San Joaquin Valley, the Broadview Water District set a 1989 water-intensity target at 10 percent below its 1986–88 average for each crop, and enforced a stiff surcharge on excess water use. Water use per acre fell by 17 percent and total drainwater by nearly 25 percent.[29] In California, the world's largest water wholesaler, the Metropolitan Water District of Southern California, buys back "saved" water from its distributors; just one, the Imperial Irrigation District, has invested in water-saving technologies that have allowed it to sell back 32 *billion* previously wasted gallons a year.

For the big farms that in many cases demonstrably waste half their water, the most powerful efficiency response is based on technology. Many farmers are switching to a technique that waters more than half of Israel's farmland and a million acres of California's.[30] It uses calibrated "emitters" attached to buried plastic tubes to deliver water directly to plant roots one drop at a time, as needed. Howard Wuertz's Sundance Farms grows 2,360 acres of cotton, wheat, barley, milo, corn, watermelons, cantaloupes, and sweet corn with this method in Arizona's blistering Casa Grande Valley. When Wuertz started his subsurface-drip conversion in 1980, his furrow-and-flood irrigation, though better than most, made use of only half of the water applied. His durable drip system raised this to 95 percent, and resulted in higher crop yields and other valuable benefits.[31]

Subsurface drip irrigation could be a critical factor in increasing the world food supply. Two-thirds of the freshwater withdrawn for human use worldwide goes toward irrigation. Ninety-three percent of the irrigated acres receive the water by flooding, the least efficient method of delivery. Converting just half those acres to doubled-efficiency drip and sprinkler irrigation[32] could save enough water to provide the irrigation needed to feed the extra 2.6 billion people expected by about 2025.[33]

Another Israeli innovation, developed by Arava R&D, enriches its agricultural water by growing edible fish in it under evaporation-blocking and temperature-controlling giant plastic "Aqua-Bubbles." The fish don't consume water, and add nutrients that subsequently fertilize crops. Such systems can produce about 150 pounds of fish per thousand gallons per year — an impressive use of space in the desert.[34] Researchers in Israel and at Arizona's Desert Research Institute are also making exciting progress with "halophytes" — crops that prefer brackish water, which in many countries is all too plentiful.

LANDSCAPING

Parks, gardens, and landscapes need water chiefly in midsummer when it's scarcest and costliest to provide. They often account for two-fifths to four-fifths of a water utility's peak demand. But even relatively modest improvements can reduce outdoor water use by up to 50 percent.[35]

The Xeriscape movement, a design practice that creates elegant and water-efficient landscapes, now boasts state associations from California to Florida. Well-designed low-water landscaping can be not only beautiful but also provide natural cooling, fire protection, and bird and wildlife habitat. It doesn't demand radical steps like turning lawns into cactus farms; water-frugal grasses have been developed that are as attractive as traditional varieties.[36] A state-of-the-art assessment by Jim Knopf shows that landscapes costing half as much as standard irrigated ones could almost eliminate water use in Denver's yards yet lose nothing in beauty.[37] Water-efficient landscaping also saves such inputs as labor, fertilizer, herbicides, and fuel, plus agrichemical runoff, noise and fumes, cracking of pavement and foundations, and generation of yard wastes. Water-efficient median strips in Palm Desert, California, which have been well received by the public, cut water and maintenance costs by 85 percent, and have reduced road deterioration and traffic accidents (caused by skidding on wet pavements). Savings multiply further when well-chosen plants are watered with efficient technologies managed in efficient ways, and ideally using stored rainwater.

The simplest way to eliminate the need for watering landscapes is to replant them with flora that evolution actually fitted to grow there. Shared-savings retrofits have transformed corporate campuses in much of the American Midwest from standard turf lawns into plots of diverse native grasslands,[38] creating a tourist magnet — a "panorama of grasses and wildflowers, producing a . . . diverse mixture of colors and textures throughout the seasons."[39] AT&T found that both initially and over time, such a planted prairie near Chicago would cost far less[40] than bluegrass. In addition, bluegrass was bred in moist Kentucky, so it has shallow roots that trap so little water that most rain runs off, requiring irrigation even after a rain. Prairie grasses, toughened for drought and hardpan, have soil-anchoring roots over ten feet deep that water the plants for free.

BUILDINGS

Houses and commercial buildings, including their outdoor uses, account for 12 percent of America's freshwater withdrawals. A typical U.S. single-family home uses about 70 gallons per person per day indoors. This would fall to about 52 with minimal improvements, or to 40 (of which 20 can be returned as graywater[41] reusable for watering outdoor plants) by introducing a more efficient toilet, clothes washer, dishwasher, showerheads, and bathroom faucets, plus graywater toilet flushing. Even more impressive improvements are now becoming available in every one of the following fixtures and appliances.

TOILETS (26 percent of indoor household use, excluding leaky toilets). One flush of a standard U.S. toilet requires more water than most individuals, and many families, in the world use for all their needs in an entire day.[42] But toilet technology has already reduced new U.S. units from the old 5–7 U.S. gallons per flush (gpf) to 1.6 or fewer, with no degradation of performance.[43] There are also three different methods to implement functional and attractive toilets that use *no* water: waterless urinals, separating toilets, and composting toilets.

Most toilet flushes are for urine alone, which can run down the drain unaided. Public-building urinals are traditionally water-flushed by always-open valves, timers, or infrared people-sensors (1–3 gpf). But the latest waterless fiberglass models[44] use liquid-repellent coatings, subtle contours to facilitate complete draining, and a special lighter-than-urine biodegradable trap liquid to prevent odors. They work well, have a lower installed cost than water-guzzling urinals, and save about 40–60,000 gallons per unit per year.[45]

Since Thomas Crapper invented the water closet, many sanitation experts have come to view it as one of the stupidest technologies of all time: In an effort to make them "invisible,"[46] it mixes pathogen-bearing feces with relatively clean urine. Then it dilutes that slurry[47] with about 100 times[48] its volume in pure drinking water, and further mixes the mess with industrial toxins in the sewer system, thus turning "an excellent fertilizer and soil conditioner"[49] into a serious, far-reaching, and dispersed disposal problem.[50] Supplying the clean water, treating the sewage, and providing all the delivery and collection in between requires systems whose cost strains the resources even of wealthy countries, let alone the 2 billion people who lack basic sanitation. The World Health Organization has stated that waterborne sanitation cannot meet *any* of its declared objectives — equity, disease prevention, and sustainability[51] — and suggests that only with more modern (waterless) techniques can the world's cities be affordably provided with clean water for drinking, cooking, and washing.[52] Meanwhile, a new, village-affordable solar-powered water purifier can stop the tragedy of waterborne disease.

A more sensible design than obsolete flush toilets has been introduced by modern Swedish toilets. These feature a two-compartment bowl to separate urine, which contains most of the nutrient value in human wastes,[53] from feces: The two leave the body separately, and should be disposed of that way. It is then a straightforward procedure to collect or sell the urine (stored in a small tank) from a tap outside the building as a valuable fertilizer,[54] and to dry and bag, compost, or otherwise treat the 20-odd pounds of feces per person per year. In Sweden, a country noted for hygienic and aesthetic refinement, more than 50,000 dry/composting systems have been sold in 42 models from 22 manufacturers; they cost scarcely more to buy and can cost less to install than a nonseparating toilet plus its sewer connection.[55] If the new urine-diverting toilets (used by the hundreds in Sweden and Mexico) are likewise perfected, they could greatly reduce toilets' water use, perhaps even to zero as some of the popular dry/composting models have already done. The toilets would save sewage-collection, sewage-treatment, and agricultural costs and would improve topsoil.

SHOWERS (18 percent of indoor use). The great American shower traditionally used about 6–8 gallons per minute (gpm), and many still do. Since 1992, the legal maximum for new units has been 2.5 gpm. But today you can take a shower just as pounding, needly, or whatever pattern you prefer by choosing from over 30 marketed models of high-performance showerheads that use only 1.0–1.5 gpm or even less.

A high-performance showerhead retails for about $13 but pays for itself in mere months from water-heating energy savings alone.

Some advanced showerheads[56] have only a single orifice made of slippery plastic, so they can't clog even in the hardest water. Their mixing chamber emits a powerfully wetting and massaging combination of air and water. One variant offers a satisfying shower with just a few pounds of pressure per square inch — produced by the gravity head from an attic tank — yet uses only 1.5–2.0 gpm.[57] Also available for the frugal or curious are clip-on "taximeters" that measure flow and temperature and display elapsed dollars.

SINKS (15 percent of indoor use). Sinks are another big water user, but faucet retrofits are among the cheapest and easiest savers. A screw-on one-dollar gadget combines the water with air to make a foamy mixture that wets better with about half as much water. A little flip-valve allows the flow to be turned off momentarily, then return to the preset temperature without wasting water readjusting the hot/cold mix. Alternatively, internal baffles and channels in a 1.5–2.5-gpm "laminar flow" device[58] deliver a smooth, solid stream of water that sticks to and wets things just as well with half the water, but turning it up to full flow can fill a pot with no delay.

CLOTHES WASHING (23 percent of indoor use) and dishwashing (1 percent). Washing machines have changed little in a century. The standard American vertical-axis design agitates clothes in a big tubful of water. In contrast, horizontal-axis machines, common overseas and in U.S. laundromats, put about 40–75 percent less water into the bottom of a tub and rotate the clothes through it.[59] Soap works better in these machines because it's more chemically concentrated. Clothes last longer because they're not agitated; tangling is also eliminated, and more space is available for bulky items. Spin cycles become shorter, better balanced, and more effective. These advantages, and the spur of federal standards, led most U.S. manufacturers of washers to introduce horizontal- or diagonal-axis machines in 1996–98. Such resource-efficient machines recently yielded a 3.5-year payback in a Portland, Oregon, laundromat, whose customers report lower wash costs and cleaner clothes.[60]

The widely available enzymatic detergents that eat fat, protein, and starch are able to clean dishes better and faster with less and cooler water. Dishwashers are improving, too, with some models adjusting water use to match the dirtiness of the load.[61] In the late 1980s, one firm[62] even invented a small countertop dishwasher needing *no* electricity — just the line pressure of hot water from the kitchen sink faucet — to needle-spray hot water onto the dishes in a several-minute cycle followed by self-drying. Running so silently that it can be used one course at a time during the meal, that "Ecotech" could reduce water use by severalfold. That product didn't make it to market, but ultrasonic dishwashers are already being installed in American kitchens, with ultrasonic clothes washers probably close behind.

OTHER INDOOR AND SYSTEM SAVINGS. Old, neglected pipes tend to leak. Even good urban distribution systems lose a tenth of their water; the average U.S. city, about a quarter; Bombay, one-third; Manila, over half.[63] During fiscal year 1990–91 alone, New York City put 26 people and $1.5 million to work in a survey of more than 90 percent of the city's 57,000 miles of water mains. This resulted in repairs to 66 breaks and 671 leaks, and saved 49 million gallons per day.[64] Since then the whole system has been rescanned every three years, and leaks have decreased by 75–80 percent. Magnetic locking caps on fire hydrants have also reduced tampering rates to less than 10 percent, saving upward of 100 million gallons on hot summer days (if disappointing neighborhood kids). Such efficiency improvements are steadily shrinking losses, making costly supply expansions unnecessary.[65]

A tenth of typical U.S. household usage[66] is leaks from toilet valves, dripping faucets, and aging pipes.[67] Toilets are the biggest offenders, often wasting as much as 750 gallons a month versus 300 for a typical leaky faucet.[68]

Automated building leak-monitoring techniques are now becoming available, often integrated with cost-saving automatic meter-reading. In this system, acute leaks trigger alarms to customers, utilities, or plumbers.[69] Insurance companies like this concept and may ultimately share its cost or waive deductibles for customers who adopt it.

TECHNOLOGY *PLUS* BEHAVIOR. Efficiency technologies that are already commercially available can in combination double or triple water efficiency, with no loss of service or convenience, no change in the source of water, and no reliance on recovery of departing wastewater.[70] Yet water efficiency depends not only on technology but also on behavior — which in turn is influenced partly by letting people know how much water they're using, for what purposes, at what cost, with what consequences.

Over the past decade, previously unmetered cities like Denver and much of New York have been installing water meters. Charging households for their actual use, rather than a flat rate, typically saves up to a third of their water. Charges that rise with consumption ("inverted" tariffs), rather than quantity discounts, can save even more.[71] Santa Barbara's emergency tariff increased price geometrically with usage, up to 27 times the base level.[72] Often the best strategy is charging marginal cost *and* educating customers. Palo Alto saved 27 percent of its water use in drought years not only by surcharges but by hiring college students to teach high-usage homeowners about their efficiency opportunities.[73] A 1994 experiment in South Africa's arid Kruger National Park[74] used simple, unsophisticated technologies, education, and metered charges to save 74 percent of the water and 52 percent of the electricity compared with standard technologies, no education, and a flat rate. The combined effect appeared to be greater than the sum of its parts. In contrast, providing only written educational materials without introducing better technologies or price signals didn't help (water use *increased* by 3 percent).

WATER-QUALITY BENEFITS. Overpumping groundwater not only depletes the resource but also tends to draw chemical contamination toward wells. This created a water crisis for Fresno's 360,000 people, who had to shut down 35 wells and retrofit water efficiency into 125,000 homes to slow the creep of the agricultural biocide dibromochloropropane.[75] In San Simeon, California, efficiency that reduced groundwater pumping by 28 percent in one year alleviated the intrusion of salt water into freshwater wells.[76] Irrigation efficiency in Nebraska's Central Platte Natural Resource District reduced the leaching of nitrogen fertilizer into aquifers, cutting dangerous nitrate levels in wells.[77]

Water efficiency can likewise relieve an overloaded sewage-treatment plant without costly upgrades or expansions, and can usually allow the plant to function better, because of reduced flows. Efficiency enables individual septic systems to work better, too. One 12-house survey found that saving a quarter to a half of household water use greatly reduced malfunctions of septic systems, made their treatment more effective, and would probably lead to lower long-run operating costs.[78] In states like Florida, where about two-fifths of households use individual, on-site wastewater treatment, this triple bonus — better water quality as well as more secure and more affordable supplies of water and energy — is of strategic importance.

INDUSTRY

The graph on page 217 likewise illustrates the dramatic water savings that have been achieved by American industry. These have often included reductions in pollutant discharges too. In 1995, nonagricultural businesses withdrew 38 percent less water than in 1970, while producing 69 percent more real output, which represents a 63 percent reduction in water intensity.[79] California's industries achieved even faster savings in the 1980s — a 46 percent reduction in water intensity in only ten years.[80] Further examples suggest that far greater savings are still achievable:

- Pacific Coca-Cola reduced a can line's need for rinsewater by 79 percent by using air instead of water to clean the insides of cans before filling.[81]

- A Calvert County, Maryland, senior citizens' center proposed to build 50 more apartments. New water and sewer hookups were going to cost $135,000. Instead, retrofitting 1.6-gpf toilets into existing units saved 58 percent of the center's water, which freed up the needed capacity at a cost of only $16,000.[82]

- A North German manufacturer of paper products for packaging almost *eliminated* its water use by completely recycling its base supply in a sophisticated process that successively sediments, floats, and filters the fiber and particulate loads from the water. Only 1.5 pounds of water per pound of paper is still needed to offset evaporation and provide the water content of the paper itself. This residual water requirement is 600 times smaller than the European norm in 1900, or about 15–20 times below the recent German norm.[83]

- During the years 1972–93, Gillette Company reduced the water used to make a razor blade in its South Boston Manufacturing Center by 96 percent. During the years 1974–93, Gillette's water use to make a Paper Mate pen also fell by 90 percent.[84]

- Armco's Kansas City steel mill, now called the GST Steel Plant, uses its water at least 16 times over, purifying it in between uses in settling ponds. It now takes in only 3.6 million gallons a day even though it uses 58 million gallons a day. Additional clarifiers and settling ponds are planned to increase water recycling still further and achieve zero discharge ahead of tightened standards.[85]

- Even in making microchips — one of the industries with the most stringent requirements for water purity — water recycling up to 85 percent has been effectively achieved.[86]

RECOVERING RAINWATER AND GRAYWATER

Whenever it rains, naturally distilled water falls on buildings. It flows off their impervious roof surfaces, is guided into gutters, is quickly sent into sewers to be combined with human and industrial wastes, and is then "taken away" at great expense.

In contrast, the roof of Mike McElveen's house in Austin, Texas, collects the local average of 32 inches of rain a year into two 8,400-gallon tanks. When full, they can provide a hundred gallons a day — enough for two people in his moderately water-efficient household[87] — even if it doesn't rain for five and a half months. Unlike the region's well water, rainwater is soft and pure, and requires no treatment.[88] The system has met all the needs of his two-person household since 1988, and even worked well during a three-year drought. The capital cost of the tank, plumbing, and enhanced water-catching surface was less than the cost would have been for redrilling the well or tapping into a newly formed rural water district. The water bills are zero, and the tanks, obviously oversized, have never fallen below 70 percent full.[89] Such on-site systems may even yield other savings because their big containers, which are often positioned at a height that can gravity-feed a hose, can reduce fire-insurance premiums.

Harvesting rainwater, common in the nineteenth-century United States, remains standard practice today even for affluent households in Hawai'i and in such islands as Bermuda, where many areas have no public water supply. In many regions of Australia, rainwater collection systems are mandatory. Rainwater-holding cisterns are affordable when measured against the water-supply and storm-water-drain investments they make unnecessary. A case study[90] in Byron, Australia, found that cisterns devoted half to supply and half to storm-water detention — the cisterns are normally kept half empty to leave room for storm water — would be cost-effective for the drainage authority to pay for. They could reduce sewer-pipe sizes, and would be almost cost-effective for the water supplier compared to other supply alternatives. These savings together could finance private cisterns from avoided public costs.

Rainwater could even be captured at the scale not just of a single house but of a whole basin. One day in August 1998, while the rest of Los Angeles sweltered under a clear summer sky, Mrs. Rozella Hall's 1920s bungalow in the South Central inner city suddenly experienced an isolated 28-inch cloudburst — 8,000 gallons in 20 minutes.[91] It came from fire hoses. A project led by Tree People was demonstrating several retrofit techniques. Two 1,700-gallon electronically controlled cisterns,[92] redirected downspouts, retention grading (slightly sunken and bermed lawn areas to hold rainwater until it can percolate into the ground), a driveway drywell (to recharge groundwater but first catch engine-oil drippings), and a grassy or mulched swale for further filtration kept all the surface water on-site. Such measures can sponge up deluges from winter storms and make them last all year. Replicated citywide, this could cut the city's water imports by 50–60 percent, help control flooding, and reduce toxic runoff to the ocean. It would improve air and water quality, save energy, cut by 30 percent the flow of yard wastes to landfills (it would instead be mulched and composted as a water-catcher and soil-builder), beautify neighborhoods, and create direct jobs (perhaps including 50,000 "urban watershed managers"). An interactive software package now enables city managers to quantify the multiple benefits of such management practices.[93] In a city like Los Angeles, where two agencies that hadn't talked to each other are spending a billion dollars a year to import water and a half billion dollars a year to take it away ("flood control"), closing the water loop could save money at both ends.[94]

Another ubiquitous but normally wasted water resource is the "graywater" from showers, sinks, tubs, and washing machines — in effect, all of a household's discharged water except "blackwater" from toilets. After widespread droughts in the 1980s and 1990s, the California legislature, following the lead of Santa Barbara and other localities, passed statewide guidelines in 1994 for the safe use of graywater for subsurface irrigation. The California Plumbing Code[95] now defines how graywater should be controlled to protect public health, keeping it underground and off food crops. Typical recovery and reuse rates average about 50 gallons per house per day, cutting total water use about in half, and saving even more in multifamily and commercial buildings where graywater is used to flush toilets. Such a system at the Roseland III office park in Essex County, New Jersey, cut the 360,000-square-foot complex's water use by 62 percent.[96]

Many buildings in Salt Lake City deliver brackish water in a separate plumbing system specifically for flushing toilets. The utility in St. Petersburg, Florida, developed a similar dual distribution system to use reclaimed water for nonpotable needs, providing about 20 million gallons a day, or one-third of the city's total consumption, for such functions as irrigation and cooling. This plan will eliminate the need for new water sources and expansions to water facilities until 2025.[97] In the Los Angeles area, sanitation districts resell an annual average of 63 million gallons per day of reclaimed tertiary-treated effluent that is virus-free and meets or exceeds bacterial and other drinking-water standards. It's used at more than 140 sites for such nonpotable purposes as irrigating parks, golf courses, and food crops, watering livestock, filling recreational lakes, running industrial processes, supplying cooling towers, construction, and for groundwater recharge.[98] In early 1998 San Diego announced America's first major municipal project to reroute reclaimed tertiary-treated wastewater directly back into reservoirs. Throughout the United States, more than a thousand projects reclaim water, but they provide less than one percent of total usage. In contrast, Israel's reclaimed total was 4 percent in 1980, and 8 percent (reclaiming 40 percent of total wastewater) in 1998.[99]

RECOVERING WATER FROM LOCAL BIOLOGICAL TREATMENT PLANTS

The World Bank has stated that North American and European sewage-treatment practices

> ... do not represent the zenith of scientific achievement, nor are they the product of a logical and rational process. Rather, [they] ... are the product of ... a history that started about 100 years ago when little was known about the fundamental physics and chemistry of the subject and when practically no applicable microbiology had been discovered. These practices are not especially clever, not logical, nor completely effective — and it is not necessarily what would be done today if these same countries had the chance to start again.[100]

Most sewage-treatment systems are large, centralized, and capital-intensive: Los Angeles alone collects a billion gallons a day through 6,500 miles of pipe. Studies have already shown that when an electrical system is similarly designed, its economics suffer, for reasons that appear equally applicable when what is flowing is not electricity in wires but water or sewage in pipes: In both cases, the connection to the customer is too long and costs too much.[101] There is growing evidence that smaller water delivery and wastewater treatment systems — often at the scale of the neighborhood or even the single building — can provide cleaner water at much lower cost and without environmental or safety hazards. An official study in Adelaide, the capital of South Australia, found that while typical large sewage-treatment plants do gain some economies of scale, they also gain bigger diseconomies because they must pay for the sewer network to collect wastes from a larger area. That network's pipes and pumps often account for about 90 percent of the total cost of wastewater treatment. Designed to capture only the advantages of treatment-plant size without counting its collection costs, standard designs are probably at least tenfold, and may even be a thousandfold, larger than an economic optimum.[102] Small-scale systems "can be more readily developed and appear able to compete against the existing systems."[103]

Some experts believe that the whole concept of sewage has been called into question by the new composting and separating toilets described above. But since most people in developed countries already use flush toilets, and probably will for a long time, the more favorable economics of smaller-scale sewage treatment[104] are leading to a rethinking of the sewage-treatment *process*. This includes measures like switching from chemical engineering to biological techniques that already — even at their relatively early stage of development — offer striking ecological and economic advantages.

The leading practitioner of this approach, Living Technologies, Inc.,[105] designs, builds, and operates innovative wastewater treatment systems called Living Machines that eliminate the need for the chlorine, polymers, aluminum salts (alum), and the other chemicals used in conventional wastewater treatment plants. A biological treatment plant costs about the same or less to construct, especially for small-capacity systems. It yields valuable fertilizers and soil amendments instead of toxic chemical hazards, looks like a water garden, greenhouse, or wetland, doesn't smell bad, and yields safer, higher-quality water.

Invented by biologist Dr. John Todd, the Living Machine treats wastewater as it moves through a series of mainly open tanks, typically located in passive-solar greenhouses. The tanks are populated by an increasingly complex series of organisms: bacteria and algae, then plant communities, and finally miniature, engineered ecosystems, including large fish and shellfish. Fixed film substrate, plant roots, and tank surfaces anchor plant roots while water moves past. The resulting controlled ecological system maximizes biological degradation of contaminants by treating them not as waste but as food. These ecosystems provide a higher degree of biodiversity than previous biological treatment technologies (which were based on only a few species), thereby treating a wider range of contaminants with greater stability and resilience. Some plants, such as bullrushes and certain flowers, sequester heavy metals, secrete antibiotics that kill pathogens, or otherwise protect human health. A simple ozone or ultraviolet treatment of the final output water (usually stored in an attractive pond or wetland habitat) would even make it potable.

Living Machines deliver higher effluent quality than conventional secondary sewage-treatment systems. Operating costs are roughly the same and sometimes less. Energy consumption is similar, but a few advances likely in blowers and system design (on the line of the "big pipes, small pumps" in chapter 6) may give Living Machines an advantage. As advanced as this technology is over conventional wastewater treatment, it represents only the beginning of what is possible. At present, only a fractionally small number of organisms are being drawn upon to produce these results. After a more complete assay of the earth's biota, we may expect to see great improvements in efficiency including a diverse array of saleable compounds and by-products.

By 1998, the company had installed twenty-three systems in the United States and six other countries. They are permitted in seven states, and existing designs serve from one household to ten thousand. Being odor-free and aesthetically pleasing, the systems should face less local resistance than conventional wastewater treatment plants, and present no chlorine or other chemical hazard. In chilly South Burlington, Vermont, a 6,400-square-foot Living Machine that reached full design flow in April 1996 is treating 80,000 gallons of municipal sewage per day, outperforming all its design targets and proving compatible with a residential neighborhood.

The technology also lends itself to integration into normal commercial settings. Visitors could enter an elegant corporate headquarters through a garden of cascading water flows, featuring a series of landscaped tanks full of flowers, fish, water plants, and other organisms — discovering only later that the garden was actually the building's sewage-treatment plant. Oberlin College's new Environmental Studies Center building and the Body Shop in Toronto have adopted this very strategy. The ability to integrate Living Machines into the landscape also suits them to industrial and food-processing use. The Mars Company's positive experience treating difficult industrial wastes in Henderson, Nevada, and Waco, Texas, has spurred the firm to order three additional systems for plants in Brazil, Australia, and the United States.[106]

IMPLEMENTATION

Many water efficiency programs had their origins in water shortages, because the threat of running dry does tend to concentrate people's minds. (Water efficiency professionals speak of the "hydro-illogic cycle": drought, concern, rain, apathy, drought, concern, rain, apathy. . . .) Nonetheless, many of the most successful efforts worked not because they exploited a teachable moment but because they, like other kinds of resource efficiency, provide better services at lower cost.[107]

In Goleta, California, drought and the threat of a multimillion-dollar expenditure to meet EPA sewage-treatment standards spurred a $1.5 million municipal program that provided information and incentives to the town's 74,000 citizens to reduce water waste. Technical improvements, plus some emergency drought measures (peak-season surcharges and a little rationing),[108] cut citywide water consumption within the single year from 1989 to 1990 by 30 percent, from an average of 135 to 90 gallons per person per day — twice the targeted savings. Sewage flow fell by over 40 percent, enabling the existing plant to run within its rated capacity and EPA secondary standards.[109] The proposed plant expansion was indefinitely deferred. The total water savings later grew to 40 percent. In the dry summer of 1990, while some nearby communities were forced to cut their water use by 30–45 percent, Goleta had only to set a 15 percent goal, avoiding disruption or hardship.

In large cities, broadly based efforts at fixture replacement, leak reduction, metering, technical advice, and rate restructuring have yielded steady improvements. Despite population growth, New York's water use is 18 percent below its peak and falling[110] — relieving pressure on sewage-treatment plants, five of which were overloaded and six about to become so. Boston has inexpensively saved 24–27 percent of its water through leak repairs and retrofitting nearly half the housing stock with leak reductions, better showerheads, faucet aerators, and toilet dams (full toilet retrofits would save even more). The more than 1,000 facility engineers and managers whom Boston trained and networked will also apply their knowledge over the course of many years, as will the next generation of Bostonians, now being educated with multimedia campaigns, teacher training, and new school curricula.

In the poor, mainly African-American and Hispanic neighborhoods of East Los Angeles, a unique partnership between community groups and a for-profit third-party firm, CTSI Corporation,[111] was formed in 1992. The coalition tackled the problem that $100 utility rebates for toilet replacements didn't help the many customers who couldn't afford to pay the balance, or those who had to wait two months for the rebate to be delivered. CTSI arranged with the utility to bulk-buy 1,000 initial toilets and use their rebates to pay for more toilets that nonprofit community groups like Mothers of East LA Santa Isabel (MELA-SI) could then give away. Soon people were lining up at convenient sites, often run by their neighbors, to bring in their decrepit, inefficient old toilets (which got recycled into road base) and exchange them for new ones plus high-performance showerheads and compact fluorescent lamps. This swap cut water and energy bills by about $30–120 per household per year, putting money back into residents' pockets and into community economies. The Metropolitan Water District of Southern California contracted with CTSI to make the program available throughout Los Angeles and Southern California. MELA-SI and eight other community groups that later joined the program earned over $1 million participating in the programs. They used these earnings to hire and train local staff, some from the unemployment rolls, and to fund such community benefits as immunizations, graffiti abatement, day care, scholarships, and inner-city business development. High-school students also marketed one-day distribution "events" at their schools — earning one school, through $15-per-toilet fees, $30,000 to re-fund student activities that had fallen victim to budget cuts. By the beginning of 1996, community groups working with CTSI had distributed more than 300,000 toilets, saving over 3 billion gallons of water per year and creating over a hundred jobs. Utility rebates in various communities citywide brought the Los Angeles total of 1.6-gpf toilet retrofits by January 1998 to about 33 percent.[112]

With indoor water as with landscape design and energy, "service contractors" are available who will choose, install, and maintain energy-efficient technologies in schools, hotels, and apartments in return for a share of the savings.[113] Denver, Colorado, is encouraging such entrepreneurs by incentivizing retail water distributors, the city's parks department, and the private sector with payments for however much water they save. Businesses and irrigators can then use the payments to hire contractors to design, implement, combine, and measure the savings.[114]

Community programs that are successful typically involve a variety of constituencies and kinds of expertise. Western Australia has mobilized plumbers, who have practical knowledge of the subject, as the vanguard of the water efficiency education and installation effort. Other potential allies include water, wastewater, energy, religious, labor, economic development, social justice, environmental, fish and wildlife, and real estate organizations. There are also new methods of implementation that create markets in saved water, and promote competition to capture the cheapest opportunities first. For example, in Connecticut, Washington, and California, different utilities that provide water, wastewater treatment, electricity, and gas are teaming up to share the tasks and costs of distribution, marketing, administration, and product selection for water-efficiency programs that benefit them all.[115]

As usual, the greatest benefits from saving water emerge from the broadest vision of connections and the widest integration of design. The natural drainage control and water storage described in chapter 5 not only saves capital and irrigation water; it creates better places to live. It also avoids vast investments in storm drains, funding reinvestments for even greater value. From Chicago to Chattanooga to Curitiba (chapter 14), this new approach to urban hydrology is starting to capture rain as it falls, put it back into groundwater, and green the city.

Letting water flow wherever it belongs on the Water Planet is a key part of the wisdom of natural capitalism. For as Carol Franklin of the landscape architecture firm Andropogon puts it, water is not, as most civil engineers assume, mere gallons of H_2O, to be taken away as quickly as possible in large concrete pipes. Water is *habitat*. Water is life.

CHAPTER 12

Climate
Making Sense *and* Making Money

*A droplet of air — The atmospheric bathtub — Flapping molecules —
A tea-cozy for earth — What we can't model — Protecting climate at
a profit — In God we trust; all others bring data — More than efficiency — Why nuclear power can't help — If Karnataka can do it —
Almost everyone wins*

FROM SPACE, THE EARTH IS BLUE BECAUSE IT IS COVERED MAINLY BY WATER.
However, were it not for certain trace gases in the atmosphere, the earth
would be a frigid icy white, and life as we know it would not exist.

Our dependable local star radiates energy in all directions, a bit of
which[1] falls on our own planet. As it turns and wobbles and wanders
through an unimaginably chilly universe, the earth soaks in solar
warmth.[2] Billions of years of this cosmic rotisserie nurtured an enormous diversity of living forms and processes that, through photosynthesis and respiration, helped create an atmosphere. It is that band of
gases that keeps life as we know it pleasantly warm.

The earth's atmosphere seems vast to a person sheltered beneath it,
but astronauts and cosmonauts see how tissue-thin it is against the
black vastness of space. Conservationists Jacques Cousteau and David
Brower give us this helpful perspective: If the earth were the size of an
egg, then all the water on the planet would be just a drop; all the air, if
condensed to the density of water, would be a droplet only one-fortieth
as big; and all the arable land would be a not-quite-visible speck of
dust. That drop, droplet, and speck are all that make the earth different
from the moon.

Incoming solar energy, nearly a fifth of a quadrillion[3] watts, hits the
outer atmosphere at about 14,000 times the total rate at which all the
people on earth are burning fossil fuels.[4] This ratio makes the amount of
fossil fuels being consumed sound insignificant. In fact, though, this
burning turns roughly 6½ billion tons a year of carbon — carbon that

was fixed by photosynthesis in ancient swamps over tens of millions of years, then locked deep underground as coal, oil, and natural gas — into carbon dioxide.[5] Some advocates argue that even this quantity is insignificant compared to the far vaster amounts of carbon dioxide that are released as part of the natural cycle of life. Indeed, the constant exchange between the growth of green plants and their combustion, digestion, and decay does involve tens of times more annual flow of carbon dioxide than is released by fuel-burning. However, augmenting natural carbon cycles, even with relatively small amounts of fossil carbon, tends to increase disproportionately the amount of CO_2 in the atmosphere. An explanation for this phenomenon can be found in your bathroom.[6] If you fill your bathtub exactly as fast as the water runs down the drain, the flow of water in and out will be in equilibrium. But if you open the tap even a little more, your bathtub will ultimately overflow.

Because there is plenty of room for the CO_2 we're adding, there is no danger of its overflowing. But as it slowly accumulates, it is gradually double-glazing our home planet. Earth's atmosphere, not counting its water vapor, contains by volume about 78 percent nitrogen, 21 percent oxygen, 0.9 percent argon, and 0.039 percent other trace gases. Nitrogen, oxygen, and argon have no greenhouse effect; thus 99 percent of the atmosphere provides virtually no insulation. Of the atmosphere's main natural constituents, only water, carbon dioxide, and ozone have warming properties. These three warming gases share a common characteristic — they each have three atoms. All molecules absorb energy at the frequencies at which they naturally vibrate. Simple two-atom molecules like nitrogen and oxygen vibrate at high frequencies, like tight little springs, so they don't absorb much of the waste heat that leaves the earth as lower-frequency infrared energy. In contrast, CO_2, H_2O, and ozone (O_3) absorb heat rays especially well, because their three atoms create a triad configuration that can flap, shimmy, and shake at the right rate to absorb and re-radiate most of the infrared rays that the warm earth emits.[7] For the same reason, other three-atom pollutants like nitrous oxide (N_2O) and sulfur dioxide (SO_2) are strong greenhouse gases, too.[8]

Carbon dioxide makes up just 1-2,800[th] of the atmosphere. Together with the other trace gases, even that tiny amount makes the earth's surface[9] about 59F° warmer, so even a relatively small additional amount can raise the temperature of the planet significantly. Before the industrial revolution, trace gases (including carbon dioxide) totaled 0.028

percent of the atmosphere. Since then, burning fossil fuel, cutting and simplifying forests, plowing prairies, and other human activities have increased that CO_2 concentration to 0.036 percent, the highest level in the past 420,000 years, and the CO_2 concentration is steadily rising by half a percent per year, though the rate of emissions fell slightly in 1998.[10]

This concentration matters because energy from the white-hot sun is a mixture of roughly half visible light and half invisible infrared heat rays. If the atmosphere had no greenhouse gases, nearly all solar radiation striking the outer edge of the atmosphere would reach the earth's surface, and all of it would promptly escape back into space. That's what makes the airless moon so frigid: It absorbs solar energy four times better than the earth (partly because the moon has no clouds), but its surface averages 63F° colder because there is no atmosphere to hold the heat. In contrast, the earth's atmosphere, like a superwindow, is relatively transparent to most of the radiation coming in from the sun but is nearly opaque to the very long wavelengths of infrared rays that radiate back to space. The atmosphere holds that heat like a semi-transparent blanket. The resulting exchange of energy back and forth between the atmosphere and the earth is 47 percent larger than the solar energy arriving from the sun, which is why the earth's surface averages about 59°F rather than 0°F. It's also why life is possible. Those few hundredths of one percent of the atmosphere that are carbon dioxide play a critical role in this heat balance.

The warmed surface of the earth tries to radiate its heat back into space, just as a hot teapot radiates heat until it gradually cools to the temperature of the kitchen. Putting more carbon dioxide into the air is like putting a tea-cozy over the pot: It blocks the escaping heat. But this particular teapot is still on the stove, as more solar heat is added daily. The better the tea-cozy blocks the escaping heat, while the stove continues to add more heat at the same rate, the hotter the tea becomes. The atmosphere works in the same way. Suppose we add more heat-trapping CO_2 to the atmosphere. Then more of the outgoing infrared rays get absorbed and reradiated downward to warm the earth's surface. The air above the surface is also warmed, which enables it to hold more water vapor, which means even more greenhouse heat-trapping and possibly more clouds. Depending on their height, latitude, and other factors, those additional clouds may further warm the earth beneath them or may cool it by bouncing away more incoming sunlight. Either way, more water vapor in the air means more precipitation.[11] Hotter air makes the water cycle and the weather machine run faster, which leads to more intense storms and more rainfall. In round numbers, each Fahrenheit degree of global warming will increase global mean precipitation by about one percent, but some places will get much more.

Over the past century, as accumulating greenhouse gases have trapped two to three more watts of radiant heat over each average square meter of the earth, its surface has become about 1F° warmer.[12] Amazing the climatologists, in the single year 1998 — the hottest year since record-keeping began in 1860, and, according to indirect evidence, in the past millennium — the earth's average temperature soared by another quarter of a Fahrenheit degree, to about 1¼F° warmer than the 1961–90 average. *Each* of the 12 months through September 1998 set a new all-time monthly high-temperature record.[13] Seven of the ten hottest years in the past 130-odd years occurred in the 1990s — the rest after 1983 — despite such strong countervailing forces as the eruption of Mt. Pinatubo, a dip in solar energy, and the depletion of stratospheric ozone, a greenhouse gas. In 1998, at least 56 countries suffered severe floods, while 45 baked in droughts that saw normally unburnable tropical forests go up in smoke from Mexico to Malaysia and from the Amazon to Florida.[14] Many people's intuition that weather is shifting and becoming more volatile is confirmed by meteorological measurements. Spring in the Northern Hemisphere is coming a week earlier; the altitude at which the atmosphere chills to freezing is rising by nearly 15 feet a year; glaciers are retreating almost everywhere.[15]

Warming the surface of the earth changes every aspect of its climate, especially the heat-driven engine that continually moves vast seas of air and water like swirls in hot soup. Some places get hotter, others colder, some wetter, others drier. Rainfall patterns shift, but when it does rain, it tends to rain more heavily. A warmer earth probably also means more volatile weather with more and worse extreme events of all kinds. Nobody knows *exactly* how these changes will play out, especially in a particular locality, but some of the general trends are already apparent.

Warmer oceans, for example, can cause currents to shift and change, more frequent and severe tropical hurricanes and typhoons to form, and perhaps more frequent or more intense El Niño events to occur. Warmer oceans kill coral reefs (which when healthy metabolize and thus sequester CO_2). The warmed ocean can actually release more CO_2, just as happens when you open a soda warmed by the sun. This is important because oceans contain about 60 times as much CO_2 as the atmosphere does. Warmer soil, especially at high latitudes, speeds up plant decomposition, releasing more CO_2. It also means drier soil and hence shifts in vegetation. In any given ecosystem, more CO_2 increases growth of those plants that can best take up more CO_2, but at the competitive expense of other plants. This unpredictably changes the composition of plant populations, hence that of animal populations and soil biota. Different vegetation also alters the land's ability to absorb sunlight and to hold rainwater. This can affect erosion patterns under heavier rains. Parched forests, bad grazing practices, and late rains cause more forest and grassland fires, more carbon release, and more smoke, as happened in Southeast Asia and Australia in 1997–98.

As the planet traps more heat, it drives more convection that transports surplus heat from equatorial to the polar areas (heat flows from hotter to colder), so temperature changes tend to be larger at the poles than at midlatitudes. Warmer poles mean changes in snowfall, more melting icecaps and glaciers (five Antarctic ice sheets are already disintegrating),[16] and more exposed land and oceans. Ice-free oceans, being dark, absorb more solar heat and therefore don't refreeze as readily. Rising amounts of runoff from high-latitude rivers lower ocean salinity. This can shift currents, including the Gulf Stream, which makes northern Europe abnormally cozy for its Hudson's Bay latitude, and the Kuroshio Current, which likewise warms Japan.[17] Warmer oceans raise sea levels, as ice on land melts and warmer water expands; sea levels have risen by about four to ten inches in the past century. Warmer oceans probably bring more and worse storms, more loss of coastal wetlands that are the nurseries of the sea, and more coastal flooding. "Thirty of the world's largest cities," writes Eugene Linden, "lie near coasts; a one-meter rise in the oceans . . . would put an estimated 300 million people directly at risk."[18] That would include 16 percent of Bangladesh — a country that spent much of the summer of 1998 up to two-thirds underwater.

Now consider the contributions of the many other trace gases that also absorb infrared rays. Methane comes from swamps, coal seams, natural-gas leaks, bacteria in the guts of cattle and termites, and many other sources. Its concentration has risen since the eighteenth century from 700 to 1,720 parts per billion and is increasing at a rate of about one percent a year. Methane is a greenhouse gas 21 times more potent per molecule than CO_2. Nitrous oxide is over 100 times as potent as CO_2; CFCs (the same synthetic gases already being phased out because they also destroy stratospheric ozone), hundreds to thousands of times; their partly or completely fluorinated substitutes, hundreds to tens of thousands of times. Near-surface ozone and nitric oxide, familiar constituents of smog, absorb infrared, too. Together, all these gases have had a heat-trapping effect about three-fourths as significant as that of CO_2 alone.

Many trace gases can react chemically with others and with one another to make new gases. The resulting 30-odd substances can undergo more than 200 known reactions. These occur differently at different altitudes, latitudes, seasons, concentrations, and, of course, temperatures, which is what the very presence of the gases affects. How various gases dissolve in or react with the oceans also depends on temperatures, concentrations, and currents. Warmer oceans, for example, hold less nitrate, slowing the growth of carbon-absorbing phytoplankton. Also, if high-latitude tundras get much warmer, ice-like compounds called methane hydrates trapped deep beneath the permafrost and offshore in the Arctic could ultimately thaw and start releasing enormous amounts of methane — more than ten times what is now in the atmosphere. Long before that could happen, though, even slight changes in Arctic bogs' water levels can increase their methane production by 100-fold. Meanwhile, the mass of frigid air above the North Pole could get even colder and more persistent, favoring ozone-depleting chemical reactions that could destroy up to 65 percent of Arctic ozone — a deeper loss than has occurred in the Antarctic.[19]

The dance of heat between sun, sky, and earth is affected not only by transparent gases and clouds but also by dust from volcanoes, deserts, and the burning of fossil fuel. Most dust, like the clouds of sulfate particles that are also produced by fossil-fuel combustion, tends partly to offset CO_2's heat-trapping effect. So far, on a global basis the dust has approximately canceled the warming effect of additional non-CO_2 greenhouse gases.

The atmosphere, ocean, land, plant, and animal systems all interact in countless complicated ways, not all of which are yet known and many of which are not yet fully understood. Most of the interactions are nonlinear, and some appear to be unstable. Modern computer models are sophisticated enough to be able to model some historic shifts in climate quite well, but they're far from perfect, and getting them close to perfection will take longer than performing the global climate experiment already under way.[20] Many scientists suspect that relatively small changes in certain forces that drive the climate — notably CO_2 concentrations, especially if they happen fast enough — may trigger large and sudden changes in the world's weather, for example by shifting ocean currents. Such changes could even lead to the onset of ice ages in mere decades: They seem to have happened this abruptly before, and therefore must be possible, but such situations are difficult to model reliably.

A few scientists believe there might be a number of still unknown climate-stabilizing mechanisms at work. However, no important ones have yet been found, and all the promising candidates have been eliminated one by one. Instead, almost all the known climate feedback mechanisms appear to be positive — warmer begets warmer still. Many uncertainties remain, but uncertainty cuts both ways. The climate problem may be less serious than most scientists fear, or it could be even worse. Stratospheric ozone depletion turned out to be worse, once the unexpected "ozone hole" over the Antarctic was noticed and found to be growing rapidly. It required emergency action in the 1980s to phase out the proven culprit — CFCs and a few related compounds, such as Halon in fire extinguishers.

What's beyond doubt is that the composition of the atmosphere is now being altered by human activity, more rapidly than it's changed at any time in at least the past 10,000 years. The present state of knowledge suggests that, even if emission rates are reduced somewhat below their 1990 levels, we will still gradually reach about triple the preindustrial CO_2 concentration. If the world's nations wanted to stabilize the atmosphere in its present disrupted state, they would need to cut CO_2 emissions immediately by about three-fifths. To return to preindustrial levels, we'd have to reduce emission rates promptly to severalfold *below* current ones. Further research may disclose either bigger safety margins, allowing that ambitious goal to be relaxed, or smaller ones, requiring it to be tightened. For now, no one knows what might constitute a "safe" rate of, or limit to, changing the atmosphere's CO_2 concentration. What is clear is that the transformations now under way are part of a risky global experiment, and that their effects on the planet's life-support systems, whatever they turn out to be, may be irreversible.

A broad scientific consensus has already acknowledged the existence of a potentially serious climate problem.[21] About 99.9 percent of the world's qualified climate scientists agree that the infrared-absorbing gases that human activity is releasing into the air are cause for concern — if not now, then soon. Most believe that those emissions are probably already beginning to disrupt the earth's climate in observable ways. The many remaining scientific uncertainties create plenty of room for interpretation about exactly what might happen, how, and when, let alone its effects on people and other life-forms. All these issues are vigorously debated among thousands of climate scientists because that's how science works: From debate, observation, hypothesis, experiment, mistake, discovery, more debate, and reassessment ultimately emerges truth. The laypeople who don't like what the science is predicting, or who don't understand the scientific process, can easily seize on details of that debate and conclude that climate science is too immature and uncertain a discipline to support any broad conclusions yet. They'd be wrong.

However, the terms and outcome of the climate-science debate don't ultimately matter. Because of the resource productivity revolution, the actions and requirements needed to protect the climate are profitable for business right now, no matter how the science turns out and no matter who takes action first. Arguments that it would be too expensive and economically harmful to mitigate the rate of increase in greenhouse gases are upside down. It costs less to eliminate the threat to our global climate, not more.

REFRAMING THE CLIMATE DEBATE

On May 19, 1997, John Browne, the chief executive of British Petroleum — then the world's third-largest, now its second-largest, oil company — announced at Stanford University: "[T]here is now an effective consensus among the world's leading scientists and serious and well informed people outside the scientific community that there is a discernible human influence on the climate, and a link between the concentration of carbon dioxide and the increase in temperature." He continued: "[W]e must now focus on what can and what should be done, not because we can be certain climate change is happening, but because the possibility can't be ignored."[22] Obviously, "what should be done" is mainly to stop raising and start lowering the rate of burning of fossil fuels, the source of 84 percent of America's and 75 percent of the world's energy.[23] Mr. (now Sir John) Browne went on to announce that BP had increased its investments in solar technology, which it expects to grow markedly in the decades to come. His lead on both the climate issue and energy alternatives has since been followed by several other oil companies.

Three months earlier, eight Nobel laureates had led some twenty-seven hundred fellow economists in declaring what all mainstream studies have found: Market-oriented policies to protect the climate by saving energy can raise American living standards and even benefit the economy.[24] They were largely ignored. Instead, a coal-led industrial lobby, the Global Climate Coalition, saturated the airwaves with ads that scared almost the entire press corps and the U.S. Senate into *presuming* that protecting the climate would be prohibitively costly. The prospect of having to reduce carbon emissions has subsequently aroused dismay, foreboding, and resistance among many in the business community, who fear it would hurt earnings and growth.

As economic columnist Robert J. Samuelson asserted in *Newsweek*: "It would be political suicide to do anything serious about [climate]. . . . So shrewd politicians are learning to dance around the dilemma."[25] In Samuelson's widely held view, carbon emissions would probably be cut only if companies were levied with a tax of roughly one hundred dollars for each metric ton of carbon they emitted. Even then, he warns, such a burdensome tax might only reduce 2010 emissions back to 1990 levels. Thus, "Without a breakthrough in alternative energy — nuclear, solar, something — no one knows how to lower emissions adequately without crushing the world economy." Congress, wrote Samuelson, "won't impose pain on voters for no obvious gain to solve a hypothetical problem. And if the United States won't, neither will anyone else."

Samuelson, like many businesspeople, believes climate protection is costly because the best-publicized (though not most broadly accepted) economic computer models say it is. Few people realize, however, that those models find carbon abatement to be costly *because that's what they assume.* This assumption masquerading as a fact has been so widely used as the input for supposedly authoritative models, which have duly disgorged it as their output, that it's often deemed infallible.

What is less well publicized is that other economic models derive the opposite answer from more realistic assumptions (including what international treaties and U.S. policy actually say), rather than from worst-case hypothetical conditions. Better yet, an enormous body of overlooked empirical data, including government-sponsored studies[26] and the results of worldwide business practice, tells an excitingly different story, one more positive than *any* of the theoretical models predict. As previous chapters have described, the technological breakthroughs that Samuelson seeks have already happened. America could shed $300 billion a year from its energy bills using existing technologies that deliver the same or better services and are rewarding at today's prices. The earth's climate can thus be protected *not at a cost but at a profit* — just as many industries are already turning the costs of environmental compliance into gains from pollution prevention.

America is confronted, as Winston Churchill said, by insurmountable opportunities. Because there are practical ways to mitigate climatic concerns *and* save more money than such measures cost, it almost doesn't matter whether you believe that climate change is a problem or not: These steps should be taken simply because they make money. Together, the following opportunities can turn climate change into an unnecessary artifact of the uneconomically wasteful use of resources:[27]

· Well over half of the threat to climate comes from the CO_2 released by burning fossil fuels. It disappears if customers use energy as efficiently as is cost-effective. Alternatively, much of this part of the threat disappears if low-carbon fuels (natural gas) or no-fossil-carbon fuels (biomass or other renewables) are substituted for more carbon-intensive fossil fuels (coal and oil) and if fossil fuels are converted more efficiently into electricity. These complementary approaches are all profitable in most circumstances. In general, it's cheaper to save fuel than to buy it, no matter what kind it is. Moreover, even inefficiently used low-carbon and some no-carbon fuels are increasingly competitive with oil and coal.

· Another one-fourth or so of the climatic threat is the result of carbon dioxide and other trace gases that are embodied in soil, trees, and other biological capital and put into the air through soil erosion, logging, and poor grazing, farming, or ranching practices. This problem can be addressed by adopting farming and forestry practices that do not release carbon from the soil, but take carbon out of the air and put it back where it belongs. Most soil-conserving and -building practices simultaneously decrease other greenhouse gas emissions, notably of methane and nitrous oxide from biological sources. These superior practices are generally at least as economical as soil-depleting, chemical-dependent methods,[28] making all their climatic benefits at least an economic break-even.

· The rest of the climatic threat nearly vanishes if CFCs are replaced with the new substitutes that are already required by a ratified and functioning global agreement, the 1988 Montreal Treaty, in order to protect the stratospheric ozone layer on which all life depends. Thanks to industrial innovation, these substitutes, including some with little or no greenhouse effect, now work the same as or better than their predecessors and typically cost about the same or less. Similar opportunities exist for the whole range of non-CO_2 heat-trapping synthetic gases.[29]

In December 1997, the world's national governments met in Kyoto, Japan, to negotiate a treaty to start dealing seriously with climate change. Its details, which will be elaborated and probably strengthened in the coming years, create a framework in which reduced emissions of any significant greenhouse gas — carbon dioxide, methane, nitrous oxide, and three kinds of fluorinated gases — can be traded between companies and between countries under agreed national emissions caps. The U.S. target is to reduce its net emissions in 2010 to 7 percent below 1990 levels. Countries that want to emit more than their quota will be able to buy permits at a market price from those that are emitting less. As with any market, trading will mean the least expensive ways of abating carbon will tend to be purchased first. It means you can undertake initiatives such as increasing energy efficiency or reforestation, and get paid extra for them by selling their carbon reductions to a broker. Improved farming, ranching, and forest practices emitting less CO_2, nitrous oxide, and methane will also earn credits under Kyoto trading rules. Thus, such carbon "sinks" as adding trees and building topsoil can produce a steady additional income, invigorating ecological restoration. The sequestration of CO_2 by injecting it into secure underground reservoirs will also become a business opportunity.

The menu of climate-protecting opportunities is so large that over time, they can overtake and even surpass the pace of economic growth.[30] Over the next half-century, even if the global economy expanded by 6- to 8-fold, the rate of releasing carbon by burning fossil fuel could simultaneously decrease by anywhere from one-third to nine-tenths below the current rate.[31] This is because of the multiplicative effect of four kinds of actions. Switching to natural gas and renewable energy, as fast as Royal Dutch/Shell planners consider likely, would cut by one-half to three-quarters the fossil-fuel carbon in each unit of primary energy consumed. The efficiency of converting that energy into delivered forms, notably electricity, could meanwhile rise by at least half, thanks to modern power plants and recapturing waste heat. The efficiency of converting delivered energy into desired services would also increase by about 4- to 6-fold if improvements simply continued at rates that have been historically sustained, in the United States and abroad, when people were paying attention.[32] Finally, the amount of satisfaction derived from each unit of energy service might remain unchanged, or might perhaps be doubled by delivering higher-quality services and fewer unwanted ones. All four of these steady, long-term improvements are profitable and already under way. Together, and combined with ways to abate or store other greenhouse gases, they will make it feasible to achieve not merely the modest interim targets set at Kyoto, but also the far greater ones needed to stabilize the earth's climate.

IN GOD WE TRUST; ALL OTHERS BRING DATA

The common assumption of diminishing returns — more efficient means costlier, cheap savings will quickly be exhausted, and efficiency is a dwindling rather than an expanding resource — stalls action. Yet actual experience is a strong antidote.

In 1981, Dow Chemical's 2,400-worker Louisiana division started prospecting for overlooked savings. Engineer Ken Nelson[33] set up a shop-floor-level contest for energy-saving proposals, which had to provide at least a 50 percent annual return on investment (ROI). The first year's 27 projects averaged 173 percent ROI. Nelson was startled, and supposed this bounty must be a fluke. The following year, however, 32 projects averaged 340 percent ROI. Twelve years and almost 900 implemented projects later, the workers had averaged (in the 575 projects subjected to audit) 204 percent ROI. In later years, the returns and the savings were both getting *larger* — in the last three years, the average payback fell from six months to only four months — because the engineers were learning faster than they were exhausting the cheapest opportunities. By 1993, the whole suite of projects taken together was paying Dow's shareholders $110 million every year.

Almost everyone responsible for buying new equipment *assumes* that more energy-efficiency models will cost more. In fact, careful scrutiny of actual market prices reveals that even at the component level, many technical devices — motors, valves, pumps, rooftop chillers, et cetera — show no correlation whatever between efficiency and price.[34] A 100-hp American motor, for example, can be cheaper at 95.8 percent efficiency than an otherwise identical 91.7 percent-efficient model.[35]

But if you didn't know that to be true — if you assumed, as economic theory and engineering handbooks predict, that more efficient models always cost more — then you probably wouldn't have shopped for a more efficient model. It is easy to calculate the cost of not getting just one more efficient motor. If it's to run continuously, using electricity that costs 5 cents a kilowatt-hour, just multiply its percentage points of potential efficiency gain by its horsepower rating. Multiply the result by $50. That will give you roughly how many dollars you just failed to add to your company's bottom line (over the long term, but expressed as a lump sum worth the same today, called the "present value"). In this example, not choosing the most efficient 100-hp motor can cost a company $20,000. Many factories contain hundreds of such motors. They're the tip of a gigantic iceberg. Motors use three-fourths of industry's electricity, and slightly more U.S. primary energy than highway vehicles. This consumption is highly concentrated: About half of all motor electricity is needed by the million largest motors, and three-fourths by the 3 million largest. Since big motors use their own capital cost's worth of electricity every few *weeks*, switching to more efficient models can pay back quickly. Adding another 30-odd improvements to make the whole motor *system* optimally efficient typically saves about half its energy with about a 190 percent annual after-tax return on investment.[36]

Whether at the level of a single component or an entire factory, previous chapters documented an unexpectedly large potential to increase energy efficiency in almost every application. Profitable and demonstrated Factor Four, Factor Ten, or greater improvements were described for commercial and residential buildings and equipment, lighting, heating, cooling, pumping, and ventilation. Carbon-saving opportunities were large in industries ranging[37] from microchips to potato chips, refineries to foundries — all further amplified by dramatic reductions in materials flows to deliver the same services. Such opportunities for *using* delivered energy more productively can also be compounded by *supplying* that energy in lower-carbon and more efficient ways[38] — a combination that in microchip fabrication could profitably cut CO_2 per chip by about 99 percent.[39] Across the whole economy, two supply-side improvements alone could about meet America's Kyoto targets:

· America's power stations turn fuel, mostly coal, into an average of 34 percent electricity and 66 percent waste heat, throwing away an amount of heat equal to the total energy use of Japan, the world's second-largest economy. In contrast, Denmark, which gets two-fifths of its electricity from "cogeneration" plants that recover and use the heat as well (and projects this fraction will increase to three-fifths by 2005), converts 61 percent of its power-plant fuel into useful work. The American firm Trigen does even better: Its small, off-the-shelf turbines produce electricity, then reuse their waste heat to provide other services. Such a system now powers, heats, and cools much of downtown Tulsa, Oklahoma. Such "trigeneration" can increase system efficiency by about 2.8-fold. It harnesses 90–91 percent of the fuel's energy content, and hence provides very cheap electricity (half a cent to two cents per kilowatt-hour). Fully adopting just this one innovation wherever feasible would reduce America's *total* CO_2 emissions by about 23 percent.[40]

· However industrial processes are fueled and powered, reselling their waste heat to other users within affordable distances[41] could cost-effectively save up to about 30 percent of U.S. industrial energy or 11 percent of America's total energy.

WHAT IF EFFICIENCY ISN'T ENOUGH?

Such firms as British Petroleum, Shell, and Enron are investing heavily in renewable sources of energy, for good reason.[42] As London's Delphi Group has advised its institutional-investor clients, alternative energy industries not only help "offset the risks of climate change" but also offer "greater growth prospects than the carbon fuel industry."[43] Group Planning at Royal Dutch/Shell considers it "highly probable" that over the next half century, renewables could become so competitive a commodity that they'd grow to supply at least half the world's energy.[44] Even today, renewable energy is Europe's fastest-growing source,[45] and California gets 9 percent of its electricity from renewable sources other than hydroelectricity.[46] The world's fastest-growing energy technologies, outpacing even energy savings, are windpower, increasing by about 26 percent a year,[47] and photovoltaics (solar cells), whose annual growth has lately ranged from 23 to 42 percent as manufacturers struggle to keep pace with strong demand.

These and similar private-sector conclusions are echoed by the two most thorough assessments conducted by the United States, or probably any other, government. In 1990 five U.S. National Laboratories reported that either fair competition plus restored research priority, or a proper accounting of its environmental benefits, could enable renewable energy to supply three-fifths of today's total U.S. energy requirements at competitive prices. Renewables could even supply one-fifth *more* electricity than the United States now uses.[48] In 1997, the labs further sharpened these conclusions.[49]

Sunlight is most abundant where the majority of the world's poorest people live. Numerous scientific studies have shown that in every part of the globe between the polar circles, this freely distributed renewable energy, if efficiently used, is adequate to support a good life continuously, indefinitely, and economically using present technologies.[50] The potential of solar photovoltaic power, once considered visionary, is starting to be validated in the marketplace. The cost of solar cells has fallen by 95 percent since the 1970s and is expected to fall by a further 75 percent in the next decade through straightforward scaling up of established production technologies. Bostonians can now buy electricity from Sun Power Electric, an entirely photovoltaic utility. Auctions to supply the Sacramento Municipal Utility District have yielded contracts to cut the delivered price of solar electricity to 9–11 cents per kilowatt-hour (1999 $) — competitive with conventional retail residential electricity.[51] If one counts some of the dozens of kinds of "distributed benefits," those cells are cost-effective right now in many uses.[52] The Sacramento electric utility even found it cheaper to hook alley lights to solar cells than to the existing wires. Most electric utilities could cut their carbon emissions by as much as 97 percent by adding solar cells and other advanced renewables, with comparable reliability and essentially unchanged cost.[53]

Meanwhile, doubled-efficiency combined-cycle gas turbines, with half the cost and only one-fourth the carbon intensity of coal-fired power plants,[54] have quietly seized most of the electric utility market for new power stations. Closing fast on the outside, the new dark horse in this area is the low-temperature polymer fuel cell being developed also for Hypercars. Fuel cells are at least as efficient but are silent, clean, reliable, scaleable to virtually any size desired, and ultimately capable of costs five to ten times below those of combined-cycle gas turbines.[55]

In contrast, the energy technologies that are the product of socialized costs and central planning have not fared well. The world's slowest-growing energy source is nuclear power — under 1 percent in 1996, with no prospect of improvement.[56] Its global capacity in 2000 will be a tenth, and orders for new plants are now a hundredth, of the lowest official forecasts made a quarter century ago. America's civilian nuclear technology cost a total of a trillion federal dollars yet delivers less energy than wood. It is dying of an incurable attack of market forces: *The Economist* says of nuclear power plants that "not one, anywhere in the world, makes commercial sense."[57] The only question is whether at least a third of U.S. nuclear plants will retire early. Many have already done so (operable units have been declining since 1990, with twenty-eight closed by the end of 1998), because their operating and repair bills make them uncompetitive to run. Worldwide, 90-odd nuclear plants have already retired after serving fewer than seventeen years. Even in France, the world's acknowledged leader in nuclear dependency, nuclear expansion has been outpaced two to one by unheralded, unnoticed, unsupported, but more cost-effective energy efficiency.

The collapse of nuclear power — once the great hope for displacing coal-burning — might at first appear to be a setback for climate protection. Actually it's good news. Since nuclear power is the costliest way to replace fossil fuels, every dollar spent on it displaces less climatic risk than would have been avoided if that same dollar were spent instead on techniques to use energy more efficiently, because those methods cost far less than nuclear power.[58] For example, if a kilowatt-hour of nuclear electricity cost six cents (optimistically low), while saving a kilowatt-hour through efficiency cost two cents (pessimistically high), then the six cents spent to buy a single nuclear kilowatt-hour could instead have bought three kilowatt-hours of savings, displacing three times as much coal-burning. This opportunity cost is why investing in nuclear power does not address climatic threats effectively but on the contrary retards their abatement.

FROM THE FIRM TO THE NATION

Whole countries, especially heavily industrialized ones, can attain big energy savings and climatically benign energy supplies simply by adding up many small individual achievements. During the years 1979–86, in the wake of the second oil shock, America obtained nearly five times as much new energy from savings as from all net expansions of supply. In those years the country got 14 percent more energy from sun, wind, water, and wood and 10 percent less from oil, gas, coal, and uranium. The economy grew 19 percent, but total energy use shrank 6 percent. By 1986, CO_2 emissions were one-third lower and annual energy costs were about $150 billion lower than they would have been at 1973 efficiency levels. Sustaining that pace today would by itself meet America's Kyoto target on time and at a profit; additional opportunities could achieve manyfold more.

All that impressive progress in the 1980s was only a first step toward what was possible from thoroughly applying cost-effective efficiency measures. In 1989 the Swedish State Power Board, Vattenfall, published — without, by order of its CEO, the usual disclaimer saying it didn't represent official policy — a thorough and conservative technical study of Sweden's further potential to save electricity and heat (which Sweden often cogenerates).[59] The study found that if the country fully used only mid-1980s energy efficiency technologies, it could save half of its electricity, at an average cost 78 percent lower than that of making more. Adopting that strategy plus switching to less carbon-intensive fuels and relying most on the least carbon-intensive power stations could enable Sweden simultaneously to

- achieve the forecast 54 percent GDP growth during the years 1987–2010,
- complete the voter-mandated phaseout of the nuclear half of the nation's power supply,
- reduce the utilities' carbon releases by one-third, and
- reduce the private internal cost of electrical services by nearly $1 billion per year

If this is possible in a country that is full of energy-intensive heavy industry, cold, cloudy, very far north, and among the most energy-efficient in the world to start with, then nations not so handicapped can obviously make even more impressive advances. Indeed, a year later, a study for the Indian state of Karnataka found that simple efficiency improvements, small hydroelectric plants, cogeneration of electrical power from sugarcane waste, methane gas generated from other wastes, a small amount of natural gas, and solar water heaters would achieve far greater and earlier development progress than would the fossil-fueled plan of the state utility. The alternatives would require two-fifths less electricity, cost two-thirds less money, and produce 95 percent less fossil-fuel CO_2.[60] These Indian and Swedish analyses studied two dramatically different types of societies, technologies, climates, wealth, and income distribution. Yet they both found that efficiency combined with renewable energy could meet each country's energy needs with greater savings and lower carbon emissions. Similar findings have emerged worldwide.[61]

The Karnataka study exposes the error made by critics of climate protection when they point to the growing world population, many of its members desperately poor, and argue that these people must use far more energy to attain a decent standard of living. In this view, climate change is a problem of industrial countries, and reducing developing countries' carbon emissions would inequitably cripple economic growth. In fact, the only way developing countries will be able to afford to increase their living standards is to avoid the wasteful practices of the industrialized nations. Investing now in greatly increased energy efficiency offers even greater advantages in the South than in the North, and meets an even more urgent developmental need, because the South, on average, is three times less energy-efficient to begin with, yet is far less able to afford such inefficiency. That's why key developing countries, including China, have been quietly saving carbon about twice as fast in percentage terms as the Western developed countries have committed to do, and possibly faster than the West even in absolute terms.[62]

Among the strongest economic advantages of focusing on energy productivity instead of energy production is that building, for example, superwindow and efficient-lamp factories instead of power stations and transmission lines requires about a thousandfold less capital per unit of extra comfort or light, yet these businesses are considerably more labor-intensive.[63] Such demand-side investments also pay back their cost about ten times as fast for reinvestment, reducing the effective capital needs by closer to ten thousandfold. This best-buys-first strategy can liberate for other development needs the one-fourth of global development capital now consumed by the power sector.[64] An important way to support this outcome would be for industrialized countries to stop the "negative technology transfer" of exporting obsolete equipment to developing countries. Denmark has recently led in this respect by banning the export of technologies (such as a coal-fired plant to India) that it would not consider economically and environmentally sound to use on its own territory. Companies and countries should do as some smart American utilities already do: Buy up obsolete appliances and scrap them, because they're worth far more dead than alive. Extending this euthanasia to inefficient old industrial equipment would be a major step for global development.[65]

What of America's own progress toward a sound long-term energy future? The graph on page 252 shows how the half-century transition along a "soft energy path" outlined in 1976 is already well under way. At

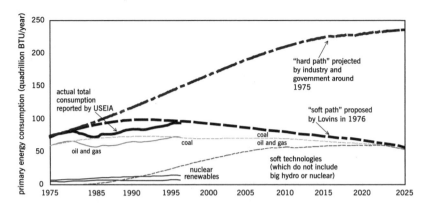

TWO ALTERNATIVES FOR U.S. ENERGY FUTURES AND PROGRESS SO FAR

the time, the energy industries heavily criticized the heretical suggestion[66] that rather than following official forecasts of rapid energy growth for inefficient use (top curve), the United States could stabilize and then reduce its energy consumption by wringing out losses in converting, distributing, and using it (next curve down). Meanwhile, efficiently used fossil fuels would bridge to appropriate renewable sources — "soft technologies" — that would gradually take over. That's roughly what happened. The actual total of U.S. energy use (third line down) is now virtually identical to this "soft-path" trajectory: with energy efficiency, as with water efficiency, the savings are being realized pretty much on schedule. However, the potential for efficient use of energy is now far greater than anyone imagined in 1976 or even in 1996. Despite falling energy prices and often hostile government policy, renewable energy has also made great strides. Balancing its delay against today's even brighter prospects for the next quarter-century, the natural-capitalist energy goals envisaged in this 1976 graph — a prosperous economy fueled by efficiently used, benign, and restorative energy sources — now seems more achievable and advantageous than ever.

ENERGY PRICES, NATIONAL COMPETITIVENESS, AND THE MARKETPLACE

Companies now dump carbon into the air without paying for it (except in their fuel bills). Even if they did have to pay, and even if not all countries had to pay, neither Americans nor anyone else need fear losing the

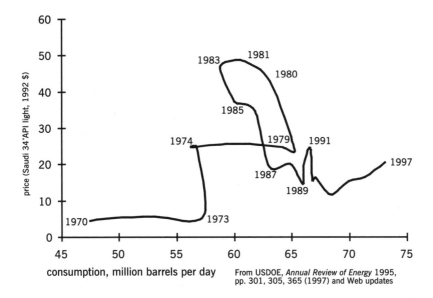

From USDOE, *Annual Review of Energy* 1995,
pp. 301, 305, 365 (1997) and Web updates

WORLD CRUDE-OIL CONSUMPTION VS. REAL PRICE, 1970–1997

ability to compete in global markets, for three main reasons: The price difference would be small, would be offset by efficiency gains it would stimulate, and wouldn't impel firms to relocate.[67]

Moreover, the basic premise is mistaken: Protecting the climate doesn't require higher energy prices in the first place. Sharp price hikes do get everyone's attention and have driven major shifts in the energy system since 1970. The graph above shows the almost textbook-perfect relationship worldwide between the price of oil and the consumption of oil. The first price shock in 1973 cut the rate of growth in consumption by 58 percent; the second in 1979 caused consumption to shrink, creating so much excess supply that prices went back down, whereupon consumption resumed its upward drift.

Between about 1975 and 1985, most new U.S. energy-using devices — cars, buildings, refrigerators, lighting systems, et cetera — *doubled* their efficiency. Many utilities became very skilled at delivering efficiency to their customers.[68] Their success fueled 35 percent economic growth with essentially zero energy growth during the years 1973–86. But then the resulting 1986 energy price crash dampened further savings,[69] virtually stagnating U.S. energy efficiency for the next decade. It was as if the price signal were the spigot that turned efficiency gains first on and then off. Seeing such evidence, it's easy to assume that the only way to return to rapid energy savings is to return also to costly energy.[70] Yet price, while helpful, isn't the only tool available: Energy efficiency can be improved very rapidly by raising prices, or paying attention, or both. Alert companies can pay attention without being hit over the head by a price signal. Even with cheap energy, efficiency gains can regain their former momentum through today's better technologies, smarter delivery methods,[71] and keener competitive and environmental pressures.

The importance of influences other than price is proven by the experience of two American metropolises.[72] From 1990 through 1996, Seattle City Light, which delivers the cheapest power of any major U.S. city, helped its customers save electricity via a variety of incentives and educational tools. Those customers' smarter choices reduced their need for electricity at peak load periods nearly twelve times faster than people in Chicago achieved, and reduced annual electric usage more than 3,600 times as fast as in Chicago, even though Seattle's electricity prices are about half of Chicago's. This behavior is the opposite of what conventional economists would have predicted from relative prices. But it proves that creating an informed, effective, and efficient market in energy-saving devices and practices can be an even more powerful stimulus than a bare price signal. That is, *price is less important than ability to respond to it.* (The reverse is also true: Higher energy prices do not automatically yield major energy savings, even after long adjustment times. That's why identical electricity-using devices and practices prevail in different cities that pay severalfold different electricity prices, and why DuPont found identical efficiency potential in its U.S. and European plants in the 1990s despite long-standing energy prices that are twice as high in Europe.)[73]

By now, most readers are probably wondering why, if such big energy savings are both feasible and profitable, they haven't all been exploited. The simple and correct answer is that the free market, effective though it is, is burdened by many subtle imperfections that inhibit the efficient allocation and use of resources. The following chapter details scores of specific obstacles to using energy in a way that saves money. But it also specifies the sensible "barrier-busting" public policies and corporate practices that can turn those obstacles into business opportunities. Mindful of this need to make markets work properly, national climate policy already emphasizes the need "to tear down barriers to successful markets and . . . create incentives to enter them" so that "protecting the climate will yield not costs, but profits; not burdens, but benefits; not sacrifice, but a higher standard of living."[74] As George David, chairman of United Technologies, put it, "we can be efficient, much, much more efficient in both our energy production and . . . the operation of equipment consuming that energy. . . . Greenhouse gases are a problem, and it's time for the usual and effective American solution"[75] — intelligent use of highly productive technologies.

ALMOST EVERYONE WINS

Using energy far more efficiently does mean that less fossil fuel would be sold than if we continued to consume it at current rates. Lower physical volumes sold do not necessarily mean lower sales for fuel vendors, but most vendors do fear that they would make less money than expected if demand grew more slowly, or stabilized, or even declined — as it would have done eventually from depletion. Where is it written, however, that coal companies or OPEC countries have an inalienable right to sell ever larger quantities of their product — or, as their apologists and OPEC itself now urge, to be compensated for lost profits if their hoped-for growth in demand slackens or reverses?

The United States has never been good at helping workers or industries in transition, and now might be a good time to improve that record with regard to prospective climate-induced shifts in policy. A failure to help coal miners, depressed communities, and even disappointed shareholders would encourage them to oppose measures that benefit society as a whole. But those measures should generate sufficient revenues to enable society, if it chooses, to afford to ease their difficulties.[76] Actually, climate policies threaten miners' jobs much less than do the coal companies, which during the years 1980–94 eliminated 55 percent of their miners' jobs, while coal output rose 25 percent. The companies continue reductions at a rate that, with no climate policy even in place, has eliminated more than nine thousand mining jobs per year.

Sound public policies can and do readily cope with much larger job losses than that.[77] As Professor Steven DeCanio, senior staff economist for President Reagan's Council of Economic Advisers, notes:

> . . . [T]he U.S. economy creates about one and a half to two million net new jobs per year, and the gross number of jobs created and destroyed through the normal process of economic change is larger. . . . If the rate of job decline in coal were to double[,] it would still be less than 1.5 percent of the normal

annual rate of total net job creation. Without minimizing the hardships of adjustments to displaced coal workers, this sort of incremental change in the sectoral distribution of jobs would not be difficult for the economy to absorb, and it would be sensible to include transitional support for displaced workers (such as retraining expenses) as an integral part of any national greenhouse-gas reduction policy. . . .

Instead of a threat to jobs, reducing the economy's dependence on fossil fuels can be seen as an investment and job-creation *opportunity*, because of the new equipment and technologies that will be required. The conversion can be accomplished without any net loss of jobs; the role of policy is to minimize transition costs and to ensure that any such costs do not fall disproportionately on narrow segments of the population such as coal industry employees.[78]

As for the shareholders, hard-nosed free-marketeers might argue that they should have foreseen climate would become an issue (some of us have been saying so since 1968), so they should have invested earlier in natural gas, efficiency, or renewables instead of coal, or in gas pipelines instead of coal-hauling railways. If efficient energy use costs less than coal, then coal will lose in fair competition, and no proponent of a thriving economy should wish otherwise.

But the best outcome, especially for the workers, would be to encourage the companies at risk in the transition to start selling a more profitable mixture of less fuel *and* more efficiency in using it. A few oil companies and hundreds of electric and gas utilities are already successfully doing so to improve both customer service and their own earnings. It is this logic that has also led the likes of ABB, BP, DuPont, Ford, Norsk Hydro, Shell, Tokyo Electric, and Toyota to fund both internal and consortium research into how to protect the climate while advancing their own business interests.[79]

PROTECTING THE CLIMATE FOR FUN AND PROFIT

A proper understanding of the practical engineering economics of energy efficiency, and of other climate-stabilizing opportunities, can thus give nearly all the parties to the climate debate what they want. Those who worry about climate can see the threats to it ameliorated. Those who don't can still make money. Those who worry about the costs and burdens of redesigning their businesses will see those investments rewarded. Those who want improved jobs, competitiveness, quality of life, public and environmental health, and individual choice and liberty can get those things, too. By emphasizing energy efficiency, and climate-protecting grazing, farming, and forestry practices based on natural systems, we can responsibly and profitably address not only climate but about 90 percent of EPA's pollution and public-health concerns — smog and particulate emissions, toxic emissions, runoff from agrichemicals, and many more. These actions are vital to a vigorous economy, national security,[80] a healthful environment, sustainable development, social justice, and a livable world.

Pragmatists suggest that we have at hand — and should elevate to the central role in climate policy — the market-transformation tools that can turn climate into a business opportunity, at home and abroad. These can, but need not, include raising energy prices. (In fact, both the Kyoto Protocol and the Clinton administration's climate policy *exclude* the carbon taxes that critics of both plans have been attacking.) Innovative, market-oriented public policies, especially at a state and local level, can focus chiefly on barrier-busting — the alchemy of turning implementation obstacles into business opportunities — to help markets work properly and reward the economically efficient use of fuel.[81] This strategy would require much *less* intervention in the market than is now mandated by regulatory rules and standards. It properly assumes that the role of government is to steer, not row, and that market actors guided by clear and simple rules can best figure out what will make sense and make money. (Two millennia ago, Lao-tzu rightly counseled: "Govern a great country as you would fry a small fish: Don't poke at it too much.") But we need to steer in the right direction — the line of least resistance and least cost — guided by a detailed and precise map that charts the barriers now blocking energy efficiency. The next chapter begins to draw that map.

A bizarre irony lurks beneath the climate debate. Why do the same people who favor competitive markets in other contexts seem to have the least faith in their efficacy for saving fossil fuels? Recall what happened the last time such a gloom-and-doom attitude prevailed. In 1990, just before Congress approved the trading system for reducing sulfur-dioxide emissions[82] — the model for the international trading framework adopted in the Kyoto climate treaty seven years later — environmentalists predicted that sulfur reductions would cost about $350 a ton, or ultimately, said the optimists, perhaps $250. Government economic models predicted $500–750; the higher figure was the most widely cited. Industry models upped the ante to $1,000–1,500 or more. The sulfur-allowance market opened in 1992 at about $250 a ton; in 1995, it cleared at $130 a ton; in 1996, it fell to $66; by 1999, it had been bid back up to $207. National sulfur emissions have fallen 37 percent in just the past decade despite an unprecedented economic boom.

In short, Congress's fierce 1990 debates about where to set the target for sulfur reductions are long forgotten, because modelers can't reliably plan how economies work. What mattered is that Congress set up an efficient trading mechanism to reward sulfur reductions and to reward early achievers. As a result, the United States is now two-fifths ahead of its sulfur target, *at a small fraction of the projected cost.* Electric rates, which industry feared would soar, have instead fallen by one-eighth and show every sign of continuing to fall indefinitely. Much the same is happening with CFCs, whose replacement was predicted to wreck the economy. The targeted CFC cuts have actually been surpassed in every year, with no significant cheating, at roughly zero net cost.[83]

The genius of private enterprise and advanced technologies reduced sulfur and CFC emissions billions of dollars more cheaply than by using government regulation. It can do so again, now that the Kyoto Conference has adopted the principle of encouraging international competition to save the most carbon at the lowest cost. The Kyoto Protocol sent a strategic message to business: Pay attention to carbon reductions and they can improve the bottom line. In boardrooms around the world, savvy executives are already planning: If we're going to have carbon trading, how can our company benefit?[84] America's largest producer of chemicals, DuPont, has already answered that question. While the United States was reluctantly agreeing in Kyoto to cut its annual greenhouse-gas emissions to 7 percent below their 1990 level by around 2010, DuPont's technologists were planning how their firm, as it recently announced, will cut its own emissions to "much less than half" of their 1991 level by 2000. These reductions lead to direct savings — each ton of avoided carbon (or equivalent) emissions has so far saved DuPont over $6 in net costs — but better yet, under the Kyoto trading regime, DuPont could become able to earn marketable emissions credits that could someday contribute billions to its net earnings.[85] Moreover, many firms in related businesses are exploring a further business opportunity unrelated to either cutting energy costs or trading emissions: gaining market share by marketing "climate-safe" products,[86] as some electricity providers are already successfully doing.[87]

There are strong reasons to predict that the framework adopted in Kyoto in 1997 for trading carbon reductions will work even better than the one adopted by Congress in 1990 for trading sulfur reductions. First, carbon trading will rely mainly on how efficiently many end users employ their resources. Buying and selling sulfur permits was set up as a business for utilities, and opportunities for energy efficiency to compete with top-of-smokestack sulfur reductions were limited. With carbon trading, however, factories, cities, farms, ranchers, foresters, and myriad other users and savers of carbon will be allowed to participate. Further, saving carbon, unlike saving sulfur, is intrinsically profitable, because saving fuel costs less than buying fuel.

The hypothesis that saving carbon will prove cheaper than saving sulfur (or indeed will cost less than zero because of savings on fuel bills) is empirical and testable. The test has already begun. By the end of 1998, a dozen private market-makers were already trading carbon reductions and sequestrations. Undaunted by diplomats' wrangling over the details of international trading rules, the traders simply did what traders do: They made their own rules in rough-and-ready ways adequate to protect their own financial interests. So how long did top traders think it would take before they'd learned enough from actual market transactions to foresee the actual cost of meeting the Kyoto Protocol's goals? Around twelve to eighteen months.[88] Thus well before the climate negotiators and politicians have decided how to implement carbon trading, the marketplace is likely to have leapfrogged over the negotiations and set an actual price. This will expose the gloomy theoretical economic models — which underlie so much of the political friction over climate protection — to what may prove a withering market test.

In just the past fifty years, the world's annual carbon emissions have quadrupled. But in the next half century, the climate problem could become as faded a memory as the energy crises of the seventies are now, because climate change is not an inevitable result of normal economic activity but an artifact of carrying out that activity in irrationally inefficient ways. Climate protection can save us all money — even coal miners, who deserve the just transition that the nation's energy savings could finance a hundred times over.

If we vault the barriers, use energy in a way that saves money, and put enterprise where it belongs, in the vanguard of sound solutions, climate change will become a problem we can't afford, don't need, and can avoid with huge financial savings to society.

CHAPTER 13

Making Markets Work

Ceaseless market vigilance — How cheap a future — The myth of free markets — Skewed markets mean lost capital — Fiddling with the switches — An ordered arrangement of wastebaskets — "Satisficing" — When regulation fails — Golden carrots — Plain vanilla motors — Making a market in nega-resources — Alternative annual report

CHURCHILL ONCE REMARKED THAT DEMOCRACY IS THE WORST SYSTEM OF government — except for all the rest. The same might be said of the market economy. Markets are extremely good at what they do, harnessing such potent motives as greed and envy — indeed, Lewis Mumford said, all the Seven Deadly Sins except sloth. Markets are so successful that they are often the vehicle for runaway, indiscriminate growth, including the growth that degrades natural capital.

A common response to the misuse, abuse, or misdirection of market forces is to call for a retreat from capitalism and a return to heavy-handed regulation. But in addressing these problems, natural capitalism does not aim to discard market economics, nor reject its valid and important principles or its powerful mechanisms. It does suggest that we should vigorously employ markets for their proper purpose as a tool for solving the problems we face, while better understanding markets' boundaries and limitations.

Democracies require ceaseless political vigilance and informed citizenship to prevent them from being subverted or distorted by those who wish to turn them to other ends. Markets, too, demand a comparable degree of responsible citizenship to keep them functioning properly despite those who would benefit more from having them work improperly. But the success of markets when they do work well is worth the effort. Their ingenuity, their rapid feedback, and their diverse, dispersed, resourceful, highly motivated agents give markets unrivaled effectiveness. Many of the excesses of markets can be compensated for by steering their immense forces in more creative and constructive directions. What is required is diligence to understand when and where markets are dysfunctional or misapplied, and to choose the correct targeted actions to help them to operate better while retaining their vigor and vitality.

This book has often argued that most of the earth's capital, which makes life and economic activity possible, has not been accounted for by conventional economics. The goal of natural capitalism is to extend the sound principles of the market to all sources of material value, not just to those that by accidents of history were first appropriated into the market system. It also seeks to guarantee that all forms of capital are as prudently stewarded as money is by the trustees of financial capital.

The notion that much of the remedy for unsustainable market activities is the adoption of sustainable market activities may offend both those who deny that markets can be unsustainable and those who deny that markets and profits can be moral. Yet worldwide experience confirms an abundance of market-based tools whose outcomes can be environmentally, economically, and ethically superior. These tools include institutional innovations that can create new markets in avoided resource depletion and abated pollution, maximize competition in saving resources, and convert the cost of a sulfur tax or a carbon-trading price into profits realized from the sale and use of efficient technologies.

Ensuring that markets fulfill their promise also requires us to remember their true purpose. *They allocate scarce resources efficiently over the short term.* That is a critical task, especially as the logic of natural capitalism changes the list of which resources are genuinely scarce. But the continuity of the human experiment depends on more than just success in the short term, and efficiently allocating scarce resources does not embrace everything people want or need to do.

For all their power and vitality, markets are only tools. They make a good servant but a bad master and a worse religion. They can be used to accomplish many important tasks, but they can't do everything, and it's a dangerous delusion to begin to believe that they can — especially when they threaten to replace ethics or politics. America may now be discovering this, and has begun its retreat from the recent flirtation with economic fundamentalism. That theology treats living things as dead, nature as a nuisance, several billion years' design experience as casually discardable, and the future as worthless. (At a 10 percent real discount rate, nothing is worth much for long, and nobody should have children.)

The 1980s extolled a selfish attitude that counted only what was countable, not what really counted. It treated such values as life, liberty, and the pursuit of happiness as if they could be bought, sold, and banked at interest. Because neoclassical economics is concerned only with efficiency, not with equity, it fostered an attitude that treated social justice as a frill, fairness as passé, and the risks of creating a permanent underclass as a market opportunity for security guards and gated "communities." Its obsession with satisfying nonmaterial needs by material means revealed the basic differences, even contradictions, between the creation of wealth, the accumulation of money, and the improvement of human beings.

Economic efficiency is an admirable means only so long as one remembers it is not an end in itself. Markets are meant to be efficient, not sufficient; aggressively competitive, not fair. Markets were never meant to achieve community or integrity, beauty or justice, sustainability or sacredness — and, by themselves, they don't. To fulfill the wider purpose of being human, civilizations have invented politics, ethics, and religion. Only they can reveal worthy goals for the tools of the economic process.

Some market theologians promote a fashionable conceit that governments should have no responsibility for overseeing markets — for setting the basic rules by which market actors play. Their attitude is, let's cut budgets for meat inspection and get government off the backs of abattoirs, and anyone who loses loved ones to toxic food can simply sue the offenders. Let's deregulate financial markets, and self-interested firms will police themselves. Let straightforward telephone, cable TV, and airline competition replace obsolete regulatory commissions. Those seduced by the purity of such theories forget that the austere brand of market economics taught by academic theorists is only tenuously related to how markets actually work. The latest illustrations of that principle include the Wild West wreck now looming in Russia, mad-cow disease, savings and loan fraud, phone scams, and crash-by-night airlines. By the time textbook simplifications get filtered into political slogans, their relationship to actual market behavior becomes remote. A dose of empiricism is in order.

THE FREE MARKET AND OTHER FANTASIES

Remember the little section toward the beginning of your first-year economics textbook where the authors listed the assumptions on which the theory of a perfect free market depends? Even as abstract theories go, those conditions are pretty unreasonable. The main ones are:

1. All participants have perfect information about the future.[1]
2. There is perfect competition.
3. Prices are absolutely accurate and up-to-date.
4. Price signals completely reflect every cost to society: There are no externalities.
5. There is no monopoly (sole seller).
6. There is no monopsony (sole buyer).
7. No individual transaction can move the market, affecting wider price patterns.
8. No resource is unemployed or underemployed.
9. There's absolutely nothing that can't be readily bought and sold (no unmarketed assets) — not even, as science-fiction author Robert Heinlein put it, "a Senator's robes with the Senator inside."
10. Any deal can be done without "friction" (no transaction costs).
11. All deals are instantaneous (no transaction lags).
12. No subsidies or other distortions exist.
13. No barriers to market entry or exit exist.
14. There is no regulation.
15. There is no taxation (or if there is, it does not distort resource allocations in any way).
16. All investments are completely divisible and fungible — they can be traded and exchanged in sufficiently uniform and standardized chunks.
17. At the appropriate risk-adjusted interest rate, unlimited capital is available to everyone.
18. Everyone is motivated solely by maximizing personal "utility," often measured by wealth or income.

Obviously the theoretical market of the textbooks is not the sort of market in which any of us does business. Actually, if there *were* such a place, it would be pretty dull. No one could make more than routine profits, because all the good ideas would already have been had, all the conceivable opportunities exploited, and all the possible profits extracted — or, as the economists put it, "arbitraged out." It's only because actual markets are so *im*perfect that there are exceptional business opportunities left.

Just how imperfect *are* the markets in which we all actually live? Let's run a quick check on that list of eighteen theoretical requirements:

1. Perfect information about the future? If anyone had it, he or she'd be barred from elections and stock markets — and probably not given any credence by the rest of us.

2. Competition is so imperfect that exceptional profits are commonly earned by exploiting either one's own oligopolistic power or others' oversights, omissions, and mistakes.

3. Markets know everything about prices and nothing about costs.

4. Most harm to natural capital isn't priced, and the best things in life are priceless.

5. No monopolies? Microsoft, airlines' fortress hubs, and your managed-health-care provider come close.

6. No monopsonies? Consider your utility, the Peanut Marketing Board, and the Federal Aviation Administration.

7. No market-movers? What about Warren Buffet and the Hunt Brothers?

8. Thirty percent of the world's people have no work or too little work. (Economists justify this by calling them "unemployable" — at least at the wages they seek.)

9. Most of the natural capital on which all life depends can be destroyed but neither bought nor sold; many drugs are bought and sold in a pretty effective free market, but doing either can jail you for life.

10. The hassle factor is the main reason that many things worth doing don't happen.

11. Does your insurance company always reimburse your medical bills promptly? Does your credit-card company credit your payments immediately?

12. Worldwide subsidies exceed $1.5 trillion annually — for example, America's 1872 Mining Act sells mineral-bearing public land for as little as $2.50 an acre and charges no royalties.

13. It's hard to start up the next Microsoft, Boeing, or GM — or to get out of the tobacco business.

14. The world's regulations, put on a bookshelf, would extend for miles.

15. The Internal Revenue Code exists.

16. You can't buy a single grape at the supermarket, nor an old-fashioned front porch in most housing developments.

17. Many people are redlined, must resort to loan sharks, or have no access to capital at any price.

18. So why does anyone fall in love, do good, or have kids, and why do three-fifths of Americans attend weekly worship services?

Actually, the market works even less perfectly than the above counter-examples suggest, for two reasons. First, corporations that benefit from subsidies, externalizing their costs, avoiding transparency, and monopolizing markets tend to ignore market realities and lobby for making new rules, or overlooking old ones, that will best achieve their private benefits. Second, people are far too complex to be perfectly rational benefit/cost maximizers. They are often irrational, sometimes devious, and clearly influenced by many things besides price.

For example, suppose you put a group of individuals in hot, muggy apartments with air conditioners and tell them that both the air conditioners and the electricity are free. What would you expect them to do? Won't they just turn it on when they feel hot and set it at a temperature at which they feel comfortable? That's what economic theory would predict; if cooling is a free good, people will use lots of it whenever they want. But only about 25 to 35 percent of individuals actually behave that way. Many others don't turn on the air conditioner at all. Most do run it occasionally, but in ways that are essentially unrelated to comfort. Instead, their usage depends largely on six other factors: household schedules; folk theories about how air conditioners work (many people think the thermostat is a valve that makes the cold come out faster); general strategies for dealing with machines; complex belief systems about health and physiology; noise aversion; and (conversely) wanting white noise to mask outside sounds that might wake the baby.[2]

Theoretical constructs are, after all, just models. The map is not the territory. The economy that can be described in equations is not the real economy. The world that conforms to eye-poppingly unreal assumptions about how every economic transaction works is not the real world. The sorts of economists who lie awake nights wondering whether what works in practice can possibly work in theory are not the sorts who should define your business opportunities.

Previous chapters have documented 100 to 200 percent annual returns on investment in energy efficiency that haven't yet been captured, as market theory presumes they must already have been. Previous chapters documented improvements in U.S. vehicles, buildings, factories, and uses of materials, fiber, and water that could probably save upward of a trillion dollars per year. These efficiency gains are available and highly profitable but haven't yet been captured. Chapter 3 even suggested that waste, in a more broadly defined sense, in the U.S.

economy could amount to at least one-fourth of the GDP. Such prominent examples of market failure suggest that the standard question of how to make markets more perfect should be turned around: Are there ways to address the *im*perfections in the marketplace that would enable people to capture the profit potential inherent in those flaws? It's time to identify the real-world obstacles to buying resource efficiency, and determine how to turn each obstacle into a new business opportunity. The attractive scope for doing this will be illustrated by examples about energy and occasionally water, but most of the implementation methods and opportunities described could be extended to saving any kind of resource.

CAPITAL MISALLOCATION

The lifeblood of textbook capitalism is the flow of capital.[3] In theory, capital flows to the best risk-adjusted returns just as automatically as water flows downhill. In theory, theory and practice are the same, but in practice they're not. In practice, even the major global institutions that handle most of the world's large capital flows have significant distortions and imperfections.[4] Realistically, most of us can't attempt to solve these problems on a global scale, but we can notice and address similar ones at the level of the firm or community.

Without managerial attention, not much happens. Most managers pay little attention to such seemingly small line-items as energy (one to two percent of most industries' costs). Similarly, most manufacturing firms choose investments that increase output or market share in preference to those that cut operating costs.[5] What both these habits overlook is that saved overheads drop from the top to the bottom line, where even small cost savings added back to profits can look a lot bigger. When the CEO of a Fortune 100 company heard that one of his sites had an outstanding energy manager who was saving $3.50 per square foot per year, he remarked, "That's nice — it's a million-square-foot facility, isn't it? So he must be adding $3.5 million a year to our bottom line." In the next breath, he added: "I can't really get excited about energy, though — it's only a few percent of my cost of doing business." He had to be shown the arithmetic to realize that achieving similar results in his 90-odd million square feet of facilities worldwide could boost that year's net earnings by 56 percent. The energy manager was promoted to spread his practice companywide.

Once managers do start paying attention, how do they determine how much energy efficiency is worth buying? Many supposedly sophisticated firms, it turns out, don't decide very carefully: They make all routine "small" purchases based on initial cost alone. Thus 90 percent of the 1.5 million electric distribution transformers bought every year, including the ones placed on utility poles, are bought on the basis of lowest first cost. Buying the less expensive and less efficient transformers passes up an opportunity to earn an after-tax return on investment of at least 14 percent a year plus many operational advantages. Nationwide, it also misallocates $1 billion a year.[6] Every first-year business student knows that the correct way to allocate capital is to compare investments' results over the long run, not choose the option that requires the least initial investment regardless of future return. Every computer spreadsheet contains net-present-value functions that perform this calculation automatically. Yet most companies don't buy energy efficiency using these principles.

Typically, energy-saving devices are chosen by engineers at the firm's operating level, using a rule-of-thumb procedure called "simple payback," which calculates how many years of savings it takes to repay the investment in better efficiency and start earning clear profits. Four-fifths of the American firms that even think about future savings (instead of just initial capital cost) use this method. Moreover, they do so with the expectation of extremely quick paybacks — a median of 1.9 years.[7] Most corporate officers are so immersed in discounted-cash-flow measures of profitability that they don't know how to translate between their own financial language and the engineers' language of simple payback.[8] They therefore may not realize that a 1.9-year simple payback is equivalent to a *71 percent* real after-tax rate of return per year, or around *six times* the cost of additional capital.

Most firms are therefore not purchasing nearly enough efficiency. They invest every day in ways to increase production or sales that don't return anywhere near 71 percent a year after tax; yet they continue to insist, often unknowingly, that energy efficiency leap this lofty hurdle. One remedy is to teach the energy engineers how to speak financial language. When the engineer goes to the comptroller and says, "Wow, have I got a deal for you — a risk-free return of 27 percent after tax!," he or she'll almost certainly get the capital that wouldn't have been obtained had the savings been expressed as a 3.4-year payback.

Many capital-constrained industries use hurdle rates even more absurd than two years: In some, the energy managers can't buy equipment that yields anything beyond a six-*month* payback. Yet at least in buildings, it's now possible to obtain capital for energy- or water-saving investments entirely from outside sources without committing any capital of one's own. In 1997, top finance firms joined the U.S. Department of Energy to create the International Performance Measurement and Verification Protocol,[9] which has since been adopted in more than 20 other countries, including Brazil, China, India, Mexico, Russia, and Ukraine. This voluntary industry-consensus approach standardizes streams of energy- and water-cost savings (in buildings and in most industrial processes) so they can be aggregated and securitized, just as FHA rules standardize home mortgages. The protocol is creating a market where loans to finance energy and water savings can be originated as quickly as they can be sold into the new secondary market. For an individual company, achieving energy savings can therefore be affordably financed and needn't compete with other internal investment needs. The protocol's metering and monitoring procedures will also help maximize savings and guarantee their longevity by providing more accurate feedback to building and factory operators.

But the misallocation of capital away from very attractive returns in energy efficiency has an even larger implication. While most business owners, just like most Americans in their own homes, typically want to get their money back from energy-saving investments within a few years, utilities and other large energy companies have traditionally been content to recover power-plant investments over the course of twenty to thirty years — about ten times as long. Our society, therefore, typically requires roughly tenfold higher returns for saving energy than for producing it.[10] Equivalent to a tenfold price distortion, this practice skews the economy by making us buy far too much energy and too little efficiency. Until the late eighties, the United States wasted on uneconomic power plants and their subsidies roughly $60 billion a year worth of capital investment, or about twice as much as it invested annually in all durable-goods manufacturing industries, thus badly crimping the nation's competitiveness.

However, in that distortion lurks another business opportunity. Arbitrageurs make fortunes from spreads of a tenth of a percentage point. The spread between the discount rates used in buying energy savings and supply are often hundreds of times larger than that —

enough to overcome the transaction costs of marketing and delivering large numbers of individually small savings. Scores of utilities proved this in well-designed eighties and early-nineties programs that delivered efficiency improvements at a total cost less than the *operating* costs of existing thermal power stations.[11] The spread in discount rate is also the basis of the Energy Service Company (ESCO) concept, where entrepreneurs are paid to cut energy bills. They charge nothing up front for their services but are paid by sharing the measured savings they achieve. Like the shared-savings landscape-retrofit and water-efficiency firms mentioned in chapter 11, skilled ESCOs are flourishing worldwide, although America's ESCO industry is still in its shakeout phase. Many federal agencies, though authorized to hire ESCOs, don't yet do so because of rigid procurement habits and procedures. This may change under President Clinton's July 25, 1998, order to remove those blockages, maximize ESCO deals, and — a major incentive — let agencies keep half of their resulting savings.

Individuals have an even harder time allocating capital to energy efficiency investments than firms do. Few people will pay fifteen to twenty dollars for an efficient lightbulb when an ordinary one sells for fifty cents, even though the efficient model, over its thirteenfold-longer lifetime, will save tens of dollars more in energy bills than its cost and will keep a ton of CO_2 out of the air. But there are ways to jump over that hurdle. Southern California Edison Company gave away more than a million compact fluorescent lamps, a measure that saved energy more cheaply than existing power stations could produce it. To broaden the market even further, SCE then cut the lamps' retail price via a temporary subsidy paid not to buyers but to lamp manufacturers, thus leveraging all the markups and lowering the retail price by more than threefold.[12] Some other utilities lease the lamps for, say, twenty cents per lamp per month, with free replacements; customers can thus pay for efficiency over time — just as they now pay for power stations — but the lamps are cheaper.

Similar workarounds are needed for larger investments. Few families can afford to buy photovoltaics, which are the equivalent of buying twenty-plus years' worth of electricity up front, any more than they could buy twenty years' worth of food in advance. Only 10 percent of American car buyers pay cash; all the rest finance or lease. When financing or leasing solar power becomes as cheap and easy a process as leasing a car, it will become as common and viable a commodity — as is happening in Sacramento, where the municipal utility not only finances photovoltaics but even rolls them into the mortgage.[13]

Everything from vending machines to photocopiers, trucks to airplanes, office space to its furniture and equipment is now commonly leased. With more money chasing deals than good deals to chase, the almost riskless opportunities in financing energy and resource efficiency will inevitably become more attractive to investors, especially when offered as a kind of evolving service. Rapidly growing new investment funds, partly funded by the insurance industry to avert the possibility of climate change, are now investing directly in "leapfrog" efficiency-plus-solar power systems in developing countries. Those systems often cost less than villagers are already paying for lighting kerosene and radio batteries,[14] and represent a new market of 2 billion people.

Some of the biggest capital flows in the world — investments in energy supply and other primary resource acquisition or provision — beg for review. Those capital flows are largely misallocated today because most international opportunities to invest in, say, national or utility-level electric power systems consider only supply-side, not demand-side, options and have no meaningful way to compare the two.[15] The resulting misallocation sends far too much money to the supply side. It's a bit like the recipe for Elephant and Rabbit Stew — one elephant, one rabbit. The remedy, as explained below, is simply to reward the best buys, not the worst.[16]

ORGANIZATIONAL FAILURES

A famous company that hasn't needed steam for years still runs a big boiler plant, with round-the-clock licensed operators, simply to heat distribution pipes (many uninsulated and leaking) lest they fail from the stresses of heating up and cooling off; nobody has gotten around to shutting down the system. Why should one manager stick his neck out when the status quo seems to work and nobody's squawking? The litany of excuses for not attending to problems like these in a large organization is all too familiar and unproductive.

Billion-dollar fabrication plants ("fabs") speed the latest microchips to market by cramming design and construction into twelve to eighteen months — too fast for actual design. The chief engineer of a huge chip-plant design firm was once told by phone about such proven technologies as a cleanroom that uses manyfold less energy yet performs better, costs less, and builds faster. His rapid-fire reply: "Sounds great, but I pay a $100,000-an-hour penalty if I don't have the drawings for our next plant done by Wednesday noon, so I can't talk to you. Sorry. Bye." The sad and ubiquitous result is "infectious repetitis" — the copying of old drawings — which leaves huge savings untapped.[17] The most painful but effective discipline for such sloppiness is bankruptcy: Once major improvements enter a cozily complacent market, laggards must improve or perish. In autumn 1997, an East Asian hard-disk-drive factory was using $7 worth of electricity per drive while a similar plant nearby used only 13.5 cents' worth.[18] Such a 54-fold energy cost disparity couldn't be sustained. The inefficient plant went broke two months later.

A safer remedy is to move early to substitute leadership for management. Leaders can arise at any level in an organization. Columbia University had its own entrenched practices until a tough new energy director, Lindsay Audin, was told to cut 10 percent off its $10 million-a-year energy bill, with uncompromised service and no capital budget. Authorizations were painfully slow until Audin showed that the delays were costing $3,000 a day in lost savings, more than the delayers' monthly paychecks. Five years later he was saving $2.8 million a year, 60 percent of it in lighting alone; had won 9 awards and $3 million in grants and rebates; and had brought 16 new efficiency products to market.[19]

The late economist Kenneth Boulding defined a hierarchy as "an ordered arrangement of wastebaskets, designed to prevent information from reaching the executive." But letting information flow to those who can best act upon it stimulates intelligence and curiosity — as in the factory where merely labeling the light switches, so that everyone could see which switches controlled which lights, saved $30,000 in the first year. No one had wanted to fiddle with the switches, lest they inadvertently cause interruptions, but labels proved to be both cheap and effective.

Another part of the reform package in any organization should be to encourage individual risk-taking. In 1994, Mitsubishi Electric tackled this problem head-on by changing how it evaluates employees' performance. Mistakes were explicitly offset by successes, so risk-takers whose boldness paid off would be rewarded. The resulting speed-up in organizational learning enabled the firm to achieve its five-year strategic goals a year early.[20] Rewards can also be institutional: Washington State routinely shares savings among their achievers, the General Fund, and an account reserved for reinvestment in more savings. This allows innovators to save even more without having to go back to the capital budgeting process.

The ultimate form of risk-taking is research: As Einstein remarked, "If we knew what it was we were doing, it wouldn't be called 'research,' would it?" A peculiar blind spot in many organizations leads to abysmally low R&D investments that lock in stagnation. The U.S. building and construction-materials industries, for example, reinvest only about one percent of their revenue in R&D, compared with ten to twenty times that for cutting-edge industries like electronics and pharmaceuticals. No wonder their techniques and materials are so antediluvian. Recent U.S. Congresses share this shortcoming, regularly slashing energy-efficiency R&D budgets that have historically yielded taxpayer returns of thousands of percent per year: Just a handful of the technologies developed at the Center for Building Science at Lawrence Berkeley National Laboratory have already ensured energy savings worth hundreds of times the center's total cost.[21]

A common problem in introducing innovation is determining who's actually going to do the work. How many economists does it take to screw in a compact fluorescent lamp? None, goes the joke — the free market will do it. But we all know that somebody actually has to get the lamp from shelf to socket; otherwise the wealth isn't created. In the 1990s many firms, assuming they'd already carried out all their worthwhile energy savings and noticing that energy prices were continuing to fall, downsized their energy managers right out of their jobs. Their responsibilities were shifted onto other overloaded agendas, and predictably ceased to be a priority. Often the loss isn't simply of a warm body; it's of a devoted champion of efficiency without whom little will happen.

Individual initiative can still be defeated by bureaucracies. Many who propose changes discover that, because resource-saving equipment must be purchased from one budget, while its savings will benefit another budget, they can't get approval. Federal buildings similarly separate their construction from their operating budgets, and managers may be forbidden to share investments that reduce taxpayers' total costs. More generally, large organizations often behave in ways individuals would never dream of. A multinational company benchmarked its plants worldwide, for example, and discovered that one of them was five times as efficient as most others. It soon found itself under internal pressure to "dumb down" its planned new plants toward the poorer ones' levels of performance so that their managers wouldn't look as bad.

Organizational economists have classified and explained such seemingly bizarre behaviors.[22] As Nobel economist Herbert Simon learned, many firms do not fully maximize earnings but rather resort to "satisficing" — doing just well enough to get by and to satisfy all the parties they need to. The inherent complexities of their environment and the limits of their authority to make and execute decisions make this timidity inevitable. Shareholders, for example, hold diversified asset portfolios, but managers whose careers ride on the success of *specific* projects are far more risk-averse, so they select only extremely high-return investments — and so on down the hierarchical chain of control. Subordinates bear the personal risks of failure, while superiors see just the results and know which projects were chosen but not why. This sort of hierarchy leads to systematic suboptimization — to second-best solutions that are less profitable overall than they should be but are also less risky individually. Rewarding individuals' net success, as Mitsubishi Electric did, is one answer. Another is to create a broader alignment between corporate and personal objectives. One utility that started paying its efficiency marketing staff a dollar for every measured kilowatt saved quickly found that verified savings got bigger and cheaper — both by an order of magnitude.

REGULATORY FAILURES

Another portion of the seemingly irrational behavior that takes place in the business world occurs because companies are forced to obey not just the invisible hand of the market but also the all-too-visible hand of the regulator, and some regulation inadvertently produces the opposite of the intended results.

All but a handful of states and nations, for example, reward regulated energy utilities for selling more energy[23] and penalize them for cutting bills. This gives shareholders and customers the opposite goals, with predictable results. Many proposed utility restructuring efforts (often misnamed "deregulation" or "competition," though most would actually inhibit those goals)[24] are missing a unique opportunity to mend this flaw. Instead they would enshrine the same perverse incentive in commodity-based market rules, rewarding the sale of as many kilowatt-hours as possible at the lowest possible price, rather than rewarding better service at lower cost.[25] But a straightforward and proven remedy does exist. Where retail price remains regulated, simple accounting innovations in a few states have decoupled retail electricity distributors' earnings from their sales volumes, so those utilities are no longer rewarded for selling more energy or penalized for selling less. The utilities keep part of whatever they save off their customers' bills. Through this plan, the nation's largest investor-owned utility, Pacific Gas and Electric Company, added over $40 million of riskless return to its 1992 bottom line while saving customers nine times that much. In California alone, the Public Utilities Commission found that, during the period 1990–93, efficiency investments rewarded and motivated by this incentive system's emulation of efficient market outcomes had saved customers a net present value of nearly $2 billion. Thoughtful utility restructuring can accomplish the same everywhere. Even without retail price regulation, it can create truly competitive conditions of diverse sellers, easy entry and exit, fair access to monopoly bottleneck facilities and to market information, effective antitrust enforcement, and continuing scrutiny to prevent abuses of market and political power.[26]

Another problem with regulations is that they are often obsolete[27] and even more often misinterpreted. Standards meant to establish a "floor" have with time come to be interpreted as a ceiling or as an economic optimum. For example, almost all U.S. buildings use wire sizes that conform to National Electrical Code (NEC) minimum requirements, because the wire size is selected and its cost passed through by the low-bid electrician. But the NEC minimum standard was chosen to prevent fires; to save money over time, wire one or two sizes fatter should be selected to reduce electrical resistance. The fatter wire costs more to buy but less to operate. In a typical office lighting circuit, the next larger wire size yields about a 193 percent-per-year after-tax return on its additional cost.[28] Few electricians know this and fewer care, since their reward for proposing higher-efficiency wires is typically a lost engagement: General contractors hire the low bidder. This situation is just another example of ubiquitous "split incentives," where people who choose technologies often aren't the same people who will pay the bills.

This problem can be solved by better regulation, such as rewriting the NEC — a slow and difficult process — or by introducing the fee-bates described in chapter 5, which focus the developer's attention up front on designing the building for maximum efficiency. A solution could also be found without regulation, in at least two ways. The project's manager could instruct the general contractor to calculate bids on minimum life-cycle cost, so more copper up front gets offset by electrical savings later — or, better still, could include properly sized wire in the specifications to which all bidders must adhere. There are also intermediate levels of solutions: Financiers or their lawyers could put optimally sized wire on their due-diligence checklist, or the local utility could provide attractive energy-efficiency incentives only for projects that are wired using a socially optimized wire-size table instead of the NEC table. Where can the developer or contractor get such a revised wire-size table? From the organization with a direct interest in turning optimal wire size into its member companies' profits — the Copper Development Association.[29]

Minimum acceptable conditions, like "meets code" (euphemism for "the worst building you can put up without being sent to jail"), or the British expression "CATNAP" (Cheapest Available Technology Narrowly Avoiding Prosecution), should have provisions to reward even better performance. Regulators often have indirect ways to address such minimal-compliance issues. To encourage developers to exceed the minimal energy-saving requirements of building codes, Santa Barbara County entitled those overcomplying by 15–45-plus percent to jump ahead in the queue for approvals, saving them a lot of time. This is a valuable reward for the builders, but it cost the county nothing.

INFORMATIONAL FAILURES

Another reason for the reluctance of business to invest in resource efficiency may be a lack of accurate and up-to-date information. Do you know where to get everything you would need to optimize your own energy use, how to shop for it, how to get it properly installed, who would stand behind it? If any of this book's examples of large, inexpensive savings surprised you, you've just witnessed a considerable market barrier: If you don't know something is possible, you can't choose to do it.

Labeling helps to address the information problem by telling buyers how competing models compare. In the United States, major appliances carry mandatory efficiency labels (though often with outdated information). A number of voluntary labeling systems, such as were used for measuring the efficiency of a quarter million San Francisco houses in 1978–80, have also found their way to the market as buyers started questioning the value of any houses that *weren't* labeled. EPA's voluntary Energy Star standard for office equipment is now embraced by over 2,000 products from more than 400 manufacturers. The efficient machines work better, yet cost the same or less, and are therefore mandated for federal purchasing. They're saving a half billion dollars a year, could nearly double that amount by 2000, and promise a ten-million-ton-a-year carbon savings by 2005.

Other voluntary programs that provide a more comprehensive system of informational, technical, and trade-ally support, like EPA's Green Lights,[30] are succeeding because they create competitive advantage. Involving more than 2,300 organizations and 7 percent of U.S. buildings, Green Lights' retrofits typically save over half of a company's lighting energy with 30 percent ROI and unchanged or improved lighting quality. Green Lights firms also show stronger earnings growth than nonparticipants.[31] The national potential for this effort is a $16 billion annual savings, plus a 12 percent reduction in utilities' carbon and other emissions.[32] In 1998 alone, Green Lights and Energy Star Buildings participants were expected to cut their energy cost by more than $280 million, and reduce air-polluting emissions by over 5 billion pounds.[33]

How much do you pay at home for a kilowatt-hour of electricity, and how many kilowatt-hours does your refrigerator — typically the biggest single user in the household — consume each year? If you don't know, because you're too busy living to delve into such minutiae, then you're part of another market barrier. To make such decisions more efficient — and because most appliances are bought not by billpayers but by landlords, homebuilders, and public housing authorities — Congress, by a near-unanimous vote, approved mandatory efficiency standards for household appliances. For the same reason, these are starting to be extended to some commercial and industrial devices, too. Utilities can also reinforce standards by rewarding customers for beating them.

VALUE-CHAIN RISKS

Manufacturers often hesitate to take the risk of developing and producing new energy-saving products because of their uncertainty that customers will buy them in the face of many of the obstacles listed in this chapter. To overcome this reluctance, Hans Nilsson, then an official of the Swedish energy-efficiency agency NUTEK, pioneered contests for bringing efficient devices into the mass market. Under his terms, a major public-sector purchasing office, Statskontoret, would issue a request for proposal, which committed to buy a large number of devices, bid at certain prices, if they met certain technical specifications, including energy savings that would be highly cost-effective to the user. This explicit expression of market demand elicited many innovations, giving a strong advantage to Swedish industry in both home and export markets. Following the Swedish example, the "golden carrot" program, devised by Dr. David Goldstein of the Natural Resources Defense Council, improved U.S. refrigerator design.[34]

Another way to encourage cities to try pioneering technologies could be an analogue of a public-guarantee system the EPA has used. This assured the first adopters of an innovative wastewater treatment system that they would receive a free replacement with a conventional alternative if the novel one didn't work. Such risk management is often the key stimulus needed to start a rising spiral of demand and production.

Efficient equipment often isn't available when and where customers need it — as anyone knows who's tried to get an efficient replacement for a burned-out water heater, furnace, air conditioner, or refrigerator on short notice. Distributors frequently reject the risk of carrying non–"plain vanilla" inventory that may sell slowly or not at all. Thus British Columbia Hydro found that the huge motors in that province' s mining and pulp-and-paper mills were virtually all inefficient, simply because they were the only product that local vendors stocked. More efficient motors had to be special-ordered, which took much longer than the mills could afford to wait. In 1988, though, B.C. Hydro started paying distributors a small, temporary subsidy to stock only efficient models, covering their extra carrying cost. In three years, premium-efficiency motors' market share soared from 3 percent to 60 percent. The subsidy was then phased out, supported by a modest backup standard. Similarly, PG&E found in the eighties that rather than paying customers a rebate for buying efficient refrigerators, it could improve the rate of adoption of efficient refrigerators, at less than a third the cost, by paying retailers a fifty-dollar bonus for each efficient model stocked but nothing for stocking inefficient ones.

FALSE OR ABSENT PRICE SIGNALS

One of the best methods to start reducing the self-deception that accompanies subsidies and other distortions is to account scrupulously for the factors that economists call externalities. Nobody knows exactly how much value to place, say, on the effects of air pollution on human health or on ecosystems. But recognizing that zero is not the right number, utility regulators in about 30 states now take some externalities into consideration in assessing utilities' proposed resource acquisitions, since most utilities don't. Until the "polluter pays" principle, accepted in principle by all industrialized countries since the 1970s, is actually implemented in energy pricing, however, prices will continue to reflect the tacit assumption that, as local energy official Randy Udall puts it, "the future is worthless and the environment doesn't matter." Calculations of cost-effectiveness based solely on private internal cost will continue to be "a value system masquerading as mathematics."[35]

Price signals are inadequate in many more immediately practical ways, too. Utility bills are seldom itemized: You can no more determine the running cost of each piece of equipment, in total or at different times of day, than you could shop sensibly if your supermarket bill showed only a grand total but no details of what you'd bought. Few firms track energy costs as a line item for which profit centers are held accountable. Firms in rented space may have energy bills prorated rather than submetered. Many companies, especially chains and franchises, never see their energy bills, which are sent directly to a remote accounting department for automatic payment. Some large firms even assume that utility bills are a fixed cost, not worth examining. But new bill-paying and bill-minimizing service companies have recently been springing up, many of which provide submetering of specific machines, times, and sites, and two-way, real-time communications to help managers pinpoint opportunities for improvement. Just ensuring that each meter generating a bill is actually in use and on the customer's premises often yields substantial savings.

Price *levels* make a difference, but so do price *structures*. Utilities often manipulate tariff structures to discount higher use or to penalize efficiency. Many did so for decades, even when their own costs increased with greater sales, believing this strategy would increase their profits, which traditional rate-of-return regulation tied to greater energy sales. Getting the incentives right so that rewards are granted for what we want — lower *bills* — and not the opposite — higher *sales* — will make such distortions counterproductive and rare.

One final class of distortions to energy choices comes from lopsided tax policy. For example, energy purchases are treated as deductible business expenses, while investments to save energy get capitalized.

However, such rules, with some effort, can be changed. When the Japanese government wanted to clean up sulfur emissions from power plants, it reportedly allowed scrubbers to be expensed in a single year. Analogous U.S. initiatives to speed the installation of efficient and environmentally sound devices and the retirement of inefficient or polluting ones are already under consideration.[36]

INCOMPLETE MARKETS AND PROPERTY RIGHTS

Even perfectly accurate prices are useless without markets in which buyers and sellers of resource efficiency can meet and do business — markets that offer a level playing field where all options can contend fairly at honest prices. As of now, such arenas don't exist. There's not yet any significant market in saved energy: "Negawatts" — electricity saved by reducing inefficiencies in its use — aren't yet a fungible commodity subject to competitive bidding, arbitrage, secondary markets, derivatives, and all the other mechanisms that make for relatively efficient markets in copper, wheat, and sowbellies. Although tradable emission rights and credits are starting to emerge, as noted in the previous chapter, you can't yet go bounty-hunting for wasted energy, nor bid negawatts (or their futures and options) against expansions of energy supply.

The existence of such markets could be a business bonanza, if the parties whose joint transactions could create the savings were introduced to each other. Thus when Morro Bay, California, ran short of water in the late 1980s, it simply required any developer wanting a building permit to save, at some other site in town, twice as much water as the new building would use. Developers then discovered what saved water is worth, because the town had established a market in it. One-third of the houses in Morro Bay got retrofitted with efficient plumbing fixtures in the first two years and two-fifths in the first four years. This plan could as well have been implemented in a larger area, via water-savings brokers. Fantasy? It's already happening. A few states — notably California, Oregon, and Montana — have reformed their "use-it-or-lose-it" water laws to allow saved water to be sold or leased without penalty. Brokers are now emerging to handle those save-and-resell deals.

Instead of just marketing negawatts (saved electricity) — a business now worth some $5 billion per year in the United States — utilities should begin to make markets *in* negawatts. This would not only maximize the number of customers saving but would also maximize *competition* in who saves and how, driving cost down and quality up. In the

1980s, Central Maine Power Company started the trend by offering cash grants to those industrial customers that pledged to save the most electricity per dollar of grant. This auction grew into one featuring "all-source bidding," later practiced in some eight states, where all ways to make or save electricity could compete. A utility that wanted more power would ask, "Who out there wants to make or save electricity at what price?" — and take the low bids until its needs were met. Around 30 states also ran auctions just for supply. They were typically offered, at attractive prices, many times as much as they wanted. Where efficiency was allowed to bid against new supply, it almost always won, permitting valuable "decongestion" of crowded grid capacity.[37]

Every form of avoided resource depletion and prevented pollution is a potential candidate for an entrepreneur to find and exploit inefficiencies. Establishing markets in saved oil could induce arbitrageurs to exploit the spread between the cost of lifted barrels and saved barrels. Dams could bid against showerheads, clear-cuts against duplex copiers. Carbon and cobalt, tungsten and trees, reefs and rainforests, are all ripe for trading savings. Just as with subatomic particles, for every resource there is an equal and opposite "antiresource": For every activity there is an abatement, arguably meriting a value and a market in which to express it. Few of those markets yet exist, but creating them can make traders prosper and all of us better off. Making markets in saved resources and avoided pollution can support powerful entrepreneurial innovations that turn each obstacle to resource productivity and loop-closing into an opportunity.[38] The bigger the problem, the bigger the potential gain, whether in energy and water, fibers and minerals, or land and mobility.

CREATIVE POLICY FRAMEWORKS

In 1991, President Bush signed into law the Intermodal Surface Transportation Efficiency Act, which mandates least-cost choices for solving local transportation needs, thus allowing federal transport dollars to flow to the best buys, not only to highways. In about thirty states, this legislation is effectively not in force because the federal funds must usually match state funds that are legally restricted to road building. It may take decades of bruising fights with highway lobbies to bring about compliance in every state.

Even better than such specific, necessary, but tedious state-by-state reforms are initiatives that can solve many other problems simultaneously. For example, resource policy consultant Dr. Mohamed El-

Gasseir has devised, and financial adviser Andrew Tobias has promoted in California, an innovative way to signal American gasoline's true social cost while reducing everyone's bills.[39] Their proposal is called "pay-at-the-pump" car insurance. Most Americans currently pay more per mile for car insurance than for gasoline, and most of that insurance is related to collisions, whose risk increases with miles driven. In Dr. El-Gasseir's plan, states can distinguish between two parts of the insurance premium. The collision-related part is charged at the gas pump, then forwarded to the private insurance companies in proportion to their market share. The remaining premium, for theft and casualty risks, would be paid through the mail to each consumer's chosen company in the usual way. A truing-up term on each bill would reflect differences in what coverage a customer wanted, how competitive the issuing insurance company's pricing was, and how good a driving record the insured had. Such insurance could also be made no-fault, paying the injured rather than the lawyers. Under the proposal, the apparent price of gasoline would rise by perhaps thirty to eighty cents a gallon — to a level still about the lowest in the industrial world but a more accurate price signal than now. Yet the increase is *not* a gasoline tax; on the contrary, the total cost of driving would go *down*, because there would no longer be any need to socialize the cost of accidents by uninsured motorists, who now constitute perhaps a fourth to a third of all U.S. drivers. Under pay-at-the-pump, everyone who buys fuel automatically buys collision and liability insurance. This is simply a smarter way to pay for automobile insurance — and it reminds us, whenever we fill up, that insurance is a part of the cost of driving.

By creating markets in negamiles and negatrips, society could discover what it's worth to pay people to stay off the roads so we needn't build and mend them so much. For that matter, as suggested by Douglas Foy, who directs the Conservation Law Foundation of New England, why not privatize each transit mode into one or more regulated public utilities that are rewarded, like Oregon's electric utilities, not for providing a bigger volume of service but for minimizing social cost? Automatic electronic billing could easily charge drivers for these social costs. This system could eliminate all transport-related subsidies and make each mode pay its own way. It contains the further possibility of converting all modes of mechanized travel from a burden on taxpayers into a stream of payments or royalties from the privatized utilities back to the public sector that built the infrastructure.

FAIR RULES MAKE MARKETS WORK

As the mafia-and-robber-barons era being reenacted in contemporary Russia should remind anyone who has forgotten a similar period of American history, market competition, like any sport, works only if there is a rulebook adhered to by all the players and enforced by honest umpires. Flagrant American abuses of market power in the early part of the century — Rockefeller in oil and Insull in electricity, among many others — led the United States to enact a series of antitrust rules and utility regulations. Devastating frauds and deceptions that fleeced millions of their life's savings led to the establishment of the Securities and Exchange Commission, the Federal Trade Commission, and other watchdogs of the public interest. Tragedies in public health and safety regularly confirm the need for a Food and Drug Administration and a Federal Aviation Administration. The market relies on these and other regulatory institutions for overseeing fair dealing, providing trustworthy information, and dedication to issues of the public good that private markets were never designed to protect. Otherwise, in a worst-case scenario, unchecked avarice can all too easily exploit and destroy a people's willingness to let markets work. Without care, this could be the fate of the Russian experiment with capitalism.

Of course, these institutions, like all others, need constant renewal. Recent trends toward forming rules and regulatory bodies that are supranational, secretive, and unaccountable threaten the basic principles of open markets that they are supposed to support. When the world's traders make rules for their own conduct in closed hearings before the World Trade Organization, the rule of law suffers. When the financiers prohibit any government interference with capital flows on grounds of mere national social interest (as the proposed Multilateral Investment Agreement would mandate), they are creating conditions that will allow them to go about their business more conveniently. But these are, in fact, the very practices — opacity and elimination of public scrutiny — that will destroy their own legitimacy, and even their ability to harness the marketplace of ideas to devise sound and farsighted decisions. Elevating the objectives of trade above the transparency and accountability that democracy requires will ultimately destroy at least one of these institutions, if not both.

Markets are, in the most basic sense, little more than a way of exchanging information about what people have and what they want. Markets are a system of rules and mechanisms for comparing preferences and opportunities to see if they can be rearranged in a better way that makes somebody better off and nobody worse off — a condition that economists call a "Pareto improvement." But there are also other means to achieve improvements without fancy arrangements using price signals: The objective can instead be signaled more directly, without the mediation of prices.

Systems without feedback are, by definition, stupid. But systems with feedback of even the most rudimentary sort can grow smarter in a hurry. How clean a car would you buy if its exhaust pipe, instead of being aimed at pedestrians, fed directly into the passenger compartment?

A factory that discharges pollution into a river is more likely to clean up if its water intake is downstream of its outfall. In fact, why not just hook the two pipes together? If it's clean enough for the public to use, why isn't it also clean enough for the factory to use? Some major chemical firms have even considered requiring their plant managers to reside at the downwind site boundary, exposing them to the same risks to which the plant exposes the public — much as Mr. DuPont built his house near his original explosives factories. This way lies the logic of the second principle of natural capitalism — eliminating the *concept* of waste and toxicity. Simple ways to use feedback to minimize risk and cost are almost unlimited. The U.S. Navy's early nuclear submarines had problems with the quality of their hull welds — until Admiral Rickover announced that the welders would be aboard the maiden dives. Swedish publisher Mariefriske's office workers avoid occupational maladies because the same department budget that includes ergonomic investments also includes workplace health services.[40]

Another effective example of creating informative feedback loops was the work of Greenpeace International scientist Dr. Jeremy Leggett, who introduced senior climate scientists to leaders of the European insurance and reinsurance industry. The information given them helped insurers to understand the connection between two things: their rapidly rising casualty claims from major storms, floods, and other instances of climatic volatility, and the prediction of all reputable climate simulation models of the effects of adding more greenhouse gases to the atmosphere. Those European reinsurers have become among the strongest private-sector forces lobbying for strong climate-protection policies. The insurance and reinsurance industry worldwide is larger financially than the oil and coal industries put together. Now it is starting to make a third linkage: investing some of its huge financial flows in the advancement of climate protection[41] — including the developing-country solar-power initiatives mentioned earlier, energy efficiency (not least for the industry's vast portfolio of commercial properties), and renewable energy. As such green investment expands because of its double dividend — high returns *and* reduced insurance risks — those who lose in capital competition will be compelled to take notice.

Cybernetics — the science of communications and control in machines and living things — studies not only feedback but also goals. A feedback system defines a "reference state" to which an operation is to aspire, and measures the difference between what is and what should be. It then generates from that difference an "error signal" that, fed back, tells the system how to change in order to get closer to the goal. People function this way. Companies do also; that's why they prepare strategic and business plans. There are ways to help them do it better.[42] Suppose, for example, that a business were to prepare — initially for internal use, since it would contain proprietary material — an *Alternative Annual Report*. The traditional annual report describes, in a widely accepted narrative and financial format, what the firm accomplished during the previous year. The alternative version would describe, in the same format, what the company would *like* to have been able to report it had accomplished, had all the internal and external obstacles been removed that make what's good for the shareholders in the short run diverge from what's good for future generations worldwide. If that gulf between reality and intention could be bridged, if the company could be run entirely with heart and without compromise, what outcomes would emerge? Since the *Alternative Annual Report* covers the past, it doesn't require any wild projections about future developments; it's just an as-if look back at what could have been done differently and better. It focuses attention on what's getting in the way of making dreams come true. Leaders may discover, for example, that they would have been able to run the company much more sustainably and honorably under different rules, such as ecological accounting and tax-shifting. If a number of companies tried this exercise, such common experiences and observations could emerge — and perhaps even the nucleus of a constituency for mending what's broken.

If we don't change where we're going, we may get there. If we want to go somewhere else, we need stars to steer by. Perhaps the first step is to describe the sort of destination we want to reach.

CHAPTER 14

Human Capitalism

Parachuting cats into Borneo — Stopping the waste of people — Curitiba's web of solutions — Faster travel without freeways — Subways on the surface — Simple, fast, fun, and cheap — When garbage isn't garbage — No hunger pangs — A place for living — A symbol of the possible

WHAT DESTINATION DOES OUR SOCIETY WANT TO REACH, AND HOW WILL IT get there? Lessons in what *not* to do can often be found in cities, where most officials, overwhelmed by a flood of problems, try to cope by naming and solving them one at a time. If they are faced with congestion, their answer is to widen streets and build bypasses and parking garages. Crime? Lock up the offenders. Smog? Regulate emissions. Illiteracy? Toughen standards. Litter? Raise fines. Homelessness? Build shelters, and if that seems to fail, jail the loiterers. Insufficient budget to fund all these competing priorities? Raise taxes or impose sacrificial austerity, to taste. Disaffected voters? Blame political enemies.

Sometimes single-problem, single-solution approaches do work, but often, as previously described, optimizing one element in isolation pessimizes the entire system. Hidden connections that have not been recognized and turned to advantage will eventually tend to create disadvantage.

Consider what happened in Borneo in the 1950s. Many Dayak villagers had malaria, and the World Health Organization had a solution that was simple and direct. Spraying DDT seemed to work: Mosquitoes died, and malaria declined. But then an expanding web of side effects ("consequences you didn't think of," quips biologist Garrett Hardin, "the existence of which you will deny as long as possible") started to appear. The roofs of people's houses began to collapse, because the DDT had also killed tiny parasitic wasps that had previously controlled thatch-eating caterpillars. The colonial government issued sheet-metal replacement roofs, but people couldn't sleep when tropical rains turned the tin roofs into drums. Meanwhile, the DDT-poisoned bugs were being eaten by geckoes, which were eaten by cats. The DDT invisibly built up in the food chain and began to kill the cats. Without the cats, the rats multiplied. The World Health Organization, threatened by potential outbreaks of typhus and sylvatic plague, which it had itself created, was obliged to parachute fourteen thousand live cats into Borneo. Thus occurred Operation Cat Drop, one of the odder missions of the British Royal Air Force.[1]

Too often, cities similarly find that the cause of their problems is prior solutions that have either missed their mark or boomeranged, like the bigger road that invites more traffic, the river channelization that worsens floods, the homeless shelter that spreads tuberculosis, and the prison that trains criminals in more sophisticated techniques. Rather, our goal should be to solve or avoid each problem in a way that also addresses many more simultaneously — without creating new ones. This system approach not only recognizes underlying causal linkages but sees places to turn challenges into opportunities. Communities and whole societies need to be managed with the same appreciation for integrative design as buildings, the same frugally simple engineering as lean factories, and the same entrepreneurial drive as great companies.

This wide focus can help people protect not only the natural capital they depend upon but also their social fabric, their own human capital. Just as ecosystems produce both monetized "natural resources" and far more valuable but unmonetized "ecosystem services," so social systems have a dual role. They provide not only the monetized "human resources" of educated minds and skilled hands but also the far more valuable but unmonetized "social system services" — culture, wisdom, honor, love, and a whole range of values, attributes, and behaviors that define our humanity and make our lives worth living.[2] Just as unsound ways of extracting wood fiber can destroy the ecological integrity of a forest until it can no longer regulate watersheds, atmosphere, climate, nutrient flows, and habitats, unsound methods of exploiting human resources can destroy the social integrity of a culture so it can no longer support the happiness and improvement of its members. Industrial capitalism can be said to be liquidating, without valuing, both natural *and* human capital — capturing short-term economic gains in ways that destroy long-term human prospect and purpose. An overworked but undervalued workforce, outsourced parenting, the unremitting insecurity that threatens even the most valued knowledge workers with fear of layoffs — these all corrode community and undermine civil society.

Previous chapters have described how the worthier employment of natural resources can protect and enhance ecosystem services. Are there also worthier ways to employ people, so as to protect and enhance social-system services? Is there a social version of the principles of natural capitalism: of resource productivity, mimicking natural processes, the service and flow economy, and reinvestment in natural capital? Are there ways to restructure economic activity that reward social enrichment and that reinvest in social systems' capacity to evolve ever more diverse and creative cultures?[3] Can reversing the waste of resources and of money also reinforce efforts to stop wasting people? How can ways of eliminating all these three kinds of waste reinforce one another? How — most challengingly — can we accomplish these goals in places where the population and its problems far outweigh available funding and time?

Basic human needs can be satisfied by a combination of products, forms of political and social organization, values and norms, spaces and contexts, behaviors and attitudes.[4] Industrial capitalism rewards only the sale of monetized goods and services, so it naturally focuses on tangible, material ways to meet human needs. To be sure, material goods are useful, and up to a point indispensable, but only so far as they serve people, not the reverse: When physical production and economic growth turn from means into ends, they yield outward affluence accompanied by inner poverties expressed as social pathologies. The shopping mall is a pale substitute for the local pub, TV sitcoms for family conviviality, security guards for safe streets, insurance for health.

The health of societies depends not only on choosing the right means to satisfy human needs but also on understanding the interlinked pattern of those means. Traditional cultures, having more limited means to satisfy human needs, tend to meet as many needs as possible with as few resources as possible. In contrast, industrial capitalism emphasizes the creation of specialized products that fight for market niches to fill needs that, as often as not, cannot be satisfied by material goods.[5] Successful societies require that each action they take answers many needs simultaneously. In effect they adopt the same design philosophy, and achieve the same elegant frugality, with which whole-system engineering meets technical demands by delivering multiple benefits from single expenditures, or lean thinking meets organizational needs by purging them of the *muda* of unneeded and counterproductive tasks. The context is different, but the logic, purpose, and result of this social form of whole-system design are similar.

In the developing countries of the South, such whole-system thinking is at a premium, because the new pattern of scarcity that is the cornerstone for the arguments of this book — abundant people but scarce nature — has arrived there early and with a vengeance. For the developing world, most acutely, the relevant question will be: How many problems can be simultaneously solved or avoided, how many needs can be met, by making the right initial choices? And how can those choices be linked into a web of mutually supporting solutions, creating a healthy economic, social, and ecological system that develops both better people *and* thriving nature?

WEAVING THE WEB OF SOLUTIONS: THE CURITIBA EXAMPLE

Curitiba is a southeastern Brazilian city with the population of Houston or Philadelphia. It shares with hundreds of similar-sized cities[6] a dangerous combination of scant resources plus explosive population growth. Curitiba' s metro-area population grew from about 300,000 in 1950 to 2.1 million in 1990,[7] when 42 percent of the population was under the age of 18. Another million residents are expected by 2020.

Most cities so challenged, in Brazil as throughout the South, have become centers of poverty, unemployment, squalor, disease, illiteracy, inequity, congestion, pollution, corruption, and despair. Yet by combining responsible government with vital entrepreneurship, Curitiba has achieved just the opposite. Though starting with the dismal economic profile typical of its region, in nearly three decades the city has achieved measurably better levels of education, health, human welfare, public safety, democratic participation, political integrity, environmental protection, and community spirit than its neighbors, and some would say than most cities in the United States. It has done so not by instituting a few economic megaprojects but by implementing hundreds of *multi*purpose, cheap, fast, simple, homegrown, people-centered initiatives harnessing market mechanisms, common sense, and local skills. It has flourished by treating all its citizens — most of all its children — not as its burden but as its most precious resource, creators of its future. It has succeeded not by central planning but by combining farsighted and pragmatic leadership with an integrated design process, strong public and business participation, and a widely shared public vision that transcends partisanship. The lessons of Curitiba's transformation hold promise and hope for all cities and all peoples throughout the world.[8]

At 6:00 on a Friday evening in 1972, an hour after the law courts had closed, the renewal of Curitiba began. City workmen began jackhammering up the pavement of the central historic boulevard, the Rua Quinze de Novembro. Working round the clock, they laid cobblestones, installed streetlights and kiosks, and planted tens of thousands of flowers. Forty-eight hours later, their meticulously planned work was complete. Brazil's first pedestrian mall — one of the first in the world — was ready for business. By midday Monday, it was so thronged that the shopkeepers, who had threatened to sue because they feared lost traffic, were petitioning for its expansion. Some people started picking the flowers to take home, but city workers promptly replanted them, day after day, until the pillage stopped. The following weekend, when automobile-club members threatened to retake the street for cars, their caravan was repulsed by an army of children, painting watercolors on mall-length rolls of paper unfurled by city workers. The boulevard, now often called Rua das Flores, the Street of Flowers, quickly became the heart of a new kind of urban landscape. The children of those children now join in a commemorative paint-in every Saturday morning. The city is blessed with twenty downtown blocks of pedestrian streets that have regenerated its public realm and reenergized its commerce and its polity.

Of the many initiatives that changed the city's direction, the historic boulevard's bold resurrection, just before it was to have been destroyed for an overpass, was the most emblematic. At that time nearly every city in the world was demolishing its historic core so bigger roads could handle the onslaught of cars carrying people between districts zoned for disparate activities. But in 1971, when Brazil was still under military dictatorship, the governor of Paraná State had chosen as mayor of its capital city a thirty-three-year-old architect, engineer, urban planner, and humanist named Jaime Lerner. Cheery, informal, energetic, intensely practical, with the brain of a technocrat and the soul of a poet, Lerner was selected not only for his knowledge of the city's needs but also for his supposed lack of political talent: The governor wanted someone politically nonthreatening. Unexpectedly, Lerner turned out to be a charismatic, compassionate, and visionary leader who ultimately ended his three terms, totaling a record twelve years, as the most popular mayor in Brazilian history.[9]

His terms alternated with those of three other mayors because of Brazil's single-consecutive-term limit. Since then, Lerner has been twice elected governor of Paraná. From that loftier position, he and the new mayor, his protégé Cassio Taniguchi, are seeking to coordinate the state's and city's responses to migration, sewage, and other joint issues that neither can address alone. Now Lerner is spoken of as a plausible candidate for president of Brazil. He has also helped train, inspire, and propagate a generation of disciples whose influence extends far beyond Brazil.

The effectiveness, common sense, and political resonance of Lerner's policies, and their reliance on wide participation, were made possible by earlier and vibrant public debate to form a broad and durable political consensus. As a result, all six post-1971 mayors of Curitiba, though politically diverse — one was an outright opponent of Lerner's — have followed compatible policies, each respectfully advancing prior achievements while adding his own stamp. Five of the six were architects, engineers, or planners who treated the city and its political leadership as a design problem, continuously unfolding as the city's 1965 master plan shed its rigidities and evolved to meet changing needs. Those six mayors' twenty-eight years (and counting) of good management have generated a flow of interconnected, interactive, evolving solutions — mostly devised and implemented by partnerships among private firms, nongovernmental organizations, municipal agencies, utilities, community groups, neighborhood associations, and individual citizens. Curitiba is not a top-down, mayor-dominated city; everyone respects the fact that, while it is served by leaders, many of the best ideas and most of their implementation come from its citizens. It encourages entrepreneurial solutions.

Lerner believed, as the late ecologist René Dubos put it, that "trend is not destiny." Rejecting the destruction of people-centered cities to rebuild them around cars, Lerner aimed to regain the vibrancy and diversity of the street life he'd enjoyed as a child, playing outside his Polish immigrant father's dry-goods store on the street of the main railway station. Having served previously as the president of the Curitiba Research and Urban Planning Institute (IPPUC),[10] the nucleus of the city's innovative design ideas since the mid-1960s, he and his design colleagues saw Curitiba as a living laboratory to test their novel concept; but there was no time to lose. With its human population doubling each decade but with no new vision of urbanism, the city was rapidly developing clogged streets, bad air, and a dwindling sense of community. Lerner knew that to reverse these symptoms of excessive automobility, he had to move quickly and take risks. The revitalization of the Rua Quinze provided a symbolic focus for emerging attitudes about the purpose of both cities and their inhabitants.[11] Residents and observers consider it a model worth emulating.

TRANSPORTATION AND LAND USE

Curitiba's best-known innovations are in "growing along the trail of memory and of transport," as Lerner puts it. "Memory is the identity of the city, and transport is the future." Transportation, he realized, is not only a way to move people but also a way to guide land-use and control growth patterns, so as to influence not just traffic routes and modes but also origins and destinations. Heretically, rather than expropriating and demolishing centrally located buildings to widen roads — the "urban renewal" that in so many cities has created a desolate, grid-locked core fed by overcrowded highways — Lerner's administration chose to adapt existing streets, losing only a few buildings throughout the city. Along the center of each of five interlinked growth axes, three parallel avenues were modified. The middle one carried express buses both ways, flanked by local traffic. The other two, one block to either side, were one-way high-capacity roads to or from downtown. This express-avenue system achieved the performance of a huge thorough-fare nearly two hundred feet wide by spreading it over three existing adjacent streets. The construction it required was completed in only four years.

Matching the density of population to the capacity to transport it, new zoning specified that the buildings nearest the bus avenues could have up to six times as much floorspace as land area, grading down to a ratio of one for properties farthest away from transit. Extra density — up to two additional stories' worth in a few specific areas with enough infrastructure to support it — was later sold by the city at 75 percent of its market value, paid in cash or land that was then reused to build low-income housing. Parks were renewed to revitalize the arts, culture, and history of the urban core. Many historic buildings were protected and refurbished; owners were reimbursed for the foregone land develop-ment rights, which were transferred to other districts. The city's rich ethnic heritage was honored and preserved. A ceremonial gate and spe-cial center was created for each main culture, operated mainly by its descendants. Mixed use was encouraged, ensuring the availability of downtown housing and a match of densities between housing and commercial needs. The city financed a special block-long covered arcade of shops open twenty-four hours a day to help keep the downtown lively throughout the night. The urban core, relieved of commercial pressures that would otherwise generate extreme densities, was returned to pedestrian priority as the focus of a renewed sense of community. Ordinary streets remained small and human-scaled; the historically evolved patterns and varying sizes of streets meant that the ratio of street area to private land remained far smaller than in a grid layout.

The axial road/transit corridors shaped the city's subsequent evolution. But before developing those corridors and hence boosting land values, the city strategically bought nearby land in selected areas and built low-income housing on it so as to ensure affordable access to jobs, shops, and recreation. In addition, the city built schools, clinics, daycare centers, parks, food distribution centers, and cultural and sports facilities throughout its suburbs, democratizing amenities previously available only to those who journeyed downtown. It thereby reduced the need to travel and strengthened the outlying neighborhoods, which also gained a great diversity of convenient shops. Small-scale, low-income housing was blended throughout the city in an effort to foster equity and social integration. The open availability of land-use plans and rules reduced uncertainty and thus discouraged land speculation. A further recent blow was struck against speculation by introducing a public Geographic Information System that gives everyone equal access to information about all the land in the city. To help keep that database up-to-date, building permits require disclosure of job, traffic, parking, and other specifics needed for sound urban and budget planning. (The city runs mainly on property taxes.) Zoning has been based on considerations including geography, hydrology, topography, climate, winds, and cultural and historical factors — not just the tax base, political pressures, or developers' proposals.

Even with this orderly development pattern, how could a city provide its rapidly growing population with transportation without choking the higher-density areas? What Curitiba did *not* do was to turn over its destiny to traffic engineers, who seldom adequately understand the complex urban dance between land use and society, space, and movement. Instead, Lerner relied on urbanists and architects, mainly from IPPUC, all of whom approached transportation and land use, hydrology and poverty, flows of nutrients and of wastes, health and education, jobs and income, culture and politics, as intertwined parts *of a single integrated design problem.* In addressing needs for transportation — considered as access, not necessarily as mobility — they followed a set of simple principles: Favor universal access over private cars. Support human needs; don't promote particular transport modes. Meet the requirements of the poorest. And don't spend money you don't have.

Curitiba started its transportation overhaul with buses because it *had* buses and couldn't afford anything else; but first it needed different buses. The old vehicles, originally built on truck chassis designed as much for hauling animals as people, were noisy, bumpy, uncomfortable, slow, and awkwardly high off the ground. Passengers had to crowd up steep stairs and jam through doors narrowed to discourage fare evasion. But the IPPUC architects and engineers devised a wholly new kind of bus, optimized for people, comfort, economy, and rapid flow. Their double- or (since 1991) triple-length express buses, "articulated" with pivoted sections for rounding corners, have up to five extrawide doors. Locally assembled by Volvo, they can carry up to 270 passengers, using 42 percent less fuel per seat-mile — even less per seat-*trip,* because they cover their routes in one-third the time.

Curitiba's system for *using* buses, dating back to 1928, also needed to be fundamentally reconceived, from routes to boarding procedures, administration to finance, politics to policies. A jumble of mismatched regional concessions had to be melded into an integrated and efficient transport system built on simple new technologies. Manual routing and scheduling were switched to homegrown software, later commercialized. On the express routes, buses now pull up alongside an invention of Lerner's team, called a "tube station"[12] — an elevated glass cylinder parallel and adjacent to the bus lane, entered through a turnstile, displaying clear maps, and accessible by the handicapped. Matched doors open on both station and bus. There are no stairs: Both floors are at the same height, like a subway and its platform. All the departing passengers disembark through one end of the tube station and board from the other, again just like a well-run subway. Depending on the time and route, this switch takes an average of about thirty seconds — as long as a bus conductor would need to collect fares from roughly seven passengers if they hadn't previously paid their fares on entering the tube stations. Instead, the bus needs only a driver, so it can carry more passengers, faster, at lower cost. Rush-hour express buses leave once a *minute*. The bigger bus, wider doors, and tube station, plus automatic controls — the buses operate traffic lights to maintain their priority — achieve three times the average passengers-per-hour, and the average speed, of a traditional bus. This reduces idle capital (69 percent fewer buses do the same job), fuel, pollution, noise, and cost, and shaves about 40 minutes off a typical daily commute. The whole system is designed not just to deliver its passengers pleasantly and safely but to do so quickly, so they'll have more time for family, friends, and enjoying life.[13]

Each lane of express buses carries 20,000 passengers per hour. That's about as many as a subway carries; indeed, it's just like a subway, except that it costs at least 100 times less (tenfold less than a surface train) and can be installed in six months, not a generation. Rio built subways that carry one-fourth as many passengers as Curitiba's buses yet cost 200 times as much. By avoiding those huge capital costs, and their perpetual operating costs, Curitiba instead freed up funds for many of its social improvements.

Curitiba is widely believed to have the finest bus system, if not the finest public transportation system, in the world. More than 1,250 buses of 9 varieties are matched to their specific duties so as to leave fewer empty seats. Two hundred forty-five carefully integrated radial, loop, and connector routes of 12 color-coded kinds, linked by 25 terminals, blanket the entire city and its environs. The buses make 17,300 daily trips on nearly 500 route-miles, covering 230,000 bus-miles per day — a distance of nine times around the world. The British *Guardian* newspaper reported that Curitiba's efficient bus service "makes London seem antediluvian. Bus jams never happen, vandalism is unknown" — even to the beautiful but deliberately fragile glass tube stations — because of pervasive civic pride. People could easily evade the bus fare, too, by walking into either open end of the terminals, but they don't, because they reciprocate the city's palpable respect.

The bus system is entirely self-financing from fares; the city contributes only the streets, stations ($4.5 million for all 200-odd stops), and lights. It sets the fare, routes, schedules, and operating standards. The forty-five-U.S.-cent fare covers all other costs, including the $45 million fleet of buses, plus a profit to the ten private operating firms. The rate structure repays one percent of the operator's fleet investment per month — a strong incentive to reinvest. Financial controls on the operating companies are strict, audited, open to public inspection, and easily understood. The two-page operating license is revocable at any time, a deterrent that helps eliminate bad entrepreneurs. Banks unwilling to invest in other cities' buses are comfortable with Curitiba's.

The bus system succeeds both financially and socially because it gets the basic incentives right. The division of total fares between the ten bus companies rewards not how many people they carry but *how many miles of route they cover,* so they have an inducement to be comprehensive, and not to indulge in destructive competition over routes already well served. The flat-rate, unlimited-transfer fare (each rider averages 1.4 segments) effectively uses shorter commutes by the middle class to subsidize longer commutes by the poor. This is one of many reasons why a poor person in Curitiba typically enjoys a higher standard of living than a poor person in São Paulo, who has essentially the same purchasing power but must spend over twice as much of it on transportation.

The Curitiban bus system is the most densely traveled in Brazil, carrying three-fourths of all the city's commuters — 1.9 million passengers per weekday, more than New York City's — with 89 percent user satisfaction.[14] By 1991, the system's attractions had encouraged enough switches from car to express-bus commuting to increase bus riders and decrease car drivers by about one-fourth. The same survey showed that 28 percent of bus users do have cars but choose not to commute in them despite the rarity of congestion.

Curitiba still has a half million cars — one for every 2.6 people, the highest rate of automobile ownership in Brazil except in Brasília itself, which was specifically designed around cars. Yet Curitiba also has no traffic problem, for thanks to benign neglect of cars, Curitiba now enjoys Brazil's lowest rate of car drivership and cleanest urban air. It saves around 7 million gallons of fuel a year, and uses one-fourth less fuel per capita than other Brazilian cities to achieve better access. Not bad for starters — and imagine the results that could be obtained with Hypercars and Hyperbuses.

And Curitibans have a multitude of mobility options beyond cars and buses. The city has over 2,200 taxis, two-thirds radio-dispatched and 90 percent driver-owned. Cyclists use 100 miles of well-designed, traffic-separated bike paths of two types — level for the leisurely, hilly for the athletic — all integrated with streets, buses, and parks. Special buses, taxis, and other services are provided for the handicapped, including travel to 32 specialized schools.

WATER, WASTEWATER, AND GREEN SPACE

Designing land-use in conjunction with transport reduced congestion and smog, saved energy, revitalized neighborhoods, and solidified civic spirit. But the success of the plan depended also on a less visible dimension: water. Curitiba lies between two major rivers and contains five smaller ones. For two centuries, people and rivers lived in harmony. But in the 1950s and 1960s, migrants from failed coffee plantations — displaced by mechanically harvested crops like soybeans — started settling in floodplain shantytowns. Meanwhile, impervious surfaces and other encroachments on natural drainage caused worsening floods through the city center. Multimillion-dollar channelization projects proved of minimal benefit. The problem had become acute when Lerner first took office. His designers decided to switch from fighting flooding to exploiting the water as a gift of habitat. They passed stringent riparian-zone protective laws, turned riverbanks into linear parks, and used small ditches and dams to form new lakes, each the core of a new park. This "design with nature" strategy stopped the flooding, and cost far less than traditional flood-control methods. Now, planners quip, heavy rains just make the ducks in the parks float a meter higher. Unused streamside buildings were meanwhile turned into sports and leisure facilities. Community groups sprang up to protect the parks, use them for environmental education, and integrate this into school programs. The flood-control greenways also worked well as antipollution buffers from nearby slums.[15] A strategic objective throughout has been to protect the giant Iguaçu basin from serious contamination, since this river within the city provides nearly all of the metro area's drinking water. Sixteen parks, cherished as public assets, form the first line of defense for this vital water resource.

At the same time, the city introduced a five-yard setback requirement (intended as a space for gardens) for all new buildings outside the core. It limited residential construction to 50 percent of a site's area, and banned impervious paving of open space. It provided permanent protection for vegetation in the low-density one-third of the city, and tax relief for woods and gardens: Over 1,100 private woodlands are now registered, and the tax-relieved private green space exceeds four square miles. All these features allow rainwater to soak in where it falls, and massively greened the city. Curitiba also planted hundreds of thousands of trees everywhere: "We provide the shade, you provide the water." The trees are the city's lungs, cleaning the air and blocking noise.

One-sixth of the city is wooded. Two nurseries provide 150,000 tree and shrub seedlings and 2.2 million plant seedlings per year. Without a permit, no one may cut down a tree, even on his or her own land, and the permit requires replanting two trees for every one that is removed.

Complementing the private gardens and woods is public green space, which in 25 years, even as the city's population grew 2.4-fold, expanded from five to 581 square feet per person — four times as much as the UN recommends or New Yorkers enjoy. The city protects nearly seven square miles of parks, nine forests, a Botanical Garden, five Environment Gardens, two Environmentally Protected Areas totaling five square miles along major rivers, 282 squares, and 259 pocket gardens. Curitiba's CD-ROM catalogs the 242 species of birds known and the 48 more suspected to live in the city; many have fled into the city's parks from encroaching suburbs. There's a profusion of amphibians and mammals and 50 kinds of snakes, and once-native species of various animals are being reintroduced. After a month's residence in the city, author Bill McKibben reported that "From every single window in Curitiba, I could see as much green as I could concrete. And green begets green; land values around the new parks have risen sharply, and with them tax revenues."

INDUSTRY AND COMMUNITY

Curitiba's economy was traditionally that of an agricultural market town and food processor. But in the past 20 years it's become an industrial and commercial powerhouse as well, linked to other cities in South America by rail, road, and two airports — one of them highly computerized and the second-largest in Brazil. Situated 190 miles southwest of São Paulo, Curitiba lies within 800 miles of the producers of 70–80 percent of Brazil's GDP, and nestles between the capitals of Brazil, Argentina, Uruguay, and Paraguay — a total market of 200 million people.

Mayor Lerner realized early on that to serve and employ its burgeoning population, the city would need to balance its commercial and service businesses with new light and medium industry. Before land speculators could move in, the city therefore planned in 1972 and bought in 1975 sixteen square miles of land, six miles west of downtown Curitiba, for its Industrial City. To ensure affordable housing near the jobs, it preinstalled low-income dwellings, schools, services, cultural facilities, streets, bus links (including a special one to the largest poor neighborhood), and protected open space: Nearly as much of the

Industrial City is occupied by woods as by factories. The city then recruited more than 500 nonpolluting industries, which provide one-fifth of its total jobs — 50,000 directly and 150,000 indirectly. To encourage firms to reduce, reuse, and recycle, they're all required to dispose of their solid wastes on their own land. Workers can walk or bike to work from their nearby homes at no cost and use their monthly transport vouchers to buy bikes. Companies are attracted by Curitiba's marketing cachet. International firms are well represented, partly because of the high quality of life: Executives reckon they save twenty commuting hours a week compared to what they would experience in São Paulo, or nine years per lifetime.

Curitiba didn't begin its urban development significantly richer or poorer than other cities in southern Brazil. In 1980, its per-capita GDP was only 10 percent above the Brazilian average. But by 1996, that margin had surged to 65 percent. More important, the effectiveness of municipal services had increased poor citizens' monthly household income from, say, $300 to the equivalent of $400 or even $500. What created this huge margin of advantage for poor Curitibans? Not direct transfer payments from the city's municipal budget, which in 1992 stood at a quarter billion dollars for a city of 1.3 million, or $156 per capita — one-eighth that of Detroit. Rather, Curitiba's funding for social services is spent more effectively than in probably any city in the North.

The municipal government is dedicated to solutions that are *simple, fast, fun, and cheap,* to what McKibben calls "constructive pragmatism." Lerner, convinced that hope is sustained by visible change for the better, inculcated a culture of speed: "Credit cards give us goods quickly, the fax machine gives us the message quickly — the only thing left in our Stone Age is the central governments." City Hall's credibility in Curitiba comes from its creating a big park in only twenty days, or launching a vast recycling program within months of its conception. Curitibans have also come to expect what is too often a rarity in Brazil: transparent, honest, and accountable government. Any politician foolish enough to stray from these ideals would be promptly skewered by the wags of the Boca Maldita — a picturesque section of the Luiz Xavier mall devoted to public grousing. The real and powerful deterrent is that the city has built what planner Jonas Rabinovitch calls "genuine mechanisms . . . to give broad-based legitimacy to its interventions. One example: People vote for the improvements they would like to see in their neighborhood when they pay property taxes."

Since the rapidly changing value of the inflation-prone national currency can be hard to calculate, some Curitiban commentators measure urban investments in a novel unit: the cost of asphalting one kilometer of street, or about a half million dollars. For example, a tube station costs the equivalent of 0.5 km; a Lighthouse of Knowledge, 0.2 km. The latter is a brightly colored, 52-foot-high, lighthouse-shaped library of about 7,000 volumes, including the *Lições Curitibanas* — a ten-volume text on Curitiba's history, culture, civics, and environment that's a fundamental element of all primary schooling. Poor students obtain their set in exchange for recyclable garbage. Its print run of enough copies to instruct at least a third of a million children (over four years) sounds like a good use of the cost of 3 km of asphalt. The Lighthouses are also gaining Internet connections, and house Brazil's first public terminals. The top of each Lighthouse is a nighttime watchtower containing a light and a policeman, keeping the neighborhood safe for the children to come and go. Lighthouses of Knowledge are sprouting around the city, with the aim of having one within walking distance of every child's home.

In Curitiba, everything is recycled. A gunpowder magazine became a theater. A mansion was converted into the planning headquarters, an army headquarters into a cultural foundation, a foundry into a popular shopping mall, and the oldest house into a publications center. The old railway station became a rail museum, and a glue plant a Creativity Center where children make handicrafts (which the city's tourist shops then sell to fund social programs). A quarry became a famous amphitheater and a cable-and-polycarbonate-birdcage opera house (built in 60 days). A garbage dump was converted into the noted 11-acre Botanical Garden that is home to 220,000 species, and another derelict quarry into the Free University of the Environment. Constructed of old tires and utility poles, the Free University provides courses for everyone — shopkeepers, building managers, journalists, teachers, homemakers, and (mandatorily) taxi drivers — on the land-use and environmental issues related to their work.

Curitiba's buses get recycled, too. The average vehicle in service is only 3.5 years old, compared with the Brazilian average of eight and the legal limit of ten. Curitiba's depreciated buses often become mobile job-training centers. Parked in the slums and reoutfitted, they are called *Linha do Ofício* ("The Jobs Route" or "The Line to Work"), and staffed by locally recruited, frequently rotated teachers who offer training in more than forty in-demand trades or disciplines to more than 10,000 people a year, mainly on nights and weekends. A three-month course costs only two bus tokens — less than a dollar. Other recycled buses become clinics, classrooms, baby-sitting centers, food markets, soup kitchens, and coaches for weekend excursions in the parks.

These innovations owe much to the staffing of the city's municipal departments. They're often led by women and are heavily populated by architects — professional problem-solvers — rather than by the more traditional sorts of bureaucrats skilled at explaining why problems can't be solved. The interdisciplinary charrette — the architect's standard design process — is Curitiba's primary problem-solving mechanism. Conceptual tests of new ideas lead quickly to their application. Risks are taken in the expectation that mistakes will be made, quickly detected and diagnosed, and corrected. When budgets can't support an entire new program, it's launched anyway so that learning can begin while more resources or economies are sought. Failures are frequent, hard lessons constant, struggles to improve unrelenting. Guided by the reservoir of experience in IPPUC and by the collective wisdom of its diverse citizenry, Curitiba experiments and improves as assiduously as any startup company. From the outside, it may look easy, but it's not. Rabinovitch emphasizes the many challenges that Curitiba's government has regularly faced. The *process* by which it seeks to overcome them, however, through persistent application of whole-system thinking, is far more important than particular successes.

CHILDREN AND HEALTH, GARBAGE AND NUTRITION

Many of Curitiba's children and adolescents have concerns as fundamental as where their next meal is coming from. As an island of decency and success in a slough of despondency, the city gave rise by the early 1990s to some 209 slum areas, containing one-ninth of its population, which were starting to suffer from diseases borne by rats and contaminated water. By Lerner's third term (1989–92), he therefore faced a doubled population and heightened social challenges. His response was to redouble Curitiba's long-standing efforts to support its poorest citizens, especially its children, who were the special concern of the city's First Lady.

The city's emphasis on its children starts with discreetly provided family-planning advice and continues with early prenatal and postnatal care. Medical improvements have cut infant mortality by nearly one-fifth in four years. By 1996 it was still slightly over twice the U.S. average, but one-third the Brazilian average, the lowest in the country, and being steadily reduced. Poor children receive regular visits from health workers and obligatory free checkups, recorded in a personal health book, until age five. Preventive health care is emphasized throughout the schools, day-care, and childhood/teen centers. The city has 88 health stations, five of which operate round-the-clock. Each has a drugstore that distributes 81 commercial and traditional medicines for free — 3 million doses per month, covering four-fifths of the most common conditions, and bulk-purchased to save packaging costs.

Because health depends critically on sanitation and nutrition, Curitiba found a creative way to fund both by turning garbage into value. Experts warned that when the city exceeded a million inhabitants, it would need not only subways but also a costly mechanical plant for separating its 800 daily metric tons of garbage. On both scores, Curitiba chose a different path. The 1989 "Garbage That Isn't Garbage" initiative led more than 70 percent of households to sort recyclables for thrice-weekly curbside collection by the green trucks of the private firm that won a public competition for the franchise. Organics go in one plastic bag; paper, metal, glass, and the like in another. Two-thirds of the separately bagged recyclables are recovered and sold. This loop-closing offset over half the system's operating cost, which previously often represented the largest item in the municipal budget. Sorting stations, built from secondhand parts, hire the homeless, the disabled, and recovering alcoholics. Landfill use has been reduced by one-sixth in weight, and even more in volume. Groundwater is protected from contamination by leaching garbage. Curitibans' paper recycling alone saves 1,200 trees a day.

The city also funds a Garbage Purchase Program[16] from what it would otherwise have paid to collect trash in the poorer neighborhoods, where normal collection was next to impossible because trucks couldn't reach unpaved alleys. Now, in the "Green Exchange" project, a small truck pulls up in one of more than 100 squatter sectors of the city and rings its bell. Tens of thousands of the area's citizens respond by bringing bags of garbage to swap for food: 60 kilograms of trash earn 60 tickets, enough for a month's food (or bus tokens, school notebooks, or Christmas toys) for an entire family. Two kilos of recyclables earn one kilo of food. Similar exchanges, all totaling close to 100 metric tons a month, occur at schools and factories. McKibben quotes the ticket book's cover: "You are responsible for this program. Keep on cooperating and we will get a cleaner Curitiba, cleaner and more human. You are an example to Brazil and even to the rest of the world."

These food exchanges address many needs at once. The rice, beans, potatoes, onions, oranges, garlic, eggs, bananas, carrots, and honey they supply are seasonal surplus produce bought from local farmers, helping keep them on the land. Public health is served by encouraging the clearance of litter from hard-to-reach land, mainly near the rivers. That effort is supplemented by a temporary-jobs-for-cleanup program called "All Clean," funded by the city but organized by 135 neighborhood associations, which hires unemployed or retired people who need the income. With cleanup, too, comes community pride: vegetable gardens, dug by out-of-school children and coached by now-employed peasants, sprout from former dumps. All these initiatives rely not on capital-intensive mechanization but on public participation.

Nutrition is improved not just by Green Exchange but by diverse efforts reaching many of the city's 700,000 poorest residents. Some families can get garden plots in the suburbs, through the neighborhood-association-centered Community Orchards Program, to grow food for their own use and for sale. One such program has established farms next to day-care, school, and neighborhood association buildings where city agronomists provide seeds, materials, tools, and advice. Another effort organizes restaurants and others to distribute meals and surplus produce to the needy. The City Department of Health offers instruction in homegrowing medicinal plants. To help the poor stretch their budgets and to discourage price-gouging, the city has tried a computerized phone system that informs shoppers of the current prices of 222 staples in the dozen largest supermarkets. Family Warehouses even bulk-buy food, toiletries, and cleaning goods for resale to low-income families at 30 percent below retail.

EDUCATION, DAY CARE, AND JOBS

With nearly 100 children born daily, Curitiba must spend 27 percent of its budget on education. Its 120-odd schools, many reused for adult education at night, have achieved one of Brazil's highest literacy rates (over 94 percent by 1996) and lowest first-grade failure rates. Environmental education, too, starts in early childhood and is not just taught in isolation but integrated across the core curriculum. A top priority of the city since 1971, it portrays the environment not just as parks but as the place and the social setting that forms tomorrow's citizens. Dozens of Centers for Integrated Education operate near conventional schools, providing half of each student's instructional time from better-trained teachers.

Schooling is only one element in an extensive network of child-oriented social services. More than 200 day-care centers, free for lower-income families and open 11 hours a day (long enough to support working parents), are situated next to many schools and provide four meals a day for some 12,000 children who would otherwise wander the slums while their parents were away at work. (Their hunger pangs could also lead them, as in other Brazilian cities, to sniff glue — an ultimately fatal practice. Curitiba recently tackled this addiction by working with the leading manufacturer to add a foul-smelling substance to its glue, a step that has gone far toward eliminating glue-sniffing nationwide.) The centers also offer instruction in caring for younger children and growing vegetables. Many companies and individuals receive tax waivers for sponsoring day-care positions through vouchers, helping to finance new centers. One measure of the community's solidarity is that through patient negotiation, without police involvement, local gangs that initially committed some vandalism to the day-care centers ended up getting involved in their work. Similarly, when gangs initially tore up flower beds at the new Botanical Garden, interpreting their vandalism not as a venting of hostility but as a cry for help led to hiring them as assistant gardeners.

Boarding schoolchildren can work part-time from their own dormitories, delivering newspapers and magazines (which also promote literacy); half their earnings are banked for them until they're older. Or they can work in a uniformed service either delivering packages or carrying parcels for shoppers in the street markets. Working schoolchildren can also get school support, sports, culture, and computer courses. Older children are given apprenticeships, entry-level jobs, and job training, often in environmental skills — forestry, ecological restoration, water pollution control, public health. They can earn half the minimum wage in parks, flower shops, and private gardens. The

Program for Childhood and Adolescence Integration (PIÁ — a pun on *pía*, Guarani slang for "kid"), an 8-to-6 effort for school dropouts aged 7–17, has 64 centers. Half teach with an environmental emphasis, reaching more than 4,000 children. Altogether, PIÁ serves some 30,000 children. As in the city's other social programs, loop-closing abounds: For example, kids learn gardening by growing flowers (the city provides the seeds), sell them to city parks, earn money and self-respect, gain skills, and qualify for real jobs.

Curitiba's few hundred street children — far fewer than in other Brazilian cities — are registered and are well known to street-smart social workers, who seek to win their trust and enroll them in the many programs, shelters, and foster arrangements that offer food, love, and support. Children who stay in school are given scholarships in the form of family food baskets, and can get part-time entry-level jobs plus health care, transportation, and job training.

STRAGGLERS AND ARRIVALS

A similarly impressive range of efforts supports the homeless and the needy elderly and disabled, with many programs achieving multiple aims. For example, Dial Solidarity stands ready to pick up any second-hand furniture and appliances, which will be repaired by apprentices in carpentry and upholstering, then resold at nominal cost in street markets in the neediest neighborhoods (or sometimes donated). The oldest slum contained for a time a traveling circus tent in which children made toys — for themselves, day-care centers, and others in need — out of recyclables. The toys were based partly on prototypes created by industrial design students: A plastic mineral-water bottle turned into a toy tube station. Programs for the elderly ("Third Age") are designed not as mere recreation but as a foundation for an independent and active life, promoted by such physical activities as yoga, dance, and physiotherapy.

Another key goal is to give an economic role to marginal and potentially alienated or resentful individuals — integrating them as active, self-reliant citizens with pride in their contribution to the community. Job markets match up employers with qualified applicants, but the seventeen hundred peasants arriving monthly from the countryside, though offered basic orientation, often have trouble finding work. The city is trying to organize a thousand poor handcart collectors of recyclables to help them get a fair price. Shoeshiners and street vendors are similarly organized and offered good sites at regular times: Rather than being expelled or harassed, Curitiba invites them to take their place in the fabric of the city, licenses them, and gives them the status, stability, and business advantage of stalls and pushcarts.

In a 170-household pilot project, some poor families constructed their own decent cottages with municipal long-term land-and-materials financing, at a cost equivalent to two packs of cigarettes a month. With a dwelling upstairs and a shop downstairs, these small "trade villages" brought vital services into the slums, fostered dignity, and turned their residents into active citizens with a stake in their neighborhood. Lerner is now leading Paraná State toward a policy of providing microcredit and land tenure in new rural villages that are expected to receive one-fourth of the state's landless peasants by 1999, delaying by at least a generation their flow to the city.

Nonetheless, that flow has continued to overwhelm Curitiba's ability to house migrants in some 14,000 low-income dwellings dispersed through existing neighborhoods. The city therefore recently created a new district, planned to lodge up to 30,000 additional migrant families. Since many peasants arrive with building skills, the city created a build-it-yourself program that gives each poor family a plot of land, a title deed, building materials, two trees — one fruit, one ornamental — and an hour's consultation with an architect. The custom design, with advice on the sequence of later room-by-room expansion, bears no additional cost and yields a vastly better result than impersonal cinder-block hovels. Each house's uniqueness in layout, appearance, and even building technology (samples of which line a Technology Street) signals the personal validation of each of the neighborhood's new citizens. And among the district's first building projects was the tube station linking it into the rest of the city. As Lerner says, a city with ghettos — ghettos of poor or of rich — isn't a city. Despite its Teutonic heritage of conservatism, Curitiba doesn't begrudge its generous help for the poor, because it's frugally and effectively carried out. Nor do taxpayers complain that government can't work, because their government so clearly does. Curitiba is a city short on cynics and long on citizens.

IDENTITY AND DIGNITY

Strengthening civil society is the focus of many other important programs in Curitiba. The larger bus terminals contain "Citizenship Streets" — clusters of satellite municipal offices that bring City Hall to its constituents where they change bus lines. (Suburban "neighborhood

City Halls" came even earlier.) The Citizenship Streets also offer information on training, business loans, and job opportunities; the largest one is even integrated with a street market. This decentralization of services to the most local possible level reflects the user-friendly, customer-service orientation of all municipal services. Their design is streamlined to save citizens' time, so that a sick mother, for example, can schedule a clinic or specialist appointment, day care, and any other required support with a single phone call. The 4,500 beds at 36 hospitals, and 1,700 daily doctor's appointments, are also centrally dispatched for users' convenience.

Another strong emphasis, from childhood up, is the availability of public information, on the sound principle that "the better citizens know their city, the better they treat it." The city's array of telephone- and Web-based resources and hotlines — and the responsiveness of the city workers and volunteers taking the calls — would do credit to a metropolis ten times its size. There are hotlines not just for kids at risk, potholes, and gas leaks but also for air, water, noise, land pollution, ugliness, and bandit tree-cutting. The social lines alone handle 28,000 calls a day — six per citizen per year. The resulting sense of participation is so ingrained that instead of graffiti scrawled on public walls, Curitibans politely tape poems to utility poles. In comparison with Americans who often don't know their next-door neighbors, Curitibans consider one another all neighbors, and in contrast with their historical reserve, are starting to show signs of downright gregariousness. As McKibben puts it, this vibrant city is "a habitat, a place for *living* — the exact and exciting opposite of a mall."

These, then, are some of the ways in which Curitiba's creative, coherent, highly integrated design approach turns isolated problems — public transport and housing, trash and food, jobs and education — into interrelated generators of new resources and social cohesion. Even a task like mowing the parks' grass reflects the goals of an integral philosophy: Instead of running noisy, smelly, oil-consuming mowing machines, a municipal shepherd moves his flock of thirty sheep around as needed. In due course, the wool and the sheep too are recycled, turning surplus grass into more income for social programs.

SYNTHESIS

Teasing apart the strands of the intricate web of Curitiban innovation reveals the basic principles of natural capitalism at work in a particularly inspiring way. Resources are used frugally. New technologies are adopted. Broken loops are reclosed. Toxicity is designed out, health in. Design works with nature, not against it. The scale of solutions matches the scale of problems. A continuous flow of value and service rewards everyone involved in ever-improving efficiency. As education rejoins nature and culture to daily life and work, myriad forms of action, learning, and attitude reinforce the healing of the natural world — and with it, the society and its politics. For Curitiba has discovered a way to transcend natural capitalism, supplementing its principles and practices with others that start to achieve what we may call human capitalism. Walter Stahel notes that traditional environmental goals — nature protection, public health and safety, resource productivity — can together build a sustainable *economy*. But, he adds, only by adding ethics, jobs, the translation of sustainability into other cultures — and we would add, citizenship — can we achieve a sustainable *society*.[17]

How, finally, is the city working? In early-1990s surveys, over 99 percent of Curitibans said they wouldn't want to live anywhere else, 70 percent of São Paulo residents thought life would be better in Curitiba, and 60 percent of New Yorkers wanted to leave their glittering city. Among Curitiba's noteworthy achievements,[18] benchmarked annually to spur further gains, are 95 percent literacy, 96 percent basic vaccination, 99.5 percent of households with drinking water and electricity, 98 percent with trash collection, 83 percent with at least a high-school education, three-fourths of households owner-occupied, one-third the national average poverty rate, and 72-year life expectancy. Curitibans enjoy 86 percent weekly newspaper circulation, 25 radio stations, 14 cable and TV stations, three orchestras (even a famous harmonica orchestra), 20 theaters, 30 public libraries, 74 museums and cultural buildings. The Culture Foundation's monthly program of events, generally with free or very cheap admission, exceeds 40 pages. With a 1996 per-capita GDP of only $7,827 — 27 percent of America's — Curitibans have created what the well-traveled Bill McKibben calls "one of the world's great cities."

Of course, Curitiba has significant problems still ahead of it: A third of metro-region houses are unsewered, 8 percent of its citizens still live in slums (compared with one-third in Rio), and nearly half its children are not yet completing grade school. Because of its success, Curitiba attracts much of the surrounding misery of southern Brazil, and cannot possibly handle all of it. But on the whole, its imperfections are of the variety that McKibben quotes from the Brazilian newsmagazine *Veja:* "It rains a lot, the streets are slippery, and drivers still go through red lights. Its virtues, however, are unbeatable."[19]

Curitiba doesn't present itself as a turnkey model for literal replication, for no two cities are alike enough for such copying to work. Rather, Lerner calls his city "not a model but a reference."[20] Perhaps its most impressive achievement is that a simple philosophy and persistent experimentation and improvement have created a First World city in the midst of the Third World — breaking what Lerner calls the "syndrome of tragedy" that paralyzes progress, and replacing it with dignity and hope. Curitiba's central political principle since 1971 has been consistent and profound: to *respect* the citizen/owner of all public assets and services, both because all people deserve respect and because, as Lerner insists, "If people feel respected, they will assume responsibility to help solve other problems." Closing the broken loop of politics, this principle recycles the poor and hungry, the apathetic and illiterate, into actively contributing citizens.

Lewis Mumford called cities a "symbol of the possible."[21] On the southern plateau of Brazil, one city has hauled itself out of tough circumstances by the strength of good design. Its design mentality treats a wide variety of needs not as competing priorities to be traded off and compromised but rather as interlinked opportunities for synergies to be optimized. In Curitiba, its results show how to combine a healthy ecosphere, a vibrant and just economy, and a society that nurtures humanity. Whatever exists is possible;[22] Curitiba exists; therefore it is possible. The existence of Curitiba holds out the promise that it will be first of a string of cities that redefine the nature of urban life.

CHAPTER 15

Once Upon a Planet

Cassandra meets Dr. Pangloss — Expert's dilemma — Blues and reds, greens and whites — Assembling the operating manual — The world's largest movement — A hidden curriculum — Reversing several hundred years — Reclaiming the future — Mandates, principles, and declarations — Because it is possible

THE ENVIRONMENTAL DEBATE IS CONDUCTED IN A PREDICTABLE CYCLE: Science discovers another negative human impact on the environment. Trade groups and businesses counter, the media reports both sides, and the issue eventually gets consigned to a growing list of unresolved problems. The point is not that one side is right and the other wrong but that the episodic nature of the news, and the compartmentalization of each successive issue, inhibit devising solutions. Environmentalists appear like Cassandra, business looks like Pandora, apologists sound like Dr. Pangloss, and the public feels paralyzed.

The Worldwatch Institute's *1998 State of the World* report again reported that the trend in environmental indicators was downward: "Forests are shrinking, water tables are falling, soils are eroding, wetlands are disappearing, fisheries are collapsing, rangelands are deteriorating, rivers are running dry, temperatures are rising, coral reefs are dying and plant and animal species are disappearing."

Predictably, Worldwatch's critics argued that the report was unduly gloomy. "In every single report in 15 years, [Worldwatch has] said we are outgrowing the planet's capacity. For 15 years, that's proved to be absolutely in every way false [sic]," retorted Jerry Taylor of the libertarian Cato Institute. Taylor cited increased life expectancy, decreasing child mortality, and improved nutritional intake as proving that standards of living improve as population grows.[1]

Ignored by the media is the likelihood that both sets of data are correct. It is unquestionable that humanity has made astonishing progress. Average life spans continue to increase, a middle-class person can travel the world, and people in developed countries have the highest standard of living in history. But those facts do not make the Worldwatch observations wrong. Seemingly contradictory trends in the environment and society should not be portrayed as mutually exclusive. Both sets of data are credible and can be explained by the concept of overshoot: the ability to exceed temporarily the carrying capacity of the earth can help people to live longer, but put our natural capital into decline. Stated in another way, the ability to accelerate a car that is low on gasoline does not prove the tank is full.

Although such debates make good fodder for reporters and can help expose gaps in knowledge, the cacophony has unfortunate effects. One is the "expert's dilemma." If you went for your annual physical and were diagnosed by two doctors who fought and argued every step of the way as to whether you were sick or healthy, you would come away confused, numbed, and probably angry. When citizens who are not experts in climatology watch *Nightline* and hear one scientist state that automotive emissions of CO_2 could lead to killer hurricanes and massive crop loss while the other says that not using carbon-based fuels will signal the end of Western civilization, the citizens are left confused and disheartened. Mediagenic arguments allow little room for consensus or shared frameworks. Though great for ratings, such media-devised wrangling ignores the possibility that innovative, pragmatic solutions might exist that can satisfy the vast majority of Americans and make the wrangling irrelevant.

Remembering Einstein's dictum on mind-sets, cited at the beginning of this book, it might be useful to review a matrix of four worldviews on the emotional and intellectual frameworks that business, citizens, and governments use to negotiate and choose about economics and the environment. Biophysicist Donella Meadows, adjunct professor of environmental studies at Dartmouth College, outlined them in *The Economist*. She stated that she has become less interested in winning the environmental debate and more concerned with the "intransigent nature of the discussion." Each of the worldviews discussed below — which are color-coded with only a slight bias — is a systems view reflecting a perspective common among business, labor, environmentalists, and synthesists, in that order.[2]

The *Blues* are mainstream free-marketers. Such people have a positive bias toward the future based on technological optimism and the strength of the economy. They are armed with a strong statistical case, based on the vigorous and dynamic economies of Western and (until

1998) Asian nations. Their approach is deeply rooted in conventional economics, and their number-crunching reveals a world vastly improved and rapidly ascending. Blues believe that reliance on innovation, investment, and individual freedom will ensure a shining future for humankind, and a level of material well-being that has strong appeal to virtually everyone in the world. Their optimism also extends to the environment, believing that in most cases, markets will send strong and appropriate price signals that will elicit timely responses, mitigating environmental damage or causing technological breakthroughs in efficiency and productivity.

The *Reds* represent the sundry forms of socialism. Although one might expect them to have been discredited by the downfall of the erstwhile Soviet Union, their worldview is very much alive. They find validation in the chaotic and horrific economic conditions that the rise of bandit capitalism has brought to contemporary Russia, a country whose economic machinery now benefits a minority at the expense of a materially and socially disadvantaged majority. The growing and worldwide gap between rich and poor confirms the Reds' analyses, which are as accurate about poverty and suffering as the Blues' observations are accurate about growth and change. While Blues focus on the promise of growth and technology, Reds focus on its shadow and try to discern its root causes. They view labor — one aspect of human capital — as the principal source of wealth and see its exploitation as the basis of injustice, impoverishment, and ignorance. The Reds generally have little to say about the environment, seeing it as a distraction from fundamentally important social issues.

The *Greens* see the world primarily in terms of ecosystems, and thus concentrate on depletion, damage, pollution, and population growth. They focus on carrying capacity and want to bring about better understanding of how large the economy can grow before it outstrips its host. Their policy focuses on how many and how much, the number of people, and the amount of impact each person can have upon the environment. Greens are not usually technophobes; most see technology as an important tool to reduce human impact. More recently, some have become interested in free-market mechanisms, and want externalities presently borne by society to be fully integrated into producer costs and consumer prices so that markets become, in David Korten's phrase, "mindful." The Greens, and to some extent the Reds, host bigger tents in that they hold a bolder and broader diversity of views. But this also keeps them splintered and self-canceling, as Greens tend to unite their enemies and divide their friends, a good formula for political failure. They are often portrayed as caring less for people than animals, more about halogenated compounds than waterborne diseases.

The *Whites* are the synthesists, and do not entirely oppose or agree with any of the three other views. With an optimistic view of humankind, they believe that process will win the day, that people who tell others what is right lead society astray. Since Blues, Reds, and Greens all fall into that category, Whites reject them all, preferring a middle way of integration, reform, respect, and reliance. They reject ideologies whether based on markets, class, or nature, and trust that informed people can solve their own problems. On the environmental level, they argue that all issues are local. On business, they say the fabled level playing field never existed because of market imperfections, lobbying, subsidies, and capital concentration. On social problems, they argue that solutions will naturally arise from place and culture rather than from ideology. Leadership in the White world is reminiscent of the Taoist reminder that good rulers make their subjects feel as if they succeeded by themselves. Environmental and social solutions can emerge only when local people are empowered and honored.

While many individuals have traits of two or more of these typologies, the different views tend to become isolated and to define the others by their own internal logic. Blues see Reds as anachronistic, even fascistic. Reds return the compliment and neither think much of the Greens, who they say are hindering progress and speaking for a privileged minority. Blues win points (among Blues) by lumping Greens in with the Reds. All three tend to ignore the Whites but will take credit when any White-type scheme works in their sphere. Meadows asks:

> What would we see if we were willing to approach the question of human population growth and planetary limits purely scientifically? What if we could divest ourselves of hopes, fears, and ideologies long enough to entertain all arguments and judge them fairly? What we would see, I think, is that all sides are partly right and mostly incomplete. Each is focusing on one piece of a very complex system. Each is seeing its piece correctly. But because no side is seeing the whole, no side is coming to wholly supportable conclusions.
>
> The Greens are correct: Population growth that causes people to level forests and overgraze lands exacerbates poverty. The Reds are correct: The helplessness of poverty creates the motivation for parents to have many children, as their only hope of providing for themselves. The Blues are right:

Economic development can bring down birthrates. The Whites are right: Development schemes work, but not when they are imposed by large bureaucratic institutions such as the World Bank. Capital can be the scarcest factor of production at some times and places, labor at other times and places, materials and energy and pollution-absorption capacity at still others. The limits the Greens point out really are there. So are the injustices that anger the Reds. So are the market and technical responses the Blues have faith in. And so is the wisdom of the people that the Whites respect.[3]

A successful business in the new era of natural capitalism will respect and understand all four views. It will realize that solutions lie in understanding the interconnectedness of problems, not in confronting them in isolation.

Moreover, it will seek a common framework of understanding about the functions of the earth itself, and the dynamics of society. While interpretation of data is subject to culture, education, and outlook, the basic principles that govern the earth are well established and commonly agreed upon by all scientists. But you would hardly know that by reading heated op-ed columns or listening to legislative debates. Although you can go to a bookstore and find books that explain the tenets, principles, and rules for everything from golf and dominoes to taxes, judo, and war, there's no user's manual for how to live and operate on the earth, the most important and complex system known.

David Brower, the éminence grise of the environmental movement, once humorously proposed such a manual years ago. The instructions might read: (1) The planet has been delivered in perfect working condition and cannot be exchanged for a new one. (2) Please don't adjust the thermostat or the atmosphere — controls were preset at the factory. (3) The biosphere was thoroughly tested and developed during a 3-billion-year breaking-in period and is powered by a maintenance-free fusion reactor that will supply energy for another 5 billion years. (4) Air and water are in limited supply and are not replaceable; they will cycle and purify themselves automatically if there are not too many aboard. (5) There is only one life per passenger and it should be treated with dignity. Instructions covering the birth, operation and maintenance, and disposal of each living entity have been thoughtfully provided, encoded in a computer language whose operation is fully automatic. If these instructions are lost or damaged, the filling of reorders is subject to long delays. (6) If there are too many passengers and conditions get crowded, read the emergency load manual and be ever more diligent that no foreign or toxic substances are introduced into the air, food, and water.[4]

Why would the inhabitants of earth need a manual? Ideally, it would provide everyone with a shared mental model of the system they are influencing and participating in. A generally accepted set of standards and principles in sports, finance, education, and other sectors enables society to function efficiently, harmoniously, and safely, allowing us to drive in traffic, land jumbo jets at O'Hare, and communicate globally through telephony and computers. A critical difference between a user's manual for such societal activities, however, and one for the environment is that earth's operating guidelines are inherent, not imposed. They cannot be made up, only recognized. Author Bill McKibben put it succinctly in a speech to corporate executives: "The laws of Congress and the laws of physics have grown increasingly divergent, and the laws of physics are not likely to yield."

Tens of thousands of organizations in the world have taken on the task of assembling the ingredients of a real operating manual for the planet. Some are specifically addressing the responsibilities and opportunities of business. These include: Rocky Mountain Institute, The Natural Step, The Wuppertal Institute, World Resources Institute, SustainAbility (London), CERES, Redefining Progress, Product-Life Institute, World Business Council for Sustainable Development (Switzerland), Center for Clean Products and Clean Technologies at the University of Tennessee, United Nations Environment Programme (UNEP) and Development Program (UNDP), Institute for Sustainable Design and Commerce at the University of Virginia (Charlottesville), Forum for the Future (London), International Institute for Sustainable Development (Canada), Businesses for Social Responsibility, and the Stockholm Environmental Institute. They are joined by approximately one hundred transnational corporations and tens of thousands of smaller companies that have pledged to take an active role in reshaping the role of business in the environment and society.

In addition, tens of thousands of institutes, associations, foundations, colleges, universities, churches, outdoor clubs, land trusts, and nongovernmental organizations are addressing the complete range of environmental issues. These include such remarkable groups as Ecotrust, Ashoka, the Society for Ecological Restoration, Worldwatch Institute, Friends of the River, Environmental Research Foundation, Development Alternatives (Delhi), Land Stewardship Council, The Just

Transition Consortium, Instituto de Ecología Politica (Santiago, Chile), International Society of Ecological Economics, International Institute for Industrial Environmental Economics (Lund), Earth Island Institute, Congress for the New Urbanism, American Farmland Trust, the Energy Foundation, Southwest Organizing Project, RIVM (Holland), Center for a New American Dream, One Thousand Friends of Oregon, the Cenozoic Society, Indigenous Environmental Network, World Wildlife Fund, IUCN, Friends of the Earth, and many more. Together, these thousands of organizations, however they may be collectively identified, have quietly become the world's largest and fastest-growing activist movement. Arguably they have now become the world's real capitalists. By addressing such issues as greenhouse gases, social equity, chemical contamination, and the loss of fisheries, wildlife corridors, and primary forests, they are doing more to preserve a viable business future than are all the world's chambers of commerce put together.

The largest institution addressing mental models is our schools. Colleges, universities, and public schools can change their impact on the environment in two fundamental ways. They create the citizens, MBAs, engineers, and architects that create our world. At the same time, they spend $564 billion a year to do so, including $17 billion annually in new construction on colleges and universities. Oberlin Professor David Orr, the leading spokesperson for integrating the environment and education, points out that a large segment of that money is spent to purchase energy, materials, food, and water in ways that are every bit as inefficient as this book outlines. Orr believes that changing the procurement, design, and investments made by our educational systems represents a "hidden curriculum" that can teach, as "powerfully as any overt curriculum, a more comprehensive way of seeing the world that is the foundation for a radically different curriculum than that presently offered virtually anywhere. In every respect this is a challenge of how we think which makes it a challenge for those institutions purporting to improve thinking. Much of the change in outlook and perspective called for will not happen in the time available unless schools, colleges, and education get it."[5]

Only once in the history of this planet — now — have total flows and movement of materials by one species matched or exceeded natural planetary flows. Humans place more than three hundred times more lead into the environment than can dissipate naturally, twenty-three times more zinc, and thirty-eight times more antimony.[6] Scientific analysis of bubbles in the Vostok ice core from Antarctica show CO_2 in the atmosphere at the highest level in 420,000 years; it took only 100 years of industrial combustion to bring this about.[7] Global temperatures in the next century are expected to exceed a 10,000-year record.

Traditional forecasting examines prior events and present trends and traces both forward to a probable tomorrow. Most of the time this method works, even with natural events, so long as projections don't extend too far into the future. Sometimes, however, traditional planning fails catastrophically, as when an unforeseen event changes all the terms of the equation. When the Soviet Empire fell, Southern California went into a near-depression as 250,000 defense jobs were lost. Real estate prices plummeted, taxes declined, alcoholism and abusive behavior increased among the unemployed, and the ripple effects were partly responsible for increased racism, anti-immigration laws, and the social uprising that occurred in South Central Los Angeles. Conventional economic forecasts of Los Angeles's future proved to be wrong simply because no one had projected an "optimistic" scenario in which the United States finally "won" the Cold War.

A big question for society is whether it is willing to place its faith in so-far-so-good forecasts that presume there will be no significant environmental problems in the future. Increasingly, it makes more sense to take into account possible downsides so that if some environmental crisis does occur, it will have the least possible effect. The rub here is that the environment never really goes "wrong" but merely changes according to the principles of nature. In that context, the most unlikely environmental scenario is that nothing unlikely happens. The biggest surprise would be no surprises. While it is unwise to believe in any one environmental projection of the future, it is important to bear in mind that nature bats last *and* owns the stadium.

Today, comprehensive planning is critical for any institution. Business faces increasing demands on all fronts, including globalization, shorter product life-cycles, the Internet, overcapacity, complex regulations, currency volatility, and changing governmental policies. In such a world, it is critical to have a long-term view that will be responsive to and complement future events. Businesses and governments often avoid the task of planning for issues related to the environment or society because the time frames for environmental and social change always seem over the horizon, whereas the challenges and modification times required in other areas are measured in years if not months. Yet any attempt to form a coherent assessment of the future that does not take into account what is happening to the natural and human capital is incomplete strategic thinking.

The lesson of this book with respect to forecasting is simple and clear: No matter what future one believes in, building the principles of natural capitalism into our planning will make the foundations of society firmer. In scenarios in which the environment begins to change rapidly (or in which its services are clearly declining), resource productivity can also buy time, buffering society against sudden changes. As futurist Peter Schwartz counsels, the best option for an uncertain future is the one that leaves the most options open.

University of North Carolina Business School Professor Stuart Hart has asked whether corporations are ready for the natural capitalism revolution. Typically, business revolutions do not arise within existing industries but from forces outside. Hart believes meeting the multitude of challenges facing business and society will bring about economic discontinuities that are unprecedented in rate and scope and will require business to adopt new approaches. It will have to leapfrog over existing technologies rather than incrementally improve them. This may mean abandoning research in core products while they are still "winners," simply because new products or systems offer vastly improved performance. Why would anyone have wanted to create incremental improvements in vacuum tubes when the transistor was coming over the horizon? Similarly, the Big Three automakers will have to determine at just what point the internal combustion engine will simply become uneconomical to re-engineer. That point may already be here.[8]

To understand the opportunities offered by the resource productivity revolution and the other principles of natural capitalism, business will need to move across industrial sectors and solicit cooperation from competitors, critics, and perceived adversaries alike. This may seem like something no sane business would ever do, but an increasing number of leading companies are doing just that. Such organizations as World Resources Institute and Rocky Mountain Institute consult regularly for companies as well as for governments and communities. One of the largest forest products companies in the world is meeting with Rainforest Action Network and Greenpeace, its former archenemies, to formulate a strategic plan for their futures. Mitsubishi Electric worked with 160 nongovernmental environmental organizations to forge a new vision for the company.

The success of resource productivity as a societal strategy may augur an entirely new relationship between business and government. Just as traditional industrial activity may no longer be economic when natural capital becomes the limiting factor, relaxed governmental regulations that once "benefited" business may now actually harm it. Once business realizes that its existence is threatened by decreasing functions of ecosystems, it may need to take positions diametrically opposed to its prior stands and even argue for stricter regulations. For example, the oil industry, with few exceptions, has led the fight against global emissions limits for CO_2. This strategy makes as much sense as defending typewriters. Although the oil industry faces a cloudy future in the long run, energy companies and especially energy service companies do not. But regulation can exert selective pressures favoring the agile, alert, and green. By fighting the wrong battle, most oil companies delay innovation and ensure potent new competition.

In contrast, OK Petroleum, Sweden's largest refiner and retailer of gasoline, fought for higher carbon taxes because it no longer sees itself as being in the petroleum business: It is a clean energy company. After formulating low-carbon gasoline, it found that it was being penalized by the per-liter fuel taxes levied in Sweden. Since the taxes were assessed on the quantity of the gasoline rather than the content of carbon that creates greenhouse gases, OK joined with twenty-four other companies to lobby the government to *increase* carbon taxes. Those businesses were thinking long-term. Having already achieved large improvements in resource productivity, they wanted a "boost" from incentives to go further. By raising resource prices, Swedish companies also thought they (like Germany and Japan before them) might gain greater advantages over their competitors in the United States, rendered somnolent by artificially cheap energy. Similarly, the U.S. firms working to create totally recyclable or compostable carpets are all fierce competitors, yet if they jointly lobbied for prohibitions on landfilling carpet, it would give them a competitive advantage, seriously putting the screws to laggards in their industry.

Just as businesses are beginning to see the loss of natural capital or ecosystem function as harmful to both their short- and long-term interests, they may also come to realize that social inequities are harmful to their interests as well. When the African writer Ken Saro-Wiwa and seven of his colleagues were hanged by the Nigerian military dictatorship after being convicted in a kangaroo court for leading the protests against the environmental degradation in Ogoniland caused by multinational petroleum companies, Shell stations in Germany were burned to the ground, boycotts in Holland slashed sales, and employees in London were chastised by family and friends. Since that time, Shell has begun to reexamine all its racial, economic, and environmental policies. Nevertheless, Shell has yet to apologize for its actions in Nigeria that helped lead to Saro-Wiwa's execution, and protests against the company continue.

While facing such challenges, it is easy to overlook the social part and go straight to the technical. Social issues are human and messy. Social includes children, women, the elderly, the next generation, and government. It is hard to grapple with what may seem unrelated issues, starting with the rights, health, education, and economic opportunities available to women. But the example of Curitiba shows that design integration of social and technical innovations is necessary and can enhance both.

It will not be trivial to establish sensible policies. Emphasizing resource productivity will require the reversal of two hundred years of policies in taxes, labor, industry, and trade meant to encourage extraction, depletion, and disposal.[9] Trade policies will need to be recast so as to protect environmental capital, cultural heritage, indigenous rights, and social equity.[10] At present, worldwide trade policies are going in exactly the opposite direction. The global economy that is presently envisaged and imposed upon the world can, in Wendell Berry's words, "only institutionalize a global ignorance, in which producers and consumers cannot know or care about one another and in which the histories of all products will be lost. In such a circumstance, the degradation of products and places, producers and consumers is inevitable."[11]

In finance, central banks, lenders, investors, pension funds, and regulatory agencies will need to be engaged so that capital allocations properly account for the loss of natural and social capital. These institutions will need to create a financial system where all value is placed on the balance sheet, and where nothing is marginalized or externalized because social or biological values don't "fit" into accepted accounting procedures.

In a decade characterized by mega-mergers in the banking industry, one hopeful sign has been the vigorous emergence of the community development finance movement. From small-scale loan funds to start-up banks, and with private and federal support, a whole set of new community institutions provide credit in innovative ways at the community level, rebuilding human and social capital in hundreds of towns and cities. Not surprisingly, it is here rather than in mainstream commercial banks that banking with a natural capital focus has taken root. Shorebank Corporation, the community development pioneer, teamed up with Portland, Oregon, based Ecotrust to create ShoreBank Pacific, a commercial bank dedicated to community development and environmental restoration in the coastal and metropolitan Pacific Northwest. The bank and its nonprofit affiliate Shorebank Enterprise Pacific have together lent millions of dollars to small and medium-size businesses that enhance profitability through improved environmental management and dedication to social equity. The bank's loans are backed by "ecodeposits" from all fifty states.

In short, business has to begin to take on and engage in questions and dialogue that it has, until now, largely avoided. If natural capital is diminishing while manufactured capital is expanding, business must ultimately create production and distribution systems that reverse the loss and eventually increase the supply of natural capital. That will involve more than product design, more than marketing and competition. It will mean a fundamental reevaluation of business's roles and responsibilities.

As this book has shown, however, business will find large, unexpected benefits. While increasing labor productivity to improve competitiveness requires huge investments in capital, materials, and energy supplies to sustain its momentum, increasing resource productivity frees up large amounts of capital that can be invested in strengthening the company and in rebuilding human capital and restoring natural capital. Businesses that are moving toward advanced resource productivity are also discovering an unexpected cultural consequence to their actions. Yes, they save energy and money, create competitive advantage, and help restore the environment. But even more important, they also save people. Not only do they rebalance the roles of workers and of resource-fed machines, but they also create a renewed sense of purpose and mission. For the first time, employees' activities at work are fully and directly aligned with what is best for their children and grandchildren at home.

In a few decades, historians may write a history of our times that goes something like this: Now that the private sector has taken its proper place as the main implementer of sustainable practices, simply because they work better and cost less, the 1970s and 1980s approach of micromanagement by intensive government regulation is only a bad memory. Battles between industry and environmentalists are confined to backward countries, where inefficient and polluting industries cling to life beneath a shield of central planning. Today, the central issues for thoughtful and successful industries — the two being increasingly identical — relate not to how best to produce the goods and services needed for a satisfying life — that's now pretty well worked out — but rather to what is worth producing, what will make us better human beings, how we can stop trying to meet nonmaterial needs by material means, and how much is enough.

For many, the prospect of an economic system based on increasing the productivity with which we use natural capital, eliminating the concept of waste, and reinvesting in the earth's living systems and its people is so upbeat that it calls into question its economic viability. To answer that question, just reverse it and ask: How is it that we have created an economic system that tells us it is cheaper to destroy the earth and exhaust its people than to nurture them both? Is it rational to have a pricing system that discounts the future and sells off the past? How did we create an economic system that confuses capital liquidation with income? Wasting resources to achieve profits is far from fair, wasting people to achieve higher GDP doesn't raise standards of living, and wasting the environment to achieve economic growth is neither economic nor growth.

To make people better off requires no new theories, and needs only common sense. It is based on the simple proposition that *all* capital be valued. While there may be no "right" way to value a forest, a river, or a child, the wrong way is to give it no value at all. If there are doubts about how to value a seven-hundred-year-old tree, ask how much it would cost to make a new one. Or a new atmosphere, or a new culture. What is remarkable about this period in history is the degree of agreement that is forming globally about the relationship between human and living systems. The tens of thousands of organizations that are working toward a sustainable world are, on the whole, diverse, local, underfunded, and tenuous. Scattered across the globe, from Siberia to Chile to Kenya to Bozeman, Montana, people and institutions are organizing to defend human life and the life of the planet. Although largely uncoordinated and mostly disconnected, the mandates, directives, principles, declarations, and other statements of purpose drafted by these groups are extraordinarily consonant. Now they are being joined by the deeper voices of international organizations, and companies, large and small. The Brundtland Report ("Our Common Future"), the World Conservation Strategy by the International Union for the Conservation of Nature, the CERES Principles, the Siena Declaration, the United Nations World Charter for Nature, the Convention on Biological Diversity and the Framework Convention on Climate Change from the Earth Summit, the Hannover Principles, and hundreds more documents obscure and known are being published, circulated, and acted upon. They are important for three reasons. First, the statements are not just about preferences: Often they suggest practical solutions that flow from the principles of whole-system thinking and design. Second, the statements represent a broad consensus that is emerging from the breadth of society rather than only from its ruling structures. Third, never before in history have such disparate and independent groups created common frameworks of understanding around the world. This has never happened in politics, economics, or religion, but it is happening in the growing movement — increasingly joined now by both religion and science — toward what is being called "sustainability." Businesspeople and governments should pay close attention. In these statements, the future is writ large and in the plainest of languages.

Ernst von Weizsäcker, member of the German Bundestag, has put it this way: "We are entering the century of the environment, whether we want to or not. In this century everyone who considers himself a realist will be forced to justify his behavior in light of the contribution it made toward the preservation of the environment."[12]

Away from the shrill divisiveness of media and politics, people are remarkably consistent in what kind of future they envision for their children and grandchildren. The potential outcome of natural capitalism and sustainability also aligns almost perfectly with what American voters are saying: They want better schools, a better environment, safer communities, family-wage jobs, more economic security, stronger family support, lower taxes, more effective governments, and more local control. In this, we are like all people and they are like us.

Natural capitalism is not about fomenting social upheaval. On the contrary, that is the consequence that will surely arise if fundamental social and environmental problems are not responsibly addressed. Natural capitalism is about choices we can make that can start to tip economic and social outcomes in positive directions. And it is already occurring — because it is necessary, possible, and practical.

NOTES

Chapter 1: The Next Industrial Revolution

1. Marine Conservation Biology Institute 1998, U.S. National Academy of Sciences and British Royal Society 1992.
2. Daily 1997.
3. Coral Reef Alliance 1998.
4. Worldwide Fund for Nature (Europe) 1998.
5. Costanza et al. 1997, using 1994 dollars in which the value was at least $33 trillion.
6. Details are in World Bank 1995 at 57–66, and 1997.
7. Deane & Cole 1969.
8. Vitousek et al. 1986, 1997.
9. International Labor Organization 1994.
10. Daly 1997.
11. Schmidt-Bleek et al. 1997.
12. Present at the Club in September 1996 were: Jacqueline Aloise de Larderel, Director, UNEP-IE, Paris; Willy Bierter, Director, Institut für Produktdauer-Forschung, Giebenach, Switzerland; Wouter van Dieren, President, Institute for Environment and Systems Analysis, Amsterdam; Hugh Faulkner, formerly Executive Director, Business Council for Sustainable Development; Claude Fussler, Vice President/Environment, Dow Europe; Mike Goto, Director, Institute of Ecotoxicology, Gakushuin University, Tokyo; Leo Jansen, Director, Dutch Sustainable Technology Programme; Ashok Khosla, President, Development Alternatives, New Delhi; Franz Lehner, President, Institute for Labor and Technology, Gelsenkirchen, Germany; Jim MacNeill, MacNeill & Associates, formerly Secretary General, Brundtland Commission, Ottawa, Canada; Wolfgang Sachs, Chairperson, Greenpeace Germany; Ken Saskai, Osaka University; Friedrich Schmidt-Bleek, Vice-President, Wuppertal Institute; Walter Stahel, Director, Institute de la Durabilité, Geneva; Paul Weaver, Director, Centre for EcoEfficiency and Enterprise, University of Portsmouth; Ernst Ulrich von Weizsäcker, President, Wuppertal Institute; Jan-Olaf Willums, Director, World Business Council for Sustainable Development, Geneva; Heinz Wohlmeyer, President, Austrian Association for Agroscientific Research; Ryoichi Yamamoto, President of MRS-Japan, Institute of Industry Science, University of Tokyo.
13. Gardner & Sampat 1998 at 26 provides a useful summary of many such initiatives.
14. Romm & Browning 1994.
15. Ayres 1989.
16. American Institute of Physics 1975, adjusted for progress and new insights since then.
17. Stahel & Reday-Mulvey 1981.
18. Friend 1996.
19. Stahel also coined the term "extended product responsibility" (EPR), which is cradle-to-cradle from the manufacturer's point of view. EPR is now becoming a mandated or voluntary standard in many European industries.
20. Stahel & Børlin 1987.
21. Emerson 1994 at 26.
22. As far as we know, the term "technical nutrient" was first used by Michael Braungart in a conversation with William A. McDonough.
23. Stahel 1981.
24. Womack & Jones 1996; Womack, personal communication, 28 February 1999.
25. *San Francisco Chronicle* 1998.
26. Kaplan 1994, 1997.
27. Yergin 1991.
28. Gleick 1998.

Chapter 2: Reinventing the Wheels

1. Those desiring a generic shorthand alternative to this term, a service mark of Rocky Mountain Institute, may use "ultralight hybrid."

2. James Womack, personal communication, February 23, 1999.

3. Williams, Moore & Lovins 1997.

4. This electricity is typically stored temporarily in a relatively small and lightweight "load-leveling device." This buffer-storage device also smooths out temporary fluctuations between the rates at which power is generated and required, decoupling the engine from the demands of driving and thus allowing the engine to become smaller.

5. Cumberford 1996, Brooke 1998, Lovins 1996a, Moore 1996, 1996a, 1997, Moore & Lovins 1995, Mascarin et al. 1995, Brylawski & Lovins 1995, 1998, Lovins et al. 1997, Cramer & Brylawski 1996, Fox & Cramer 1997, Williams et al. 1997.

6. Lovins 1996a, Fig. 1.

7. A nonproprietary current chronology is maintained at www.hypercarcenter.org.

8. Brooke 1998.

9. Designed for battery-electric cars like GM's EV-1, these high-pressure tires can grip the road well, despite the lighter car's pressing down less on them, because they're narrower — keeping the pressure on the contact patch about the same — and contain special gripping compounds like silica.

10. Mascarin et al. 1995, Lovins 1997, Lovins et al. 1997.

11. Brylawski & Lovins 1995, 1998, Lovins et al. 1997. Efforts to validate this hypothesis are under way.

12. Lugar & Woolsey 1999.

13. We describe here the Proton-Exchange Membrane (PEM) type of fuel cell because it has the clearest prospects of very low cost in high-volume production. Several other types of fuel cells are in commercial or experimental use, and some show promise of potentially low cost as well. See generally Cannon 1995, and, for the entire hydrogen transition strategy, Lovins & Williams 1999.

14. Port 1998.

15. Several independent studies (e.g., Lomax et al. 1997) have used standard industrial engineering techniques to calculate costs around $20–35/kW for the fuel-cell stack. Simplified accessories would increase this only modestly.

16. Williams et al. 1997.

17. This consists of a "reformer" — a thermochemical, often catalytic, reactor that extracts the hydrogen from a hydrocarbon fuel — and devices to remove residual carbon monoxide, sulfur, and any other impurities that could poison the fuel cell's catalyst.

18. Lovins & Lehmann 2001.

19. Directed Technologies, Inc. 1997.

20. James et al. 1997.

21. Bain 1997.

22. President's Council of Advisors on Science and Technology (PCAST) 1997 at 6–34.

23. Williams 1996.

24. Lovins & Lovins 1991, Lovins et al. 1981, Samuels 1981, *Automotive News* 1983, Goldenberg et al. 1983.

25. Such as the enclosed two-person Swiss Twike and S-LEM vehicles: www.twike.com and www.s-lem.ch/. By spring 1998, these makers were selling ten a week at SF12,000 each.

26. Such as the experimental CyberTran: von Weizsäcker et al. at 124–125 and Plate 10; Dearian & Plum 1993, Dearian & Arthur 1997. CyberTran Development Co., 1223 Peoples Ave., Troy NY 12180, 518/276-2225, fax -6380, transit@transit21.com, www.cybertran.com.

27. Lovins 1998.

28. Lovins et al. 1997.

29. Today's propane and natural-gas feedstocks for polymer production could be replaced by vegetable carbohydrates: Lugar & Woolsey 1999. Henry Ford built a vegetable-composite car in 1941, and today's materials are better: *Carbohydrate Economy* 1998.

30. Lovins et al. 1997.

31. Cramer & Brylawski 1996, Fox & Cramer 1997.

32. This term, a combination of "fee" and "rebate," is credited to Dr. Arthur H.

Rosenfeld. The concept is credited to him, to Amory Lovins in the 1970s, and perhaps even earlier to IBM scientist Dr. Richard Garwin.

33. In 1989, the California legislature agreed, approving a "Drive+" feebate bill by a 7:1 margin, although outgoing governor Deukmejian vetoed it. Two years later, the Province of Ontario set the precedent by introducing a feebate supported by labor, automakers and dealers, other industry, environmentalists, and government, though like Austria's, the Ontario feebate is weak: Flavin & Dunn 1997 at 33–34.

34. A rebate of several thousand dollars for each 0.01-gallon-per-mile difference would pay about $5,000 to $15,000 of the cost of an efficient new car. That would rapidly get efficient, clean cars on the road and inefficient, dirty cars off the road: The dirtiest fifth of the car fleet produces perhaps three-fifths of its air pollution. Such "accelerated-scrappage" incentives have many variants.

35. Lovins et al. 1997. Hypercars are good news for such industries as electronics, systems integration, aerospace, software, petrochemicals, and even textiles with automated fiber-weaving techniques. Generally, while there would be some shifts in the types of work Hypercars provide, the total number and quality of jobs should improve, employment opportunities could be far more widely distributed by location and occupation, and some jobs should shift from manufacturing to the aftermarket — customization and upgrading businesses analogous to those in the computer industry. There would be less of the dangerous and mindless metal-bashing and the awkward, tedious assembly labor, more craft in lightweighting every part and optimizing all the software. In general, the dynamic new industries created should provide at least as many and as good jobs as are likely to be lost under current trends within the existing auto-related industries.

36. *Business Week* 1998.

37. Flavin & Dunn 1997 at 13–14.

38. Schafer & Victor 1997.

39. Johnson 1993.

40. MacKenzie et al. 1992, Ketcham & Komanoff 1992, Cobb 1998.

41. According to the 1996 annual Global Burden of Disease study by the World Health Organization, World Bank, and Harvard School of Public Health (Reuters 1997). In New York City, the leading cause of death among children aged 5–14 is pedestrian automobile accidents (Walljasper 1998).

42. Gibbs 1997.

43. *The Economist* 1997.

44. Case studies from Association for Commuter Transportation, ACTHQ@aol.com, 202/393-3497.

45. *Financial Times* 1998, Shoup 1997a; Prof. Donald Shoup, personal communication, 10 August 1998, Dept. of Urban Planning, UCLA, 310/825-5705.

46. Shoup 1997.

47. Buerkle 1998.

48. Id.

49. *The Economist* 1996.

50. Buerkle 1998; May & Nash 1996. (Flavin & Dunn 1997 mention Krakow as another interesting example.)

51. Gibbs 1997.

52. Newman & Kenworthy 1992; *cf.* Plowden & Hillman 1996.

53. *New Urban News* 1997, 1997a.

54. Durning 1996 at 24.

55. Komanoff & Levine 1994.

56. Gardner 1998.

57. Lowe 1990.

58. Komanoff & Levine 1994, Gardner 1998, Brown et al. 1997.

59. Gardner 1998 at 19, citing Todd Litman, Victoria (B.C.) Transport Policy Institute.

60. Gardner 1998 at 21–22.

61. von Weizsäcker et al. at 128–130, Petersen 1994; Stattauto.Hamburg.Reese@t-online.de.

62. The effects are of course wider and more complex: Cairncross 1997, Mokhtarian 1997.

63. North 1997.

64. Holtzclaw 1998.

65. Nivola 1999.

66. Gibbs 1997.

67. Seal-Uncapher et al. 1997 at 69.

68. Id., Kinsley & Lovins 1995.

69. Goldstein 1996.

70. Holtzclaw 1998, 1994, Holtzclaw & Goldstein 1991.

71. Tyson 1998.

72. Durning 1998.

Chapter 3: Waste Not

1. Womack & Jones 1996.

2. Anderson 1998.

3. Kranendonk & Bringezu 1993.

4. Liedtke 1993.

5. Wackernagel & Rees 1996.

6. Weber 1996.

7. Rathje & Murphy 1992 at 3–9.

8. Wernick & Ausubel 1995.

9. Private correspondence, Collins & Aikman, Inc.

10. Nadis & MacKenzie 1993.

11. Chemical Manufacturers Association 1993.

12. United States Bureau of the Census 1993.

13. USGS, 1995, http://h2o.er.usgs.gov/public/watuse/graphics/octo.html.

14. Water alone accounts for 1.2 million pounds per person per year. Most analyses of materials flow understandably leave water out because it dwarfs all other inputs and outputs and because it's ultimately more or less cyclic. Nevertheless, water as a material requires energy to move it to and from the processes required (Gleick 1994), and should be included in overall studies because the water is no longer potable or pure. At least 20 percent of water (3 billion tons) is so hazardous that it cannot be released into the environment and is injected into the ground.

15. *New York Times* 1995, Eckholm 1998.

16. *New York Times* 1996a; Mark Miringoff, personal communication, 914/332–6014, December 21, 1998. The index, reported with a two-year lag, was 76.9 in 1975 (for 1973) and 43.1 in 1998 (for 1996), up slightly from 37.5 in 1996 (for 1994).

17. Data from http://europa.eu.int/comm/dg05/empl&esf/docs/joint.htm.

18. Wilson 1996.

19. Mergenhagen 1996.

20. *San Francisco Chronicle* 1998a.

21. *Criminal Justice Newsletter* 1995.

22. Rowe 1996.

23. This occurred at a speech to The Conference Board given by Paul Hawken, February 1994, New York City.

24. Schor 1991.

25. L. Mishel et al. 1997.

26. By the late 1990s, half of all U.S. households, and about 80 percent of all African-American and Hispanic households, had less than three months' financial reserves.

27. *The Economist* 1996.

28. Lovins 1990.

29. Pear 1993.

30. *New York Times* 1994.

31. Pear 1993.

32. Brody 1995.

33. *New York Times* 1996.

34. Perlman 1998.

35. Drug Policy Foundation 1994.

36. Butterfield 1996.

37. Rowe 1996.

38. Daly 1997, 1998.

39. Halstead, Rowe, & Cobb 1995.

40. As quoted in Abramovitz 1998.

Chapter 4: Making the World

1. Other than in nuclear fission, where the mass difference is extremely small.

2. Interlaboratory Working Group 1997 at 4.35.

3. Sheldon 1994. Microfluidics (Amato 1998) can even make yields approach 100 percent, permitting orders-of-magnitude reductions in capital and energy costs by eliminating the need to separate undesired byproducts.

4. *Wall Street Journal* 1998; Stein et al. 1998.

5. Lovins 1998a.

6. Eng Lock Lee, personal communication, December 28, 1997 (he guided this and the following project); Zagar 1998; and proprietary data, respectively.

7. Robertson et al. 1997. We relied heavily on this reference, and discussion with its senior author, for much of the rest of this section.

8. Interlaboratory Working Group 1997 at 4.1, 4.35.

9. In the Air Sentry bistable-vortex design (Lab Crafters, Inc., 2085 5th Ave., Ronkonkoma, NY 11779, 516/471-7755, fax -9161). Further improvements of comparable size are available by complementary means (Lunneberg 1998, p. 9, methods 3 and 4), raising the saving to 70–80 percent (J. Stein, E source, personal communication, 4 August 1998). Fume hoods often account for 50–75 percent of laboratories' total energy use.

10. The Sentry, from Progressive Technologies, 200 Ames Pond Dr., Tewksbury, MA 01876-1274, 978/863-1000.

11. Arbeus 1998.

12. Thompson 1998.

13. Interlaboratory Working Group at 4.39.

14. Id. at 4.43.

15. Dr. Michael Braungart, personal communication, February 8, 1998.

16. Amato 1998.

17. Service 1998, 1998a.

18. Jim McCloy, then head of strategic planning, Georgia Power Co., personal communication, late 1980s.

19. Interlaboratory Working Group at 4.36.

20. Wann 1990, Abe et al. 1998.

21. Atmospheric Pollution Prevention Division (USEPA) 1997.

22. See Pollard 1979.

23. Alternatively, at about 480°F by autoclaving olivine in steam (Kihlstedt 1977).

24. Benyus 1997 at 98ff.

25. Id. at 135.

26. *New York Times* 1998.

27. Prof. Dr. Hanns Fischer (personal communication, December 4, 1997), Physikalisch-Chemisches Institut der Universität Zürich, Winterthurerstraße 190, CH-8057 Zürich, Switzerland, fax ++ 41 1 + 362–0139, hfischer@pci.unizh.ch. We are indebted to Dow Europe's vice president, Dr. Claude Fussler, for this example. See Fischer 1991, 1991a, 1994, and Kating & Fischer 1995.

28. Brown & Levine eds. Interlaboratory Working Group 1997 at 4.41.

29. Full implementation of this project is currently on hold.

30. Bob Salter, Osmotek, PO Box 1882, Corvallis, OR 97339, 541/753-1297,

rsalter@praxis.com, personal communications, 1998.

31. McDonough & Braungart 1998.

32. Foresight Institute, http://www.foresight.org/homepage.html.

33. This paragraph is paraphrased from Dr. Benyus's keynote address to the E source Members' Forum, October 8, 1998, Aspen, Colorado (www.esource.com).

34. Gardner & Sampat 1998 at 35, citing analyses by Walter Stahel's group.

35. Willis 1996.

36. Womack & Jones 1996 at 20.

37. Seissa 1991.

38. Perhaps a little sprue or flashing to be trimmed away and recycled, but far less than foundry and machining scrap for metals.

39. Roodman & Lenssen 1995 and RMI 1998 at 303.

40. Interlaboratory Working Group at 4.45.

41. Id. at 4.40.

42. Williams, Larson & Ross 1987 at 112.

43. Womack & Jones, 1996 at 316, n. 10.

44. Joel Makower (publisher of *Green Business Newsletter,* www.greenbiz.com), personal communication, February 3, 1998, citing company data.

45. The Design Council 1997 at 13.

46. OTA 1992 at 28.

47. Anderson (1998) says as much energy as the factory required, but ecometrics later discovered that the nylon saved was twice the amount originally thought (Jim Hartzfeld, personal communication, January 7, 1999).

48. Krol 1997; see also Young & Sachs 1994.

49. Id. at 3.

50. According to Warshall (1997), about 10 million pounds of floor carpet goes to the world's landfills every day.

51. Baldwin 1996.

52. Interagency Workgroup 1998 (citing a study by the Fraunhofer Institute in Stuttgart).

53. Interagency Workgroup 1998. The size estimate is due to Professor Robert Lund at Boston University (Deutsch 1998), and will doubtless be updated by the new

Remanufacturing Industries Council International.

54. OTA 1992 at 41.

55. Originally dubbed "Phoenix," this business has been renamed Miller SQA, standing for Simple, Quick, Affordable (www.sqa.net).

56. Deutsch 1998.

57. Interagency Workgroup on Industrial Ecology 1998.

58. Rocchi 1997 at 19.

59. McLean & Shopley 1996.

60. John Elter (VP New Business Development, Xerox Corporation), personal communication, November 1997. His 350 engineers designed the product after a week's wilderness course.

61. Deutsch 1998.

62. Nielsen & Elsbree 1997. Digital Equipment Corp., 111 Powdermill Rd, MSO2–3/C3, Maynard, MA 01754.

63. Gardner & Sampat 1998 at 37.

64. Id. at 45.

65. Graedel & Allenby 1996a at 99.

66. Rocchi 1997 at 20. The firm also developed a new type of soldering paste whose binder sublimes at soldering temperature. It can then be condensed and recovered, eliminating customers' need for a cleaning line.

67. McLean & Shopley 1996.

68. Gardner & Sampat 1998 at 46. This illustrates the importance of "industrial ecosystems," like the well-known archetype in Kalundborg, Denmark: If industries aren't close enough for one's waste actually to become another's food, the connectivity of their "ecosystem" is lost, and the potential food rots as waste.

69. *Green Business Letter* January 1998, reporting First American Scientific Corp.'s Kinetic Disintegration Technology.

70. Andreeva 1998.

71. *Automotive Industries* (1995) summarized from its 1928 coverage: "Ford used scrap lumber from shipping containers in his vehicles, cut smaller pieces for shipping containers, and ground the smallest scraps for cardboard. Tools were often reworked eight to ten times, mop pails were made from old paint cans and conveyor belt scraps were used in his cars to stop squeaks and rattles. . . . He dumped all metal scrap from rolling mills, billet trimmings, machine shop shavings and even nails into his furnaces, creating a steel mix of which nearly 50% was recycled."

72. Recycling steel takes one-third to two-thirds less energy than making it from ore, so two-fifths of crude steel worldwide is currently recovered from scrap. A similar switch to stackable, instead of single-use, packing crates that are returned and reused is heading for a 95 percent reusable container rate at Mitsubishi's Diamond Star Motors, and Mitsubishi Motor Manufacturing of America has reduced its use of wooden shipping containers by 99 percent, from 345 to 0.6 tons per year, by reusing wood and switching to steel: Kim Custer, Mitsubishi Motor Sales America (Cypress, CA), kcuster@mmsa.com, personal communications, 1995 and 1998.

73. Gardner & Sampat 1998 at 45.

74. The firm is developing a "reverse distribution network" to feed its 50,000-ton-a-year North Carolina plant. Since 1991, such innovation has helped the films business move from near failure to the top of a 57-firm marketplace while more than doubling its revenues. Goodman 1998.

75. Interagency Workgroup on Industrial Ecology 1998. Between 1970 and 1993–94, U.S. lead use rose by 15 percent, but recycling rose by 120 percent, use in gasoline was nearly eliminated, other dissipative uses were reduced, and in all, lead losses fell by 44 percent. Of course, a good goal would be to eliminate this toxic material altogether, as today's best technologies are very close to permitting.

76. From Phenix Biocomposites, Inc., St. Peter, Minnesota, 800/324-8187. Other interesting biomaterials are listed on p. 16 of the Summer 1997 *Whole Earth*.

77. Conventional packaging can be so complex that it's very hard or impossible to recycle. For example (OTA 1992), a standard snack-chips bag just two thousandths of an inch thick, can consist of nine layers — copolymer, polypropylene, copolymer, inks, polyethylene, aluminum metallization, copolymer, polypropylene, and copolymer. In contrast, a new technique (from Energy Conversion Devices in Troy, Michigan) can provide an excellent air barrier (to prevent oxidation of the food) with a silica coating just a few atoms thick on a single layer of fully biodegradable plastic. Put in a landfill, it soon decomposes into soil.

78. Roodman & Lenssen 1995 and RMI 1998 at 299.

79. For example, less steel to make the Hypercars, less cement to make the roads on which to haul the steel, less steel to make the steel and cement mills, et cetera. Using the 1970s technology still prevalent in much of the world, making a pound of nitrogen fertilizer requires not only operating energy equivalent to about five pounds of coal but also an initial plant investment of a pound of steel. Hauling and spreading it takes more work. Thus, organic farming and healthier soil mean less fertilizer, less energy, and less steel, then less transportation, road capacity, et cetera. Very little research has been done on the input-output structure of an economic equilibrium with radically reduced materials intensities.

80. American Institute of Physics 1975.

Chapter 5: Building Blocks

1. Browning 1992, Rocky Mountain Institute 1998.

2. Corbett 1981.

3. These three projects are among 84 featured in a book called *Green Development: Integrating Ecology and Real Estate* (RMI 1998).

4. Id. at 299, citing Roodman & Lenssen 1995 at 22.

5. RMI 1998 offers many examples.

6. Id.

7. Cramer-Kresselt Research 1996, cited at 2–10 in National Laboratory Directors 1997. See also Houghton 1995.

8. Romm & Browning 1994.

9. Browning 1997, 1997a.

10. Id., Romm & Browning 1994.

11. Romm & Browning 1994, Browning 1997.

12. A "ton" is a U.S. unit of the rate of cooling provided by an air conditioner or similar refrigerative system. Measured as 12,000 BTU per hour, or 3.52 thermal kilowatts, it is the rate at which cooling is delivered by melting a short (2,000-pound) ton of ice, the nineteenth-century cooling method, during a 24-hour period.

13. Houghton et al. 1992, Lovins 1992a.

14. Eley 1997.

15. Lovins 1992a.

16. Id.

17. At www.usgbc.org.

18. von Weizsäcker et al. 1997 at 191–197.

19. See www.pge.com/pec/act2/ acsaasum.html.

20. In the Antioch building, it saved 38 percent, and cost one-sixth less than it saved.

21. Kerry Tremain (ktremain@ earthlink.net), personal communication, May 29, 1999.

22. Lovins & Sardinsky 1988, Piette et al. 1989.

23. Jim Rogers PE, personal communications, February 5 and October 6, 1998 (jimrogers@mediaone.net, 508/256-1345, FAX -2226, 1 Blacksmith Rd., Chelmsford, MA 01824).

24. Komor 1996, Lovins & Heede 1990.

25. Franta & Anstead 1996.

26. Strong 1996 at 54.

27. See von Weizsäcker et al. 1997 at 62, Houghton et al. 1992 at 9. For the same building, the best design submitted in PG&E's Design Challenge, by ENSAR Group, would have saved about 87 percent of the total energy use. Other buildings described below have achieved 100 percent cooling reductions in hot climates.

28. Even in very large buildings, this is often feasible in hot climates, especially if the hottest days are also dry, and if the design uses displacement ventilation and one hundred percent outside air — both advantageous in many other respects.

29. *The Economist* 1998.

30. Froeschle 1998 and Lynn M. Froeschle AIA, personal communication, January 14, 1998.

31. RMI 1998 at 299 citing Roodman & Lenssen 1995 at 22.

32. *Environmental Building News* 1995.

33. RMI 1998 at 300–301.

34. Of ten recent case studies of recycling construction wastes, six showed unchanged and four showed reduced construction costs: *Environmental Design & Construction* 1998.

35. Id.

36. *Pacific Northwest Energy Conservation & Renewable Energy Newsletter* 1997. See also www.etbl.lbl.gov/aerosol-commercialaps.

37. Rosenfeld 1999.

38. Heederik 1998, Rosenfeld 1999, Aeroseal Inc. (www.aeroseal.com, Austin, TX, 512/445-2504).

39. Butti & Perlin 1980.

40. Lovins 1991b.

41. In Göteborg and Malmö, according to *Svenska Dagbladet,* July 30, 1998.

42. Boonyatikarn 1997.

43. www.pge.com/pec/act2/astansum.html.

44. See von Weizsäcker et al. 1997 at 25–26.

45. Atmospheric Pollution Prevention Division 1997.

46. Bancroft et al. 1991.

47. EPRI (www.kcpl.com/about/microwave.htm), updating Lamarre 1997.

48. For more details, see von Weizsäcker et al. 1997 at 33–36, and George et al. 1996 at 39.

49. Effective in 2001, though in April 1997, the Department of Energy relaxed this to 29 units. Nonetheless, by then, compared with the levels of efficiency prevailing in 1974 (but not counting the then-expected 6 percent annual growth in usage per refrigerator as they became bigger and fancier), the U.S. standards are expected to have saved the U.S. the equivalent of 45 one-thousand-megawatt power stations: Rosenfeld 1999.

50. See Shepard et al. 1990, Stickney 1992.

51. Nørgård 1989, summarized in von Weizsäcker et al. 1997 at 29–33.

52. von Weizsäcker et al. 1997 at 93, citing research by Walter Stahel.

53. Chelman 1998.

54. *New Urban News* 1997, 1997a, Walljasper 1998.

55. Durning 1996.

56. Oldenburg 1997.

57. Rosenfeld et al. 1996.

58. Rosenfeld 1999.

59. Id., n. 8.

60. Mott-Smith 1982.

61. Wassman 1999.

62. Rocky Mountain Institute 1998, Weissman & Corbett 1992.

63. Real Estate Research Corporation (RERC) 1974. See also Frank 1989.

64. Including roads (20 instead of 30 feet wide), driveways, street trees, sewers, water services, and drainage.

65. W. D. Browning, personal communication, January 6, 1999.

66. In Tannin (Orange Beach, Alabama): Chapman 1998. See also *Wall Street Journal* 1996, *New Urban News* 1997b, 1997c, RMI 1998.

67. Kinsley 1992.

Chapter 6: Tunneling Through the Cost Barrier

1. Design Council 1997a at 20.

2. Romm 1994.

3. Romm & Browning 1994.

4. Lovins 1995, 1996.

5. Lovins & Sardinsky 1988, Piette et al. 1989.

6. Mr. Lee is technical director of Supersymmetry Services Pte Ltd, 26 Ayer Rajah Crescent #05/02, 139944 Singapore, 65/777-7755, fax 779-7608.

7. More precisely, the Davis house would cost less to build if done as a normal construction project rather than a unique scientific experiment, and the Lovins house did cost less to build in 1983 with respect to its 99 percent saving of space-heating energy without its other savings.

8. Lovins 1991b.

9. Davis Energy Group 1994.

10. This phrase is due to solar designer Ed Mazria.

11. Lovins 1995. The air-conditioner downsizing was empirically confirmed elsewhere: RMI 1998 at 43, 50.

12. Including buildings (chapter 5), lighting systems (Lovins & Sardinsky 1998), motor systems (Lovins et al. 1989), hot-water systems (Bancroft et al. 1991), car design (chapter 2), and even computer design; see also Lovins 1993.

13. Lovins et al. 1989, Lovins & Sardinsky 1988.

14. See Lovins & Sardinsky 1988.

15. See Houghton et al. 1992 or Cler et al. 1997.

16. Berry 1981.

17. Alexander 1977.

Chapter 7: *Muda*, Service, and Flow

1. Womack & Jones 1996, summarized 1996a. See also Romm, who made many similar arguments (1994) and closely related them to clean production concepts.

2. Womack & Jones 1996. We are also grateful for Dr. Womack's helpful comments on this chapter; he is president of the Lean Enterprise Institute. www.lean.org.

3. Ohno 1988.

4. Womack & Jones 1996 at 66.

5. The mistake is caused by using the wrong metrics. As Womack & Jones remark (1996 at 60), "machines rapidly making unwanted parts during one hundred percent of their available hours and employees earnestly performing unneeded tasks during every available minute are only producing *muda*."

6. Womack & Jones 1996 at 216.

7. Naturalists have long known this: Haldane 1985, Colinvaux 1978.

8. Lovins & Lehmann 2001.

9. Womack & Jones 1996 at 24.

10. Womack, Jones, & Roos 1990.

11. Csikzentmihalyi 1990.

12. Lenssen & Newcomb 1996, citing Fédération Nationale de la Gestion des Equipements de l'Energie et de l'Environnement (FG&E) (undated).

13. Sprotte 1997 at 18.

14. For Otis Elevator's riposte, see Davis & Meyer 1998 at 24–25.

15. Lacob 1997 describes a next step.

16. Rocchi 1997 at 26.

17. See www.epa.gov/opptintr/greenchemistry/asrca98.htm.

18. Ron van der Graaf, director, Van Vlodrop Milieutechnologie (Vierlinghweg 32, 4612 PN Bergen op Zoom, Netherlands, ++31 164 + 265550, fax + 258125), personal communications, 1998.

19. Rocchi 1997 at 20.

20. Id. at 21.

21. Id. at 18.

22. Deutsch 1997.

23. Sprotte 1997.

24. Jan Agri (project manager, environmental Affairs, Electrolux, Stockholm), personal communications, March 9 and August 1, 1998, jan.agri@notes.electrolux.se.

25. Davis & Meyer 1998 at 14.

26. Id. at 21.

27. Id. at 183ff.

28. Agri, loc. cit. supra; Sjöberg & Laughran 1998.

29. Interface recommends that its carpet tiles be free-laid, but some installers may use an adhesive anyway. Around 1993, in an effort to mitigate fumes from broadloom installation, Interface had already introduced water-based glues, which were quickly adopted by most of the industry.

30. Personal communication, December 23, 1998.

31. Anderson 1998. The ultimate step, Anderson hopes, is to go back to the landfills and mine the 4 billion pounds of carpets arriving annually — a resource out of place.

32. Womack, personal communication, February 27, 1998.

33. Id. We are grateful for his important contribution to this discussion of stabilization of the business cycle.

34. James Womack, personal communication, February 27, 1998.

Chapter 8: Capital Gains

1. Meadows et al. 1972.

2. Ayres 1996a, 1998. Actually, the MIT team's model did include price feedback for resources, pollution cleanup, health care, and other investments. In the original resource submodel (Behrens 1973), for example, the price linkage was explicit: as *The Limits to Growth* explained at 63, that submodel "takes into account the many interrelationships among such factors as varying grades of ore, production costs, new mining technology, the elasticity of consumer demand, and substitution of other resources." *Limits* then gave an example (at 63–67) explaining the relationships between price, cost, and technology. Yet most readers ignored these references to price. That's partly because when

submodels revealed no significant difference between modeling price feedback explicitly and doing so implicitly via lookup tables, the researchers adopted the condensed form for simplicity (Behrens 1973, Meadows & Meadows 1973, Meadows al. 1992 at 165).

3. What the press interpreted as predictions of resource depletion were explicitly presented as mathematical illustrations of exponential-growth arithmetic, and were absolutely correct on the assumptions stated. The prospects for and effects of increased reserves, for example, as a consequence of increased scarcity, price, exploration, and technology, were also clearly described at 62 and 66. The conclusion drawn about resource depletion was merely (66–67, emphasis altered) that "given present [1970–72] consumption rates *and the projected increase in these rates,* the great majority of the currently important nonrenewable resources will be extremely costly 100 years from now . . . regardless of the most optimistic assumptions about undiscovered reserves, technological advances, substitution, or recycling, *as long as the demand for resources continues to grow exponentially.*" That properly qualified statement was correct in 1972 and remains correct today. Unfortunately, many people got it mixed up with the initial illustrations.

4. "Reserves," as the MIT team was well aware, are an economic concept whose numerical size shifts over time: They are the part of the geological resource base whose location is known and that can be profitably extracted at present prices using present technologies.

5. *World Oil* 1997.

6. Meadows et al. 1972.

7. The MIT team's 1972 summary conclusions were not a prediction of anything but an explanation of choices and their consequences. The book specifically included, emphasized, and advocated a feasible transition to sustainability, based largely on strong and rapid improvements in resource productivity. That is, the authors issued a warning but also conveyed "a message of promise" that their analysis "justified . . . then and still justifies" twenty years later, but that in hindsight could now be even more strongly stated: Meadows et al. 1992 at xiii, xv–xvi. However, the fictitious "prophecy of doom" image dominated press coverage of the book and has shaped most people's perceptions of its message ever since.

8. Recer 1996, Ehrlich et al. 1997.

9. One economist who didn't believe this was invited to climb into a large bell jar with as much money as he wanted and see how long he'd last.

10. Calvin 1998.

11. A clear explanation of nonlinear response in social systems (Gladwell 1996) illustrates the concept from everyday experience: "Tomato catsup / In a bottle, / First none'll come, / and then the lot'll."

12. Stevens 1998.

13. Ayres 1995. Exceptionally, nuclear reactions do convert mass into energy, but so far as is known, their sum remains constant.

14. Technical readers will recognize this concept as "negentropy," rigorously analyzed by Nicolas Georgescu-Roegen in his dense text *Entropy and the Economic Process.*

15. Hillel 1991.

16. Gardner 1998a.

17. UNEP 1996.

18. Abramovitz 1998.

19. *San Francisco Chronicle* 1998c.

20. The primary references are reviewed in Brown et al. 1998 at 52.

21. Yoon 1998.

22. These organisms, such as algae, slime molds, and flagellates, have cell nuclei but are neither animals, plants, nor fungi.

23. Eisenberg 1998 at 27–28.

24. Id. at 23.

25. Stuart & Jenny 1999.

26. Eisenberg 1998. For the same reasons, the root system of one young rye plant was found to have 6,875 square feet of surface area — 130 times that of the aboveground plant — and the network of fungi in one ounce of rich forest soil, if it could be unraveled, could easily extend for two miles: Id. at 24.

27. As quoted by Margulis and Sagan 1997 at 18.

28. As quoted in Daily 1997.

29. Abramovitz 1998.

30. Gary Paul Nabhan and Steven Buchmann have formed the Forgotten Pollinators Campaign to educate the public about the growing threat human activities place on domestic crops and wild plants. Forgotten pollinators include the 4–5,000 wild bees native to North America but also hummingbirds, butterflies, beetles, moths, bats, and even certain species of flies. The Forgotten Pollinators Campaign, Arizona-Sonora Desert Museum, 2021 N. Kinney Road, Tucson, AZ 85743; 520/883-3006, fax -2500, fpollen@azstarnet.com.

31. McHugh 1998.

32. Newman 1997.

33. De Groot 1994 (this is an amended and reworded rendition of de Groot's list of Regulation, Carrier, Production, and Information Functions); Cairns 1997 (which contains a very useful framework for understanding conditions for sustaining natural capital, based in part on the work of Dr. Karl-Henrik Robèrt, founder of The Natural Step).

34. The analysis published in *Nature* included sixteen specific biomes — geographical regions containing specific communities of flora and fauna — and identified the value of seventeen ecosystem services by economic activity within each biome. The biomes included marine and terrestrial environments: open ocean (33.2 million hectares), estuaries (180 million hectares), seaweed and algae beds (200 million hectares), coral reefs (62 million hectares), continental shelves (2.6 million hectares), lakes and rivers (200 million hectares), tropical forests (1,900 million hectares), temperate forests (2,955 million hectares), grasslands and rangelands (3,898 million hectares), tidal marshes and mangroves (165 million hectares), swamps and floodplains (165 million hectares). The economic values included net income, replacement cost, market value, resource production, real estate value in the case of cultural services, damage prevention, shadow prices, external costs mitigated, direct or estimated revenues in the case of recreation, avoided costs and damages, lost income in the case of erosion, restoration costs in cases of erosion control, option value, rents, opportunity costs, dockside prices for marine products, flood damage control, and energy flow analyses. One hundred seventeen prior studies, surveys, and papers were used as primary data and valuation sources for the paper. The study did not include the value of nonrenewable fuels and minerals or of the atmosphere itself.

35. Noss et al. 1995, Noss & Peters 1995.

36. We are indebted to Susan Meeker-Lowry, who made this point eloquently in a letter to the editor regarding Jane Abramovitz's article in *Worldwatch* cited earlier (Abramovitz 1998): "Nature doesn't provide us with services, like a waitress or mechanic or doctor. The diverse species and processes that make up ecosystems do what they do naturally. . . . Putting a price tag on it is terribly misleading, because in the end we cannot buy nature because we cannot create it."

37. Peter Raven, private correspondence, February 15, 1999.

38. As quoted in Hobsbawm 1996.

39. Daly at 22 in Jansson et al. 1994.

40. Id.

41. Myers 1998.

42. Id. and Roodman 1996.

43. World Bank 1995 at 48.

44. Rocky Mountain Institute first thoroughly analyzed federal subsidies to the U.S. energy sector for FY1986, then helped the Alliance to Save Energy update to FY1989. The only official assessments, whether by the U.S. government or by such international bodies as the International Energy Agency, OECD, UN, and World Bank, continue to omit most of the subsidies, partly on the specious grounds that some of them are also available to certain other industries (though not for, say, investments in saving energy). Transparency in subsidies is becoming somewhat greater in a few European countries.

45. *The Economist*, December 6, 1997. In fairness, the federal subsidies to the U.S. oil industry, unlike other fossil-fuel industries, are approximately offset by federal excise taxes collected on its retail products.

46. Myers 1998.

47. Roodman 1996.

48. U.S. Congress 1998; Friends of the Earth 1998.

49. Kinsella et al. 1999.

50. *The Economist,* December 13, 1997.

51. Id.

52. Sarah Gray, Farm Service Agency, USDA, personal communication, December 1998.

53. All these examples are from the World Bank (1995) at 55–65.

54. Caulfield 1989.

55. Zepezauer 1996.

56. Id.

57. Randy O'Toole, correspondence April 1998. The Thoreau Institute. www.ti.org. This number is an approximation of the annual losses from National Forest timber sales.

58. Bagby 1996.

59. Ayres 1996a, 1998.

60. Id.

61. Gardner & Sampat 1998 at 48.

62. Axelsson 1996.

63. Gardner & Sampat 1998 at 43.

64. Roodman 1998.

65. One of the best recent works in the area of tax shifts is Hammond et al. 1997.

66. Myers 1998; *San Francisco Chronicle* 1998b.

67. Anderson 1997.

68. In the fifth year, various external circumstances unrelated to Interface's sustainability work hurt the company, but it remained profitable.

Chapter 9: Nature's Filaments

1. McPherson 1994.

2. Walton 1999.

3. Warshall 1997 at 4–7, plus supplementary materials 8–21.

4. Niklas 1996 and Willis 1996.

5. Warshall 1997 at 6.

6. Id. at 7.

7. *Earth Impact* 1997, Harmony Catalog Newsletter, www.simplelife.com.

8. von Weizsäcker et al. at 88–89.

9. Chouinard & Brown 1997.

10. *Organic Cotton Directory 1998–99.*

11. Warshall 1997 at 7, 10.

12. Wernick & Ausubel 1995.

13. The Sustainable Forestry Working Group's 1998 U.S. case studies are available from Island Press, www.islandpress.org. See also Chipello 1998.

14. Nilsson 1997 at 121.

15. U.N. Food and Agriculture Organization 1995.

16. World Resources Institute 1994 at 15.

17. Or 20,000 acres per year with 5-day-a-week cutting. This assumes 117.4 ft^3 of wood is used per ton of pulp, a U.S. average of 1,550 ft^3 of wood per acre, and a large chemical pulp mill with a 1,000-short-ton-per-day production capacity. Based on figures cited in: Haynes 1990 at 52, 262.

18. Grieg-Gran et al. 1997.

19. According to the American Forest & Paper Association, www.afandpa.org, downloaded February 15, 1998.

20. International Institute for Environment and Development (IIED) 1995; summarized in Grieg-Gran et al. 1997; cited in Rice 1995 at 103.

21. Rainforest Action Network (RAN) 1995 at 10; and Recycled Paper Coalition 1993.

22. The Paper Task Force (Duke University, Environmental Defense Fund, Johnson & Johnson, McDonald's, The Prudential Insurance Company of America, Time Inc.) 1995 at 54. Summarized by Blum et al. 1997.

23. Lotspeich 1995 at 26.

24. Macht 1997. Hire Quality is at 773/281-6924.

25. Torben Petersen, information technology manager, Oticon A/S (Strandvejen 58, DK-2900 Hellerup, fax 45 39 27 79 00), personal communication, March 24, 1998.

26. Leica AG, CH-9435 Heerbrugg, Switzerland, fax ++ 41 71 + 727-3127.

27. BankAmerica 1997.

28. The DesignSuite catalog is described in Port 1998.

29. Dudley & Stolton 1996; cited in Brown 1997 at 68, n. 12. Prof. Paul Barten of the Yale School of Forestry and Environmental Studies estimates this as about 100 acres of pulp trees (personal communication, October 25, 1995).

30. Paper Task Force 1995 at 57–58.

31. Rice 1995 at 60; RAN 1995 at 10; Ayres & Ayres 1996 at 219; Friends of the Earth 1993.

32. IIED 1995, Richert & Venner 1994.

33. Puder 1992.

34. Brownstein et al. 1997, a report of a 1995–98 independent inquiry coordinated by RMI called the Systems Group on Forests, and seeking ways to reduce pressure on primary forests in a way that would also benefit forest-products companies. The formula summarized here is heuristic, not exhaustive. For example, it doesn't include improving the weather-protection and hence the lifetime of outdoor structural wood, nor indirect methods, such as saving forests by using electricity more efficiently instead of flooding forests for hydroelectric dams. The formula's linear structure assumes that the variables are independent of one another, while in fact its eight terms have complex interactions through both price and physical (by-product, coproduct, et cetera) relationships. The terms of this formula also don't account for all of the kinds of pressure on forests: Forests are degraded or destroyed in many other ways than simply extracting fiber from them or clearing them for small farms. There are also ambiguities about where among the eight terms a given innovation should be classified, though that's probably not important so long as each option is counted once and only once.

35. Brownstein et al. 1997.

36. IIED 1995 reports partial duplexing cut AT&T's paper cost by about 15 percent.

37. Penzias 1995.

38. Warshall 1997.

39. Brownstein et al. 1997.

40. Calculated as $(1 \div 0.9)$.

41. For example, from 3 to 15 m³/ha-y wood production; cf. Sedjo 1994 at 11; these yields are within average or typical ranges. For example, the average U.S. harvest from natural forest, about 110 m³/ha, is roughly one-sixth of the standing volume at harvest of a good New Zealand plantation of 30-year-old softwoods. Wood production at an average rate (over the stand life) of 20 m³/ha-y is "routinely achievable in temperate softwoods (to produce about 700 m³/ha

at 30 years)" (Andy Pearce, Landcare Research New Zealand Ltd., personal communication, September 8, 1998).

42. Cf. EDF example in Paper Task Force Final Report at 57. Basis weight measures the amount of fiber per unit area.

43. For heuristic simplicity this term has been moved here from its usual position among the materials-cycle improvements.

44. Chapter 4, www.pge.com/pec/act2/adavssum.html, and Davis Energy Group 1994 at App. F.

45. Davis Energy Group 1994, PG&E 1993.

46. Gorman 1998.

47. www.bellcomb.com or 612/521-2425. The firm currently sells only smaller, non-building components, but has demonstrated the concept's suitability for small buildings.

48. Composites News 1995.

49. Machalaba 1998, Resource Conservation Alliance 1998.

50. For example, Eastman Kodak's pallet and stacking-pattern redesign saved over 7 million pounds of wood and $380,000 in a single year: Inform Reports Fall/Winter 1997.

51. At 1809 Carter Ave., Bronx, NY 10457, 212/222-7688, fax -2047.

52. RAN 1995 at 29–30.

53. American Forest & Paper Association 1994.

54. That's just for paper as such; by 1993, recycling was already over 50 percent for newspapers and nearly 60 percent for corrugated cardboard.

55. U.N. FAO 1998 (1996 data).

56. Warshall 1997 at 6. This comparison is uncorrected for differing moisture content, and uses removals data for 1991 from Haynes et al. 1995, table 34, at 41, using conversion factors from Haynes 1990, table B-7, at 262.

57. Joe Haworth, Sanitation District of Los Angeles County, 562/908-4202, personal communication, 1999.

58. Boxboard Containers 1993 at 44–45; Pulp & Paper Week 1993 at 24–28.

59. 59 Fountain St., Framingham, MA 01702, 508/620-0421, www.decopier.com.

60. The ink was first suggested as an experiment by German chemist Michael Braungart. Although practically possible, it has not been pursued as far as the authors know, primarily because of the institutional barriers to its acceptance.

61. Mann 1998 at 60; Horrigan et al. 1998.

62. Sedjo 1995 at 177–209 in Bailey ed. 1995 at 180. At p. 202 he gives total world forest area as "just a bit below 4 billion hectares," or nearly 9.9 billion acres. Definitions and data on this point differ widely, and also change over time: Brown 1997 at 96 cites 8.5 billion acres of forests, excluding woodlands, which have trees but no closed canopy. For present purposes we adopt Sedjo's higher estimate.

63. This implies a productivity of 8 m^3/ha-y (114 ft^3/acre-y). *Average* U.S. temperate and boreal software forest productivity is only 2 (Roger Sedjo, Resources for the Future, personal communication, September 12, 1996) or 3 (Haynes 1990, 1986 data in Fig. 29 at 54) m^3/ha-y. However, fast-growing species and plantations commonly provide more than 20 m^3/ha-y — Northwest poplars can yield 30–50, Louisiana cottonwood 30–45 — and genetic engineering already well under way is expected to provide two to three and a half times higher productivity still (40–70 m^3/ha-y or 572–1,000 ft^3/acre-y). Consistent with Sedjo's line of reasoning, IIED found that plantations could in principle provide the world's entire pulpwood needs, about half the total industrial harvest, from an area of only 100 million acres, equivalent to the land area of Sweden plus Paraguay (IIED 1996 at 64–66). That's only 1 percent (they called it 1.5 percent) of world forest area, or about one-third the *present* area of tree plantations, or less than four times the present area of all high-yield ones.

64. Assuming 40–70 m^3/ha-y. The lower end of this range "is available . . . in some temperate and tropical hardwood plantations, especially eucalyptus both temperate and tropical" (Andy Pearce, loc. cit.), while the higher end may be achievable in "extremely short rotation pulpwood tropical plantations" whose long-term sustain-

ability is not yet established. Warshall (1995) found that plantations recently occupied about 100–135 million ha, including 40 million ha of industrial plantations, of which 11–14 million ha were high-yielding. Plantations accounted for at most 4 percent of world forest area, but yielded about 34 percent of the total harvest.

65. Taking this loss to be 12.8 million ha/y: U.N. FAO 1997.

66. Sedjo 1997 at 10, 30.

67. However, Pearce (loc. cit.) correctly notes that a given forest cannot, in general, simultaneously reduce floods, recharge groundwater, *and* yield more surface water: "[T]he water balance is a fixed sum game and generally you can't have all three of these together." These services may, however, be provided to a significant degree in different places or times.

68. Krause et al. 1989 at I.3–49.

69. Pearce (loc. cit.) says that for 1.2 million hectares of New Zealand exotic softwood plantations, fiber value was about 40 percent of ecosystem value, but those plantations are about six times as productive of fiber as a typical U.S. natural forest, and being less ecologically diverse, may be presumed to have a lower natural capital value.

70. Wang & Hu 1998.

71. Warshall 1997 at 12.

72. Atchison 1995.

73. Smith 1997 at 76, citing U.N. Food & Agriculture Organization 1993.

74. Ayres 1993 at 6.

75. Warshall 1997 at 7.

Chapter 10: Food for Life

1. Naylor 1996 — the main source for the next three paragraphs.

2. Berry 1999.

3. Benyus 1997 at 20, 53.

4. U.N. FAO 1998. Nitrogen fertilizer now accounts for half the on-farm energy used to grow high-yield crops.

5. Ayres 1996 at 12. Berner & Berner 1996, at 101, show 158 million metric tons of human and 123 million metric tons of natural nitrogen fixation per year.

6. Conway 1997 at 33; see also 108–139.

7. Lal et al. 1998 at 17.

8. Id. at 18–19.

9. Soil scientists Lal et al. (1998 at 32) state that U.S. cropland's soil erosion rate fell by about one-third during the years 1982–92.

10. Lal 1995.

11. Eisenberg 1998 at 31.

12. Id. at 26.

13. Naylor 1996 at 117.

14. Id. at 111.

15. Sears 1935, Carter & Hale 1974, Hillel 1991.

16. Eisenberg 1998 at 31.

17. Reddy et al. 1997, at 47, citing WRI 1992. A further 1.8 billion acres is lightly degraded and can be restored by good soil conservation practices.

18. Naylor 1996.

19. Sedjo 1997 at 27. That drop was offset by more efficient processing later.

20. Diamond 1997 at 132.

21. Wes Jackson notes that about 85 percent of human caloric intake comes from a 65-million-year-old family of grasses, none of which happens to be poisonous.

22. Benyus 1997.

23. A few small nonprofit groups like Seed Savers Exchange (3076 N. Winn Rd., Decorah, IA 52101, http://nj5.injersey.com/~jceres/garden/sse.html) are making heroic efforts to preserve such biodiversity, but their resources are far smaller than the task.

24. Graedel & Allenby 1996 at 331.

25. National Research Council 1996.

26. Prof. David Pimentel (Cornell U.), personal communication, September 1998.

27. Specter 1998, citing estimates by the U.N. World Food Program.

28. Benyus 1997 at 18.

29. Id. In addition, nearly 50 weed species now resist herbicides (Conway 1997 at 209).

30. DeVore 1996 offers instructive examples.

31. *Gene Exchange* 1998, citing Gould et al. 1997 and Tabashnik et al. 1997, 1997a; Mellon & Rissler 1998. Beneficial insects can also be harmed: Halweil 1999.

32. Conway 1997 at 153.

33. Prof. Richard Harwood (Michigan State U.), personal communication, November 12, 1998.

34. That is about three-fifths as great as their consumption of iron and steel: Wernick & Ausubel 1995 at 470.

35. Daily & Ehrlich 1996.

36. Krause et al. 1989 at I.3–14.

37. Conway 1997, Lovins & Lovins 1991.

38. Successfully tested at the USDA Grain Marketing Research Laboratory, 1515 College Ave., Manhattan, KS 66502, 785/776-2728; contact agricultural engineer Harry Converse.

39. Bloome & Cuperus 1984.

40. von Weizsäcker et al. at 51–53, based on work by Wouter van Dieren and Geert Posma, and on personal communications with the former.

41. Wade 1981; see also UNDP 1996.

42. von Weizsäcker et al. at 117–121.

43. National Laboratory Directors 1997 at B-33.

44. Frantzen 1998, Lane 1998.

45. Eisenberg 1998 at 23, 29. See also Warshall 1999 and accompanying articles.

46. Epprecht 1998; see also Ho & Steinbrecher 1998, Ho et al. 1998, and www.ucsusa.org.

47. Prof. Robert M. Goodman (U. of Wisconsin), personal communication, October 7, 1998.

48. Bintrim et al. 1997.

49. Worster 1993.

50. Warshall 1999.

51. Lovins & Lovins 1991.

52. Krause et al. 1989 at I.3–32. Contrary to the conservative assumption made by Harmon et al. (1990), the data cited by Krause do show a 10 percent soil-carbon loss when the natural forest becomes managed.

53. Ross & Steinmeyer 1990.

54. Lal et al. 1998 at iv.

55. Id. at vi.

56. Id. at 83 estimate that the total carbon sequestration and offset potential from the roughly 337 million acres of U.S. cropland is 120–270 million metric tons of carbon per year, or 0.4–0.8 metric tons per acre per year.

57. Id.

58. For comparison, USDA/Beltsville test plots in the 1980s showed 0.2–0.6 percent carbon gain per year through light (40 t/ha-y) applications of compost and manure.

59. Id. at 92, Lal 1997.

60. Krause et al. 1989, p. I.3–20, Gardner 1998a.

61. Gardner 1998a.

62. Haruki Tsuchiya (personal communication, June 22, 1998) estimates that the animals' respiration emits 3 billion metric tons of CO_2 per year, compared with 2 billion for the earth's human population, 5 billion for cars, and 21 billion for all fossil-fuel combustion.

63. Krause et al. 1989, EPA 1989.

64. Crutzen et al. 1986.

65. Soden 1988.

66. Browning 1987.

67. EPA 1989 at VII-270.

68. Krause et al. 1989 at I.3–19.

69. Gardner 1998a.

70. Id.

71. Savory & Butterfield 1999; Center for Holistic Management, 1010 Tijeras NW, Albuquerque, NM 87102, 505/842-5252, center@holisticmanagement.org.

72. Dana Jackson, Land Stewardship Project, personal communication, September 30, 1998; DeVore 1998.

73. DeVore 1998a.

74. Id.

75. Gardner 1998.

76. These more than doubled in rotational vs. continuous grazing in one Wisconsin experiment: Dansingburg & DeVore 1997.

77. Quoted in DeVore 1998.

78. NRC 1989. Similar economic benefits have been found in many hundreds of diverse U.S. and German farms: Brody 1985, Bechmann 1987, Bossel et al. 1986.

79. NRC 1989.

80. Jackson et al. 1984.

81. Conway 1997 at 200. The success of this approach naturally depends on addressing not only agricultural but also contextual social needs, especially the role of women, microcredit, and land tenure.

82. von Weizsäcker et al. at 99–101, The Land Institute 1993, Ecology Action 1993.

83. Benyus 1997 at 36–37, Fukuoka 1978.

84. Conway 1997 at 177–178.

85. Id. at 279.

86. Such as nitrogen-fixing blue-green alga *Anabaena azollae* in rice culture: Conway 1997 at 231–232.

87. Krause et al. 1989 at I.3–23, 24.

88. Benyus 1997 at 12–13.

89. Id. at 36–46.

90. Id. at 25.

91. von Weizsäcker et al. at 97–99, The Land Institute 1993.

92. Pimentel 1997.

Chapter 11: Aqueous Solutions

1. The rest of the freshwater 35 million cubic kilometers is in the polar icecaps and inaccessibly deep aquifers. See generally U.N. Commission on Sustainable Development (UNCSD) 1997.

2. Some 3.3 million people, three-fourths of them babies and children, die each year of diarrhea, and 1.5 billion people are infected with intestinal worms similarly spread by fecal-oral contamination: Simpson-Herbert 1996 at 47–53, citing World Health Organization 1995. In 1990, WHO estimated that 1.3 billion people in the developing world lacked access to safe and plentiful drinking water and 2.6 billion to adequate sanitation: http://206.168.2.226/information.html, downloaded January 14, 1998; UNCSD 1997; Gleick 1998 at 40. Pollution is often gross, large-scale, and industrial: In China, four-fifths of the major rivers are too toxic to support fish (Brown & Halweil 1998). In the United States in 1997, after decades of cleanup, only 16 percent of the 2,111 watersheds in the lower 48 United States had "good" water quality, 36 percent were "moderate," 21 percent had more serious problems, and 27 percent were indeterminate. (The U.S. Environmental Protection Agency's 1997 Index of Watershed Indicators is available at http://www.epa.gov/surf/iwi; Surf your Watershed is one level up [no iwi]. Additional instructions and hard copy [the Index is publication #EPA-841-R-97-010] are available from the National Center for Environmental Publications and Information, PO Box 42419, Cincinnati, OH 45242-2419, 513/489-8190, fax -8695.) The U.S. Department of Agriculture considers 46 percent of all U.S. counties, with 54 million people who drink water from underground, susceptible to groundwater contamination from farm chemicals, chiefly the herbicide atrazine and the insecticide aldicarb: *U.S. Water News,* November 1997. Half of all Americans rely on groundwater for their drinking water (Benyus 1997 at 19). Not surprisingly, U.S. imports of bottled water have more than doubled in the past decade (Kummer 1998).

3. Chao 1995, cited by Gleick 1998 at 70.

4. Brown et al. 1998 at 169.

5. Id. at 5–6.

6. Brown & Halweil 1998.

7. Gleick 1998 at 125–131, a compilation of five millennia of water conflicts.

8. Gleick 1994 reports that desalination, the last-resort technology for those lacking freshwater but rich in money and energy, provides only one-thousandth of the world's freshwater use. The economics of greatly increasing that fraction are discouraging. The minimum energy theoretically required to desalt a thousand gallons of seawater is 10.6 megajoules — the energy contained in ten ounces of oil. However, the best large-scale desalination plants operating in 1994 used about 30 times the theoretical limit, and are unlikely to improve by more than another threefold.

9. Postel et al. 1996.

10. Id., estimating a potential 10 percent increase in accessible runoff over the next 30 years, while population grows by about 45 percent.

11. In mixed current dollars: Rogers 1993.

12. Bredehoeft 1984 at 17.

13. Rogers 1993, paraphrased in Gleick 1998 at 6.

14. These two are somewhat analogous and often related: Gleick 1994.

15. Postel et al. 1996 estimate that the fraction of the earth's accessible water runoff appropriated for human use could rise from 54 percent in 1995 to more than 70 percent by 2025.

16. Gleick et al. 1995. Reisner (1986/93) estimated that enough water to meet the

needs of Los Angeles's 13 million people was being used to irrigate California pastures for feeding livestock.

17. Jackson 1980.

18. The Ogallala provided one-tenth of America's total irrigation, and watered two-tenths of the nation's irrigated land.

19. Bredehoeft 1984 at 38–39.

20. Thanks to Dr. Wes Jackson of the Land Institute (Salina, KS 67401) for these insights. Prof. Jackie Giuliani of Antioch University (Los Angeles) notes that preparing and serving a single fast-food order of a hamburger, fries, and a soda requires over 1,500 gallons.

21. *U.S. Water News,* April 1992; the sample size exceeded 700 operations in four states.

22. Id.

23. Gleick 1998 at 10.

24. Solley et al. 1998.

25. Gleick 1998 at 12.

26. Brown & Halweil 1998.

27. Pinkham & Dyer 1993 at 9–10.

28. From 1.4 to 0.2 million acre-feet per year by 1991. Due to the 1992–96 drought, the depletion rate rebounded to 0.6–0.8 Maf/y by 1997, but steady efficiency improvements are continuing. Wayne Wyatt, High Plains Water District, 2930 Ave. Q, Lubbock, TX 79405, 806/762-0181, personal communication, February 16, 1998, and Laird & Dyer 1992 at 4–5.

29. Largely through canal lining and better management: Laird & Dyer 1992 at 5–7, Pinkham & Dyer 1994 at 10–12.

30. Gleick 1998 at 23.

31. For further case studies, see Gleick 1999.

32. Such designs as low-energy precision application can boost sprinkler efficiencies from 60–70 percent to 95 percent (Postel 1997).

33. Polak 1998, courtesy of RMI Director Dr. Michael Edesess.

34. DeSena 1997.

35. The Global Cities Project 1991 at 61. See generally Chaplin 1994.

36. *U.S. Water News* 1992.

37. Knopf 1999.

38. Patchett undated; *Midwest Real Estate News* 1992.

39. Jim Patchett, personal communications, 1997–98.

40. Installation is typically 4–23 times and maintenance 7–21 times cheaper, depending on local conditions.

41. Relatively clean but nonpotable water, filtered and recovered from sinks, bathtubs, showers, and clothes- and dishwashers.

42. Postel 1997, Jones 1993.

43. Osann & Young 1998; Pape 1998; *Australian Plumbing Industry* 1992; see also Ecos Catalog, "Tools for Low-Water and Waterless Living," 152 Commonwealth Ave., Concord, MA 01742-2842, 978/369-3951.

44. Waterless Co. LLC, 1223 Camino del Mar, Del Mar, CA 92014, 800/244-6364, www.waterless.com.

45. A 42-unit retrofit to avoid replumbing an old building when replacing continuous-flow urinals saved 42–54,000 gal/unit-y, with a 3.4-year payback without or 1.7 y with a rebate from the Seattle Water Department: Nelson 1995.

46. Drangert 1997 in Drangert et al. 1997. A person excretes about 500 liters of urine and 50 liters of feces (3/4 water) per year.

47. This greatly complicates the safe, economical, and sustainable handling of both: Jönsson 1997, in Drangert et al. 1997.

48. According to "On-Site Waste Treatment — What Are the Benefits?" Clivus Multrum, Inc., 15 Union St., Lawrence, MA 01840, 978/725-5591, 800/962-8447, fax 978/557-9658, www.clivusmultrum.com/. Id. gives the ratio as about 36–360 in Swedish practice.

49. Simpson-Hebert 1996. The nutrients in a person's annual excreta roughly equal those required to grow enough cereals to feed that person for a year: Drangert et al. 1997; Jönsson 1997.

50. In developing countries, 95 percent of sewage is discharged untreated: World Resources Institute 1992. Even the wealthiest countries cannot afford tertiary treatment and safe disposal of industrially contaminated sludge.

51. Simpson-Hebert 1996.

52. Rogers 1997, Kalbermatten et al. 1982.

52a. WaterHealth International, 1700 Soscol Ave., Suite 5, Napa, CA 94559, 707/252-9092, fax -1514, www.waterhealth.com. Alternatively, very inexpensive house-scale water purifiers have been developed by Susan Murcott, murcott@mit.edu.

53. About 88 percent of N, 67 percent of P, and 71 percent of K: Jönsson 1997. Urine also releases far less ammonia if not exposed to an enzyme secreted by *Micrococcus urea*, a bacterium in feces.

54. Even if diluted 10:1 with water, one person's urine may be right for fertilizing as little as 10–20 square meters of intensive garden. Such a mixture of urine with household graywater is an essentially perfect fertilizer that can close the nutrient loop for growing a person's food: Drangert 1997 in Drangert et al. 1997.

55. Id.; Del Porto & Steinfeld 1999. Carol Steinfeld informs us that urine-diverting models are offered by Ekologen and Dubbletten in Sweden.

56. For example, those from Energy Technology Laboratories, 2351 Tenaya Drive, Modesto, CA 95354, 800/344-3242, www.savewater.com.

57. The range depends on pressure; the vendor is ETL (previous note).

58. Omni Products, Chronomite Laboratories, 1420 W. 240th St., Harbor City, CA 90710, 800/447-4962, provides models with nominal flow rates of 1.5, 2.0, and 2.5 gpm.

59. U.S. models in early 1998 included Maytag's "Neptune" (http://neptune.maytag.com), Amana's "LTA85" (www.raytheon.com/rap/amana), and Frigidaire's "Gallery" (www.frigidaire). See Lamarre 1997a.

60. Posh Wash, evenings 503/257-9391.

61. *Consumer Reports* 1997.

62. Hart Industries of Laguna Hills, CA, now apparently defunct; but the idea seems feasible.

63. *U.S. Water News* April 1992 at 18.

64. Ian Michaels, New York City Department of Environmental Protection, Room 2454 Municipal Bldg, 1 Center St., New York, NY 10007.

65. Liebold 1995.

66. North American Residential End Use Study (see Nelson 1997).

67. Chernick 1988.

68. City of Boulder, "Water Conservation Facts and Tips," P.O. Box 791, Boulder, CO 80306, 303/441-3240.

69. Watersense and Northern Indiana Public Service Company are undertaking 1998 pilot installations of a programmable system, WatersOff!, that can trigger shutoff or notification on detecting major leaks (typically over 1 gpm) and can also recognize slow leaks (down to 0.05 gpm). Notification can be integrated with an emergency plumber call arranged by the utility. Kevin Shea, Watersense, Inc., 83 Second Ave., Burlington, MA 01801, 617/273-2733, kevinshea1@aol.com.

70. Fritz 1984–89.

71. U.S. Water News 1998.

72. Bill Ferguson, Water Development Planner, Public Works Dept., PO Box 1990, Santa Barbara, CA 93102, 805/564-5460.

73. Beth O'Connor, Utilities Market Services, City of Palo Alto, P.O. Box 10250, Palo Alto, CA 94303, 650/329-2549.

74. Preston 1994.

75. Vickers 1990.

76. John Wallace, Office Administrator, San Simeon Acres Community Services, Rt. 1, Box S17, San Simeon, CA 93452, 805/544-4011.

77. By an average of 0.22 ppm per year since 1987. Pinkham 1994 and personal communication, February 6, 1998, Ron Bishop, General Manager, Central Platte Natural Resource District, 215 N. Kaufmann Ave., Grand Island, NE, 308/385-6282.

78. Sharpe et al. 1984 at 12, Rubin 1982.

79. See also Postel 1992, citing Wilson 1997 at 10.

80. Gleick 1998 at 20–21.

81. Preliminary test data from Philip Paschke, Community Services Division, Seattle Public Utilities, 206/684-7666, personal communication, February 5, 1998. The site's operations manager is John Terry, 206/455-2000.

82. Dennis Brobst, Director, Water and Sewer Division, Calvert County, 175 Main Street, Prince Frederick, MD 20678, 410/535-1600.

83. von Weizsäcker et al. 1997 at 82–83.

84. Id. at 83, with thanks to Wendy Pratt of California Futures (Sacramento).

85. Alan Niebrugge, personal communication, 1994. Then Manager of Environmental Services. Contact Mike McMahan, GS Technologies, 8116 Wilson Road, Kansas City, MO 64125, 816/242-5638.

86. By Intel: http://www.intel.com/intel/other/ehs/management.html.

87. Using the new AWWA 44.6 gpcd average; a "nonconserving" household averages 64.6.

88. That's the rural Texas norm, although Dr. McElveen, a physician, uses ultraviolet light to treat the water.

89. U.S. Water News 1992a.

90. Wymer 1997.

91. For comparison, the canonical 133-year flood is 10 inches in 24 hours.

92. These can respond to local demand or be remotely "dispatched" by city water managers. Such dispatch of a "networked reservoir" could also empty cisterns in time for anticipated storms.

93. The TREES software package and related information are available from Tree People (12601 Mulholland Drive, Beverly Hills, CA 90210, 818/753-4600) or project administrator PS Enterprises (310/393-3703, fax -7012). TREES stands for Transagency Resources for Environmental and Economic Sustainability, and comprises diverse government, community, and environmental groups.

94. Jeff Wallace and Andy Lipkis, personal communication, October 30, 1998.

95. Re safety, see City of Los Angeles 1992, Warshall 1995a.

96. John Irwin, Thetford Systems, Inc., Box 1285, Ann Arbor, MI 48106. The project serves more than 1,100 people.

97. Joe Towry, Public Utilities Department, 290 16th St. N, St. Petersburg, FL 33713, 727/892-5095.

98. Chuck W. Carry, Sanitation Districts of Los Angeles County, Box 4998, Whittier, CA 90607.

99. Adler & Mace 1990; Prof. Avner Adin (Hebrew U. of Jerusalem, Div. of Environmental Science, personal communication, December 23, 1998).

100. *Sanitation and Disease,* quoted by David Venhuizen, PE (5803 Gateshead Drive, Austin, TX 78745, 512/442-4047, fax -4057, waterguy@ix.netcom.com).

101. Lovins & Lehmann 2001.

102. Clark & Tomlinson 1995.

103. Clark, Perkins, & Wood 1997 at 70–71; Clark 1997.

104. Venhuizen 1997 and in his 1996 paper "Is 'Waste' Water Reclamation and Reuse In Your Future?," http://www.geocities. com/RainForest/Vines/5240/Future-Water Use.html, downloaded 5 February 1998.

105. Living Technologies, Inc., 431 Pine St., Burlington, VT 05401, 802/865-4460, fax -4438, http://www.livingmachines.com, jtodd@cape.com.

106. Wilson & Malin 1996 at 13–17.

107. Osann & Young 1998 at 27–52 present numerous case studies. Santa Monica's Baysaver Program, for example, returned about two dollars in savings per dollar invested, and has retrofitted nearly 60 percent of its toilets. For a general implementation guide, see Rocky Mountain Institute Water Program 1991.

108. Its goal of a 15 percent overall reduction was met by allocating 0–45 percent residential, 10–20 percent agricultural, and 15 percent commercial and industrial reductions depending on customers' current usage. Households that were already moderately water-efficient were therefore unaffected by the restrictions.

109. Larry Farwell, former Water Conservation Coordinator for the Goleta Water District, now a private consultant: 2476 San Marcos Pass Road, Santa Barbara, CA 93105, 805/964-8486, lfarwel@earthlink.net.

110. Per-capita consumption fell 16 percent during 1991–97: Osann & Young 1998 at 38.

111. CTSI Corporation, 2722 Walnut Ave., Tustin CA 92780, 714/669-4303; Chaplin 1995.

112. Osann & Young 1998 at 35, Gomez & Owens-Viani 1998. This effort installed over 750,000 new toilets just in the first four years.

113. Water Management, Inc. (117 Claremont, Alexandria, VA 22304, 703/658-4300, fax -4311, www.watermgt.com) is a typical "water service company," or WASCO.

114. Jim Reed (Water Conservation Speciaiist, Denver Water, 1600 W. 12th Ave., Denver, CO 80254, 303/628-6347, www.state.co.use/gov+dir/oec), personal communication, February 3, 1998.

115. Jones & Dyer 1994; Jones et al. 1993 at 17–21.

Chapter 12: Climate

1. The fraction of total solar radiation that's intercepted by the earth's disk is 3×10^{-10}.

2. The earth also receives 0.018 percent of its warmth from heat flowing up from its interior, driven by radioactive decay, and 0.002 percent from the friction of the tides (moonpower). Berner & Berner 1996 at 10.

3. That is, about 2×10^{17} watts.

4. In 1990, fossil fuels accounted for about 87 percent of the world's commercial primary energy use. Noncommercial energy use added another estimated 11 percent to commercial energy use. Reddy et al. 1997 at 110.

5. This doesn't include 0.5–2.5 billion metric tons from deforestation and other net decreases in standing biomass. For these and other data in this simplified introduction to climatology, see Intergovernmental Panel on Climate Change (IPCC) 1990, 1992, 1996, 1996a, and continuing supplements.

6. This metaphor is provided by Matthias Schabel.

7. IPCC 1990.

8. Some of the best and most accessible descriptions of the history and science of global warming are contained in Weiner (1990) and Schneider (1997).

9. This does not mean that the *air* becomes warmer. Because downward reradiation of heat trapped by atmospheric CO_2 warms the surface, it cools the atmosphere equally, except near the surface where the air is directly heated by its proximity to the earth.

10. Approximately 30 percent of the increase during 1850–1990 came from such land-use changes as deforestation and eco-

logical simplification, the rest from industry. Of the total increase, about 65 percent has come from the developed countries that currently comprise one-fifth of the world's population (Austin et al. 1998).

11. The average column of air contains water vapor equivalent to an inch of rain, removed by precipitation and replenished by evaporation every eleven days.

12. IPCC 1996. Satellite measurements now match surface measurements: Wentz & Schabel 1998, Hansen et al. 1998.

13. Stevens 1998a, citing a World Metereological Organization compilation of data from the NASA Goddard Institute for Space Studies, the British Meteorological Office, the U.S. National Climatic Data Center, the NASA Marshall Space Flight Center and University of Alabama, the International Research Institute (New York), and the Climatic Prediction Center (Washington, D.C.). Data from October 1998 were the latest available as this book went to press.

14. Flavin 1998.

15. McKibben 1998.

16. Vaughan & Doake 1996.

17. Kerr 1998.

18. Linden 1996 at 65.

19. Shindell et al. 1998.

20. Schneider 1997.

21. IPCC 1990, 1994, 1996.

22. Browne 1997.

23. The President's Council of Advisors on Science and Technology (PCAST) 1997.

24. Arrow et al. 1997; for a splendidly clear explanation of why theoretical models differ, see Repetto & Austin 1997.

25. Samuelson 1997.

26. E.g., Lovins et al. 1981, ICF 1990, Okken et al. 1991, Evans 1992, IPSEP 1993 & 1994–8, Koomey et al. 1991, Krause 1996, Brown & Levine 1997.

27. Detailed documentation on each of these matters, omitting only the newest developments such as Hypercars, is in the 188 references of an earlier survey paper in the journal of record: Lovins & Lovins 1991. Many older but still useful references are in its decade-earlier predecessor, Lovins et al. 1981.

28. NRC 1989, Lovins & Lovins 1991.

29. For example, just during 1990–96, while its earnings and stock prices soared, DuPont halved its total greenhouse gas emissions per unit of production, mainly by phasing out CFCs, of which it was the main manufacturer. During 1996–2002, it expects to save more than half the remaining greenhouse-gas emissions from its plants while continuing to decrease the greenhouse effects of its products per unit output (Krol 1997). During its first six months of operation at just one plant (the Sabine River Works in Texas), an "abater" that turns by-product nitrous oxide into air saved the equivalent of 7 *billion* pounds of CO_2. That's the same as taking three million cars off the road. Meanwhile, Monsanto's Solutia spinoff found in 1997 that nitrous oxide is not just an unwanted, climate-threatening nuisance, but also a valuable reagent for turning benzene into competitively priced phenol — a classic conversion of lemons into lemonade.

30. There are six gases, each of which can be emitted less or stored or sequestered more. Either approach offers many methods — many kinds of efficiencies, process changes, substitutions, et cetera. Some methods also offer many different kinds of savings for the price of one: Lovins & Lovins 1991.

31. Lovins 1997a.

32. A 4- to 6-fold improvement over fifty years implies an average annual improvement by 2.8 to 3.6 percent. Americans actually reduced the primary energy used per dollar of real GDP by 3.4 percent per year during the years 1979–86. Preliminary data, not weather-corrected, for the short period 1997–99 suggest the possibility that comparably rapid savings may be starting to recur, driven this time not by price but by skill, attention, and competition.

33. Nelson 1993; now at KENTEC, Inc., 8118 Oakbrook Drive, Baton Rouge, LA 70810, 225/761-1838, fax -1872, kentech@compuserve.com.

34. Mills et al. 1991 (Swedish household refrigerators); U. of Lund data noted by T. B. Johansson, 1992, and recent industry data from Gunnar Hofstadius of ITT Flygt (personal communication, August 31, 1998) (industrial pumps); Howe et al. 1996 at 133, Fig. 8-8 (motors; the MotorMaster staff have privately confirmed the lack of efficiency/ price correlation up to at least 200 hp); Houghton & Hibberd 1998 at 9, Fig. 6, for 5.4–20-ton packaged rooftop air-conditioning units. Valves are illustrated by the commonplace observation that full-port ball valves have far lower frictional head than globe valves but cost about half as much.

35. Howe et al. 1996.

36. Lovins et al. 1989, Fickett et al. 1990. This doesn't count the savings further downstream, which are usually larger and cheaper, and should be done first.

37. Interlaboratory Working Group 1997.

38. Lovins 1998a.

39. STMicroelectronics Vice President Murray Duffin (1998) has publicly presented a similar strategy.

40. Casten 1997.

41. Groscurth & Kümmel 1989.

42. Johansson et al. 1993, Romm & Curtis 1996.

43. Mansley 1995.

44. *Shell Venster,* Jan./Feb. 1998, the Shell external-relations newsletter, which states: "In 2050 a ratio 50/50 for fossil/ renewables is a probable scenario, so we have to enter this market now!" *Cf.* Kassler 1994.

45. *The Economist* 1998a.

46. Flavin & Dunn 1997 at 47, citing California Energy Commission data from October 1997.

47. Brown et al. 1997 at 52; see also PCAST at 6-14; National Laboratory Directors at 2-38.

48. SERI 1990.

49. Interlaboratory Working Group 1997, e.g. at 1.14.

50. Sørensen 1979, Lovins et al. 1981, Reddy & Goldemberg 1990, Johansson et al. 1989 & 1993.

51. Flavin & O'Meara 1998 at 25.

52. Lovins & Lehmann 2001.

53. Johansson et al. 1993 at 23ff.

54. See also Prophet 1998.

55. Williams et al. 1997, Lovins 1998.

56. Edwards 1997.

57. *The Economist* 1998.

58. Keepin & Kats 1988, 1988a.

59. Bodlund et al. 1989.

60. Reddy & Goldemberg 1990.

61. Such studies are at scales ranging from California (Calwell et al. 1990) and New England (Krause et al. 1992) to western Europe (IPSEP 1993, 1994–98) and the world (Lovins et al. 1981, Goldemberg et al. 1988).

62. Reid & Goldemberg 1997, Flavin & Dunn 1997 at 26–29. See also Levine et al. 1993, Reddy et al. 1997, Yergin 1997.

63. Gadgil et al. 1991.

64. Lovins & Gadgil 1991.

65. Id.

66. Lovins 1976, Nash 1977.

67. Lovins & Lovins 1997.

68. For example, during the years 1983–85, ten million people served by Southern California Edison Company, aided by a comprehensive slate of financing, information, and other support, raised their electrical efficiency so quickly that if all Americans did as well, then *each year* they'd decrease the need for power supplies ten years later by about 7 percent. Implementing these savings would cost the efficiency about one-tenth as much as building today's cheapest new power stations. Lovins 1985 at 180–183, Fickett et al. 1990.

69. Interlaboratory Working Group 1997 at 2.10.

70. Jaffe & Stavins 1994, Sanstad & Howarth 1994, Krause 1996.

71. von Weizsäcker et al. at 143–209.

72. Todd 1997, Brandt 1997; Lovins & Lovins 1997 at n147.

73. Stewart 1997.

74. Clinton 1997.

75. David 1997 [David, G. 1997: Address to Earth Technologies Forum, October 26].

76. The total payroll of all U.S. coal miners is about $5 billion, or 1 percent of the nation's energy bills. This is less than spontaneous gains in energy efficiency *save* in any typical year. Americans pay about $24 billion a year for coal. If the miners' worst fears came true and coal consumption fell by half, then American consumers could afford to make good the miners'

entire lost pay — with $9 billion a year left over. (For illustration, consumers could pay about $11.5 billion less each year for coal, pay $2.5 billion to cover the payroll of the out-of-work miners, and still have $9 billion left.) A more rigorous calculation would be much more sophisticated and opaque, but would give roughly the same answer.

77. Goodstein 1999.
78. DeCanio 1997.
79. *Christian Science Monitor* 1997.
80. Nitze 1997.
81. However, extensive European research suggests that a combination of price and market-transformation initiatives may interactively boost economic efficiency and welfare more than the sum of their parts: Krause 1996.
82. NREL 1997.
83. DeCanio 1997.
84. Carey 1998, Lovins 1999.
85. Cushman 1999. DuPont is now among the industries seeking an important law to ensure credits for early emission reductions.
86. Climate Neutral Network, c/o Sue Hall, 509/538-2500, suehsea@gorge.net.
87. Such as Green Mountain Power, PO Box 850, South Burlington, VT 05402, 802/660-5672, www.gmpvt.com.
88. Lovins 1999, according to Dr. Richard Sandor, Vice Chair, Chicago Board of Trade (personal communication, December 2, 1998).

Chapter 13: Making Markets Work

1. *Cf.* Buchan 1997 at 239–240.
2. Lovins 1992, citing Kempton et al. 1992, Lutzenhiser 1992.
3. Korten 1999.
4. Schmidheiny & Zorraquin 1996.
5. Interlaboratory Working Group 1997.
6. Howe 1993.
7. DeCanio 1994.
8. The magic formula is: after-tax return on investment in percent per year equals (1 − marginal tax rate in decimal form) / (simple payback in years − 1). Thus

if the total marginal tax rate (Federal, state, and local) totals, say, 36 percent or 0.36 (the value we assume), then the after-tax ROI corresponding to a two-year simple payback is $(1 - 0.36) / (2 - 1) = 0.64$, or 64 percent per year. Thus the ROI tends to infinity as the simple payback approaches one year, so for paybacks of one year or less, the ROI is conventionally set to infinity. For simplicity, the formula assumes an end-of-year convention about when investments are made and booked (a different timing assumption will change the result), and ignores such tax effects as the expensing of energy costs and capitalization of efficiency investments.

9. DOE 1997.
10. Implicit real annual discount rates for buying efficiency typically range around 30–60-plus percent: Rosenfeld & Hafemeister 1998; Koomey et al. 1991, Levine et al. 1995, Hausman 1979, Hartman & Doane 1986, Wolf et al. 1983.
11. Nadel 1990, Lovins 1994.
12. von Weizsäcker et al. at 166–167.
13. Udall 1997.
14. Lovins & Lehmann 2001.
15. Lovins & Gadgil 1991.
16. See also von Weizsäcker et al. at 155–176.
17. Proprietary engagements led by RMI and partly summarized in Lovins 1998a.
18. Rajendran 1997 and private data.
19. Audin & Howe 1994.
20. *Wall Street Journal* 1997.
21. Rosenfeld 1999, Mills 1995.
22. DeCanio 1993, 1994, 1994a, 1994b.
23. Lovins 1996.
24. Bradford 1998.
25. Moskovitz 1989, Lovins 1996.
26. Bradford 1998.
27. E.g., Sauer 1997, 1998.
28. CDA 1996.
29. Id.
30. EPA 1993.
31. DeCanio 1994b.
32. EPA 1993.
33. EPA 1998.
34. Geller & Nadel 1994.
35. Udall 1997.

36. Promoted by Byron Kennard, Executive Director, The Center for Small Business and the Environment, PO Box 53127, Washington, DC 20008, csbe2000@aol.com.

37. Lovins 1995a.

38. Arnold & Day (1998) provide a partial taxonomy of the business benefits of sustainable practices.

39. Tobias 1993. Their effort has so far been unsuccessful due to opposing lobbying efforts by industries that prefer their profits from present arrangements.

40. Gil Friend, personal communication, 1998.

41. Mills & Knoepfel 1997; Schanzenbacher & Mills 1997; and Mills 1997, http://eande.lbl.gov/CBS/Climate-insurance/GoingGreen.html.

42. Savory & Butterfield 1999. Describes a particularly comprehensive and ecologically based way to do this.

Chapter 14: Human Capitalism

1. Conway 1969, Harrisson 1965, Cheng 1963.

2. And may even help us live longer: longevity in 282 U.S. metropolitan areas has been much better correlated with relative than with absolute income, apparently reflecting links between psychosocial tensions and health (Lardner 1998).

3. This is a less modest restatement of the goals of Rocky Mountain Institute's Economic Renewal Project (1983–), which uses resource productivity and other principles to help build sustainable local economies from the bottom up. This often yields such important social side benefits as conflict resolution and leadership development. The project has shown its analytic and organizing process to be flexible and replicable, and has developed a variety of field-tested tools, including such workbooks and casebooks as Kinsley 1997, Hubbard & Fong 1995, and Cantrell 1991. A complete list of publications is at www.rmi.org.

4. Max-Neef 1992.

5. Some products even falsely pretend to satisfy a need, thereby retaining the opportunity to try again in other ways, or satisfy a need in ways that simultaneously prevent the satisfaction of other needs, creating still more market opportunities: Max-Neef 1992.

6. Midsized cities of 0.5 to 5 million hold four times as many of the world's people as do the megacities of 10 million or more: O'Meara 1998.

7. The population of the city itself quadrupled in 30 years, and by 1996 was 1.5 million out of the metro region's 2.4 million.

8. The following account draws on 1991–98 personal communications with Jaime Lerner and his former adviser Jonas Rabinovitch (now Senior Urban Development Adviser and Manager of the Urban Development Team at the United Nations Development Programme, jonas.rabinovitch@undp.org, fax 212/906-6973); the city's Portuguese-language website, www.curitiba.arauc.br; its 600-MB Portuguese/Spanish/English CD-ROM *Enciclopédia Cidade de Curitiba;* its video, *Good Morning, Curitiba;* the English-language brochures Curitiba 1997, Curitiba undated, and FAS undated; Lamounier & Figueiredo 1996; de Vega 1996; Rabinovitch 1992, 1993, 1995, 1996; Rabinovitch & Hoehn 1995 (which lists further readings); Rabinovitch & Leitman 1993, 1996; McKibben 1995 (the broadest and most accessible English-language treatment); Linden 1996; and O'Meara 1998. We are especially grateful for Jonas Rabinovitch's careful review of a draft of this chapter, but we alone are responsible for its content.

9. Linden 1996 at 62.

10. Having such a base for institutionalizing the continuous improvement of the city's strategy has proven invaluable. Now 200 strong, this independent nonprofit think tank has served as a vital incubator and reservoir of creativity, training three mayors and many of their senior advisors. (Rabinovitch joined in 1981 and rose to become its COO.) Starting with a 1965 strategic plan that won a public competition after wide public debate, IPPUC refined its fundamentals and details, ripening the plan until 1971 when, with Lerner's election, its implementation could begin.

11. Berry (1995 at 56): "If we are serious about conservation, then we are going to have to quit thinking about our work as a sequence of specialized and temporary responses to a sequence of specialized and temporary emergencies. We will have to recognize that our work is economic. We are going to have to come up with competent, practical, at-home answers to the humblest human questions: How should we live? How should we keep house? How should we provide ourselves with food, clothing, shelter, heat, light, learning, amusement, rest? How, in short, ought we to use the world?"

12. von Weizsäcker et al. at 126–128; photo, Plate 11. By mid-1998, 223 of these *estações tubo* were in use.

13. Linden 1996 at 62.

14. Linden (1996) reports that Lyons and Vancouver are among the cities considering surface subways.

15. The city is experimenting with innovative sewage-treatment methods and considering a dual-quality water supply and cistern collection, but until Lerner recently shifted to the Governorship, city/state issues prevented innovation in and decentralization of the water and wastewater systems.

16. The effort was launched by TV ads and school programs featuring actors dressed as the Leaf Family.

17. Available at www.product-life.org/history.htm. Stahel calls these last two steps "social ecology" and "cultural ecology."

18. At least, notes Rabinovitch, in the "formal city" for which good statistics exist: "It is impossible to have reliable data about the informal city, which changes on a daily basis and would present lower percentages. This fact is universal."

19. McKibben 1995 at 110.

20. Linden (1996 at 63–64) speculates that the rarity of examples like Curitiba's might reflect an unusual confluence of gifted leadership and prepared citizens.

21. Quoted id.

22. An aphorism of the late economist and iconoclast Professor Kenneth Boulding.

Chapter 15: Once Upon a Planet

1. Briscoe 1998.

2. Meadows 1994 at 25–30.

3. Meadows 1994.

4. Brower 1995 at 155–159. These are based on an endpaper published in 1975 in the *New York Times* entitled *The Third Planet: Operating Instructions* (300 Broadway, Suite 28, San Francisco, CA 94133-3312) and paraphrased here by permission.

5. D. Orr, personal communication, February 1, 1999.

6. Ayres 1992.

7. Holling, "New Science and New Investments for a Sustainable Biosphere," at 57 in Jansson et al. 1994, Callahan 1999.

8. Hart 1999.

9. Ayres 1995a.

10. Costanza, "Three General Policies to Achieve Sustainability," at 392 in Jansson et al. 1994.

11. Berry 1999.

12. von Weizsäcker 1994.

REFERENCES

Abe, J. M., Dempsey, P. E., and Basset, D. A., 1998: *Business Ecology: Giving Your Organization the Natural Edge,* Butterworth-Heinemann; The Business Ecology Network, PO Box 29, Shady Side, MD 20764-9546, 410/867-3596, fax -7956, www.naturaledge.org.

Abramovitz, J. N., 1998: "Putting a Value on Nature's 'Free' Services," *WorldWatch* 11(1):10, Jan./Feb.

Adler, R. W., and Mace, T., 1990: "Water, water . . . ," Natural Resources Defense Council, *Los Angeles Times,* Apr. 29.

Alexander, C., 1977: *A Pattern Language,* Oxford University Press, New York, NY.

Alliance to Save Energy, American Council for an Energy-Efficient Economy, Natural Resources Defense Council, Tellus Institute, and Union of Concerned Scientists 1997: *Energy Innovations. A Prosperous Path to a Clean Environment,* June, ASE, 1200 18th St. NW, Suite 900, Washington, DC 20036, www.ase.org.

Amato, I., 1998: "Fomenting a Revolution in Miniature," *Science* 282:402–405, Oct. 16.

American Forest and Paper Association 1994: *Fast Facts,* 1111 19th St. NW, Washington, DC 20036, 202/463-2737.

American Forest and Paper Association, www.afandpa.org, downloaded Feb. 15, 1998.

American Institute of Physics 1975: *Efficient Use of Energy,* American Physical Society Studies on the Technical Aspects of the More Efficient Use of Energy, Conf. Procs. No. 25, AIP, New York, NY.

Anderson, R. C., 1997: Interface Sustainability Report, Interface Corp., La Grange, GA.

——— 1998: *Mid-Course Correction,* Peregrinzilla Press, Interface Corp., Atlanta, GA.

Andreeva, N., 1998: " You Deserve a Starch Container Today," *Business Week,* p. 115, Oct. 5, dtwoct@businessweek.com.

Arbeus, U., 1998: "The N-Pump — A New Concept," *Scientific Impeller* 5:23–27, ITT Flygt AB, Solna, Sweden, ++ 46 8 + 627-6500, fax -6900.

Arnold, M. B., and Day, R. M., 1998: *The Next Bottom Line: Making Sustainable Development Tangible,* World Resources Institute, Washington, DC.

Arrow, K., Jorgenson, D., Krugman, P., Nordhaus, W., Solow, R., et al., 1997: "The Economists' Statement on Climate Change," Feb. 13, available from Redefining Progress, San Francisco, CA, 415/781-1191, www.rprogress.org.

Atchison, J., 1995: "Nonwood Fiber Could Play Major Role in U.S. Papermaking Furnishes," *Pulp and Paper* 67(9):125–131.

Atmospheric Pollution Prevention Division, USEPA 1997: "Role of Technology in Climate Change Policy," briefing paper, Washington, DC, ca. Nov.

Audin, L., and Howe, B., 1994: *Success at Zero Net Cost: Columbia University's Achievements in Energy Efficiency,* CS-94-1, E SOURCE, Boulder, CO 80301, www.esource.com.

Audin, L., Houghton, D., Shepard, M., and Hawthorne, W., 1998: *Lighting Technology Atlas,* E SOURCE, Boulder, CO.

Austin, D., Goldemberg, J., and Parker, G., 1998: "Contributions to Climate Change: Are Conventional Metrics Misleading the Debate?," *Climate Notes*, Oct., World Resources Institute, Washington, DC, http://www.wri.org/wri/climate/.

Australian Plumbing Industry 1992: "'Leading Edge' Technology," Oct./Nov.

Automotive Industries 1995: July centenary issue, p. 124.

Automotive News 1983: "Cat's 3306B Makes It Big in the Real World," Nov. 7.

Axelsson, S., 1996: *Ecological Tax Reform*, Naturskyddsföringen (Swedish Society for Nature Conservation), Stockholm, Oct.

Ayres, E., 1993: "Making Paper Without Trees," *Worldwatch* 6, Sept./Oct.

Ayres, R. U., 1989: *Technology and Environment*, National Academy of Sciences, Washington, DC.

————— 1992: "Toxic Heavy Metals: Materials Cycle Optimization," *Proc. Natl. Acad. Scis.* 89:815–820, Feb.

————— 1995: "Thermodynamics and Process Analysis for Future Economic Scenarios," *Envtl. and Res. Ecs.* 6:207–230.

————— 1995a: "Economic Growth: Politically Necessary but Not Environmentally Friendly," *Ecol. Ecs.* 15: 97–99; see also "Achieving Eco-Efficiency in Business," World Business Council for Sustainable Development, Geneva.

————— 1996: "Industrial Metabolism and the Grand Nutrient Cycles," working paper, 96/54/EPS, INSEAD, Boul. de Constance, 77305 Fontainebleau Cedex, France.

————— 1996a: "Turning Point: The End of the Growth Paradigm," Working Paper 96/49/EPS, Centre for the Management of Environmental Resources, INSEAD, Fontainebleau, France.

————— 1998: *Turning Point: The End of the Growth Paradigm*, Earthscan, London.

Ayres, R. U. and L. W., 1996: *Industrial Ecology*, Edward Elgar, Cheltenham, Glos., UK, and Brookfield, VT.

Bagby, M. E., 1996: *Annual Report of the United States of America*, HarperBusiness, New York, NY.

Bain, A., 1997: "The Hindenburg Disaster: A Compelling Theory of Probable Cause and Effect," *Procs. Natl. Hydr. Assn. 8th Ann. Hydrogen Mtg.* (Alexandria, VA), Mar. 11–13, pp. 125–128.

Baldwin, J., 1996: *Buckyworks: Buckminster Fuller's Ideas for Today*, John Wiley, New York, NY.

Bancroft, B., Shepard, M., Lovins, A. B., and Bishop, R., 1991: *The State of the Art: Water Heating*, COMPETITEK/Rocky Mountain Institute, Oct., E SOURCE, Boulder, CO 80301, www.esource.com.

BankAmerica 1997: *BankAmerica Environmental Program 1997 Progress Report*, BankAmerica, Los Angeles, CA.

Barten, P., 1995: personal communication, Oct. 25, Yale Forestry School.

Bechmann, A., 1987: *Landbau-Wende: Gesunde Landwirtschaft — Gesunde Ernährung*, S. Fischer, Frankfurt.

Behrens, W. W. III, 1973: "The Dynamics of Natural Resource Utilization," Ch. 6 pp. 141–162 in Meadows, D. L. and D. H., 1973, *Toward Global Equilibrium: Selected Papers*, Wright-Allen Press, Cambridge, MA.

Benyus, J. M., 1997: *Biomimicry: Innovations Inspired by Nature*, William Morrow, New York, NY.

Berner, E. K. and R. A., 1996: *Global Environment: Water, Air, and Geochemical Cycles*, Prentice Hall, Upper Saddle River, NJ.

Berry, W., 1981: "Solving for Pattern," in *The Gift of Good Land*, North Point Press, San Francisco, CA.

———— 1995: "Private Property and the Common Wealth," *Another Turn of the Crank*, Counterpoint, Washington, DC.

———— 1999: "Back to the Land," *The Amicus Journal* 20(4):37–40, Winter, Natural Resources Defense Council, New York; a longer version, "The Whole Horse," appeared in the British journal *Resurgence* 188, May/June 1998.

Bintrim, S. B., Ireland, J. S., Joseph, D. A., Donohue, T. J., Handelsman, J., and Goodman, R. M., 1997: "Molecular and computational analyses reveal vast phylogenetic diversity of bacteria in soil," *Proc. Natl. Acad. Scis.* 94:277–282.

Bishop, Ron, 1998: personal communication, Feb. 6, General Manager, Central Platte Natural Resource District, 215 N. Kaufmann Ave., Grand Island, NE, 308/385-6282.

Bloome, P. D., and Cuperus, G. W., 1984: "Aeration for Management of Stored Grain Insects in Wheat," #84-3517, 1984 Winter Meeting (New Orleans), Am. Soc. Ag. Eng. (2950 Niles Road, St. Joseph, MI 49085), Dec. 11–14.

Blum, L., Denison, R. A., and Rusfon, J. F., 1997: "A Life-Cycle Approach to Purchasing and Using Environmentally Preferable Paper," *J. Indl. Ecol.* 1(3):15–46, Summer.

Bodlund, B., et al., 1989: "The Challenge of Choices: Technology Options for the Swedish Electricity Sector," pp. 883–947 in Johansson, T. B., et al., eds., *Electricity*, Lund University Press, Lund, Sweden.

Boonyatikarn, S., 1997: "The Energy Conserving House," Energy Expert Co. Ltd., Feb., available from the author (Assoc. Prof. of Arch. and Dep. Dir. for Res. Affairs), Chulalongkorn U., Phyathai Rd., 10330 Bangkok, Thailand, ++ 66 2 + 218-80 90 66, fax + 254-7579.

Boulding, K.: "The Economics of Spaceship Earth," *Environmental Quality in a Growing Economy*, Jarret, H., ed., Johns Hopkins Press, Baltimore, MD.

Boxboard Containers 1993: "Case Closed," pp. 44–45, Oct.

Bradford, P. A., 1998: "No one gets out alive: the hijacking of the electric industry," Energy: Buildings, Economics, and the Earth Conference, New York, Earth Day, Apr. 21.

Brandt, M., 1997: personal communications, Aug. 13 and 21, Commonwealth Edison Company, Chicago, IL.

Braungart, M., 1998: personal communication, Feb. 8.

Bredehoeft, J., 1984: "Physical Limitations of Water Resources," pp. 17–44 in Engelbert, E. A., with Scheuring, A. F., eds., *Water Scarcity: Impacts on Western Agriculture*, University of California Press, Berkeley.

Briscoe, D., 1998: "State of the World," Jan. 10, Associated Press, Washington, DC.

Brody, J. E., 1995: "Annual Health Care Cost of Meat Is Billions, Study Says," *New York Times*, Nov. 21.

———— 1985: "Organic Farming Moves into the Mainstream," *New York Times*, p. 20, Oct. 8.

Brooke, L., 1998: "Amory Lovins: Composite Crusader," *Automotive Industries*, pp. 59–60, 63, Sept.

Brower, D., 1995: *Let the Mountains Talk, Let the Rivers Run*, HarperCollins, New York, NY.

Brown, L. R., and Halweil, B., 1998: "China's Water Shortage Could Shake World Food Security," *Worldwatch* 11(4): 10–21, July/Aug.

Brown, L. R., Renner, M., and Flavin, C., 1997: *Vital Signs 1997*, Worldwatch Institute, Washington, DC, www.worldwatch.org.

Brown, L. R., Flavin, C., and French, H., 1998: *State of the World 1998,* Worldwatch Institute, Washington, DC, www.worldwatch.org.

Browne, J., 1997: Address at Stanford University, May 19, www.bp.com.

Browning, W. D., 1987: "Steaks and Mistakes: A Study of U.S. Beef Production," Rocky Mountain Institute internal research paper.

—— 1992: "NMB Bank Headquarters: The Impressive Performance of a Green Building," *Urban Land,* Urban Land Institute, pp. 23–25, June.

—— 1997: "Giving Productivity an Energy-Efficient Boost," *Consulting-Specifying Engineer,* pp. 40–44, Jan.

—— 1997a: "Boosting productivity with IEQ improvements," *Building Design and Construction,* pp. 50–52, Apr.

Brownstein, E., Hall, S., and Lotspeich C., with Lovins, A. B., 1997: "Resource Efficiency in Wood Fiber Services: A 'Soft Fiber Path' for Forest Products Markets," Systems Group on Forests, Rocky Mountain Institute, Snowmass, CO, July, draft to be published in 1999.

Brylawski, M., and Lovins, A. B., 1995: "Ultralight-Hybrid Vehicle Design: Overcoming the Barriers to Using Advanced Composites in the Automotive Industry," Mar. 28 paper to 41st International Symposium and Exhibition, Society for the Advancement of Material and Process Engineering (SAMPE), Anaheim, CA, preprint, RMI Publication #T95–39.

Brylawski, M., and Lovins, A. B., 1998: "Advanced Composites: The Car Is at the Crossroads," paper to 43rd International Symposium and Exhibition, Society for the Advancement of Material and Process Engineering (SAMPE), May 31–June 4, Anaheim, CA, SAMPE J. 35(2): 25–36 (Mar./Apr. 1999), RMI Publication #T98-1.

Buchan, J., 1997: *Frozen Desire: The Meaning of Money,* Farrar Straus and Giroux, New York, NY.

Buerkle, T., 1998: "Using Taxes as Stick, U.K. Aims to Cut Car Travel," *Intl. Herald Tribune* (New York ed.), p. 7, July 21.

Business Week 1998: "A New Iron Age," p. 103, Jan. 12.

Butterfield, F., 1996: "Survey Finds That Crimes Cost $450 Billion a Year," *New York Times,* Apr. 22.

Butti, K., and Perlin, J., 1980: *A Golden Thread: 2500 Years of Solar Architecture and Technology,* Cheshire Books, Palo Alto, CA.

Cairncross, F., 1997: *The Death of Distance: How the Communications Revolution Will Change Our Lives,* Harvard Business School Publishing, Boston, MA.

Cairns, J. Jr., 1997: "Defining Goals and Conditions for a Sustainable World," *Environmental Health Perspectives* 105(11):1164–1170, Nov.

Callahan, R. 1999: "Ice Core Shows Greenhouse Gases," Associated Press, June 6.

Calvin, W. H. 1998: "The Great Climate Flip-Flop," *Atlantic Monthly,* Jan.

Calwell, C., Edwards, A., Gladstein, C., and Lee, L., 1990: *Clearing the Air,* Natural Resources Defense Council, San Francisco, CA, www.nrdc.org.

Cannon, J., 1995: "Harnessing Hydrogen: The Key to Sustainable Transportation," INFORM, New York, NY, ISBN 0-918780-65-9.

Cantrell, P., 1991: *The Food and Agriculture Workbook,* Economic Renewal Project, Rocky Mountain Institute Publication #ER91-7, www.rmi.org.

Carbohydrate Economy, The, 1998: "Growing Cars," 1(3):1–7, Summer, Institute for Local Self-Reliance, Chicago, www.carbohydrateeconomy.org.

Carey, J., 1998: "Look Who's Thawing in Global Climate," *Business Week,* pp. 97–98, Nov. 9.

Carter, V. G., and Hale, T., 1974: *Topsoil and Civilization*, University of Oklahoma Press, Norman.

Casten, T., 1997: Remarks to White House Climate Conference, Oct. 6, Trigen Energy Co., White Plains, NY.

Caulfield, C., 1989: *Multiple Exposures: Chronicles of the Radiation Age*, HarperCollins, New York, NY.

Chao, B. F., 1995: "Anthropogenic impact on global geodynamics due to water impoundment in major reservoirs," *Geophys. Res. Letts.* 22:3533–3536.

Chaplin, S. W., 1993: "Group Bridges Toilet Rebate Gap," *Home Energy*, p. 9, May/June.

——— 1994: *Water-Efficient Landscaping: A Guide for Utilities and Community Planners*, Rocky Mountain Institute Publication #W94-8, www.rmi.org.

Chapman, R., 1998: "New urban projects yield solid returns," *New Urban News* 3(1):1 and 8–11, Jan.–Feb.

Chelman, Chester, 1998: personal communication based on research in Traffic Engineering Society archives, White Mountain Survey, Box 440, Ossipee, NH 03864, 603/539-4118.

Chemical Manufacturers Association 1993: *United States Chemical Industry Statistical Handbook*, CMA, Washington, DC.

Cheng, F. Y., 1963: "Deterioration of Thatch Roofs by Moth Larvae after House Spraying in the Course of a Malaria Eradication Programme in North Borneo," *Bull. WHO* 28:136–137.

Chipello, C. J., 1998: "MacMillan Bloedel to Unveil Plan to Restrict Scope of Its Logging," *Wall Street Journal*, p. B2, June 10.

Chouinard, Y., and Brown, M., 1997: "Going Organic: Converting Patagonia's Cotton Product Line," *J. Indl. Ecol.* 1(1): 117ff, Winter.

Christian Science Monitor 1997: "21st Century Weather," editorial, p. 20, Aug. 6.

City of Los Angeles 1982: "Graywater Pilot Project, Final Report," Office of Water Reclamation (which was recently abolished), Nov.

Clark, R. D. S., 1997: *Water Sustainability in Urban Areas: An Adelaide and Regions Case Study, Report Five: Optimum Scale for Urban Water Systems*, Water Resources Group, South Australia Department of Environment and Natural Resources, Adelaide, July.

Clark, R. D. S., Perkins, A., and Wood, S. E., 1997: *Water Sustainability in Urban Areas: An Adelaide and Regions Case Study, Report One: An Exploration of the Concept*, Water Resources Group, South Australia Department of Environment and Natural Resources, Adelaide, July.

Clark, R. D. S., and Tomlinson, G. W., 1995: *Optimum Scale for Water Services in Metropolitan Adelaide: Part I, Least Cost Scale for Sewerage Systems*, Dept. of Environmental and Natural Resources, Water Resources Group, South Australia, Sept.

Cler, G., Shepard, H., Gregerson, J., Houghton, D. J., Fryer, L., Elleson, J., Pattinson, B., Hawthorne, W., Webster, L., Stein, J., Davis, D., and Parsons, S., 1997: *Commercial Space Cooling and Air Handling Technology Atlas*, E SOURCE, Boulder, CO, www.esource.com.

Clinton, W. J., 1997: Climate policy speech, National Geographic Society, Washington, DC, Oct. 22.

Clivus Multrum, Inc., "On-site waste treatment — what are the benefits?," 15 Union St., Lawrence, MA 01840, 978/725-5591, 800/962-8447, fax 978/557-9658, www.clivusmultrum.com.

Cobb, C. W., 1998: "The Roads Aren't Free: Estimating the Full Social Cost of Driving and the Effects of Accurate Pricing," Working Paper #3 on Environmental Tax Shifting, Redefining Progress, San Francisco, CA, www.rprogress.org.

Colinvaux, P., 1978: "Why Big Fierce Animals Are Rare," in *An Ecologist's Perspective*, Princeton University Press, Princeton, NJ.

Composites News: Infrastructure 1995: "Reinforced Glulam Beams May Cause Materials Revolution," 30:1–4, Aug. 18, Composites Worldwide, Solano Beach, CA 619/775-1372, fax -5271; see also "Composites Lead to Revolutionary Wood Beams and Bridges," 4:1–3, Apr. 11, 1994.

Consumer Reports 1997: "Less Noisy, Less Thirsty," Jan., pp. 42–45.

Conway, G. R., 1969: "Ecological Aspects of Pest Control in Malaysia," 467–488 (see 483–484) in Farvar, M. T., and Milton, J. P., eds. 1969/1972, *The Careless Technology*, Natural History Press, New York, NY.

———— 1997: *The Doubly Green Revolution*, Penguin, London; also 1999, Cornell University Press, Ithaca, NY.

Copper Development Association (CDA) 1996: "One Wire Size Up Means Big Savings," A6008/93/96, CDA, 260 Madison Ave., New York, NY 10016, 800/CDA-DATA or 212/251-7200, fax -7234, http://energy.copper.org.

Coral Reef Alliance 1998: "Reefs in Danger: Threats to Coral Reefs Around the World," Oct. 22.

Corbett, M., 1981: *A Better Place to Live*, Rodale Press, Emmaus, PA.

Costanza, R., d'Arge, R., de Groot, R., Farber, S., Grasso, M., Hannon, B., Limburg, K., Naeem, S., O'Neill, R. V., and Paruelo, J., 1997: "The Value of the World's Ecosystem Services and Natural Capital," *Nature* 387:253–260, May 15.

Cramer, D., and Brylawski, M., 1996: "Ultralight-Hybrid Vehicle Design: Implications for the Recycling Industry," *Procs. Soc. Plastics Engs. Div.'s 3rd Ann. Recycl. Conf.*, Nov. 7–8, Chicago, IL, Rocky Mountain Institute Publication #T96-14.

Cramer-Kressett Research 1996: *Facilities and Real Estate Strategies*, prepared for National Summit on Building Performance, Nov.

Criminal Justice Newsletter 1995: "30 Percent of Young Black Men Are in Corrections System, Study Finds," 26:19, Oct. 20.

Crutzen, P. J., et al. 1986: "Methane Production by Domestic Animals, Wild Ruminants, Other Herbivorous Fauna and Humans," *Tellus* 38B:271–284.

Csikszentmihalyi, M., 1990: *Flow: The Psychology of Optimal Experience*, Harper and Row, New York, NY.

Cumberford, R., 1996: "New cars for the new millennium," *Automobile* 11(7), Oct., and "Lightness is all," id. 11(8), Nov., both reprinted as RMI Publication #T96-13.

Curitiba (Prefeitura da Cidade) 1997: "Curitiba: Social and Economic Indicators 1997," Dept. of Industry, Commerce and Tourism, Rua da Glória 362, 800.030-060 Centro Cívico, Curitiba, Paraná, Brasil, ++ 055 41 + 352-4021, fax + 352-4201, sict@sict. curitiba.arauc.br.

Curitiba (Prefeitura da Cidade) undated: "Children and Teenagers — Citizens of Curitiba," Secretaria Municipal da Criança, Rua da Glória 362, Centro Civico, CEP 80030-060 Curitiba, Paraná, Brasil, ++ 55 41 + 352-4129, fax -4184, dacyla@smcr. curitiba.arauc.br, www.pr.gov.br/curitiba.

Cushman, J. H. Jr., 1999: "Industries Press Plan for Credits in Emissions Pact," *New York Times* (late N.Y. edn.), 1: 1, Jan. 3.

Custer, Kim, 1995: personal communications, Feb., Mitsubishi Motor Sales America, Cypress, CA.

CyberTran: CyberTran Development Co., 1223 Peoples Ave., Troy, NY 12180, 518/276-2225, fax -6380, transit@transit21.com, www.cybertran.com.

Daily, G., Alexander, S., Ehrlich, P., Goulder, L., Lubchenco, J., Matson, P. A., Mooney, H. A., Postel, S., Schneider, S. H., Tilman, D., and Woodwell, G. M., 1997: "Ecosystem Services: Benefits Supplied to Human Societies by Natural Ecosystems," *Issues in Ecology*, #2, Ecological Society of America, Washington, DC.

Daily, G. C., ed., 1997: *Nature's Services: Societal Dependence on Natural Ecosystems*, Island Press, Washington, DC.

Daily, G. C., and Ehrlich, P. R., 1996: "Global Change and Human Susceptibility to Disease," *Ann. Rev. En Envt.* 21:125–144.

Daly, H. E., 1994: "Operationalizing Sustainable Development by Investing in Natural Capital," p. 22 in Jansson, A., et al., eds., *Investing in Natural Capital*, Island Press, Washington, DC.

——— 1997: "Uneconomic Growth: From Empty-World to Full-World Economics," Rice University, DeLange-Woodlands Conference *Sustainable Development: Managing the Transition*, Houston, TX, Mar. 3, in press in Columbia U. Press conference volume.

——— 1998: "Beyond Growth: Avoiding Uneconomic Growth," Intl. Soc. Ecol. Ecs. 5th Bien. Conf., Santiago, Chile, Nov.

Dansingburg, J., and DeVore, B., 1997: "Canary in a Farm Field," *The Land Stewardship Letter* 15(6):1, 10–11, Dec., Land Stewardship Project, 2200 Fourth St., White Bear Lake, MN 55110.

David, G., 1997: Address to Earth Technologies Forum, Oct. 26.

Davis, S., and Meyer, C., 1998: *Blur: The Speed of Change in the Connected Economy*, Addison-Wesley, Reading, MA.

Davis Energy Group, Inc., 1994: "ACT^2 Davis Site Final Report," Report No. 008.1-93.18, Pacific Gas and Electric Co. (PGandE), 3400 Crow Canyon Road, San Ramon, CA 94583, Feb., www.pge.com.

de Groot, R. S., 1994: "Environmental Functions and the Economic Value of Natural Ecosystems," p. 151 in Jansson, A., et al., eds., *Investing in Natural Capital*, Island Press, Washington, DC.

de Vega, Z. M., 1996: "Curitiba: A World Model in Urban Development," *Iberoamericano*, EFE Agency, rough translation provided Aug. 1998 by webmaster@curitiba. arauc.br.

Deane, P., and Cole, W. A., 1969: *British Economic Growth, 1688–1959*, 2nd edn., Cambridge U. Press, Cambridge, England.

Dearian, J., and Arthur, R., 1997: "Ultra Light Rail Transit: The Wave of the Future," available from CyberTran International, www.cybertran.com.

Dearian, J. A., and Plum, M. M., 1993: "The Capital, Energy, and Time Economics of an Automated, On-Demand Transportation System," 28th Intersoc. En. Cons. Eng. Conf., Aug. 8–13, Atlanta, GA (from J. A. Dearien, c/o Lockheed INEL, PO Box 1625, Idaho Falls, ID, 83415-3765).

DeCanio, S. J., 1993: "Barriers Within Firms to Energy-efficient Investments," *En. Pol.* 21(9):906–914, Sept.

——— 1994: "Why Do Profitable Energy-Saving Investment Projects Languish?," *J. Genl. Mgt.* 20(1), Autumn.

——— 1994a: "Agency and Control Problems in US Corporations: The Case of Energy-efficient Investment Projects," *J. Ecs. Bus.* 1(1):105–123.

——— 1994b: "Energy Efficiency and Managerial Performance: Improving Profitability While Reducing Greenhouse Gas Emissions," at 86–101 in Feldman, D. L., ed., *Global Climate Change and Public Policy*, Nelson-Hall, Chicago.

———— 1997: *The Economics of Climate Change,* Redefining Progress, San Francisco, CA, Oct., www.rprogress.org.

Del Porto, D., and Steinfeld, C. 1999: *The Composting Toilet System Book,* Chelsea Green, White River Junction, VT.

Department of Energy (DOE) 1997: *IPMVP: International Performance Measurement and Verification Protocol,* DOE/EE-0081(97), Sept., U.S. Department of Energy, Washington, DC 20585, www.ipmvp.org.

DeSena, M., 1997: "Integration of Aqua-Culture and Agriculture Saves Water, Boosts Economy," *U.S. Water News* 14(11): 15, Nov.

Design Council 1997: "More for Less," Oct., p. 13, Haymarket House, 1 Oxendon St., London SW1Y 4EE, England.

Design Council, 1997a: id., p. 20.

Deutsch, C. H., 1997: "A New High-Tech Code: From Widgets to Service," *Intl. Herald Tribune,* New York, pp. 1 and 7, Jan. 8.

———— 1998: "Second Time Around, and Around," *New York Times,* pp. C1 and C3, July 14.

DeVore, B., 1996: "Reflecting on What the Land Has to Teach," *The Land Stewardship Letter* 14(5):1, 9–10, Oct./Nov., Land Stewardship Project, 2200 Fourth St., White Bear Lake, MN 55110.

———— 1998: "A Land of Milk and Money," *The Land Stewardship Letter* 16(1):1, 10–12, Jan.–Mar., Land Stewardship Project.

———— 1998a: "Rotational grazing offers financial incentive to help environment," *Minneapolis Star Tribune,* p. A11, Oct. 26.

Diamond, J., 1997: *Guns, Germs, and Steel,* W. W. Norton, New York, NY.

Directed Technologies, Inc., 1997: "Direct-Hydrogen-Fueled Proton-Exchange-Membrane Fuel Cell System for Transportation Applications: Hydrogen Vehicle Safety Report," prepared for U.S. Department of Energy by Ford Motor Co., Dearborn, MI 48121, DOE/CE/50389-502, May.

Drangert, J. O., 1997: "Perception of Human Excreta: A Point Source Pollution or Diffuse Pollution?," in Drangert, J. O., Bew, J., and Winblad, U., eds., 1997: *Ecological Alternatives in Sanitation — Procs. SIDA Sanitation Workshop,* Ballingsholm, Sweden, Aug. 6–9, Publications on Water Resources: No 9, Swedish Intl. Devel. Coop. Agency, Dept. of Natural Resources and the Environment, Stockholm.

———— : "Perceptions, Urine Blindness and Urban Agriculture," in Drangert, J. O., Bew, J., and Winblad, U., eds., 1997: *Ecological Alternatives in Sanitation — Procs. SIDA Sanitation Workshop,* op. cit.

Drug Policy Foundation 1994: "Will the Next $150 Billion Make You Safer?," *New York Times,* advertisement, Feb. 27.

Dudley, N., and Stolton, S., 1996: "Pulp Fact: The Environmental and Social Impacts of the Pulp and Paper Industry," World Wide Fund for Nature, May 8, www.panda.org/tda/forest/contents.htm.

Duffin, M., 1998: presentation to 16th Nikkei Microdevices Seminar, Tokyo, May 28, available from author, Corporate VP, TQEM, STMicroelectronics, murray.duffin@st.com.

Durning, A. T., 1996: "The Car and the City," Northwest Environment Watch Report #3, NWEW, Seattle, WA.

———— 1998: Remarks to Nordic Council Environmental Symposium, Göteborg, Feb. 28.

Earth Impact 1997: Harmony Catalog Newsletter, Winter, www.simplelife.com.

Eckholm, E., 1998: "Joblessness: A Perilous Curve on China's Capitalist Road," *New York Times,* Jan. 20.

Ecology Action 1993: *Annual Report,* 5798 Ridgewood Road, Willits, CA 95490-9730, 707/459-0150, fax -5409.

Economist 1996: "Living with the Car Survey, 'The Hidden Costs,' " June 22.

——— 1997: "Jam Today, Road Pricing Tomorrow," Dec. 6, "How Subsidies Destroy the Land," Dec. 13, and "Plenty of Gloom," Dec. 31.

——— 1998: "Power to the people," Mar. 28, pp. 61–63.

——— 1998a: "When virtue pays a premium," Apr. 18, pp. 57–58.

Edwards, R., 1997: "Nuclear Firms Want Special Treatment," *New Scientist,* June 14.

Ehrlich, P., 1996: "Ecological Economics and the Carrying Capacity of the Earth," p. 38 in Jansson, A., et al., eds., *Investing in Natural Capital,* Island Press, New York, NY.

Ehrlich, P., et al., 1997: "No Middle Way on the Environment," *Atlantic Monthly,* Dec.

Eisenberg, E., 1998: *The Ecology of Eden,* Alfred A. Knopf, New York, NY.

Electrolux 1997: *The Global Appliance Company: Environmental Report 1997,* AB Electrolux, Group Environmental Affairs, S-105 45 Stockholm, ++ 46 8 + 738-6598, fax + 738-7666, environmental.affairs@electrolux.se, www.electrolux.se.

Eley, C., AIA PE 1997: presentation on Performance-Based Fees, Eley Associates, San Francisco, 415/957-1977, fax -1381.

Emerson, R. W., 1994: *Nature and other writings,* Shambhala, Boston, MA, at 9–10.

Environmental Building News 1995: "What's New in Construction Waste Management," 4(6):14, Nov./Dec., EBN, 28 Birge St., Suite 30, Brattleboro, VT 05301, 802/257-7300, fax -7304, ebn@ebuild.com, www.ebuild.com.

Environmental Design and Construction 1998: "10 Building Projects Follow System to Recycle Waste," 36–38, Jan./Feb.

EPA 1989: *Policy Options for Stabilizing Global Climate,* draft Report to Congress, Lashof, D. A., and Tirpak, D., eds., 2 vols., Feb.

EPA 1993: "Introducing the Green Lights Program," EPA 430-F-93-050, Nov.

EPA 1998: Green Lights advertisement, *Environmental Design and Construction,* Jan./Feb. inside back cover.

Epprecht, T., 1998: "Genetic engineering and liability insurance: The power of public perception," Swiss Re, Zurich, publications@swissre.com.

FAS (Fundação de Ação Social), undated: "Solidarity in Curitiba Has a Name: FAS," FAS, Avenida Paraná 2272 — Boa Vista, Curitiba PR, CEP 82510-000, phone and fax ++55 41 + 42/356-7272, pmcta@lepus.celepar.br, www.celepar.br/curitiba/curitiba. html.

Fédération Nationale de la Gestion des Equipements de l'Energie et de l'Environnement (FG&E), "Défense et illustration . . . d'un métier," p. 25 (5, rue de Téhéran, 75008 Paris, ++ 33 1 + 4075 0411, fax + 4075 0407).

Fickett, A. P., Gellings, C. W., and Lovins, A. B., 1990: "Efficient Use of Electricity," *Sci. Amer.* 263(3):64–74, Sept.

Financial Times 1998: p. 3, Nov. 2.

Fischer, H., 1991: "Ausbindungsintegrierter Umweltschutz durch Chemie," *Chemie in unserer Zeit* 25(5):249–256.

——— 1991a: "Environmental Protection by Practical Chemistry: A General Chemistry Laboratory Course with a Minimum of Chemical Waste," *Chimia* 45(3):77–80, Mar.

——— 1994: *Praktikum in Allgemeiner Chemie,* Verlag Helvetica Chemica Acta and VCH (Basel and Weinheim), Teile 1 and 2, ISBN 3-527-29204-7 and 3-906390-10-1, 1994–5, 2nd edn., also available in Russian.

——— 1997: personal communication, Dec. 4, Physikalisch-Chemisches Institut der Universität Zürich, Winterthurerstrasse 190, CH-8057 Zürich, Switzerland, fax ++ 41 1 + 362-0139, hfischer@pci.unizh.ch.

Flavin, C., 1998: "Last Tango in Buenos Aires," *Worldwatch* 11(6):10–18, Nov./Dec.

Flavin, C., and Dunn. S., 1997: "Rising Sun, Gathering Winds: Policies to Stabilize the Climate and Strengthen Economies," Paper #138, Worldwatch Institute, Washington, DC, Nov., www.worldwatch.org.

Flavin, C., and O'Meara, M., 1998: "Solar Power Markets Boom," *Worldwatch* 11(5):23–27, Sept./Oct.

Fox, J., and Cramer, D., 1997: "Hypercars: A Market-Oriented Approach to Meeting Lifecycle and Environmental Goals," Society of Automotive Engineers (SAE) Paper No. 971096, Rocky Mountain Institute Publication #T97-5.

Frank, J. E., 1989: *The Costs of Alternative Development Patterns: A Review of the Literature,* The Urban Land Institute, Washington, DC.

Franta, G., and Anstead, K., 1996: *Glazing Design Handbook for Energy Efficiency,* American Institute of Architects, Washington, DC.

Frantzen, T., 1998: "Deep-Bedded Facilities Changed Our Lives!," *Practical Farmers of Iowa Newsletter,* p. 33, Spring.

Friend, G., 1996: "Ecomimesis: Copying ecosystems for fun and profit," *The New Bottom Line,* Feb. 4, gfriend@igc.apc.org.

Friends of the Earth 1993: *Packaging and Packaging Waste,* Evidence to House of Lords Select Committee on the European Communities, London.

——— 1998: "Dirty Little Secrets," FOE, Washington, DC, www.foe.org/DLS.

Fritz, D., 1984–89: "Salt Ash Peak Occupancy Flow Report," Hawk Mountain Development Corp., Box 64, Plymouth, VT 05056, 802/672-3811.

Froeschle, L., 1998: "Renovating Ridgehaven into a successful green office building," *Environmental Design and Construction,* pp. 55–61, Jan./Feb.

Froeschle, Lynn M., AIA, 1998: personal communication, Jan. 14.

Fukuoka, M., 1978: *The One Straw Revolution: An Introduction to Natural Farming,* Rodale Press, Emmaus, PA; also 1985: Friends Rural Centre, Rasulia, Hoshangabad, Madhya Pradesh, India.

Gadgil, A. J., Rosenfeld, A. H., Arasteh, D., and Ward, E., 1991: "Advanced Lighting and Window Technology for Reducing Electricity Consumption and Peak Demand: Overseas Manufacturing and Marketing Opportunities," 3:6.135–6.152, *Procs. IEA/ ENEL Conf. on Advanced Technologies for Electric Demand-Side Management,* Sorrento, Apr. 2–5, publ. by OECD/IEA, Paris, and as LBNL-30389 Rev. by Lawrence Berkeley [National] Berkeley, CA, www.lbl.gov.

Gardner, G., 1998: "When Cities Take Bicycles Seriously," *Worldwatch* 11(5):16–22, Sept.–Oct.

——— 1998a: *Recycling Organic Waste: From Urban Pollutant to Farm Resource,* Worldwatch Paper 135, Worldwatch Institute, Washington, DC, summarized in Brown et al., eds., 1998, pp. 96–112, "Recycling Organic Wastes."

Gardner, G., and Sampat, P., 1998: "Mind Over Matter: Recasting the Role of Materials in Our Lives," Worldwatch Paper 144, Worldwatch Institute, Washington, DC, Dec.

Geller, H., and Nadel, S., 1994: "Market Transformation Programs: Past Results, Future Directions," *Procs. ACEEE Summer Study Energy Effic. Bldgs.* 10:187–197, American Council for an Energy-Efficient Economy, Washington, DC.

Gene Exchange, The, 1998: "New Reports Spell Trouble for Bt-Resistance Management," Union of Concerned Scientists, Agriculture and Biotechnology Project, 1616 P St.

NW, Suite 310, Washington, DC 20036-1495, www.ucsusa.org/publications/pubs-home.html#Gene.

George, K., Gregerson, J., Shepard, M., Webster, C., and David, D., 1996: *Residential Appliances: Technology Atlas,* E source, Boulder, CO 80301, 303/440-8500, fax -8502, www.esource.com.

Gibbs, W. W., 1997: "Transportation's Perennial Problems," *Sci. Amer.* 277(4):54–57 (Oct.).

Gladwell, M., 1996: "The Tipping Point: Why Is the City Suddenly So Much Safer — Could It Be That Crime Really Is an Epidemic?" *The New Yorker,* pp. 32–38, June 3.

Gleick, P. H., 1994: "Water and Energy," *Ann. Rev. En. Envt.* 19:269–299.

——— 1998: *The World's Water 1998–1999: The Biennial Report on Freshwater Resources,* Island Press, Washington, DC; updated at www.worldwater.org.

——— ed., 1999: *Sustainable Use of Water: California Success Stories,* Pacific Institute for Studies in Development, Environment, and Security, Oakland, CA.

Gleick, P. H., Loh, P., Gomez, S., and Morrison, J., 1995: *California Water 2020. A Sustainable Vision,* Pacific Institute for Studies in Development, Environment, and Security, Oakland, CA.

Global Cities Project 1991: *Building Sustainable Communities: An Environmental Guide for Local Government,* Center for the Study of Law and Politics, 2962 Fillmore St., San Francisco, CA 94123, 415/775-0791, Apr.

Goldemberg, J., Johansson, T. B., Reddy, A. K. N., and Williams, R. H., 1988: *Energy for a Sustainable World,* Wiley Eastern, New Delhi.

Goldstein, D., 1996: "Making Housing More Affordable: Correcting Misplaced Incentives in the Lending System," Natural Resources Defense Council, San Francisco, CA, www.smartgrowth.org/library/housing_afford_goldstein.html.

Gomez, S., and Owens-Viani, L., 1998: "Community/Water Agency partnerships to save water and revitalize communities," in Gleick 1999, op. cit.

Goodman, A., 1998: "New Helmsman, New Goals," *Tomorrow,* pp. 20–21, Mar./Apr.

Goodstein, E., 1999: *What Trade-Off? Fictions and Facts About Jobs and the Environment* (working title, in press), Island Press, Washington, DC.

Gorman, T. M., 1998: "Structural Products Made from Small Diameter and Under-Utilized Trees," *The Greening of Yellowstone and Beyond* conference (Bozeman, May 14–16), available from Prof. Gorman, Forest Products Dept., U. of Id., Moscow, ID 83844-1132, 208/885-7402, fax -6226, tgorman@uidaho.edu.

Gould, F., et al. 1997: "Initial frequency of Alleles for Resistance to *Bacillus thuringiensis* Toxins in Field Populations of *Heliothis virescens,*" *Procs. NAS* 94:3519–3523.

Graedel, T. E., and Allenby, B. R., 1996: *Industrial Ecology,* AT&T and Prentice-Hall, Englewood Cliffs, NJ.

——— 1996a: *Design for Environment,* AT&T and Prentice-Hall, Upper Saddle River, NJ.

Green Business Letter 1998: "First American Scientific Corp.'s Kinetic Disintegration Technology," Jan., makower@greenbiz.com.

——— 1998a: "Fade to White," Aug., makower@greenbiz.com.

Grieg-Gran, M., et. al. 1997: "Towards a Sustainable Paper Cycle," *J. Indl. Ecol.* 1(3):47–68, Summer.

Groscurth, H.-M., and Kümmel, R., 1989: "The Cost of Energy Optimization: A Thermoeconomic Analysis of National Energy Systems," Physikalisches Institut der Universität Würzburg, May 16.

Haldane, J. B. S., 1985: *"On Being the Right Size" and Other Essays,* ed. by J. M. Smith, Oxford U. Press, New York, NY.

Halstead, T., Rowe, J., and Cobb, C., 1995: "If the GDP Is Up, Why Is America Down?," *The Atlantic Monthly* 276(4):59–78, Oct.

Halweil, B., 1999: "Unintended effects of Bt Crops," *Worldwatch* 12(1):9–10, Jan./Feb.

Hammond, J., et al. 1997: *Tax Waste, Not Work — How Changing What We Tax Can Lead to a Stronger Economy and a Cleaner Environment,* Apr., Redefining Progress, San Francisco, CA, 800/896-2100 or 415/781-1191, www.rprogress.org.

Hansen, J. E., Sato, M., Ruety, R., Lacis, A., and Glascoe, J., 1998: "Global Climate Data and Models: A Reconciliation," *Science* 281:930–932, Aug. 14.

Harmon, M. E., Ferrell, W. K., and Franklin, J. F., 1990: "Effects on Carbon Storage of Conversion of Old-Growth Forests to Young Forests," *Science* 247:699–702, Feb. 9.

Harrisson, T., 1965: "Operation Cat-Drop," *Animals* 5:512–513.

Hart, S., 1999: "Global Sustainability and the Creative Destruction of Industries," accepted for publication in *Sloan Mgt. Rev.,* Mar.

Hartman, R. S., and Doane, M. J., 1986: "Household discount rates revisited," *En. J.* 7(1):139–148, Jan.

Hausman, J., 1979: "Individual Discount Rates and the Purchase and Utilization of Energy-Consuming Durables," *Bell J. Ecs.* 10(1):33–54.

Hawken, Paul, 1997: "Natural Capitalism," *Mother Jones,* Mar./Apr.

——— 1994: Speech to the Conference Board, Feb., New York, NY.

Haynes, R., coordinator, 1990: *An Analysis of the Timber Situation in the United States: 1898–2040,* U.S. Forest Service, Ft. Collins, CO, General Technical Report RM-199, Dec.

Haynes, R. W., Adams, D. M., and Mills, J. R., 1995: "The 1993 RPA Timber Assessment Update," RM-GTR-259, U.S. Forest Service, Mar.

Heederik, G., 1998: "Daddy's Duct Sealing Method," *Home Energy,* pp. 44–45, Jan./Feb.

Hillel, D., 1991: *Out of the Earth, Civilization and the Life of the Soil,* The Free Press, New York, NY.

Ho, M.-W., and Steinbrecher, R. A., 1998: *Fatal Flaws in Food Safety Assessment: Critique of the Joint FAO/WHO Biotechnology and Food Safety Report,* TWN Biotechnology and Biosafety Series 1, Third World Network, Penang, Malaysia, ISBN 983-9747-29-0.

Ho, M.-W., Traavik, T., Olsvik, O., Midtredt, T., Tappeser, B., Howard, C. V., von Weizsäcker, E. U., and McGavin, G. C., 1998: *Gene Technology in the Etiology of Drug-resistant Diseases,* TWN Biotechnology and Biosafety Series 2, Third World Network, Penang, Malaysia, ISBN 983-9747-35-5.

Hobsbawm, E., 1996: *The Age of Revolution,* Vintage, New York, NY.

Holling, C. S. 1994: "New Science and New Investments for a Sustainable Biosphere," p. 5, in Jansson, A., et al., eds., *Investing in Natural Capital,* Island Press, Washington, DC.

Holtzclaw, J., 1994: "Using Residential Patterns and Transit to Decrease Auto Dependence and Costs," Natural Resources Defense Council, San Francisco, CA, www.nrdc.org.

——— 1998: *But I Have to Drive! Why? Analysis of 3 Regions: San Francisco, Chicago and Los Angeles,* The Location Efficient Mortgage Partnership (Natural Resources Defense Council, San Francisco; Center for Neighborhood Policy, Chicago; Surface Transportation Policy Project, Washington, DC), May.

Holtzclaw, J., and Goldstein, D., 1991: "Efficient Cars in Efficient Cities," Natural Resources Defense Council, San Francisco, CA.

Horrigan, J. B., Irwin, F. H., and Cook, E., 1998: *Taking a Byte Out of Carbon: Electronic Industries Alliance, and International Cooperative for Environmental Leadership,* World Resources Institute, Washington, DC.

Houghton, D. J., Bishop, R. C., Lovins, A. B., Stickney, B. L., Newcomb, J. J., Shepard, M., and Davids, B. J., 1992: *The State of the Art: Space Cooling and Air Handling,* COM-PETITEK/Rocky Mountain Institute, Aug., supplemented and updated by Cler et al. 1997.

Houghton, D. J., and Hibberd, D., 1998: "Packaged Rooftop Air Conditioners: A Buyer's Guide for 5.4 to 20 Ton Units," TU-98-1, E SOURCE, Boulder, CO, www. esource.com.

Houghton, D. J., 1995: "Demand-Controlled Ventilation: Teaching Buildings to Breathe," TU-95-10, E SOURCE, Boulder, CO.

Howe, B., 1993: "Distribution Transformers: A Growing Energy Savings Opportunity," TU-93-10, E SOURCE, Boulder, CO, Dec.

Howe, B., Shepard, M., Lovins, A. B., Stickney, B. L., and Houghton, D. J., 1996: *Drive-power Technology Atlas,* E SOURCE. Data are periodically updated by the Motor-Master database sponsored by USDOE (800/862-2086, fax 360/586-8303, Motor Challenge Information Clearinghouse, Box 43717, Olympia, WA 98504-3171).

Hubbard, A., and Fong, C., 1995: *Community Energy Workbook,* Economic Renewal Project, Rocky Mountain Institute Publication #ER95-4, RMI, Snowmass, CO 81654-9199, www.rmi.org.

INFORM Reports 1997: 17(3), Fall/Winter, INFORM, New York, NY.

Interagency Workgroup on Industrial Ecology, Material and Energy Flows 1998: *Materials,* final report, Jan., White House Council on Environmental Quality et al., 800/363-3732, www.oit.doe.gov/mining/materials.

Interlaboratory Working Group 1997: *Scenarios of U.S. Carbon Reductions: Potential Impacts of Energy Technologies by 2010 and Beyond,* Lawrence Berkeley [National] Laboratory (Berkeley, CA) and Oak Ridge National Laboratory (Oak Ridge, TN), LBNL-40533, ORNL-444 Sept., www.ornl.gov/ORNL/Energy_Eff/ CON444.

International Institute for Environment and Development (IIED) 1995: *The Sustainable Paper Cycle,* Phase I, Review Report, Second Draft, IIED/World Business Council on Sustainable Development (WBCSD), London.

International Labor Organization 1994: *The World Employment Situation, Trends and Prospects,* press release, ILO, Washington, DC, and Geneva, Switzerland, Mar. 6.

IPCC (Intergovernmental Panel on Climate Change) 1990: *Climate Change: The Scientific Assessment,* Cambridge U. Press, Cambridge, England.

——— 1992: *Climate Change 1992,* Cambridge U. Press.

——— 1996: *Climate Change 1995: IPPC Second Assessment Report,* 2 vols., Cambridge U. Press.

——— 1996a: *The Economic and Social Dimensions of Climate Change,* Vol. 3 of *Climate Change 1995: IPPC Second Assessment Report,* Cambridge U. Press.

IPSEP 1993: *Energy Policy in the Greenhouse, Vol. II, Pt. 1: Cutting Carbon Emissions: Burden or Benefit?,* report to Dutch Ministry of Environment, International Project for Sustainable Energy Paths, El Cerrito, CA 94530, ipsep@igc.org.

——— 1994–8: *Energy Policy in the Greenhouse, Vol. II, Pt. 2–6: The Cost of Cutting Carbon Emissions in Western Europe,* id.

Jackson, W., 1980: "The Great Plains in Transition," *The Land Report* 10:29–31 (Summer 1980), The Land Institute, Salina, KS 67401, 785/823-5376, fax -8728.

Jackson, W., Berry, W., and Colman, B., 1984: *Meeting the Expectations of the Land,* North Point, San Francisco, CA.

Jaffe, A. B., and Stavins, R. N., 1994: "The Energy Efficiency Gap: What Does It Mean?," *En. Pol.* 22(10):804–810, Oct.

James, B. D., Thomas, C. E., Baum, G. N., Lomax, F. D. Jr., and Kuhn, I. F. Jr., 1997: "Making the Case for Direct Hydrogen Storage in Fuel Cell Vehicles," *Procs. 8th Ann. U.S. Hydrogen Mtg.*, National Hydrogen Association, Mar. 11–13, Alexandria, VA.

Johansson, T. B., et al., eds. 1989: *Electricity: Efficient End-Use and New Generation Technologies, and Their Planning Implications*, U. of Lund Press, Lund, Sweden.

Johansson, T. B., Kelly, H., Reddy, A. K. N., and Williams, R. H., eds., and Burnham, L., exec. ed. 1993: *Renewable Energy*, Island Press, Washington, DC.

Johnson, E. W. 1993: "Avoiding the Collision of Cities and Cars: Urban Transportation Policy for the 21st Century," American Academy of Arts and Sciences; see also "Taming the car and its user: should we do both?," *Bull. Amer. Acad. Arts and Scis.* 46(2): 13–29, 1992.

Jones, A. P., 1993: "Better toilets, fewer dams," *The Nation* (Bangkok), Jan. 31, Rocky Mountain Institute Publication #W94-7.

Jones, A. P., and Dyer J., 1994: "Partnerships on the Frontier of Innovation," Rocky Mountain Institute Publication #W94-6.

Jones, A. P., Dyer, J., and Obst, J., 1993: "Pulling Utilities Together: Water-Energy Partnerships," *Home Energy*, July/Aug.

Jönsson, H., 1997: "Assessment of Sanitation Systems and Reuse of Urine," in Drangert, J. O., Bew, J., and Winblad, U., eds., 1997: *Ecological Alternatives in Sanitation — Procs. SIDA Sanitation Workshop*, Ballingsholm, Sweden, Aug. 6–9, Publications on Water Resources: No 9, Swedish Intl. Devel. Coop. Agency, Dept. of Natural Resources and the Environment, Stockholm (author is at Dept. of Ag. Eng., Swedish U. of Ag. Scis., hakan.jonsson@lt.slu.se).

Kalbermatten, J. M., Julius, D. S., Gunnerson, C. G., and Mara, D. D., 1982: "I. Appropriate sanitation alternatives: A technical and economic appraisal" and "II. A planning and design manual," World Bank Studies in Water Supply and Sanitation, Johns Hopkins U. Press, Baltimore, MD.

Kaplan, R., 1997: "The Future of Democracy," *Atlantic Monthly*, Dec.

——— 1994: "The Coming Anarchy," *Atlantic Monthly*, Feb.

Kassler, P., 1994: *Energy for Development*, Shell Selected Paper, Shell Intl. Petroleum Co., London, Nov.

Kating, P., and Fischer, H., 1995: *Chemie in unserer Zeit* 29(2):101–106, from VCH Verlagsgesellschaft mbH, W-6940 Weinheim.

Keepin, W. N., and Kats, G., 1988: "Global Warning" [*sic*], *Science* 241:1027, Aug. 26.

——— 1988a: "Greenhouse Warming: Comparative Analysis of Nuclear and Efficiency Abatement Strategies," *En. Pol.* 16(6):538–561, Dec., and calculational supplement, "Greenhouse Warming: A Rationale for Nuclear Power?," available from RMI.

Kelly, K., 1994: *Out of Control, the Rise of Neo-biological Civilization*, Addison-Wesley, Reading, MA; see also *New Rules for a New Economy*, Penguin Group, New York, NY, 1998.

Kempton, W., Feuermann, D., and McGarity, A. E., 1992: "I always turn it on super: user decisions about when and how to operate room air conditioners," *Energy and Buildings* 18(3):177–191.

Kerr, R. A., 1998: "Warming's Unpleasant Surprise: Shivering in the Greenhouse?," *Science* 281:156–158, July 10.

Ketcham, B., and Komanoff, C., 1992: "Win-Win Transportation, A No-Losers Approach to Financing Transport in New York City and the Region," Transportation Alternatives, New York, NY.

Kihlstedt, P. G., 1977: "Samhällets Råvaruförsörjning under Energibrist," IVA-Rapport 12, Ingenjörsvetenskapsakademien, Stockholm.

Kinsella, S., ed., 1999: "Welfare for Waste: How Federal Taxpayer Subsidies Waste Resources and Discourage Recycling," Grass Roots Recycling Network (Athens, GA, zerowaste@grrn.org), Friends of the Earth, Taxpayers for Common Sense, and Materials Efficiency Project (www.cnt.org/materials) (all Washington, DC), Apr.

Kinsley, M., 1992: *Economic Renewal Guide,* Economic Renewal Project, Rocky Mountain Institute Publication #ER92-23, RMI, Snowmass, CO 81654-9199, www.rmi.org.

Kinsley, M., and Lovins, H., 1995: "Paying for Growth, Prospering from Development," Rocky Mountain Institute Publication #ER95-5.

Kinsley, M., 1997: *Economic Renewal Guide: A Collaborative Process for Sustainable Community Development,* Economic Renewal Project, Rocky Mountain Institute Publication #ER97-2.

Knopf, J., 1999: *Waterwise Landscaping with Trees, Shrubs, and Vines: A Xeriscape Guide for the Rocky Mountain Region, plus California and the Desert Southwest,* in press, spring 1999, 320 Hollyberry Lane, Boulder, CO 80303, 303/494-8766.

Komanoff, C., and Levine, J., 1994: "Where Everybody Bikes," *Transportation Alternatives,* Sept./Oct., p. 15.

Komor, P., 1996: "Cooling Demands from Office Equipment and Other Plug Loads," TU-96-9, E source, Boulder, CO 80301, www.esource.com.

Koomey, J. G., Atkinson, C., Meier, A., McMahon, J. E., Boghosian, S., et al. 1991: *The Potential for Electricity Efficiency Improvements in the U.S. Residential Sector,* LBL-30477, Lawrence Berkeley [National] Laboratory, Berkeley, CA, July.

Korten, D., 1999: *The Post-Corporate World: Life After Capitalism,* Barrett-Koehler, San Francisco, CA.

Kranendonk, S., and Bringezu, S., 1993: "Major Material Flows Associated with Orange Juice Consumption in Germany," *Fresenius Environmental Bulletin,* Aug.

Krause, F., 1996: "The Cost of Mitigating Carbon Emissions: A Review of Methods and Findings from European Studies," *En. Pol.* 24(10/11):899–915.

Krause, F., Bach, W., and Koomey, J., 1989: *Energy Policy in the Greenhouse,* report to Dutch Ministry of Housing, Vol. 1, Physical Planning and Environment, International Project for Sustainable Energy Paths, El Cerrito, CA, Sept.

Krause, F., Busch, J., and Koomey, J. G., 1992: *Internalizing Global Warming Risks in Power Sector Planning: A Case Study of Carbon Reduction Costs for the New England Region,* LBL-30797, 2 vols., Lawrence Berkeley [National] Laboratory, Berkeley, CA 94720, Nov.

Krol, J. A., 1997: Remarks at the CIED World Forum on Energy and Environment, Caracas, Nov. 18.

Kummer, C., 1998: "Carried Away," *New York Times Magazine,* pp. 38ff, Aug. 30.

Lacob, M., 1997: "Elevators on the Move," *Scientific American* 277(4):136–137, Oct.

Laird, C., and Dyer, J., 1992: "Feedback and Irrigation Efficiency," Rocky Mountain Institute Publication #A92-20.

Lal, R., 1995: "Global soil erosion by water and carbon dynamics," at 131–142 in Lal, R., Kimble, J. L., Levine, E., and Stewart, B. A., eds., *Soils and Global Change,* CRC/Lewis Publishers, Boca Raton, FL.

——— 1997: "Residue management, conservation tillage and soil restoration for mitigating greenhouse effect by CO_2 enrichment," *Soil and Tillage Res.* 43:81–101.

Lal, R., Kimble, J. L., Follet, R. F., and Cole, C. V., 1998: *The Potential of U.S. Cropland to Sequester Carbon and Mitigate the Greenhouse Effect*, Sleeping Bear Press, 121 S. Main St., Chelsea, MI 48118.

Lamarre, L. 1997: "The New Line on Laundry," *EPRI.*, pp. 14–23, Nov./ Dec.

—— 1997a: "Less Noisy, Less Thirsty," *Consumer Reports*, pp. 42–45, Jan.

Lamounier, B., and Figueiredo, R., 1996: "Curitiba: A Paradigm," rough English translation provided Aug. 1998 by webmaster@curitiba.arauc.br, original cited as published in *As cidades que dão certo: experiências inovadoras na administração pública brasiliera*, MH Comunicação, 1996.

Land Institute, The, 1993: *Annual Report*, Salina, KS 67401, 913/823-5376.

Lane, J., 1998: "Farmers, researchers put their heads together on hoops," *Leopold Letter* 10(1):10 (see also 3ff), Spring 1998, Leopold Center, Ames, IA, 515/294-3711.

Lardner, J., 1998: "Americans' Widening Gap in Incomes May Be Narrowing Our Lifespans," *Sunday Washington Post*, p. C01, Aug. 16.

Lenssen, N., 1995: *Local Integrated Resource Planning: A New Tool for a Competitive Era*, Strategic Issue Paper IV, E SOURCE, Boulder, CO 80301, www.esource.com.

Lenssen, N., and Newcomb, J., 1996: *Integrated Energy Services: The Shape of Things to Come?*, Strategic Issue Paper VIII, E SOURCE, Boulder, CO.

Levine, M. D., Koomey, J. G., McMahon, J. E., and Sanstad, A. H., 1995: "Energy Efficiency Policy and Market Failures," *Ann. Rev. En. Envt.* 20:535–555.

Levine, M. D., Liu, F., and Sinton, J. E., 1993: "China's Energy System: Historical Evolution, Current Issues, and Prospects," *Ann. Rev. En. Envt.* 17:405–435.

Liebold, W. C., 1995: "Financial and 'Integrated Resource' Planning and New York City Water Efficiency Programs," Workshop on Plumbing Fixtures and Water Conservation, American Water Works Association, Dept. of Conservation, NYC Dept. of Environmental Protection, June 9.

Liedtke, C., 1993: "Material Intensity of Paper and Board Production in Western Europe," *Fresenius Environmental Bulletin*, Aug.

Linden, E., 1996: "The Exploding Cities of the Developing World," *For. Aff.* 75(1):52–65, Jan./Feb.

Lomax, F. D., Jr., James, B. D., and Mooradian, R. P., 1997: "PEM Fuel Cell Cost Minimization Using 'Design for Manufacture and Assembly' Techniques." *Procs. 8th Annual U.S. Hydr. Mtg.*, National Hydrogen Assn. (Alexandria, VA), Mar. 11–13, pp. 459–468.

Lotspeich, C., 1995: "Economic and Environmental Aspects of Reducing Demand for Wood Fiber in the Pulp and Paper Sector," unpublished Master's Project, Yale School of Forestry and Environmental Studies.

Lovins, A. B., 1976: "Energy Strategy: The Road Not Taken?," *For. Aff.* 55(1):65–96, Fall, Rocky Mountain Institute Publication #E-1, www.rmi.org.

—— 1990: "Make Fuel Efficiency Our Gulf Strategy," op-ed in the *New York Times*, Dec. 3, Rocky Mountain Institute Publication #S90-27a.

—— 1991b: *Rocky Mountain Institute Visitor's Guide*, Rocky Mountain Institute Publication #H-1, Snowmass, CO 81654-9199.

—— 1992: "Air Conditioning Comfort: Behavioral and Cultural Issues," Strategic Issue Paper #1 (SIP I), E SOURCE, Boulder, CO 80301, www.esource.com.

—— 1992a: "Energy-Efficient Buildings: Institutional Barriers and Opportunities," Strategic Issue Paper #2 (SIP II), E SOURCE, Boulder, CO.

—— 1993: "What an Energy-Efficient Computer Can Do," Rocky Mountain Institute Publication #E93-20.

—— 1994: "Apples, Oranges, and Horned Toads: Is the Joskow and Marron Critique of Electric Efficiency Costs Valid?," *El. J.* 7(4):29–49, May.

—— 1995: "The Super-Efficient Passive Building Frontier," condensation of Centenary address, *ASHRAE J.* 37(6):79–81, June, Rocky Mountain Institute Publication #E95-28.

—— 1995a: "Comments on FERC's Mega-NOPR," July 24, Rocky Mountain Institute Publication #U95-37.

—— 1996: "Negawatts: Twelve Transitions, Eight Improvements, and One Distraction," *En. Pol.* 24(4), Apr., RMI Publication #U96-11.

—— 1996a: "Hypercars: The Next Industrial Revolution," *Procs. 13th Intl. El. Veh. Sympos.* (Osaka), Oct., Rocky Mountain Institute Publication #T96-9, downloadable from www.rmi.org.

—— 1997: "Auto Bodies Lighten Up," letter, *Technol. Rev.,* MIT, pp. 6–8, May/ June.

—— 1997a: "Climate: Making Sense *and* Making Money," keynote address to International NGOs' Research Conference "Sustainability Vision 21: Energy Policies and CO_2 Reduction Technologies," Kyoto, Dec. 6, Rocky Mountain Institute Publication #E97-13, downloadable from www.rmi.org/catalog/climate.htm (not to be confused with Lovins and Lovins 1997, id.).

—— 1998: "Putting Central Power Plants Out of Business," address to Aspen Institute Energy Forum, July 7, RMI Publication #E98-2.

—— 1998a: "Negawatts for Fabs: Advanced Electric Productivity for Fun and Profit," overhead slides of a technical presentation on energy savings opportunities in microchip fabrication plants, given to semiconductor industry, Rocky Mountain Institute Publication #E98-3, available at http://redtail.stanford.edu/seminar/presentations/lovins3/index.htm.

—— 1999: "Smart Companies Aren't Waiting Around for Climate Treaty Ratification," *Worldwatch* 12(1):7, Jan./Feb.

Lovins, A. B., Brylawski, M. M., Cramer, D. R., and Moore, T. C., 1997: *Hypercars: Materials, Manufacturing, and Policy Implications,* 2nd ed., Mar., 317 refs.; front matter, RMI Publication #T96-7 (28 pp.), downloadable from www. hypercar.com.

Lovins, A. B., and Gadgil, A., 1991: "The Negawatt Revolution: Electric Efficiency and Asian Development," Rocky Mountain Institute Publication #E91-23, abridged in *Far E. Ec. Rev.,* Aug. 1.

Lovins, A. B., and Heede, R., 1990: *Electricity-Saving Office Equipment,* COMPETITEK/ Rocky Mountain Institute, Sept.

Lovins, A. B., and Lehmann, A., 2001: *Small Is Profitable: The Hidden Economic Benefits of Making Electrical Resources the Right Size,* in press, Rocky Mountain Institute, www.rmi.org.

Lovins, A. B., and L. H., 1991: "Least-Cost Climatic Stabilization," *Ann. Rev. En. Envt.* 16:433–531, Rocky Mountain Institute Publication #E91-33.

—— 1997: "Climate: Making Sense *and* Making Money," Rocky Mountain Institute Publication #E97-13, downloadable from www.rmi.org/catalog/climate.htm (not to be confused with Lovins 1997a, id.).

Lovins, A. B., and L. H., Krause, F., and Bach, W., 1981: *Least-Cost Energy: Solving the CO_2 Problem,* report to German Federal Environmental Agency, reprinted 1989 as Rocky Mountain Institute Publication #E89-17.

Lovins, A. B., Neymark, J., Flanigan, T., Kiernan, P. B., Bancroft, B., and Shepard, M., 1989: *The State of the Art: Drivepower,* COMPETITEK/Rocky Mountain Institute, Snowmass, CO 81654-9199, updated and supplemented by Howe et al. 1996 q.v.

Lovins, A. B., and Sardinsky, R., 1988: *The State of the Art: Lighting,* COMPETITEK/Rocky Mountain Institute, Snowmass, CO 81654-9199, updated and supplemented by Audin et al. 1998, q.v.

Lovins, A. B., and Williams, B. D., 1999: "A Strategy for the Hydrogen Transition," *Procs. National Hydrogen Assn. Mtg.,* Apr. 7–9, Arlington, VA, RMI Publication #E99-7, www.hypercar.com/go/whatfgo.html.

Lowe, M. D., 1990: "Alternatives to Automobile Transport: Transport for Livable Cities," Worldwatch Institute, Washington, DC.

Lugar, R. G., and Woolsey, R. J., 1999: "The New Petroleum," *For. Aff.* 78(1):88–102, Jan./Feb.

Lunneberg, T., 1998: "High-Efficiency Laboratory Ventilation," TU-98-4, E SOURCE, Boulder, CO 80301, www.esource.com, Mar.

Lutzenhiser, L., 1992: "A Question of Control: Alternative Patterns of Room Air Conditioner Use," *Energy and Buildings* 18(3): 193–200.

Machalaba, D., 1998: "Hitting the Skids," *Wall Street Journal,* Apr. 1, p. A1.

Macht, J., 1997: "Pulp Addiction," *Inc.* 19(4):43–46.

MacKenzie, J. J., Dower, R. C., and Chen, D. D. T., 1992: *The Going Rate: What It Really Costs to Drive,* World Resources Institute, Washington, DC.

Mann, C. C., 1998: "Who Will Own Your Next Good Idea?," *Atlantic Monthly* 282(3): 57–82, Sept.

Mansley, M., 1995: *Long Term Financial Risks to the Carbon Fuel Industry from Climate Change,* Delphi Group, London.

Margulis, L., and Sagan, D., 1997: *Microcosmos: Four Billion Years of Evolution from Our Microbial Ancestors,* University of California Press, Berkeley, CA.

Marine Conservation Biology Institute 1998: "Troubled Waters: A Call for Action," MCBI, Redmond, WA, Jan., www.mcbi.org.

Mascarin, A. E., Dieffenbach, J. R., Brylawski, M. M., Cramer, D. R., and Lovins, A. B., 1995: "Costing the Ultralite in Volume Production: Can Advanced Composite Bodies-in-White Be Affordable?," International Body Engineering Conference, Detroit, Nov. 1; corrected Aug. 31 preprint, Rocky Mountain Institute Publication #T95-35.

Max-Neef, M., 1992: "Development and human needs," pp. 197–214 in P. Ekins and M. Max-Neef, eds., *Real-life economics: Understanding wealth creation,* Routledge, London.

May, A. D., and Nash, C. A., 1996: "Urban Congestion: A European Perspective on Theory and Practice," *Ann. Rev. En. Envt.* 21:239–260.

McDonough, W., and Braungart, M., 1998: "The Next Industrial Revolution," *Atlantic Monthly* 282(4), Oct.

McHugh, P., 1998: "Rare Otters Surface in S.F. Bay," *San Francisco Chronicle,* Jan. 17.

McKibben, B., 1995: Ch. 2, "Curitiba," in *Hope, Human and Wild,* Little, Brown, Boston, MA.

McKibben, B., 1998: "A Special Moment in History," *Atlantic Monthly* 281(5):55–78, May.

McLean, R., and Shopley, J., 1996: "Green light shows for corporate gains," *Fin. Times* (London), July 3.

McPherson, N., 1994: *Machines and Economic Growth,* The Greenwood Press, Westport, CT.

Meadows, D. H., 1994: "Seeing the Population Issue Whole," at pp. 23–33 in *Beyond the Numbers,* Mazur, L. A., ed., Island Press, Washington, DC.

Meadows, D. H. and D. L., 1973: "A Summary of *The Limits to Growth:* Its Critics and Its Challenge," *Futures,* Feb. (first presented at Yale U., Sept. 1972).

Meadows, D. H. and D. L., Randers, J., and Behrens, W., 1972: *The Limits to Growth: A Report for the Club of Rome's Project on the Predicament of Mankind,* Potomac Associates, Washington, DC, republished 1974 by Universe Books, New York, NY.

Meadows, D. H. and D. L., and Randers, J., 1992: *Beyond the Limits,* Chelsea Green Publishing Co., PO Box 130, Post Mills, VT 05058.

Meeker-Lowry, S., 1998: "You Can't Put a Price on Gaia," letter to the editor in response to Jane Abramovitz's article in Jan./Feb. 1998 issue, *Worldwatch* 11(2), Mar./Apr.

Mellon, M., and Rissler, J., eds., 1998: *Now or Never: Serious New Plans to Save a Natural Pest Control,* Union of Concerned Scientists, Washington, DC.

Mergenhagen, P., 1996: "The Prison Population Bomb," *Am. Demogr.,* Feb.

Midwest Real Estate News 1992: "Native Midwesterners Retake Suburban Landscape," pp. 35–36, July.

Mills, E., 1991: *An End-Use Perspective on Electricity Price Responsiveness,* PhD thesis, Department of Envtl. and En. Syst. Studies, U. of Lund, Lund, Sweden.

——— 1995: "From the Lab to the Marketplace," LBNL-758, Lawrence Berkeley [National] Laboratory, Berkeley, CA, http://eande.lbl.gov/CBS/Lab2Mkt/LabtMkt.html.

———1997: "Going Green Reduces Losses," Nov. 19, http://eande.lbl.gov/CBS/Climate-insurance/GoingGreen.html.

Mills, E., and Knoepfel, I., 1997: "Energy-Efficiency Options for Insurance Loss Prevention," LBNL-40426, Lawrence Berkeley [National] Laboratory, Berkeley, CA, June 9.

Mishel, L., et al., 1997: *The State of Working America, 1996–97,* M. E. Sharpe, New York, NY.

Mokhtarian, P. L., 1997: "Now That Travel Can Be Virtual, Will Congestion Virtually Disappear?," *Scientific American* 277(4):93, Oct.

Moore, T. C., 1996: "Tools and Strategies for Hybrid-Electric Drivesystem Optimization," *SAE (Society of Automotive Engineers) Future Transportation Technology Conference,* Vancouver, BC, SAE Paper No. 961660, Rocky Mountain Institute Publication #T96-12.

——— 1996a: "Ultralight Hybrid Vehicles: Principles and Design," *Procs. 13th Intl. El. Veh. Sympos.* (Osaka), Oct., Rocky Mountain Institute Publication #T96-10, downloadable from www.rmi.org.

——— 1997: "HEV Control Strategy: Implications of Performance Criteria, System Configuration and Design, and Component Selection," *Procs. Inst. El. and Electronic Engs. (IEEE), Control Systs. Soc. 1997 Am. Control Conf.,* Albuquerque, NM, June 4–6, Rocky Mountain Institute Publication #T97-7.

Moore, T. C., and Lovins, A. B., 1995: "Vehicle Design Strategies to Meet and Exceed PNGV Goals," *SAE (Society of Automotive Engineers) Future Transportation Technology Conference,* Aug. 4, Costa Mesa, CA, SAE Paper No. 951906, Rocky Mountain Institute Publication #T95-27.

Moskovitz, D., 1989: *Profits and Progress Through Least-Cost Planning,* National Association of Regulatory Utility Commissioners, Washington, DC.

Mott-Smith, J., 1982: "Residential Street Widths," SolarCal Local Government Commission, Sacramento, CA.

Myers, N., 1998: *Perverse Subsidies: Tax $s Undercutting Our Economies and Environments Alike,* Intl. Inst. for Sust. Devel., 161 Portage Ave. E., 6th Floor, Winnipeg, Manitoba R3B 0Y4, 204/958-7700, fax -7710, info@iisd.ca.

Nadel, S., 1990: *Lesson Learned,* New York State Energy Research and Development Authority, New York State Energy Office, Niagara Mohawk Power Corp., American Council for an Energy-Efficient Economy, Rep. 90-8, Albany, NY, Apr.

Nadis, S., and MacKenzie, J. J., 1993: *Car Trouble,* World Resources Institute, Beacon Press, Boston, MA, 1993.

Nash, H., ed., Lovins, A. B. and L. H., 1977: *The Energy Controversy: Soft Path Questions and Answers,* Friends of the Earth, San Francisco, CA.

National Laboratory Directors 1997: *Technology Opportunities to Reduce U.S. Greenhouse Gas Emissions,* Oct., www.ornl.gov/ climate_change, 2 vols.

National Research Council (NRC) 1989: *Alternative Agriculture,* National Academy Press, Washington, DC.

National Research Council (NRC) 1996: *Lost Crops of Africa: Volume I: Grains,* National Academy Press, Washington, DC.

Naylor, R. L., 1996: "Energy and Resource Constraints on Intensive Agricultural Production," *Ann. Rev. En. Envt.* 21:99–123.

Nelson, Jon Olaf, 1997: "1997, Residential Water Use Summary," downloaded Jan. 1998, http://www.waterwiser. org/wateruse/main.html, preliminary results of the North American Residential End-Use Study sponsored by American Water Works Association Research Foundation.

Nelson, K. E., 1993, "Dow's Energy/WRAP Program," Lecture at 1993 Indl. En. Technol. Conf., Houston, Mar. 24–25; now at KENTEC, Inc., 8118 Oakbrook Dr., Baton Rouge, LA 70810, 225/761-1838, fax -1872, kentech@compuserve.com.

Nelson, K. L., 1995: "Following Energy Utilities' Model, Water Cos. Offer Incentives for Efficiency," *En. User News* 20(6), June.

Newman, S., 1997: "Super Typhoon," Earthweek, *San Francisco Chronicle,* Dec. 12.

Newman, P., and Kenworthy, J., with Robinson, L. 1992: *Winning Back the Cities,* Pluto Press Australia Ltd, Leichhardt, New South Wales, Australia.

New Urban News 1997: "Narrow streets are the safest," 2(6):1 and 9, Nov.–Dec., PO Box 6515, Ithaca, NY 14851, 607/275-3087, fax 607/272-2685.

——— 1997a: "ITE prepares to tentatively endorse narrow streets," 2(5):1 and 14, and "ITE fails by ignoring street widths," id., 2.

——— 1997b: "'New Urbanism premium' identified in Kentlands," 2(6): 1 and 3, Nov.–Dec.

——— 1997c: "Neotraditional projects proliferate in many parts of the U.S.," 2(5): 1 and 5–13, Sept.–Oct.

New York Times 1994: "420,000 C-Sections a Year Called Unneeded," May 22.

——— 1995: "In China's Southwest, a Battle to Contain the Spreading Scourge of Heroin," p. A6, Nov. 15.

——— 1996: "Clean Air: Adding it Up," Dec. 1.

——— 1996a: "Index of Social Well-Being Is at the Lowest in 25 Years," p. A1, Oct. 14.

——— 1998: "Oil Spills? Ask a Hairdresser," June 9.

Niebrugge, Alan, 1994: personal communication, Mgr. of Envtl. Services, GS Technologies, 8116 Wilson Rd., Kansas City, MO 64125, 816/242-5840.

Nielsen, L. J., and Elsbree, J. F. Jr., 1997: "Integration of Product Stewardship into a Personal Computer Product Family," IEEE/Intl. Soc. Ecol. Ecs., Digital Equipment Corp., 111 Powdermill Rd, MSO2-3/C3, Maynard, MA 01754.

Niklas, C., 1996: "How to Build a Tree," *Natural History* 105(2):48–52, Feb.

Nilsson, S., 1997: "Roundtable Conclusions — So What?," *J. Indl. Ecol.* 1(3):115–123, Summer.

Nitze, P. H., 1997: "A Cold-War Solution for a Warming World," *Washington Post* op-ed, p. A22, July 2.

Nivola, P., 1999: "Fit for Fat City?: A 'Lite' Menu of European Policies to Improve Our Urban Form," Policy Brief 44, Brookings Institution, Washington, DC, Feb., www.brook.edu/es/urban/urban.htm.

Nørgård, J. S., 1989: "Low Electricity Appliances — Options for the Future," in Johansson, T. B., et al., *Electricity,* University of Lund Press, Lund, Sweden.

North, D., 1997: "Is Your Head Office a Useless Frill?," *Canadian Business,* pp. 78–82, Nov. 14.

Noss, R. F., and Peters, R. L., 1995: *Endangered Ecosystems of the United States: A Status Report and Plan for Action,* Defenders of Wildlife, Washington, DC.

Noss, R. F., LaRoe, E. T., Scott, J. M., 1995: *Endangered Ecosystems of the United States: A Preliminary Assessment of Loss and Degradation,* Biological Report 28, USDI National Biological Service, Washington, DC.

NREL 1997: "Clean Air Act Amendments: Projected versus Actual Costs," Policy and Environmental Analysis Team, Center for Energy Analysis and Applications, National Renewable Energy Laboratory, Golden, CO, July 8.

Office of Technology Assessment (OTA), U.S. Congress, 1992: *Green Products by Design,* OTA-E-541, U.S. Govt. Printing Office, Washington, DC, Oct.

Ohno, T., 1988: *The Toyota Production System: Beyond Large Scale Production,* Productivity Press, Portland, OR.

Oldenburg, R., 1997: *The Great Good Place,* Marlow and Co., New York, NY.

O'Meara, M., 1998: "How Mid-Sized Cities Can Avoid Strangulation," *Worldwatch* 11 (5): 8–15, Sept.–Oct.

Organic Cotton Directory 1998–99: Organic Trade Association/Organic Fiber Council, PO Box 1078, Greenfield, MA 01302, 413/774-7511, fax -7433, ofc@igc.org.

Osann, E. R., and Young, J. E., 1998: *Saving Water, Saving Dollars: Efficient Plumbing Products and the Protection of America's Waters,* Potomac Resources, Washington, DC, Apr., available from American Council for an Energy-Efficient Economy, 202/429-0063, fax -0193, ace3pubs@ix.netcom.com.

Pacific Northwest Energy Conservation and Renewable Energy Newsletter 1997: "Leaky Ducts: Res. Ductwork Increasingly Viewed as Promising En. Conservation Target," http://www.newsdata.com/enernet/iod/conweb/conweb13.html#cw13-5.

Pape, T., 1998: personal communication, June 1; Chair, Interior Plumbing Committee, AWWA Water Cons. Div., c/o Best Management Partners, 1704 Elm St., El Cerrito, CA 94530, 510/620-0915.

Paper Task Force 1995: "Paper Task Force Recommendations for Purchasing and Using Environmentally Preferable Paper," Final Report, Environmental Defense Fund, New York, NY. (Duke University, Environmental Defense Fund, Johnson and Johnson, McDonald's, The Prudential Insurance Company of America, Time Inc.)

Paschke, Philip, 1998: personal communication, Community Services Division, Seattle Public Utilities, Feb. 5, 206/684-7666.

Patchett, J., undated: "Cost Estimates Comparing Native Landscapes versus Traditional Landscape Treatments," Conservation Design Forum, 1750 E. Diehl Rd., Suite 102, Naperville, IL 60563, 708/955-0355.

Pear, R., 1993: "$1 Trillion in Health Costs Is Predicted," *New York Times,* Dec. 29.

Penzias, A., 1995: *Harmony: Business, Technology, and Life After Paperwork,* Harper-Collins, New York, NY.

Perlman, D., 1998: "Cost of Cardiovascular Ailments Soaring," *San Francisco Chronicle,* Jan. 1.

Petersen, M., 1994: *Ökonomische Analyse des Car-sharing,* Stattauto, Berlin.

PG&E 1993: "New Wall System at Davis Residential Site," fact sheet, ACT[2] (Advanced Customer Technology Test for Maximum Energy Effciency), Pacific Gas & Electric Co. (San Ramon, CA 94583), Dec.

Piette, M., Krause, F., and Verderber, R., 1989: *Technology Assessment: Energy-Efficient Commercial Lighting,* LBL-27032, Lawrence Berkeley [National] Laboratory, Berkeley, CA 94720, Apr.

Pimentel, P. F., 1997: "How Well Does ICI Conservation Work?," *Procs. Workshop Industrial/Commercial/Institutional Conservation: More Bang for Your Conservation Buck!,* American Water Works Assn., Feb. 3, Los Angeles, or ERI Services, Boston, MA 02111, 617/542-8567.

Pinkham, R., and Dyer, J., 1993: "Linking Water and Energy Savings in Irrigation," Rocky Mountain Institute Publication #A93-11.

Pinkham, R., 1994: "Improving Water Quality with More Efficient Irrigation," Rocky Mountain Institute Publication #A94-4.

Plowden, S., and Hillman, M., 1996: *Speed Control and Transport Policy,* Policy Studies Institute, London, available from BEBC Distribution Ltd. (PO Box 1496, Poole, Dorset BH12 3YD, UK).

Polak, P., 1998: "Putting 100 Million Acres Under Drip Irrigation by the Year 2015," notes for International Development Enterprises brainstorming meeting, Mar. 28–29 (10403 West Colfax Ave. #500, Lakewood, CO 80215, 303/332-4336, www.ideorg.org, ide@ideorg.org).

Pollard, R. D., ed., 1979: *The Nugget File,* Union of Concerned Scientists, Cambridge, MA.

Port, O., 1998: "A Warehouse of Virtual Parts," *Business Week,* p. 85, July 6.

——— 1998: "With These Gizmos, Your Cell Phone Can Run on Vodka," *Business Week,* p. 77, Feb. 16.

Postel, S. L., 1992/97: *Last Oasis,* W. W. Norton and Co., New York, NY.

Postel, S. L., Daily, G. C., and Ehrlich, P. R., 1996: "Human Appropriation of Renewable Fresh Water," *Science* 271:785–788.

President's Council of Advisors on Science and Technology (PCAST) 1997: *Federal Energy Research and Development for the Challenges of the Twenty-first Century,* Report of the Energy Research and Development Panel, Nov. 5.

Preston, G., 1994: "The Effects of a User-Pays Approach, and Resource-Saving Measures, on Water and Electricity Use by Visitors to the Kruger National Park," *S. Afr. J. Sci.* 90:558–561, Nov./Dec.

Prophet, T., 1998: "Distributed Generation as a Green House Gas Solution," AlliedSignal table #MG3228 presented at Aspen Institute Energy Forum, July 7, used by permission.

Puder, F., 1992: *The German Packaging Decree, Multi-trip System Decree and the Consequences of the EC Packaging Directive,* paper to Milieudefensie Sustainable Packaging Conference, Dept. of Waste Economics, Umweltbundesamt, Berlin.

Pulp and Paper Week 1993: "Green Bay Studying Plan to Build Series of Regional Minimills Based on Recycled Fiber," 15(20):24–28, May.

Rabinovitch, J., 1992: "Curitiba: toward sustainable urban development," *Envt. and Urbanization* 4(2):62–73, Oct.

——— 1993: "Urban public transport management in Curitiba, Brazil," *UNEP Ind. and Envt.* 18–20, Jan.–June.

——— 1995: "A sustainable urban transportation system," *En. for Sust. Devel.* 2(2): 11–17, July, Intl. Energy Initiative.

———— 1996: "Innovative land use and public transport policy: The case of Curitiba, Brazil," *Land Use Policy* 13(1):51–67.

Rabinovitch, J., and Hoehn, J., 1995: "A Sustainable Urban Transportation System: the 'Surface Metro' in Curitiba, Brazil," Working Paper #19, The Environmental and Natural Resources Policy and Training Project (EPAT) / Midwest Universities Consortium for International Activities (MUCIA), U. of Wisconsin/Madison, 608/263-4781, fax 608/265-2993, eamaurer@facstaff.wisc.edu, May.

Rabinovitch, J., and Leitman, J., 1993: "Environmental Innovation and Management in Curitiba, Brazil," Urban Management Programme Working Paper #1, United Nations Development Program/UNCHS (Habitat)/World Bank, Washington, DC, June.

———— 1996: "Urban Planning in Curitiba," *Scientific American* 26–33, Mar.

Rainforest Action Network (RAN) 1995: *Cut Waste Not Trees,* RAN, San Francisco, CA, www.ran.org.

Rajendran, V., 1997: "Energy Efficiency and Competition," address to Asean/E.U. conference (Bangkok) on behalf of Federation of Malaysian Manufacturers, available from author at Western Digital, Kuala Lumpur.

Rathje, W., and Murphy, C., 1992: *Rubbish! The Archaeology of Garbage,* HarperCollins, New York, NY.

Real Estate Research Corporation (RERC) 1974: *The Costs of Sprawl: Environmental and Economic Costs of Alternative Residential Development Patterns at the Urban Fringe,* 3 vols., prepared for President's Council on Environmental Quality, Dept. of Housing and Urban Development, and Environmental Protection Agency, U.S. Govt. Printing Office, Washington, DC.

Recer, P., 1996: "Living in Biosphere Just Didn't Work Out," *San Francisco Chronicle,* Nov. 25. *Cf.* www.biospherics.org.

Recycled Paper Coalition 1993: *Annual Report.*

Reddy, A. K. N., and Goldemberg, J., 1990: "Energy for the Developing World," *Scientific American* 110–118, Sept.

Reddy, A. K. N., Williams, R. H., and Johansson, T. B., 1997: *Energy After Rio: Prospects and Challenges,* Sales #E.97 III.B.11, ISBN 92-1-12670-1, United Nations Development Program, New York, NY.

Reddy, W. V., and Goldemberg, J., 1997: "Are Developing Countries Already Doing as Much as Industrialized Countries to Slow Climate Change?," *Climate Notes,* World Resources Institute, Washington, DC, July, www.wri.org.

Reisner, M., 1986/93: *Cadillac Desert: The American West and Its Disappearing Water,* Penguin Books, New York, NY.

Repetto, R., and Austin, D., 1997: *The Costs of Climate Protection: A Guide for the Perplexed,* World Resources Institute, Washington, DC, www.wri.org/wri/climate/.

Resource Conservation Alliance 1998: "Administration, Leahy Advocate Ban on Solid Wood Packing Material in Response to Asian Long-horned Beetle Infestation," lead story, *RCA Newswire,* Nov. 23, roselle@essential.org.

Reuters 1997: "Car crashes a growing world cause of death," 2008 ET, Dec. 2.

Rice, T., ed., 1995: *Out of the Woods: Reducing Wood Consumption to Save the World's Forests,* Friends of the Earth (FOE/UK), London, England, Apr.

Richert, W., and Venner, H., 1994: *Well Packed: Examples of Environment-Friendly Packaging Systems,* Milieudefensie, Amsterdam.

Robertson, C., Stein, J., Harris, J., and Cherniack, M., 1997: "Strategies to Improve Energy Efficiency in Semiconductor Manufacturing," preprint for *Procs. ACEEE*

Summer Study on En. Eff. in Ind., July 9–11, Saratoga Springs, NY, sponsored by The American Council for an Energy-Efficient Economy, Washington, DC.

Rocchi 1997: *Towards a New Product-Services Mix: Corporations in the Perspective of Sustainability,* MS Thesis in Environmental Management and Policy, Lund University, Sweden, Sept., simona.rocchi@cesena.nettuno.it.

Rocky Mountain Institute 1988: *Negawatts for Arkansas: Saving Electricity, Gas, and Dollars to Resolve the Grand Gulf Problem,* Executive Summary, Report to the Arkansas Energy Office, RMI Publication #U88-41.

———— 1991: *Visitors' Guide,* Publication #H-1.

———— Water Program 1991: *Water Efficiency: A Resource for Utility Managers, Community Planners, and Other Decisionmakers,* report to EPA, Rocky Mountain Institute Publication #W91-27.

———— 1998: *Green Development: Integrating Ecology and Real Estate* (by Wilson, A., Seal-Uncapher, J. L., McManigal, L., Lovins, L. H., Cureton, M., and Browning, W.), John Wiley and Sons, New York, NY. Accompanied by a CD-ROM of 100 case studies, *Green Developments,* available (as is the book) from Rocky Mountain Institute (1739 Snowmass Creek Rd., Snowmass, CO 81654, 970/927-3851, fax -4510, www.rmi.org) under publication numbers D97-11 and D97-12, respectively.

Rogers, P., 1993: *America's Water: Federal Roles and Responsibilities,* Twentieth Century Fund, MIT Press, Cambridge, MA.

Rogers, P., 1997: "Water for big cities: Big problems, easy solutions?," Harvard University draft paper, cited by Gleick 1998 p. 22.

Rogers, Jim, 1998: personal communication, Feb. 5, jimrogers@mediaone.net.

Romm, J. J., 1994: *Lean and Clean Management,* Kodansha, New York, NY, 1994.

Romm, J. J., and Browning, W. D., 1994: "Greening the Building and the Bottom Line: Increasing Productivity Through Energy-Efficient Design," Rocky Mountain Institute Publication #D94-27.

Romm, J. J., and Curtis, C., 1996: "Mideast Oil Forever?," *Atlantic Monthly* 277(4):57–74, Apr.

Roodman, D., 1996: "Paying the Piper," Worldwatch Institute, Washington, DC, Dec.

———— 1998: "Getting the Signals Right: Tax Reform to Protect the Environment and the Economy," Worldwatch Institute, Washington, DC, May.

Roodman, D., and Lenssen, N., 1995: "A Building Revolution: How Ecology and Health Concerns Are Transforming Construction," Worldwatch Paper #124, Worldwatch Institute, Washington, DC.

Rosenfeld, A. H., 1999: "The Art of Energy Efficiency," *Ann. Rev. En. Envt.,* in press.

Rosenfeld, A. H., and Hafemeister, D., 1988: "Energy-efficient buildings," *Scientific American* 258(4):217–230, Apr.

Rosenfeld, A. H., Romm, J. J., Akbari, H., Pomerance, M., and Taha, H., 1996: "Policies to Reduce Heat Islands: Magnitudes of Benefits and Incentives to Achieve Them," LBL-38679, Lawrence Berkeley [National] Laboratory, Berkeley, CA 94720.

Ross, M. H., and Steinmeyer, D., 1990: "Energy for Industry," *Scientific American* 88–98, Sept.

Rowe, J., 1996: "Major Growing Pains," *U.S. News & World Report,* Oct. 21.

Rubin, A. R., 1982: "Effects of Extreme Water Conservation on the Characteristics and Treatability of Septic Tank Effluent," *Procs. Third Natl. Symp. on Individual and Small Community Sewage Systs.,* Am. Soc. Ag. Engs., St. Joseph, MI 64501.

Samuels, G., 1981: *Transportation Energy Requirements to the Year 2010,* ORNL-5745, Oak Ridge National Laboratory, Oak Ridge, TN.

Samuelson, R. J., 1997: "Don't Hold Your Breath," *Newsweek,* p. 57, July 14.

San Francisco Chronicle 1998: "Natural Disasters Around World Cost Record $89 Billion in 1998," Nov. 28.

———— 1998a: "Number of Americans in Jail Rises Again," Jan. 19.

———— 1998b: "Lobbyists Spend $100 Million a Month," Mar. 7.

———— 1998c: "Accidental Fishing Called Huge Threat," May 21.

Sanstad, A. H., and Howarth, R., 1994: "'Normal' Markets, Market Imperfections, and Energy Efficiency," *En. Pol.* 22(10):811–818, Oct.

Sauer, G., 1997: "Cement, Concrete and Greenhouse Gas," CGLI Second Roundtable on North American Energy Policy, Apr., available from author (Sr. VP Mfg., Holnam Inc., Dundee, MI 48131, 734/529-2411, fax -5268).

———— 1998: "S.W.O.T. Analysis for Cement and Concrete Industries," *Advances in Cement and Concrete,* Engineering Foundation Conference, Banff, July 5.

Savory, A., and Butterfield, J., 1999: *Holistic Management: A New Framework for Decision-Making,* Island Press, Washington, DC; Center for Holistic Management, 1010 Tijeras NW, Albuquerque, NM 87102, 505/842-5252, www.holisticmanagement.org, center@holisticmanagement.org.

Schafer, A., and Victor, D., 1997: "The Past and Future of Global Mobility," *Scientific American* 277(4):58–61, Oct.

Schanzenbacher, B., and Mills, E., 1997: "Climate Change from an Insurance Perspective," *Update,* Dec., Inst. for Business and Home Safety; publications of the Insurance Industry Initiative, UN Environment Programme.

Schmidheiney, S., and Zorraquin, F., 1996: "Financing Change: The Financial Community, Eco-Efficiency, and Sustainable Development," World Business Council for Sustainable Development, MIT Press, Cambridge, MA.

Schmidt-Bleek, F., et al., 1997: "Statement to Government and Business Leaders," Wuppertal Institute, Wuppertal, Germany.

Schneider, S. H., 1997: *Laboratory Earth: The Planetary Gamble We Can't Afford to Lose,* Basic Books, New York, NY.

Schor, J., 1991: *The Overworked American: The Unexpected Decline of Leisure,* Basic Books, New York, NY.

Sears, P. B., 1935: *Deserts on the March,* U. of Ok. Press, Norman, OK.

Sedjo, R., 1994: "The Importance of High-Yield Plantation Forestry for Meeting Timber Needs: Recent Performance and Future Potentials," Discussion Paper 95–08, Resources for the Future Foundation, Washington, DC, Dec.

———— 1995: "Forests: Conflicting Signals," at 177–209 in Bailey, R., ed., 1995: *The True State of the Planet,* Free Press/Simon and Schuster, New York, NY.

———— 1996: personal communication, Resources for the Future Foundation, Sept. 12.

———— 1997: "The Forest Sector: Important Innovations," draft, Resources for the Future, Washington, DC, Mar. 5.

Seissa, R., 1991: presentation to U.S. National Research Council / Energy Engineering Board symposium, Committee on Fuel Economy of Automobiles and Light Trucks, Irvine, CA, on behalf of Dow Chemical Co., July 8.

SERI 1990: *The Potential of Renewable Energy,* Interlaboratory White Paper, SERI/TP260-3674, Golden, CO, Mar.

Service, R. F., 1998: "The Pocket DNA Sequencer," *Science* 282:399–401, Oct. 16.

———— 1998a: "Miniaturization Puts Chemical Plants Where You Want Them," *Science* 282:400, Oct. 16.

Sharpe, W. E., Cole, A. C., and Fritten, D. C., 1984: "Restoration of Failing On-Site Wastewater Disposal Systems Using Water Conservation," *J. Water Polln. Control Fedn.* 56(7).

Sheldon, R. A., 1994: "Consider the environmental quotient," *Chemtech,* American Chemical Society, pp. 38–47, Mar.

Shepard, M., et al., 1990: *The State of the Art: Appliances,* COMPETITEK/Rocky Mountain Institute, Aug., supplemented and updated by later editions of the *Appliance Technology Atlas,* E SOURCE, Boulder, CO 80301, www.esource.com.

Shindell, D. T., Rind, D., and Lonergan, P., 1998: "Increased Polar Stratospheric Ozone Losses and Delayed Eventual Recovery Owing to Increased Greenhouse Gas Concentrations," *Nature* 392:589–592, Apr. 9.

Shoup, D. C., 1997: "The High Cost of Free Parking," *Access* 10:2–9, Spring, U. of Ca. Transportation Center, Berkeley, CA 94720-1720, http://socrates.berkeley. edu/~uctc.

——— 1997a: "Evaluating the Effects of Cashing Out Employer-Paid Parking: Eight Case Studies," *Transport Policy* 4(4):201–216, Oct.

Simpson-Herbert, M., 1996: "Sanitation Myths: Obstacles to Progress?," in *Safeguarding Water Resources for Tomorrow, New Solutions to Old Problems,* Proceedings of Sixth Stockholm Water Symposium, Aug. 4–9, Stockholm Water Company, pp. 47–53.

Sjöberg, C., with Laughran, K., 1998: "A Crisis in the Oven," *Tomorrow,* p. 24, Nov./Dec. Further information available from Per Grunewald, Environment Director, Electrolux, per.grunewald@notes.electrolux.se, ++ 46 8 + 738-6555, fax -7666.

Smith, M., 1997: "Perspectives on the U.S. Paper Industry and Sustainable Production," *J. Indl. Ecol.* 1(3):69–85, Summer; see also *The U.S. Paper Industry and Sustainable Production: An Argument for Restructuring,* MIT Press, Cambridge, MA.

Soden, K., 1988: "U.S. Farm Subsidies," Rocky Mountain Institute Publication #A88-22.

Solley, W. B., Pierce, R. R., and Perlman, H. A., 1998: *Estimated Use of Water in the United States in 1995,* U.S. Geological Survey, Circular 1200, U.S. Government Printing Office, Washington, DC.

Sørensen, B., 1979: *Renewable Energy,* Academic Press, New York, NY.

Sprotte, K., 1997: *A Strategic Fit for Tomorrow's Eco-Efficient Service Economy,* MBA thesis, University of Strathclyde, Scotland.

Stahel, W. R., and Reday-Mulvey, G., 1981: *Jobs for Tomorrow, the Potential for Substituting Manpower for Energy,* Vantage Press, New York, NY.

Stahel, W. R., and Børlin, M., 1987: *Strategie économique de la durabilité,* Société de Banque Suisse, Geneva, Switzerland.

Stein, J., et al., 1998: "Delivering Energy Services to Semiconductor and Related High-Tech Industries," multi-client study, E SOURCE, Boulder, CO 80301, www.esource. com.

Stevens, W. K., 1998: "If Climate Changes, It May Change Quickly," *New York Times,* Jan. 27.

——— 1998a: "How Warm Was It? A Record-Book Year," *Intl. Herald Trib.* (N.Y. edn.), p. 7, Dec. 19–20.

Stewart, John W., 1997: personal communication, Oct. 9.

Stickney, B., 1992: "Super Efficient Refrigeration Systems," TU-92-8, E SOURCE, Boulder, CO 80301, www.esource.com.

Strong, S. J., 1996: "Power Windows," *IEEE Spectrum,* Oct.

Stuart, K., and Jenny, H., 1999: "My Friend the Soil," *Whole Earth* 96:6–9, Spring.

Tabashnik, B., et al., 1997: "One Gene in Diamondback Moth Confers Resistance to Four *Bacillus thuringiensis* Toxins," *Procs. NAS* 94:1640–1644.

———— 1997a: "Seeking the Root of Insect Resistance to Transgenic Plants," *Procs. NAS* 94:3488–3490.

Thompson, S., 1998: personal communication, July 28, Envirozone, Hilton Head, SC, 843/689-3101, fax -6331, envirozone@aol.com.

Tobias, A., 1993: *Auto Insurance Alert: Why the System Stinks, How to Fix It, and What to Do in the Meantime,* Simon and Schuster, New York, NY.

Todd, J., 1997: personal communication, Aug. 7, documented in annual *EMSD Accomplishment Reports,* Seattle City Light, Seattle, WA.

Tyson, A. S., 1998: "Seattle Neighborhoods Stem Suburban Sprawl," *Christian Science Monitor,* Jan. 9.

U.C.S. 1998: *A Small Price to Pay,* Union of Concerned Scientists and Tellus Institute, July, downloadable from www.ucsusa.org.

U.N. Commission on Sustainable Development, 1997: *Comprehensive Assessment of the Freshwater Resources of the World,* United Nations, New York, NY.

U.N. Development Programme (UNDP) 1996: *Urban Agriculture. Food, Jobs and Sustainable Cities,* Publication Series for Habitat II, l, UNDP, New York, NY.

U.N. Food and Agriculture Organization 1995: *Forestry Statistics: Today and Tomorrow* and *Forest Products Yearbook,* FAO, Viale delle Terme di Caracalla, 00100 Rome, Italy.

———— 1997: *State of the World's Forests,* FAO, Rome.

———— 1993: *Pulp, Paper, and Paperboard Capacity Survey, 1993–1998,* FAO, Rome.

U.S. Congress 1998: *Estimates of Federal Tax Expenditures for Fiscal Years 1999–2003,* Joint Committee on Taxation, Washington, DC.

U.S. Water News 1992: "Leakage Varies Worldwide," Apr., p. 18, "Less Watering, Less Mowing," Oct., p. 17, and "Conservation Is a Matter of Survival on High Plains," Apr., pp. 1 and 17.

———— 1992a: "Texas home lives by rain alone," 8(10):1, Apr.

———— 1997: "Freshwater Forum: Assessment of U.S. watersheds released by EPA," p. 7, Nov.

———— 1998: "California Expert Says Innovative Water Rates Key to Conservation," p. 21, Jan.

Udall, R., 1997: "The New Frontier: Grid-Connected PV," typescript, *Community Office for Resource Efficiency,* Carbondale, CO.

United Nations Environmental Program (UNEP) 1996: "Poverty and the Environment: Reconciling Short-term Needs and Long-term Sustainable Goals," Press Release, Nairobi, Mar. 1.

United States Bureau of the Census 1993: *Statistical Abstract of the United States 1993,* U.S. Govt. Printing Office, Washington, DC.

United States Geological Survey 1995: http://h2o.er.usgs.gov/public/watuse/graphics/octo.html.

Vaughan, D. G., and Doake, C. S. M., 1996: "Recent Atmospheric Warming and Retreat of Ice Shelves on the Antarctic Peninsula," *Nature* 379:328–331, Jan. 25.

Venhuizen, D., 1997: "Paradigm Shift: Decentralized wastewater systems may provide better management at less cost," *Water Envt. and Technol.* 49–52, Aug. See also "The Decentralized Concept of Wastewater Management," 1996, http://www.geocities.com/RainForest/Vines/5240/Venh_Decentralized_WW.html, downloaded Feb. 5, 1998, and "Is 'Waste' Water Reclamation and Reuse in Your Future?," http://www.geocities.com/RainForest/Vines/5240/FutureWater Use.html, downloaded Feb. 5, 1998 (5803 Gateshead Drive, Austin, TX 78745, 512/442-4047, fax -4057, waterguy@ix.netcom.com).

Venster 1998: Royal Dutch/Shell Group External Affairs newsletter, London/The Hague, Jan./Feb.

Vickers, A., 1990: "Water-Use Efficiency Standards for Plumbing Fixtures: Benefits of National Legislation," *AWWA J.*, May.

Vitousek, P., et al., 1986: "Human Appropriation of the Products of Photosynthesis," *BioScience* 34:368–73, May.

Vitousek, P. M., Mooney, H. A., Lubchenco, J., and Melillo, J. M., 1997: "Human Domination of Earth's Ecosystems," *Science* 277:494–99, July.

von Weizsäcker, E. U., 1994: *Earth Politics*, Zed Books, London.

von Weizsäcker, E. U., Lovins, A. B. and L. H., 1997: *Factor Four: Doubling Wealth, Halving Resource Use*, Earthscan, London, available in North America exclusively from Rocky Mountain Institute, Snowmass, CO 81654-9199, www.rmi.org.

Wackernagel, M., and Rees, W., 1995: *Our Ecological Footprint: Reducing Human Impact on the Earth*, New Society Publishers, Gabriola Island, BC, Canada.

Wade, E., 1981: "Fertile cities," *Development Forum*, Sept./Dec.

Wallace, John, Office Administrator, San Simeon Acres Community Services, Rt. 1, Box S17, San Simeon, CA 93452, 805/544-4011.

Walljasper, J., 1998: "Road Warriors," *Utne Reader* 10 and 12, Mar.–Apr.

Wall Street Journal 1996: "Developers Discover Old Values Can Bring Astonishing Returns," Florida edn., Dec. 4, summarized in *New Urban News*, Jan.–Feb. 1997, p. 11.

———— 1997: "Mitsubishi Electric Says It's Almost Met Goals of 5-Year Plan," p. B11A, Oct. 6.

———— 1998: "Chip-Industry Study Cites Sector's Impact on U.S. Economy," p. B13, Mar. 17.

Walton, A., 1999: "Technology Versus African-Americans," *Atlantic Monthly* 283(1): 14–18, Jan.

Wang, R., and Hu, D., 1998: "Totality, Mobility and Vitality: Feng-Shui Principles and Its Application to the Blue Network Development of Yangtze Delta," 34th International Planning Congress, Azores, 26 Sept.–2 Oct.; Research Center for Eco-Environmental Science, Chinese Academy of Sciences, Beijing 1000080, wangrs@sun.ihep.ac.cn.

Wann, D., 1990: *Biologic: Environmental Protection by Design*, Johnson Books, Boulder, CO.

Warshall, P., 1995: "Wood Supplies and Prices in the Next Decade," unpublished paper for Global Business Network, Nov.

———— 1995a: "Graywater Handbooks," Peter Warshall and Associates, City of Malibu, CA.

———— 1997: "The Tensile and the Tantric," *Whole Earth* 90:4–7 (plus supplementary materials 8–21), Summer.

———— 1999: "The Soil Bank," *Whole Earth* 96:22–24, Spring.

Wassmann, F., 1999: personal communication, Jan. 4., Studio for Ecology and Garden Art, Hofenstr. 69, CH-3023 Hinterkappelen near Bern, Switzerland, ++ 41 31 + 829-2755.

Weber, B., 1996: "At The Dump. Wish You Were Here," *New York Times*, Mar. 27.

Weiner, J. 1990: *The Next One Hundred Years*, Bantam, New York, NY.

Weissman, S., and Corbett, J., 1992: *Land Use Strategies for More Liveable Places*, Local Government Commission (909 12th St., Suite 201, Sacramento, CA 95814).

Wentz, F. J., and Schabel, M., 1998: "Effects of orbital decay on satellite-derived lower tropospheric temperature trends," *Nature* 394:661–664, Aug. 13. See also Gaffen, D. J., "Falling satellites, rising temperatures," id. 394:615–616.

Wernick, I. K., and Ausubel, J. H., 1995: "National Materials Flows and the Environment," in Socolow, R. H., Anderson, D., and Harte, J., eds., 1995: *Ann. Rev. En. Envt.* 20:463–492.

Williams, B. D., Moore, T. C., and Lovins, A. B., 1997: "Speeding the Transition: Designing a Fuel-Cell Hypercar," *Procs. Natl. Hydr. Assn. 8th Ann. U.S. Hydr. Mtg.,* Alexandria, VA, 11–13 Mar., Rocky Mountain Institute Publication #T97-9, www.rmi.org.

Williams, R. H., 1996: "Fuel Decarbonization for Fuel Cell Applications and Sequestration of the Separated CO_2," Res. Rep. No. 295, Jan., Princeton University Center for Energy and Environmental Studies, Princeton U., Princeton, NJ 08540.

Williams, R. H., Larson, E. D., Ross, M. H., 1987: "Materials, Affluence, and Industrial Energy Use," *Ann. Rev. En. Envt.* 12:99–144.

Willis, D., 1996: "Naturally Inspired," *Natural History* 105(2):53–55, Feb.

Wilson, A., and Malin, M., 1996: "Ecological Wastewater Treatment," *Envtl. Bldg. News* 5(4):13–17, July/Aug.

Wilson, A., 1997: "Water: Conserving This Precious Resource," *Envtl. Bldg. News* 10, Sept.

Wilson, W. J., 1996: *When Work Disappears,* Knopf, New York, NY.

Wolf, J. L., Reid, M., Miller, R. S., and Fleming, E. J., 1983: *Industrial Investment in Energy Efficiency: Opportunities, Management Practices, and Tax Incentives,* Alliance to Save Energy, Washington, DC.

Womack, J. P., Jones, D. T., and Roos, D., 1990: *The Machine That Changed the World,* Rawson-MacMillan and Harper-Collins, 1991.

Womack, J. P., and Jones, D. T., 1996: *Lean Thinking: Banish Waste and Create Wealth in Your Corporation,* Simon and Schuster, New York, summarized in "Beyond Toyota: How to Root Out Waste and Pursue Perfection," *Harv. Bus. Rev.* 140–158, Sept./Oct., Reprint 96511.

World Bank 1995: *Monitoring Environmental Progress: A Report on Work in Progress,* Environmentally Sustainable Development, World Bank, Washington, DC.

———— 1997: *Expanding the Measure of Wealth: Indicators of Environmentally Sustainable Development,* Environmentally Sustainable Development Studies and Monographs Series No. 17, World Bank, Washington, DC.

World Health Organization (WHO) 1995: *Community Water Supply and Sanitation: Needs, Challenges, and Health Objectives,* Report by the Director-General to the Forty-eighth World Health Assembly, Geneva.

World Oil 1997: *World Trends* 218(8), Aug., Gulf Publishing Co., Houston, TX.

World Resources Institute 1992: *World Resources 1992–1993,* Oxford U. Press, New York, NY.

World Resources Institute 1994: *Competitive Implications of Environmental Regulation of Chlorinated Releases in the Pulp and Paper Industry,* Management Institute for Environment and Business (MEB), WRI, Washington, DC.

Worldwide Fund for Nature Europe 1998: "A third of world's natural resources consumed since 1970: Report," Agence France-Presse, October.

Worster, D., 1993: "A Sense of Soil," p. 82 in *The Wealth of Nature,* Oxford U. Press, New York, NY.

Wyatt, W., 1998: personal communication, High Plains Water District, 2930 Ave. Q, Lubbock, TX 79405, 806/762-0181, Feb. 6.

Wymer, D., 1997: "Rainwater Tank Stormwater Drainage Benefit Analysis," fax from Byron Shire Council Works and Services Department, as reported and interpreted in Preferred Options, *The Rous Regional Water Efficiency Program, Final Report of the Rous Regional Demand Management Strategy,* Mar., pp. 95–98. Kindly provided by Dr. Stuart White, Director, Preferred Options (Asia-Pacific) Pty Ltd, PO Box 243, Lismore NSW 2480, Australia, ++ 61 66 + 221-211, FAX + 223-233, stuartw@peg. apc.org.

Yergin, D., 1991: *The Prize: The Epic Quest for Oil, Money, and Power,* Simon and Schuster, London.

——— 1997: Remarks to White House Climate Conference, Oct. 6, Cambridge Energy Research Associates, Cambridge, MA.

Yoon 1998: "A 'Dead Zone' Grows in the Gulf of Mexico," *New York Times,* p. F1, Jan. 20.

Young, J. E., and Sachs, A., 1994: "The Next Efficiency Revolution: Creating a Sustainable Materials Economy," Worldwatch Paper 121, Worldwatch Institute, Washington, DC.

Zagar, V., 1998: "Energy Efficiency of ST-AMK Wafer Fab Case Study," seminar on Energy Savings, Clean Technology and the Revised Tax Incentives, Institution of Engineers (Singapore), Feb. 27, available from author at STMicroelectronics, Singapore, vlatko.zagar@st.com.

Zepezauer, N. A., 1996: *Taking the Rich Off Welfare,* Odonian Press, Tucson, AZ.

INDEX